EDUCATION STUDIES

Foundations of Policy

Edited by

Robert F. Lawson
R. L. Schnell

UNIVERSITY
PRESS OF
AMERICA

Copyright © 1983 by

University Press of America, Inc.

P.O. Box 19101, Washington, D.C. 20036

ISBN (Perfect): 0-8191-2920-8
ISBN (Cloth): 0-8191-2919-4

To

The Students of

Educational Foundations 785

iv

CONTENTS

Preface vii

1   HISTORY OF EDUCATION   1

R.L. SCHNELL, Professor
Department of Educational Policy
    & Administrative Studies
The University of Calgary

2   SOCIOLOGY OF EDUCATION   73

LOIS E. FOSTER, Senior Lecturer
School of Education
La Trobe University
Australia

3   PSYCHOLOGY OF EDUCATION   175

DAVID R. EVANS, Associate Professor
Department of Psychology
University of Western Ontario

    and

MARGARET T. HEARN, Director
Department of Psychology
War Memorial Children's Hospital
London, Ontario

4   PHILOSOPHY OF EDUCATION   283

JOHN L. McNEILL, Associate Professor
Department of Educational Policy
    & Administrative Studies
The University of Calgary

5   EDUCATIONAL THEORY   339
      WILLIAM D. WINN, Associate Professor
      Department of Curriculum and
        Instruction
      The University of Calgary

6   EDUCATIONAL ADMINISTRATION   407
    Orthodoxy (and Heterodoxy)
      J.G.T. KELSEY, Associate Professor
      Centre for the Study of Administration
        in Education
      University of British Columbia

      and

      JOHN C. LONG, Associate Professor
      Department of Educational Administration
        and Foundations
      University of Manitoba

7   EDUCATIONAL KNOWLEDGE AND THE
    SCHOOL PROFESSIONAL   449
      ROBERT F. LAWSON, Professor and Dean
      Faculty of Education
      The University of Calgary

PREFACE

We are convinced that a proper understanding of the traditions of inquiry and discourse represented by the six chapters in this book are essential for undergraduates as well as graduate students in education. All too often students and school practitioners are unaware of the diversity and intellectual rigor of education as an academic enterprise. At the same time, graduate students, although appreciative of the sophistication and significance of their own specialties, fail to comprehend the nature and achievements of other disciplines and fields.

Such ignorance not only contributes to a defensive parochialism that denigrates other modes of inquiry but also to a very common inability to benefit from the sound scholarly work done outside a single specialty. As long time members of Educational Foundations and now Educational Policy and Administrative Studies Departments, the editors can attest to the intellectual stimulation and challenge provided by philosophers, sociologists, historians, comparatists, and anthropologists working within the confines of a single university unit. We now look forward to further intellectual growth by interaction with specialists in educational administration.

Indeed, the very idea of this book and the opportunity to carry it out were only possible because of the years of discussion and debate provided by colleagues past and present. To these and to the patient authors of the chapters we extend our thanks.

CHAPTER 1

HISTORY OF EDUCATION

REVOLUTION IN STYLE AND CONTENT

Educational history was one of the founding disciplines of teacher training programs. With the establishment of state maintained public schools in Europe and North America, the subject was first a basic element in normal schools and training colleges and then in university departments of education. That these early courses concentrated on the study of educational ideas is understandable given the two-fold concern with classroom management and professional attitudes. The educational theorists provided, in the age before scientific psychology, guidance not only in curriculum and instruction but also in a range of psychological problems related to student maturation and development. In addition, the writings supported a growing sense of professionalism that leading advocates of popular education saw as indispensible to its ultimate success.[1]

With the creation of new educational specialities, educational psychology and sociology, and the increased bureaucratization of public systems of schools that required new professionals and concomitant training programs, e.g., educational administration, educational history lost much of its rationale for inclusion as a requirement in the professional education of teachers. The rapid professionalization of teaching and its expression in university studies, particularly at the graduate level, challenged educationists to reconstruct offerings in educational history to bring them more in tune with the dominant purposes of a new self-conscious occupational group. Out of this challenge to make educational history relevant to the interest of teachers and administrators, educationists such as E.P. Cubberley and Paul Monroe constructed a story of educational progress that remained until the 1960s the overwhelmingly

1

accepted interpretation of schooling in western societies. As in the case of the earlier history of educational ideas, the new educational history served professional purposes.[2]

This, of course, is an endemic concern of educational history since its existence is intimately connected to the establishment of teacher-training and its worth justified almost solely on relevance to the purposes of schools and teachers. The grounds of relevance, however, have shifted over time in relation to changing societal interests and academic styles and methods. There appears to be some initial assumption that historical knowledge is/can be useful in preparing teachers. The older views of guidance in classroom management and of inspiration and uplift fade before the demands of increased bureaucratization, professional standards, and societal diversity.[3]

The creation of the social foundations of education as a composite educational specialty, first in the 1930s at Teachers College and then at School of Education, University of Illinois in the 1940s, suggested a new way of rendering educational history relevant. Social foundations specialists would cull the academic educational disciplines for materials relevant to fundamental problems of contemporary education. The new specialty would serve the two perennial issues of teacher preparation--the relation of theory to practice and the development of proper attitudes and beliefs in prospective teachers.

Although particularly provoking the ire of the second-generation of American educational historians, the social foundations approach gravely threatened the disciplinary integrity of all educational studies and, therefore, their legitimacy as university subjects. Under the pressure of assimilation, educational historians in the 1940s and 1950s engaged in a long discussion of the purpose of their specialty. Although committed to the historical study of education, these educationalists sought ways to demonstrate its relevance in

2

teacher education programs. The prolonged debate over the functions of educational history occupied a considerable portion of a number of journals--including the only one devoted to history of education.[4]

Before the debate had collapsed by the late 1950s, a series of socio-political and scholastic upheavals so radically changed the assumptions underlying the discussion as to render the whole process obsolete. First, the devolution of western world domination, the resulting Cold War and liberation movements in Asia, Africa, and America, alerted scholars outside of faculties of education to socio-economic and political functions of formal education. Increasingly schooling was seen as an instrument of national policy, both in terms of internal development schemes and in dealing with client nations in the Third World. Thus, the educational process and its institutional expressions became the object of studies by political scientists, sociologists, and economists who were examining problems in the development of the new nations and of minorities within older industrialized western nations.[5]

As schooling became a central theme in social scientific studies of contemporary societies, historians were moved to understand both the significance of schooling in American life and its potential for historical inquiry. The groundbreaking work was done by Bernard Bailyn who provided a biting critique of the existing educational historiography and a model for future studies. Bailyn's work established the legitimacy of education as a subject of historical study and a new set of research problems. Prior to Education in the Forming of American Society, the primary emphasis had been on schools as isolated self-contained social systems with their own internal logic. This perspective dovetailed with the existing state of educational history as primarily a service subject taught to undergraduate students in faculties of education. Bailyn stressed that education could not be reduced to schooling--especially where

schools were not universal compulsory institutions
--without seriously distorting historical understanding, that any academic enterprise that cut
itself off from the intellectual ferment of its
time ran the risk of alienation and stagnation,
and that central human institutions such as education could not be adequately comprehended apart
from the total network of institutions.[6] Although
a number of studies that would signal the changes
in historical scholarship were already well underway, it was Bailyn's interpretation of education
in colonial society that demonstrated how old evidence could be read in new ways. Thus, by the
early 1960s, educational history was in the process of being transformed into history of education.[7]

      The renaissance of the historical study of
education had a short moment in the academic sun.
It was almost immediately caught up in the social
and ideological upheaval of the 1960s. The Bailyn
"tradition" emphasized that education needed to be
studied with all the intellectual tools available
to the historian. In that sense, it was an assertion of the historical importance of education and
the necessity for academic rigor in its study.
Bitter controversies and unrest--associated with
militant students, Viet Nam, anti-war violence,
and the New Left--called into question some of the
bedrock assumptions underlying western liberal
society. Among those questioned were assumptions
regarding objective value-free scholarship, the
rationale for public institutions including schools
and universities, and the nature of human freedom
and dignity in capitalist society. If Bailyn had
indicted educational history for its intellectual
limitations, the new left critics condemned the
entire academic enterprise as an elaborate mechanism to justify an unjust and inhumane society.
Academic scholarship in the service of dominant
social and economic groups indoctrinated, social-
ized, and trained the rest of society to accept a
corrupt system. The monolithic interpretation of
state maintained schooling that had been successfully challenged by the Bailyn critique was given

in a perverse manner a new lease on life.[8]

Given the radical nature of the New Left critique, some instrument was needed to explain the success of a pernicious system that was able to maintain a facade of freedom and personal choice in the face of horrendous deprivation. The crucial character of modern society is the development of institutions--not basic sociological institutions such as religion--but rather concrete visible institutions that order our lives by rules and regulations. Of all the means by which we are institutionalized none is more universal and compulsory than the school. Consequently, historians of education were provided with a unique opportunity to combine radical analysis with historical inquiry.

The radical critique neatly reversed the old dominant Whig interpretation by asserting that schooling served to socialize instead of educate, to indoctrinate instead of enlighten, and to train instead of liberate. As a result, schools were not the means of uplift and mobility but rather the means by which the working classes, the poor, the radically and ethnically different were kept in their places and came to believe that their places were what they had earned for themselves. Both interpretations gave schools a central role in history and argued for their power in controlling social development.[9]

These two revolutions in historical style and perspective promised a new role and greater prestige for historians of education. At the very least, the historian by connecting the school into a network of institutions and activities gave it a new social and intellectual significance and thereby created a new attractive body of historical studies. At the other extreme, the historian emerged as a radical intellectual armed with the latest academic tools as well as critical theory. In either case, the results were bold, well researched and iconoclastic studies.[10]

But these developments were themselves

5

overtaken by two other revolutions--one demographic and the other socio-political. In the first instance, the 1970s marked the great downturn in post-World War II population. The massive and prolonged drop in the birth rate spelled an end to the dramatic growth in post-secondary enrollments that had marked the two decades since 1945. The expansion of educational provision had come to characterize not only the United States but all industrial states from Canada to Japan to France. In some cases this growth was necessarily tied into a veritable explosion in secondary education which turned formerly elitist institutions into mass ones. The tremendous expansion had created jobs, higher salaries, and seemingly unending advancement. Declining birth rates and stagnating institutions met head on the graduates of undergraduate and graduate programs geared to an ever expanding market.[11]

The upshot of such economic and social disaster had been panic and demoralization in universities and the professions. That the unease provoked by these conditions is not without grounds can be seen in the staff reductions at some institutions and in the growing realization that mobility from one institution to another has become increasingly rare. The growing closure of professional advancement and the possibility of redundancy raised anew the perennial issue of theory and practice in teacher education, and in particular, the value of history of education.

The second revolution is, of course, connected to both the declining enrollments and the radical critiques of institutions. A fundamental element of the critique was the extent to which institutions, for whatever reasons, failed to meet their professed purposes. In particular, it was noted that various school programs, e.g., reading, failed by a wide margin to accomplish their goals. In turn, the school staff claimed that their failure was tied into the failure of universities to educate and train competent staff.

6

In answer to the complaint of militant
minorities, some educational authorities have
sought new ways in which to satisfy the minorities
and to make the universities more accountable to
public authority. Given the immense investment in
state-maintained schooling, decisions to increase
its productivity or to demand great precision in
its activities appeared to be eminently sane public
policy. A major move in this direction involved
the establishment of minimum levels of student
performance in elementary and secondary schools.
Such levels were described in behavioral terms in
order to provide for adequate evaluation. In turn,
legislative pressure was placed on teacher education institutions to guarantee that their graduates would have the minimum knowledge and skills
to manage the programs of the schools.[12]

No matter how potentially enlightening or
interesting the new history of education was to
its practitioners, it needed to be justified--at
least as a component in the undergraduate preparation of teachers--in terms of its contribution to
the effective management of minimal school programs
defined in behavioral terms. Such a situation
simply reinforced the service nature of history of
education and other educational specialties in the
pre-service training of teachers. Although it
would be possible to decide on disciplinary grounds
to refuse to cooperate with such directives, the
results would be the elimination of history of
education from undergraduate programs and relega-
tion to an extremely small corner of faculties of
education and of a few departments of history.

Consequently, the tremendous intellectual
and ideological revolutions, which created a whole
new literature in history of education, have run
into obstacles that threaten the progress of the
new history of education. Although it is possible
to lament the decline of universities and the
threat to scholarship, this would only divert us
from our primary objective of examining the state
of educational historiography. The following discussion will examine the major styles and perspec-

7

tives in the new history of education, explicate
a theory of history, and then construct a history
of education program by analyzing significant
studies and subsequently synthesizing them into a
coherent historical interpretation.

INTERPRETATION: HISTORICAL FACTS AND HISTORICAL KNOWLEDGE

The dominant character of recent history of
education is the drive to overcome its scholarly
and intellectual isolation--an effort which has
taken two forms. First, the older style of educational history emphasized pedagogical organization,
practices, and ideas as elements in a self-contained social system. In that sense, it was about
chalk and desks and great educators and clearly
intended to edify. The criticism of professional
historians such as Bailyn hammered at its isolated
character and the subsequent failure to provide a
comprehensive view of educational activities.
Consequently, a new social history of education
developed that sought to understand educational
experience in terms of other major institutions
and significant social and intellectual movements.
Unlike early historians who used the larger society
to set the stage for the real point of their studies, that is, schooling, the new historians centred
their attention on how educational activities are
to be seen as expressions of major societal values
and attitudes. This has meant, for example, that
if a particular form of education is identified as
Calvinistic or elitist that the concepts involved
must be explicated. Or to use a further example,
to identify certain innovations in American education as progressive without demonstrating what
"progressivism" meant in the United States is to
lose most of the explanatory power of the concept.
In short, historians of education are more sensitive to the value of conceptual clarity and expos-
itory relationships.

The second thrust has involved a wholly new

research approach. In general, the new social
history of education emphasizes the importance of
action over ideas or--to be precise--behavior over
words, and thus can be understood a part of the
movement in historical studies to use social scientific constructs and theories and statistical techniques in the collection, organization and analysis
of aggregate data. Even in studies that do not
employ aggregate data, the emphasis is on large
collectivities that allows for generalizations
about practices or behaviors.[13]

There is, of course, a fundamental assumption behind the concentration on behavior, namely,
that it is possible to infer values from behavior,
which is extremely dubious and which will be examined later. For the present discussion, the important point is that the new social history of
education has been a necessary corrective to the
earlier obsession with ideas and legislative and
administrative refinements.

It does seem, however, that emphasis on behavior has obscured one of Bailyn's major insights,
that is, that education and schooling are not identical. Although such a statement is trite, historians of education as much as their contemporaries
find it difficult not to conflate the two. The
issue is not merely the lapse into discussing public education instead of public schooling but more
importantly the failure to understand that while
the point of school includes education it also includes socialization, training, and indoctrination.
Moreover, education even in societies with universal compulsory schooling must be understood as
broader than formal education. There is, also, a
need to use the concept of education with greater
precision and consistency.

The emphasis on aggregate data has encouraged historians to turn to schools--and particularly
to publically maintained systems of schools--since
they are the institutions with not only the records
but also with collective experience that makes
aggregate data possible. Consequently more frag-

9

mentary institutions and experiences are frequently slighted. It is understandable that historians have moved from the establishment of systems of common schools in the nineteenth century to the creation of urban school systems in the twentieth century.[14]

Interestingly, the new social historians have not moved to reconstruct the internal life of the school and the classroom in the twentieth century. Apart from individual attempts to establish dominant values which shaped school practices, there has been little work done that would parallel the historical investigations of community and family life which have become so popular in the past two decades.[15]

Finally, the preference for behavior over words has contributed to the virtual disappearance of scholarly work in the history of educational ideas. That the earlier tradition suffered from major defects or failed to pose questions significant to our own times is clear; however, there is a major need to re-examine much of the traditional content of educational ideas in the light of our own interests and in relationship with the work being done in intellectual history.

CONSTRUCTING HISTORICAL INTERPRETATIONS

One of the major problems in any discipline is the accumulation of a body of specialized studies that do not provide a comprehensive view of the object of the discipline. Although there are the occasional insightful bibliographical surveys that allow us to grasp the state of the art in a particular aspect of the discipline, the real integration of new research and perspectives is usually found in substantial studies that demonstrate how the discrete pieces of scholarship can be fitted into a new unity. Once constructed, the new synthesis provides the basis for a "generation" of scholarship to substantiate and extend it or to modify and reject it. In any case, the original creation establishes the new limits of thought and inquiry. Consequently, old works that were outside the limits of the superseded synthesis sometimes become "relevant" while those that are not apparently compatible are dropped.

As might be expected, such syntheses do not treat a total discipline and therefore it is possible to have several that integrate significant and occasionally overlapping areas. There are also magnificent works of creative scholarship that leave no progeny. These are often the studies that new syntheses resurrect and make relevant.

The view of scholarship implicit in the above discussion is one peculiarly appropriate to historical inquiry. The object of historical investigation is not to reconstruct the past but rather to construct historical knowledge. Reconstruction in historical research might seem to suggest that historians are interested in actually recreating a portion of the past so that they might experience it directly. There are, of course, some difficulties in such an undertaking, for example, the fragmentary nature of the evidence available for such recreation and the fact that hindsight transforms the recreated past. Such considerations question the possibility but not the desirability of the reconstructionist theory.16

It does seem reasonable to ask whether or not the popular understanding of reconstruction is really sensible. If the major objections are technical, there are means to circumvent them. Some evasive techniques include the massive collection of data, new means of utilizing the data, and ways of getting around the problem of knowledge of historical outcomes.

Since historians work with public events and public records of public events, they have been driven to preservation and collection of evidence. Since the essence of history is human action over time, historians seek to establish historical facts of sequence and substance. This passion for fact has led to two popular misunderstandings of historical inquiry. First, that since the principal object of historical work is the verification of fact, the true historian is one who can supply discrete data. Although historians generally react negatively to such an assumption—with clever and disparaging things to say about antiquarians and chroniclers, they have contributed to the misconception by holding that enough data will tell us directly something significant about the past. The latest technological explosion in historical study has created new procedures for utilizing data which were unmanageable prior to the development of computers and related systems. With the potential for massive data-collecting and processing, the Rankean dream of having the facts speak for themselves seems to be attainable.

The second misconception is that what historians know about the consequences of past human actions hinders historical inquiry. Such a view mistaken represents a gross misunderstanding of the work of the historian and is essentially a corollary of the data-collecting thesis. Historians today are much given to the use of innovative teaching methods—including role playing—that are to heighten our sensibilities and sensitivities. As meanings of enlivening student interest in history courses, such techniques are clearly valuable and worthwhile; however, when such procedures are offered as solutions to the problems of historical study, one needs to examine the grounds upon which the activity is justified.

To begin with, a wide range of pedagogical activities can be justified on grounds that are quite distinct from those essential to a proper understanding of historical inquiry. In brief, historians as teachers are concerned with the organization and dissemination of historical knowledge. In their role as teachers, historians use historical thinking and concepts to organize the results of historical inquiry into coherent and

12

meaningful courses and programs. What is being argued is that history courses are organized differently from other courses in the cultural sciences because they are essentially concerned with human experience over time and because although historians employ generalizations they do not seek to establish social scientific laws.

Historical inquiry seeks to establish historical facts out of an examination of evidence--written records, artifacts, and oral tradition. Historical facts appear to have two characteristics. First, they are acknowledged to be the case, that is, the information they assert is widely accepted. Secondly, they are historical facts because they are employed in the construction of historical knowledge, that is, not all facts about past events are historical facts. To be included in the class of historical facts requires that the facts make some difference in historical understanding.

The activity of transforming evidence into historical facts is only the initial step in historical inquiry. Indeed, the status of historical fact only comes if the final activity is undertaken, that is, the construction of historical knowledge. As indicated earlier, the two most popular misconceptions of history are related to mistakes about the nature of historical knowledge. The first mistake is the belief that historians establish the validity of certain discrete pieces of information about the past. The second mistake is the belief that historians seek to recreate the past or at least selected portions of it. If the first misconception is a popular vulgarity, the second is largely a creation of historians. To actually reconstruct or recreate the past would be to place the historian in the same position as the critic of contemporary society. The point of history is to understand the past. Historical understanding is no more facilitated by the amassing of facts than is the understanding of any contemporary event by the sheer accumulation of facts.

The point of historical inquiry is to understand the past by constructing interpretations that give point and meaning to past events. Using historical facts, logic, and reasonable assumptions, historians construct interpretations that are coherent and contextually related to other historical facts. Given this view of historical activity, we come to certain conclusions about the nature of historical knowledge: (1) historical knowledge and facts are not identical although the former is constructed out of the latter; (2) historical knowledge is only probable in that it is based on historical fact, logic, and assumptions, which allow human ingenuity to construct a narrative that interprets a particular set of events; and (3) the crucial element in the construction of historical interpretation is the assumptions that both guide the selection of facts and impart meaning to their order.

Consequently the appearance of seminal studies that integrate contemporary historical research must necessarily wait on the development of significant new historical interpretations. In turn, new interpretations do not grow out of new historical facts but rather out of new assumptions. In one sense, new assumptions by making different facts relevant to historical inquiry create new historical facts.

Thus, in surveying history of education as a university discipline, we may understand historical studies as serving one of two functions: the establishment of historical facts or the construction of historical knowledge. Many individual pieces of historical inquiry are so lacking in interpretative scope that they serve as coherent collections of historical data. Consequently, they require an interpretative framework that will transform them from fact to knowledge.

THEMES AND STUDIES

In the case of the history of education in western societies to begin at the beginning is wise

14

counsel. The educational practices, institutions and ideas of ancient Greece and Rome have been extensively and critically examined. Both educationists and classicists have been drawn to educational issues for distinct reasons. For the educationists, the classic world possessed a cultural and linguistic unity that was cut across by substantial intellectual and ethical considerations. Given their moral and practical concerns, educationists appreciated the manner in which these issues were dealt with in the city-states of classical Greece, in the Hellenistic kingdoms, and in republican and imperial Rome. The state of these societies provided a social laboratory in which ideas about human nature and institutions found concrete expression. For classicists, the ancient western world represented not only the first flourishing of literature, philosophy, and science, but more importantly man's first attempts to define himself and his world. The Greeks, in particular, were conscious of their social character and sought to explicate the ways in which character could be achieved by a conscious activity, i.e., by education.

The most influential recent studies have all stressed the Greek sense of culture as consciously pursued ideals which could be translated into educational terms and finally pedagogical activities.[17] An interesting aspect of Greek education was the extent to which much of it occurred in informal settings. Indeed, the strictly educational studies usually operate on a fairly high level of analysis and often ignore the development and practices of schools.[18]

It was, however, the development of educational institutions and practices hardy enough to stand the shock of transplantation that established the immense historical importance of Greek culture. Hellenistic education with its curricula, systematic organization, and methods, meant that non-Greeks could be Hellenized and that compatible cultures had the organizational framework into which their own ideals and values could be poured. From

15

the philosophic and cultural issues of classical
Greek education which provided a unity as a back-
drop to ethical and political differences, we move
easily into another unity, namely, the view of
education as the conscious attempt to form human
personality and the continuity of pedagogical institutions, practices, and ideas.[19]

To some extent, the sense of wholeness and
continuity reflects the ancient sense of time and
culture, that is, the ancients understood themselves
to be living under the same sun and participating
in the same milieu although separated by centuries.
This continuity is further enhanced by the organic
development of educational patterns from Greece
through Hellenism to Rome. The disappearance of
artistic and athletic training in Roman education
was the culmination of a marked tendency in that
direction in Hellenistic education. It might also
be noted that the concept of developing citizens
to match the particular constitution of a state
fitted admirably the needs of states that lacked
the modern sense of nationalism.

Late Hellenistic and Roman education had to
confront two new problems, i.e., Christianity and
Greek scholarship in a non-Greek society. Using
Hellenic models, Roman scholars and writers were
able to create a solid if less magnificent body of
literature upon which to build an educational system. The Roman example suggested two compatible
solutions to questions of foreign language instruction, namely, the translation of classics into the
vernacular and the potential of a vernacular to
produce authentic masterpieces.[20]

Christianity proved an intractable problem
because it represented a different world view not
only from classical culture but from all secular
societies. Out of the bitter confrontation of
Imperial Rome, classical culture, and Christianity
came an accommodation in which classical learning
became an integral part of Christian life. Needing
a literate clergy and laity, the early church accepted the classical school as a prime means for such

training. At the same time, religious education and moral training were deemed to belong to the home and the church.[21]

The integration of the political, cultural, and religious elements in the later Roman empire provided a powerful impetus to cultural continuity; however, it also raised serious practical problems for the Christian church with the decline of secular institutions. The decline of Roman authority and the weakening of the institutions of cultural transmission broke the unity of classical culture. There are, of course, a number of ways in which to understand that fateful political and social collapse. If one compares the literary and scientific level of late Roman and early medieval societies, then the Roman collapse can only be seen as an unmitigated disaster; however, if the last centuries of Roman rule are seen as the fag end of a burnt out culture without answers to a pressing series of socio-economic problems, then collapse can be viewed as the burial of a spent cultural and political entity.[22] In any event, the failure of Roman secular institutions and the survival of the Christian church in the massive demographic changes of Western Europe transformed forever the nature of European life. It was the period from 300 to 1200 that established many of the enduring characteristics of Western life that have only been finally eroded in this century. Educationally, three developments provided the framework for the creation of European society.[23]

First, as in the case of Roman contact with Greek culture, the Christian church was faced with the problem of providing classical education in a non-classical world. Given the integration of Christianity and classical learning, the church required classically trained clergy. Even a patina of Roman culture in many provinces ensured that promising boys would be trained in properly staffed schools. The demographic changes not only destroyed the schools and other cultural supports but also converted the provinces into non-Latin speaking societies. The problem of second language instruction, which the Romans had evaded by converting their schools from Greek to Latin, had to be faced up to directly. The work of Irish and English monks in the sixth and seventh centuries provided the pedagogical techniques for turning the sons of "barbarians" into classical scholars. These procedures were later introduced into the palace schools and monasteries of the continent by the educational reforms of Charlemague in the eighth century.

A second problem is related closely to the issue discussed above, that is, the gradual establishment of ecclesiastical control of education. When confronted by the need for an educated clergy, the early Christian church had decided not to establish a parallel and competing system of schools but rather to build the theological training of clergy upon the base of classic studies. The collapse of secular authority and its cultural institutions forced the church to take a hand in the training of its priests and religious. At the same time, the emerging medieval politia required educated clerks and officials as much as the church required educated clergy. Given the universality and institutional strength of the church, it possessed even in its darkest moments a layer of training that did not exist at the medieval courts. Consequently, when the medieval monarchs sought to upgrade their administrations they turned to the bishops and clergy within their realms for trained manpower. Thus, it was in the interests of the church and state to improve the efficiency and education of the clergy. In addition, it was the Church which possessed the initial manpower and experience necessary for substantial educational reform. The whole thrust from the eighth century was to expand the Church's responsibility for and control of educational institutions. By the high middle ages, the identification of Church and education had been established.

Thirdly, ancient education had emphasized rhetoric and literary studies--with scientific, philosophical and professional training occupying a very minor area. Medieval society had witnessed

18

a nearly absolute reversal of emphasis. As suggested in the discussion of the first two developments, much of the pressure for educational transformation came out of pressing practical problems. In this instance, the demand was not for cultured and refined aristocrats and landowners but for skillful and literate clergy and administrators to manage the affairs of Church and state and to provide the religious services offered by a sophisticated church. Faced with acute practical demands, medieval education developed a network of professional specialties which by a combination of apprenticeship and instruction would produce the needed personnel in medicine, law, theology, and administration.

In brief, one can understand the period from 200 to 1200 as being defined educationally by two major developments. One involved a major shift in institutional power, that is, the identification of formal education as the responsibility of the Church. Although there is evidence of a reluctance to undertake the duty, religious and secular needs were too great to resist. Once the Church assumed responsibility for education, institutional inertia and the growing realization of the importance of education in ensuring orthodoxy and religious stability tended to intensify ecclesiastical control. The other represented major intellectual changes, namely, the sustaining of Latin literature and cultural values which in time would provide the exemplar for incorporating the flourishing vernacular literatures into the curricula and the creation of new disciplines which would have a major impact on Western culture. Although the classics are often seen as inhibiting the development of vernacular languages and literatures in Europe, it is mistaken not to recognize that the institutional framework and the categories of thought were largely supplied by the transformations which have occurred around the remnants of classical learning in contact with the demographically revolutionized medieval society.

By the eleventh century, the major educational agencies that would dominate early modern Europe and its colonial offshoots were in the process of formation. The cathedral and collegiate schools of northern Europe replaced the monasteries and courts as the principal centres of learning. The next century witnessed the rise of the university on the basis of the professional disciplines, which had developed during the early middle ages, and a revival of the arts. The medieval university provided the organizational pattern and fundamental concept of higher education in the west. Although the continuity of organization is too obvious for comment, the enduring imprint on the concept of higher education is less often recognized. What was established by the medieval university was the understanding that higher education involved a unique mixture of education and training, that is, of instruction and apprenticeship. The medieval university was not a place of education--if by that is meant a concern for the total person--but rather an agency for the acquisition of certain societally and professionally useful skills and knowledge by means of lectures and apprenticeship. The active nature of this learning gave the university and its members--students as well as masters--a sense of participation in the creation of new knowledge. Although the tradition of experimental research would rise in the nineteenth century, the medieval university was from its inception a means of intellectual production. Consequently, higher education was distinguished from cathedral and other schools by the combination of instruction and apprenticeship which introduced students to the production of academic knowledge. Although the expansion of post-secondary institutions since World War II hastened to blur the distinction between secondary education and university training, the parasitic nature of the former on the results of the latter is undeniable.

The central importance of the medieval university in defining many of the enduring intellectual issues of western society provides a focus for the study of medieval education. In addition, the university in its organization and ideas reflected much of medieval society and consequently provides a useful means of linking medieval education to social and cultural developments.[24]

The persistence of university organizational patterns allows for the continuity between the Middle Ages and the Renaissance and Reformation. Although the impact of Renaissance humanism is acknowledged to have been great, the actual connection between humanism and education is a matter of dispute. The Renaissance scholar P.O. Kristeller has argued that humanism was largely an educational movement and that in Italy the humanist scholar gained a commanding role in education. This view is disputed by R.R. Bolgar, who adopting a more limited concept of humanist scholar, identified a smaller group of humanists active in formal pedagogical institutions. Both Kristeller and Bolgar agree on the essentially literary interests of the humanists and their limited impact--except for improved style and greater sophistication in using linguistic techniques--on professional and scientific studies. In a sense, the very success of humanism destroyed it as an innovating force in formal education. The production of vernacular translations of Greek and Latin classics, the work of humanist scholars, made interest in the thought of the ancients less pressing in schools and universities and ensured the dissemination of classical allusions into the growing vernacular literature. In addition, humanist learning had to accommodate the Reformation, whose concern for piety and religious orthodoxy encouraged a stress on style and form over content.[25]

The period from the triumph of humanist education in European educational institutions in the sixteenth century to the rise of national systems of schools in the nineteenth century has proved to be a difficult one for educational historians to handle as can be seen in the scholarly literature. When treating these centuries, historians depend upon analyses of educational theorists such as Montaigne, Comenius, Locke, and Rousseau, or descriptions of educational experiments, e.g., Basedow's Philanthropinum, or the rise of experimental science and the growing conviction that scientific studies held the key to transforming and controlling man's environment. The trend of these lines of scholarship has been to emphasize the general undercutting of secondary and university curricula that had been formed in the Middle Ages and Renaissance on the grounds of their irrelevance to social and intellectual conditions.[26]

Such historians have confined their interests too closely to the schools, thereby missing the significance of developments outside these institutions, and have been unable to reconcile the persistence of existing schools and the demands for change. The emphasis on strictly internal matters, i.e., curricula and methods, has distorted the analyses of theorists of failing to explicate where and how education as an institution and a process connects with larger societal elements.

Although the period suffers from a lack of synthesizing works, the framework for a unifying interpretation is found in the studies of Philippe Aries and a new generation of scholars who are examining the growth of institutional life since the Middle Ages. The idea that early modern history was marked by an absolute explosion of institutional changes is not new. A central theme of professional historical study has been the rise of the national state with all its accompanying rationalization and organization. It is, therefore, easy for us to grasp that between us and medieval society there existed an institutional gap. At the same time, we are aware that certain institutional forms existed in shapes that are clearly antecedents of present ones. These considerations have led us to a classic Whig interpretation of the centuries, that is, we have traced out the transformation of our educational institutions--with their associated patterns of ideas, activities, and beliefs--as if they were seeds needing only the proper conditions to grow into fully developed plants. Associated with that view is the assumption that related ideas, activities, and beliefs were also in embryonic forms that would eventually reach a complete mature stage.

From this perspective, every past society or civilization can only be viewed as an imperfect version of the present. Bernard Bailyn in his watershed criticism of history of education in the United States charged that educational historians lacked a sense of surprise. As discussed earlier, historians do know the outcomes of past events; therefore, the surprise that Bailyn calls for is the kind that occurs when we come to understand that the fundamental assumptions behind earlier institutions, ideas, activities, and beliefs, are essentially different from those that shape our world. The differences are not of the primitive and rudimentary to the sophisticated and mature but rather distinct but overlapping world views. What is being suggested is that such distinct views are clearly not those which separate modern "primitive" societies from modern western societies but rather that which separate us from a world which was not incompatible with modern science, technology, and rationality. In brief, the medieval world was like us but fundamentally different.

It is the genius of historians of institutional changes to have explicated the underlying assumptions and to provide an alternative to the dominant Whig view of history. The unifying interpretation develops along the following lines: first, there are certain essential activities and functions in western societies that are provided regardless of their technological or scientific sophistication, e.g., education, occupation, and social participation; secondly, these general functions are organized and conducted according to certain societal perceptions that give form to a culture's historical world; and, finally, to understand these historical worlds we must acquire a comprehension of the societal perceptions.[27]

These societal perceptions are not the historical equivalents of the results of public opinion polls. They are instead fundamental and usually inarticulated understandings about man and his environment. In the past two decades, historians have sought to determine the essential meanings of a wide range of basic concepts. For students of education, the central concepts are education.

schooling, family, childhood, adolescence, occupation, and citizenship. In particular, much of the
social change of the past four hundred years can
be organized around three concepts: childhood,
family, and schooling.[28]

Such an organization not only incorporates
much of the newest research but also assimilates
the standard literature in the field. Unless we
can comprehend how past generations were initiated
without schools into society, it is very likely
that we will see their societies as primitive.
What is needed is more than cliches about boys and
girls gaining the folk wisdom of animal life and
food-gathering from parents. What is being re-
covered is the mechanics of how people grew up and
became part of societies where schools performed a
very limited if crucial function.[29]

The three concepts allow us to interpret the
following historical facts: the explosion of
schooling in the eighteenth and nineteenth centuries that culminated in compulsory attendance legis-
lation; the increase in institutions serving and
controlling special populations; the marked rise
in sentimentality concerning family life; and the
sense of a loss of community and sociability so
characteristic of modern literature. The transformation of the school from an instrument of training
into an agency for education and enculturation required that the school became a specialized pro-
tective institution, whose clientele--if not in-
mates--were withdrawn from society, placed in an
especially controlled social setting, and prepared
to enter society at a later date. Within the school
they were classified and cared for according to the
characteristics determined by reformers, pedagogues,
and moralists. Their separation was justified on
grounds that alleged a weakness of mind and character requiring prolonged training and supervision.
Such a development had its counterparts in the
growing tendency to categorize elements within populations and to insist that their welfare demanded
separation from society and an extended, if not
permanent, minority.[30] An interesting aspect of
this drive to categorization is that it occurred

at the time of the final integration of political societies, that is, at the point in which citizenship was being universally extended under the ideology of nationalism.

It might be thought that these developments were essentially contradictory; however, the essence of the national state is completely compatible with increasing differentiation of its members. The national state is a centralizing bureaucratic polity which claims absolute responsibility for its members; therefore, no aspect of life is unworthy of its attention. The bureaucratic polity is a rational agency which meant that its actions are based on rules and rules in turn demand distinctions and categories.

Thus, it seems that the rise of the national state was a necessary condition for the institutionalization of modern societies--of which the common school is only the most universally and extensively experienced. But at the same time, such a state had to be in position to afford the institutionalization of whole populations. That is, the bureaucratic and ideological nature of the national state made categorization imperative but nineteenth and twentieth century technology made it possible.

An essential characteristic of national states is that fundamentally repressive activities are understood as liberating. The issue is not the old dilemma that freedom can only exist within a framework of laws, but rather that the function of law is positive, that is, not prohibiting but actively shaping and directing. This militant view found its way into other institutions, i.e., religion, family, and education.

In religion, the positive path has its limits since a church insisting upon vital religious commitment and fervour is led logically to inquisition or sectarianism. Unless supported by secular authority (which betrays ultimately religious independence), the inquisitional approach must falter. On the other hand, sectarianism is the path to

25

isolation and social irrelevance. In the face of the total authority of the state, the churches resorted to formal education as a means of maintaining their authority. The original identification of Christianity with the spoken word and a learned clergy was not extended to include a literate membership. The great missionary campaigns of the eighteenth and nineteenth centuries in Asia and Africa were clearly educational as well as religious efforts. Missionaries were often pedagogues as well as clergymen.[31]

Family life which we so easily identify with sentimentality and privacy also underwent a revolution in the centuries prior to the rise of mass compulsory schooling. The transformation of the family from an institution concerned primarily with the work of the world, that is, economic production and for the propertied the maintenance of their assets, to an agency of love and psychological control which paralleled the move from the medieval and Renaissance politics of subjects to the national states of citizens.[32]

The final key institution in the modernization of western society is the school. Schooling underwent two fundamental changes. First, that institutions like the family and the state had limited functions. Viewed as an articulated series of institutions, which is certainly giving it too much coherence, schooling even for those who made fullest use of it never had the same responsibility for shaping the minds and personality which we assign modern schools. The limits of formal education may be seen not only in organization, methods, and curricula, but more importantly in the writings about education from the Renaissance on.[33]

With some notable exceptions, educational theorists--before the nineteenth century--wrote about education and not schooling. (In days past, when educational treatises such as The Republic and The Emile were read in history of education courses, students often complained that their authors dealt with the whole life of the child.) Even in cases of

26

professional pedagogues such as Erasmuc and Melanch-
thon one is struck by either the extent to which
education is seen as occurring outside schooling
or the technical nature of their concerns.

In the seventeenth century, a series of
self-help tracts appeared which directly treated
schooling. An interesting aspect of these works
is that they dealt with the teaching and acquisition of basic skills of reading, writing, and computation. The books were intended either to assist
masters and others in providing very limited training to apprentices or others consigned to their
charge or to enable literate craftsmen to improve
their own skills.[34]

Thus, in neither of the cases previously
discussed was the school seen as a central agency
for education. Schools--from those providing limited literacy training to universities--had functions which involved training not education. The
limitations of universities come as no surprise to
us--even though for a brief moment in the 1960s some
people thought otherwise--since the terminology
connected with them all suggest an invitation into
a specific discipline with the acquisition of particular skills and knowledge that makes possible
the independent practice of the discipline. It is
possible that such an initiation can result in an
"educated" person but it is also equally possible
that vast numbers of trained persons lack the necessary characteristics. In that sense, the university in its most fundamental function as a research and training institution falls outside the
new concept of schooling that developed in the nineteenth century.[35]

The theorists of education--certainly from
Locke on--pioneered new sensitivities to child
nature and its proper formation. In the first
place, the idea of education as the perfection of
one's personality had been borrowed from the Greeks
and its exponents from Aristotle and Socrates to
Cicero clearly did not have school children in mind.
Secondly, the appeal to psychological ideas and

27

eventually theories that emphasized child development and the need for careful supervision and care marked a significant movement from the earlier concern with personality and the need for understanding the traits of one's students.

Whatever the source of the new sensibility, the first spokesmen wrote outside formal education. The major shift in educational thought occurred at the end of the eighteenth century with the work of Pestalozzi. The earlier theorists had assumed that a really self-conscious education was essential only for those social groups that could be expected to wield significant social and political power. The rest could obtain their training and education by means of the existing institutions which inducted them into the societies' occupations and social life. Like Locke and Rousseau, Pestalozzi was prompted by significant societal changes--in this case the disarray of the French Revolution and its aftermath--to invoke education as a means of social reform. Faced with mass poverty and social disorder, he sought educational solutions that were to be undertaken not in private homes but mass institutions.

For the first time on a significant institutional scale, the attempt was made to provide education to children. The century after Pestalozzi was truly the era of the common school institutionally and intellectually. A series of educational theorists and their disciples created a new literature and a new concept of schooling. Significant figures such as Herbart, Froebel, Dewey, and Montessori, made the school--and particularly the primary school--the central element of education. With the gradual extension of compulsory schooling into the secondary and tertiary levels, this concept was further established.

A major theoretical and organizational innovation that failed to permanently establish itself after some major successes tells us much about changing sensibilities.[36] The rise of the monitorial school movement with its societies, training

institutions, and proponents early in the nineteenth century and its total collapse by 1850 can
be seen as the failure of a pedagogical system
when confronted by growing demands for education.
Monitorialism was a rational, well-organized and
psychologically sophisticated system of instruction.
Although plagued by the stigma of being a form of
schooling for paupers, its major defect was that
it never became a system of education. Joseph
Lancaster, its principal spokesman, was able to
present a clear description of its psychological
and ethical underpinnings but was never able to
give the system creditability as an instrument of
moral and cultural development. In brief, monitorialism was more akin to the elementary instruction
of the medieval schools and the schools conducted
by masters for apprentices and others both children
and adults in the seventeenth century.

In this sense, schools were identified with
children and with the view that they had essential
cultural and moral functions. A concurrent notion,
evident in the works of Locke and Rousseau, challenged the concept of the fixity of human nature
by emphasizing the possibility of human improvement
by means of rational control and guidance of individual development. Earlier schemes of human betterment, for example, Plato and More, rested fundamentally on a utopian political and social system
which would train its citizens to fit the "constitution." The new proposals were individual and developmental, not social and static.

(This, of course, is not to question the
value or power of these classics but rather to
suggest that a major shift from theology and politics to psychology was occurring which moved the
focus of educational thought first away from a view
of education as a life-time activity and secondly
from an identification of pedagogy with training.)

Both Locke and Rousseau may be understood as
liberals and conservatives in that both sought to
ensure the stability of personal traits and habits
within a changing social framework. Locke's appeal

29

to generations of pedagogues is based on a commitment to classical educational aims as well as a
moderate and reasonable approach to them. What sets
Locke apart is the recognition that social and
political conditions that did not directly support
the desirable dispositions could be circumvented
by a carefully guided education. Rousseau's educational arguments are only comprehensible in the
context of his political and social thought in that
both Emile and Sophie are educated not for an ideal
society but for any one of the European politics.[37]

In this manner, the object of educational
thought went from theology and politics to psychology, from social structures to individual development, and from enculturation to schooling.

The major educational theorists of the past
two centuries--Pestalozzi, Herbart, Froebel, Montessori, and Dewey--have proposed reforms of pedagogical methods, curricula, and organization. It
is also significant that their greatest impact has
been in common school segment of modern educational
systems. Indeed, their failure to bring about innovations in the education of youth and adults may be
seen as both a limitation of their pedagogical vision
and the degree in which children, schooling, and
education have become interdependent.

The final element in this educational transformation from traditional to modern society was
the separation of the family from its social context. A persistent theme in literature, political
and social criticism, and social science is modern
western man's alienation, his loss of community,
and ultimately his purposelessness.[38] The dilemma
is, of course, that neither state is entirely desirable and that while truly communal societies run
counter to the essence of modern life, i.e., individuality, self-expression, and freedom from social
duty, the attempts to create ideological coherence
have led to politics that would torture and destroy
peoples and cultures for the sake of an idea.

The linkage between society and formal education underwent drastic changes in the nineteenth century. Schooling since the Sophists served an essential but limited function in western societies. It taught basic literacy and arithmetic skills, provided initiation into the domains of selected bodies of knowledge, and at the top-end produced independent and skilled professors of disciplines. But the major thrust of schooling at all levels was training rather than education. When to that is added the fact that such training was crucial to only a small proportion of society, it becomes clear that a considerable amount of education and, indeed, training took place outside agencies of formal pedagogy. The non-formal means which most readily spring to mind are apprenticeship, domestic service, and play. Such instruments of education and socialization are familiar to us principally as defeated social arrangements that fell before the forces of industrial society, i.e., science, technology, and schooling.

Apprenticeship collapsed because increasingly sophisticated technology required knowledge and skills preeminently acquired through instruction or because technology and the drive for profits destroyed the unity of crafts thereby turning them into a collection of discrete semi-skilled occupations. At the same time, political and social changes undercut domestic service as a respectable form of employment. The extension of full political rights to all citizens and the infiltration of democratic ideology into social relationships made it increasingly difficult to recruit and keep efficient domestic servants. Play in the form of adult activities functioned in many societies as an early means of inducting members into their values, beliefs, and socially significant activities. Faced with a growing fragmentation of modern society, play lost much of its relationship to the society's fundamental values, particularly regarding work, and increasingly found its expression in commercial enterprise or self-expression.

Whatever the causes, the decline signalled a major societal reorganization. A conventional

31

interpretation of the rise of schooling in the
nineteenth century is that the traditional western
family which had been a multi-purpose institution
began to give up those functions, e.g., education,
which it could no longer sustain and to transfer
them to other agencies. According to this view,
the ideal family had operated as a small self-
contained community providing except for highly
specialized activities, all the essential elements
of training and education. Seen in this light,
schools by becoming major institutions for education
as well as training began to displace the family as
the principal means of education and socialization.[39]

The evidence of the new historical demography suggests another and more intriguing interpretation.[40] The medieval social order was not
based upon an extended version of our affectionate
families. First, the family was a much more loosely
structured unit, held together more by economic and
social considerations than sentiment. Although
families served to provide the initial introduction
to the community, children were often put out to
apprenticeship or service well before puberty. Even
for those children not removed from their parents,
medieval society consisted of a multitude of social
groupings, occupational, age, and religious, that
claimed the allegiance of their members. While the
occupational bonds in the form of apprenticeship
and guilds are obvious enough, it is the age groups
that are most at variance with modern societies.
These societies served in some cases until the nineteenth century as instruments of initiation and control for young people as they were assimilated into
the general society. Although such age groupings
allowed for the release of energy and the testing
of growing strength, they did not function as a
deviant form of the general culture.

Secondly, the transformation of the family
into a sentimental and private institution meant
its withdrawal from the free flowing interaction of
medieval society. The sociability of medieval life
allowed for many institutions to participate in the
socialization and education of medieval man. The

growing privacy of the family meant not only its separation from the social milieu but also from work. Consequently, as family life became more inward and less social, men who had previously combined their occupation and family lives began to locate their offices, counting rooms, and workshops away from their living quarters. Seen in this manner, the family was not declining in the face of competing agencies but rather its success was ensured by the development of compatible institutions, i.e., schools. For the family to assert the claims of love and responsibility that have characterized western social relationship since the nineteenth century, it was necessary for it to maximize its psychological grasp by withdrawing from a too free interchange with its milieu. At the same time, contraction and withdrawal weakened the educative function of all non-formal agencies. Although a replacement was needed for the milieu and apprenticeship, it had to be compatible with the family's emphasis on love and privacy.[41]

The new school that was being given theoretical justification by educational thinkers such as Pestalozzi and Dewey was eminently suited to support the family in its socializing and educational activities. Like the new family, the new school had separated itself from the flow of society by buildings, age groupings, and psychological ideas concerning human development. Thus, the new family and the new school functioned as allies in converting traditional European communities into modern societies.[42]

Arising out of the interpretation is another way of understanding the establishment and operation of national systems of school. In the first place, the educational institutions of medieval Europe, while indispensible to the governance of secular and religious society, were not linked to social class and power in the manner of modern societies. Although not necessarily illiterate, the nobility were trained and educated by an apprenticeship to manner and morals in the big houses of their own class. The Latin schools constituted a network of

33

institutions of varying levels of instruction that were essentially more developed versions of smaller schools--from the little Latin schools to cathedral schools to the universities. The schools lacked graded articulated curricula, providing simultaneously elementary and higher instruction, and indiscriminately mixed boys with youths and adults. Designed for the training of clerics, the Latin schools served as nurseries for state officials. Given the pre-eminence of the nobility it was unnecessary for them to assure their position in secular and religious leadership by means of education. Consequently the students for Latin schools were drawn primarily from the commons, both rural and urban.[43]

At the same time, instruction in the vernacular represented a curious mixture of elementary subjects, i.e., writing and arithmetic, with quasi-legal and commercial skills such as the drafting of documents and contracts. Like the Latin schools, these institutions provided training in studies necessary for flourishing occupations. As a result, primary education that modern nations consider so essential in preparing their young for participation in society did not occur in schools. Rather as indicated earlier, it took place in apprenticeship, domestic service, and the milieu.

The expansion of schooling into education and socialization introduced questions of social distinction into institutions of formal education. Vernacular schools incorporated both the elementary training of the Latin and occupational schools as well as the socialization identified with apprenticeship and service. As educational agencies, schools were responsible for initiating children and youth into society. And a differentiated social order required a corresponding range of socialization. In particular vernacular elementary schooling with its emphasis on literacy, manners, and character, came increasingly under the auspices of religious and charitable interests and manifested itself as a form of rescue for irreligion, immorality, and pauperism. With the growing separation of family

34

and community, the vernacular school offered an alternative means of socialization and also served as a means of distinguishing between social groups.[44]

The old Latin school also underwent a transformation that made it a central experience for at first the middle classes and then the aristocracy. The social utility of humanistic education commonly identified with the grammar schools and universities was, of course, a common theme of educators and scholars from Petrarch to Milton. Much of the educational writing of the fifteenth and sixteenth centuries had emphasized the need for the "gentle born" to perfect their gifts with the proper training. Much of this literature stressed the power of a close and careful study of the classics to form the requisite moral and intellectual dispositions. The new Latin incorporated not only that emphasis but gave structural form to the humanist concern for guidance and supervision.[45]

The humanist educators who had gained notice as pedagogues had worked in small court or palace schools where they were able to control the lives of their students. But these ventures can be seen as additions to the initiation that such children and youths received in their participation at court. A real impact required institutions that would serve significant numbers of society's elite. Throughout the sixteenth and seventeenth centuries, Latin schools moved from clerical to secular, from professional preparation to education and socialization, and from peripheral to central institutions in the lives of European social and political elites. By the sixteenth century, the trend of extended schooling for socially significant boys and youth was firmly established and in succeeding centuries the old Latin schools underwent those changes that culminated into the "traditional" classical secondary schools of the nineteenth century.[46]

Essentially this meant that the schools became preparatory to participation in the society, that the theological character of the medieval school gave way to attitudes and studies more appropriate to governors of the new secular society, and that the previous distain of the aristocracy towards bookish learning was replaced by a growing belief that it was their privilege. Certainly by the nineteenth century, the identification of rank and secondary schooling had become the commonplace which it is today. The dilemma of the aristocracy concerning schooling--but not education and social-ization--was that it occupied a doubly privileged position, that is, by blood and rank it represented the best of the society and its way of life repre-sented the most desirable available to the society.

Since the aristocracy believed itself to be both biologically and culturally the "best" of the society, it was debatable that institutions could alter this matter very much. If schooling really made a difference, it called into question the whole basis of a society of ranks and orders. It would seem that fundamentally a belief in the rational control of human development, which lies at the heart of formal education, is a denial of a social order based on blood lines. The attraction of schooling is first to those social groups who possess the economic resources but not the lineage for full social and political participation. Consequently, the perennial rising middle classes of historians is a series of social groups being assimilated. That the "middle classes" did not rise once and for all is clearly substantiated by the sociological community studies which demonstrate how and when-- at least in the United States and Canada--various immigrant groups moved in significant numbers into the various social strata characterized by income, education, housing, and prestige.[47]

In large measure, the middle classes did not demand radical alterations in the unequal distri-bution of power and property. What was called for was a proper respect for and appreciation of their achievements which clearly demonstrated their right to share in the best life that society had to offer. As mentioned earlier, the aristocracy based its superiority on inherited qualities and blood and many educational theorists of the Renaissance advocated a special formal education which separated the aristocracy from the rest of society. Although admitting the necessity for the mastery of certain disciplines, the thrust of the proposals was to emphasize the development of character and mind by means of an initiation into a way of life.[48] Consequently, the focus on such education was the home either under the father's personal supervision or at least under a wise mentor chosen by the father. Locke is a late example of the blending of humanistic studies and formation in the aristocratic household. If such advice had won the day, European society would have integrated much more slowly than it did. The pressure of the centralizing bureaucratic states which required trained and literate governors, ministers, and clerks demanded that the aristocracy--as the humanists had foreseen--master those studies that would equip them to think and argue effectively, to organize and to deal conceptually with documents and facts. Both in economic and pedagogical terms, such training could not occur within households.

Schools were obviously required and once that was admitted then the institutions could not be limited to the aristocracy. Rather the original interest in them had come from those who saw them as instruments of training and then by those who recognized their power for re-socialization. The developing secondary schools pulled together the aristocracy and the social groups who because of their economic power demanded to be included in the governing classes. Although the aristocracy possessed various privileges within the schools and universities, the general tendency of schooling was to assimilate and integrate the dominant social and political classes.[49]

The process of social and political integration of the urban and rural poor also centred around the establishment of formal education. Like the aristocracy, the poor possessed a way of life most effectively entered into by participation and not by formal education. In contrast to their "betters," the lower orders were excluded from power

37

and any societal change that might move them to
action was generally opposed. Consequently except
for a select few chosen to be trained for service
to the church or state, the rationale for formal
education for the lower orders had to await the
appearance of new concepts of moral order, human
development, and social stability.[50]

The campaigns for schooling the poor had to
rest--at least in the beginning--on non-economic
grounds since both the level of technology and the
use of manpower did not require a schooled literate
populations. The reasons for the interest in educating the poor and labouring classes arose out of
religious piety, concerns for decency and deference,
and changing views of the nature of society and man.
Although the humanist concern for development and
its rational control assumed the possibility of
individual improvement, it was not until the seventeenth century that the concern was directed at the
lower orders in a pedagogical manner. The impulse
behind the early efforts at mass formal education
was religious and widespread throughout European
Christendom. In particular, the evangelical and
Catholic churches moved to provide religious instruction, character and religious formation, and
literacy training to the urban poor. Largely an
act by paternalism and Christian charity, the movement demonstrated that mass school could be sustained with an efficient administrative and pedagogical
organization.[51]

But clearly such activities saw schooling
and any related secular results were means to religious conversion and Christian witness. Although
such work was profoundly conservative in that it
sought to inculcate religious faith, develop virtues
of mind and character, train in literacy, in order
to arm their students against the evils of poverty,
that is, pauperism, irreligion, and social instability, such charity schooling with all its limitations
was severely criticized by conservatives on the
grounds that it unfitted the recipients for menial
and laborious tasks. Religious defenders of
charity schools argued that ignorance and isolation

were greater dangers to social and religious stability than a carefully guarded literacy. Such schools by providing an education that stressed personal responsibility, deference to lawful authority, and the providential nature of the social order, were claimed to innoculate their students against the social evils.[52] In brief, the campaigns rested on the assumptions that knowledge was preferable to ignorance, that truth could not fail to convince those who studied it, and that minds disciplined by elementary instruction would think and act in conformity with truth. It is important to remember that religious charity schooling was a significant development in that even in its most limited form it had moved beyond oral instruction and rote to reading. The more common forms include reading and writing with even arithmetic in many cases.[53]

Although many recent educational critics are prone to see schooling at the most advanced levels as an extremely effective means of social control, the history of the past century has demonstrated that revolutions are related to literacy and communication networks made possible by schooling. The critics of educational activities to the lower orders in the eighteenth and nineteenth centuries were correct in their conclusion that the consequences of schooling, especially literacy and a fuller perspective of the world, were to destroy the tribalism and isolation that allowed traditional political and social hierarchies to exist. Schooling permitted the growth of sentiments of culture, language and experience, in a manner that led to the identification of enduring national and cultural-linguistic groups. The gradual grinding down of tribal and village distinctions facilitated the development of nationalist feeling and prepared the way for future mini-nationalist movements that finally reached their logical conclusion in the separatist rhetoric of North American in the 1960s.

Religious sentiment underlying the early charity school movements was predicated on beliefs that although man's mind had been darkened and his will weakened these defects flowing from original

39

sin could be remedied by training, instruction, and habituation. While obviously rejecting any notion of human improveability. The gradual softening of pre-destinarianism and concepts of innate depravity among major protestant churches in the eighteenth and nineteenth centuries provided the green light for missionary activities, domestic and foreign.[54] A key element in missionary activities, Catholic and Protestant, was the assumption that catechetizing based on oral teaching, i.e., sermonizing, and rote memorization of catechism questions and answers was not sufficient. The essence of modern evangelism demanded literacy, which meant that most missionaries were pedagogues and that the missionary movements involved substantial formal education.

At the same time, currents of secular thought also supported the possibility and necessity of intervention in human life. One line of thought was based on the malleability of human nature and the potential for control inherent in a properly controlled environment. Nationalist movements and centralist tendencies in governments required the integration of all social elements within political boundaries. Together the two views justified state intervention and the creation of new institutions to ensure political and social assimilation. The absorption of religious and humanitarian educational efforts among the poor and labouring classes marked a significant watershed in schooling.[55]

First, no matter how the earlier educational activity was justified it obviously represented a charitable enterprise--the bringing of a good to the lower orders. State intervention meant that schooling was cast not only as a desirable good but moreover as an essential duty of citizenship, that is, schooling not only conferred citizenship but was demanded by it. In this sense, the identification of schooling and full social and political participation turned charity schooling into popular education.[56] Secondly, some humanitarians saw schooling and related types of formal education as having the power to bring about a series of social, moral, and political revolutions. Committed to the view that

knowledge is power, these theorists and practitioners saw formal education as a means of destroying
man's limited understanding of himself and the world
and of ending inequalities based on an incorrect
knowledge of the laws of societal life. Following
from this view was the notion that full and comprehensive education was a necessary condition of
human development, that is, popular education not
only freed men but also made humanity possible.[57]

By the late nineteenth century, the bases
for modern commitment had been securely established.
Indeed, it may be argued that schooling had become
the central institution of modern societies. Accordingly it is possible to understand developing
nations' movement toward modernization by examining
their incorporation of popular education into their
national ideology.[58] Within both developed and developing nations it is possible to construct a history of socio-economic and political integration
of social groups by examining their inclusion or
exclusion in popular education.[59]

With popular education, i.e., universal compulsory schooling, as the central and necessary institution of modern and modernizing societies, a
series of related studies examining the ideologies,
social and psychological theories, and pedagogical
ideas, from the Renaissance to the present has given
us an integrated background, a cognitive perspective, for understanding the recent studies in the
social history of education. These studies in emphasizing the growth of bureaucracy, institutional
refinement, and impersonalism have demonstrated the
triumph of the dominant notion of popular education, i.e., as the central duty of and means to
citizenship.[60] In fact, the crucial issue in the
historical studies in the social control tradition
is that compulsory schooling was the instrument of
social and political integration. Writing from the
perspective of North American capitalism, these
scholars have confused the dominant classes with
the requirements of the modern state.

Finally, the remarkable tradition of

41

dissenting educational critiques over the past two
centuries can be interpreted fundamentally as a
rejection of an assimulating social and political
order. The tendency to lump together conservative
and radical social and educational critics is to
blur a significant distinction. The conservative
critic rejects the modern state and its institutions because they mean the limitation of freedom
in all spheres of life. The radical critic identifying the state and personal aggrandisement sees
the growth of compulsory schooling as the extension
of class power.

Critics and proponents have come to see formal education within the intricate web of roles and
relationships of modern and modernizing societies.
The crucial position of schooling in understanding
that web has made history of education in all its
forms an exciting and truly foundational study for
teachers.

FOOTNOTES

1. Merle L. Borrowman, The Liberal and Technical in Teacher Education (New York: Teachers College, Columbia University, 1956); Charles J. Brauner, American Educational Theory (Englewood Cliffs, N.J.: Prentice-Hall, 1964); and Paul Woodring, "The Development of Teacher Education," in National Society for the Study of Education, Teacher Education, 74th Yearbook, Part 2 (Chicago: NSSE, 1975).

2. Sol Cohen, "The History of the History of American Education, 1900-1976: The Uses of the Past." Harvard Educational Review 46 (August 1976): 298-330.

3. Bernard Bailyn, Education in the Forming of American Society (Chapel Hill: University of North Carolina Press, 1960); Michael B. Katz, Class, Bureaucracy and Schools (New York: Frederick Praeger, 1971); and Diane Ravitch, The Revisionists Revised (New York: Basic Books, 1978).

4. Cohen, "History of the History of American Education," and Robert R. Sherman and Joseph Kirschner (eds.), Understanding History of Education (Cambridge: Schenkman, 1976).

5. Gabriel A. Almond and Sidney Verba, The Civic Culture (Princeton: Princeton University Press, 1963); Frederick Harbison and Charles A. Myers, Education, Manpower and Economic Growth (New York: McGraw-Hill, 1964); and David E. Apter, The Politics of Modernization (Chicago: University of Chicago Press, 1965).

6. Bailyn, "Education as a Discipline: Some Historical Notes," in John Walton and James L. Kuethe (Eds.), The Discipline of Education Madison: University of Wisconsin Press, 1963; Lawrence A. Cremin, The Wonderful World of Ellwood Patterson Cubberley (New York: Teachers College Press, 1965); and Brian Simon, "History of Educa-

tion," in J.W. Tibble (Ed.), The Study of Education
(London: Routledge and Kegan Paul, 1970).

7. Lawrence A. Crenin, The Transformation of
the School (New York: Alfred A. Knopf, 1961);
Raymond E. Callahan, Education and the Cult of
Efficiency (Chicago: University of Chicago Press,
1962); and Rush Welter, Popular Education and
Democratic Thought in America (New York: Columbia
University Press, 1962).

Earlier studies that should have alerted educational historians to new possibilities were because of their authorship and topics largely ignored: H.I. Marrou, A History of Education in
Antiquity (New York: Sheed and Ward, 1956), and
R.R. Bolgar, The Classical Heritage and Its Beneficiaries (Cambridge: Cambridge University Press,
1954).

8. Colin Greer, The Great School Legend (New
York: Viking Press, 1971); Michael B. Katz, The
Irony of Early School Reform (Cambridge: Harvard
University Press, 1968); and Samuel Bowles and
Herbert Gintis, Schooling in Capitalist America
(New York: Basic Books, 1976).

9. Patricia T. Rooke, "From Pollyanna to
Jeremiah--Recent Interpretations of American Educational History." Journal of Educational Thought
9 (April 1975):   15-29.

10. Marvin Lazerson, Origins of the Urban
School (Cambridge: Harvard University Press,
1972); Clarence Karier, Paul Violan, and Joel
Spring, Roots of Crisis (Chicago: Rand McNally,
1973); and David B. Tyack, The One Best System
(Cambridge: Harvard University Press, 1974).

11. Earl F. Cheit, The New Depression in Higher Education (New York: McGraw-Hill, 1971).

12. N.L. Gage and Philip H. Winne, "Perfor-
mance-Based Teacher Education," and N. Bush and
Peter Enemack, "Control and Responsibility in

Teacher Education," in NSSE, Teacher Education.

13. Robert F. Berkhofer, Jr., A Behavioral Approach to Historical Analysis (New York: Free Press, 1969), and William O. Aydelotte, Quantification in History (Reading, Mass.: Addison-Wesley, 1971).

14. Carl F. Kaestle, The Evolution of an Urban School System: New York, 1750-1850 (Cambridge: Harvard University Press, 1973); Stanley K. Schultz, The Culture Factory: Boston Public Schools, 1789-1860 (New York: Oxford University Press, 1973); and James W. Sanders, The Education of an Urban Minority: Catholics in Chicago, 1833-1965 (New York: Oxford University Press, 1977).

15. Walter Feinberg, Reason and Rhetoric (New York: John Wiley, 1975).

16. The sources of this discussion are Gordon Leff, History and Social Theory (Garden City: Anchor Books, 1966); Jack W. Meiland, Scepticism and Historical Knowledge (New York: Random House, 1965); and Peter Winch, Idea of a Social Science and Its Relation to Philosophy (London: Routledge and Kegan Paul, 1970).

17. Werner Jaeger, Paideia: The Ideals of Greek Culture, 3 vols. (New York: Oxford University Press, 1943-45), and A.W.H. Adkins, Merit and Responsibility: A Study in Greek Values (London: Oxford University Press, 1960).

18. William Frankena, Three Historical Philosophies of Education (Chicago: Scott, Foresman, 1965); William Barclay, Educational Ideals in the Ancient World (London: Collins, 1959); and E.B. Castle, Ancient Education and Today (Harmondsworth: Penguin Books, 1961).

19. Marrou, A History of Education in Antiquity; Aubrey O. Gwynn, Roman Education from Cicero to Quintilian (New York: Teachers College Press, 1966); and Stanley F. Bonner, Education in

45

Ancient Rome (Berkeley: University of California Press, 1977).

20. T.J. Haarhoff, Schools of Gaul (Johannesburg: Witwatersrand University, 1958).

21. Marrou, A History of Education in Antiquity, and Bolgar, The Classical Heritage.

22. William Carroll Bark, Origins of the Medieval World (Stanford: Stanford University Press, 1958).

23. The following discussion is based primarily on the works of Marrou and Bolgar supplemented by E. Harris Harbison, The Christian Scholar in the Age of the Reformation (New York: Charles Scribners, 1961); Pierre Riche, Education and Culture in the Barbarian West (Columbia: University of South Carolina Press, 1978); and Cora E. Lutz, Schoolmasters of the Tenth Century (Hamden, Conn.: Shoe String, 1977).

24. Hastings, Rashdall, The Universities of Europe in the Middle Ages (new edition, F.M. Powicke and A.B. Emden, Eds., 3 vols.; London: Oxford University Press, 1936); and Gordon Leff, Paris and Oxford Universities in the 13th and 14th Centuries (New York: John Wiley, 1968).

25. Paul O. Kristeller, Renaissance Thought: The Classic, Scholastic, and Humanistic Strains (New York: Harper Torchbooks, 1961); Kenneth Charlton, Education in Renaissance England Toronto: University of Toronto Press, 1965); Joan Simon, Education and Society in Tudor England (London: Cambridge University Press, 1966); Fritz Caspari, Education and Social Order in Tudor England (New York: Teachers College Press, 1968); and the old but useful studies by W.H. Woodward, Studies in Education during the Age of the Renaissance, 1400-1600 (New York: Teachers College Press, 1967); Vittorino da Feltre and Other Humanist Educators (New York: Teachers College Press, 1963), and Desiderius Erasmus Concerning the Aim and Method of

Education (New York: Teachers College Press, 1964).

26. R. Freeman Butts, A Cultural History of Western Education (New York: McGraw-Hill, 1955); H.G. Good, A History of Western Education (2nd. ed.) (New York: Macmillan, 1960); and James Mulhern, A History of Education (2nd ed.) (New York: Ronald Press, 1959).

27. David J. Rothman, The Discovery of the Asylum: Social Order and Disorder in the New Republic (Boston: Little, Brown, 1971).

28. R.L. Schnell, "Childhood as Ideology: A Reinterpretation of the Common School." British Journal of Educational Studies (forthcoming 1979).

29. John Demos, A Little Commonwealth: Family Life in Plymouth Colony (New York: Oxford University Press, 1970).

30. Gerald N. Grob, Mental Institutions in America (New York: Free Press, 1973).

31. Patricia T. Rooke, "The Christianization and Education of Slaves and Apprentices in the British West Indies: The Impact of Evangelical Missionaries, 1800-1838." (Ph.D. dissertation, University of Alberta, 1977).

32. Philippe Aries, Centuries of Childhood (New York: Vintage Books, 1965).

33. William H. Woodward (Ed.), Vottorino da Feltre and Other Humanist Educators (New York: Teachers College, 1963); Peter Gay (Ed.), John Locke on Education (New York: Teachers College, 1964); and William Boyd (Ed.), The "Emile" of Jean-Jacques Rousseau (New York: Teachers College, 1962).

34. John W. Adamson, Pioneers of Modern Education in the Seventeenth Century (New York: Teachers College, 1971).

47

35. R.S. Peters, Ethics and Education (London: George Allen and Unwin, 1966).

36. Carl F. Kaestle (Ed.), Joseph Lancaster and the Monitorial School Movement: A Documentary History (New York: Teachers College, 1973).

37. Victor G. Wexler, "'Made for Man's Delight': Rousseau as Antifeminist." American Historical Review 81 (April 1976): 266-291; Ernest Cassirer, The Question of Jean-Jacques Rousseau (Bloomington: Midland Books, 1963), and Rousseau, Kant and Goethe (New York: Harper Torchbooks, 1963); and Charles W. Hendel, Jean-Jacques Rousseau: Moralist (Indianapolis: Bobbs-Merrill, 1962).

38. Jean Paul Sartre, Existentialism and Humanism (1948) and Nausea (1964).

39. Bailyn, Education in the Forming of American Society.

40. Edward Shorter, The Making of the Modern Family (New York: Basic Books, 1975).

41. Philippe Aries, "La Famille: A Report from France." Encounter 45 (August 1975): 7-12; and Jacques Mousseau, "The Family: Prison of Love." Psychology Today (August 1975): 53-58.

42. Barbara Finkelstein, "Pedagogy as Intrusion: Teaching Values in Popular Primary Schools in Nineteenth Century America." History of Childhood Quarterly 2 (Winter 1975): 349-378; and "The Fear of Childhood: Relations Between Parents and Teachers in Popular Primary Schools in the Nineteenth Century." Ibid. 3 (Winter 1976): 321-335.

43. J.H. Hexter, Reappraisals in History (New York: Harper Torchbooks, 1961).

44. M.G. Jones, The Charity School Movement (London: Frank Cass, 1964).

48

45. Fritz Caspari, Humanism and Social Order in Tudor England (New York: Teachers College, 1968); and Arthur B. Ferguson, The Articulate Citizen and the English Renaissance (Durham: Duke University Press, 1965).

46. Charles R. Bailey, French Secondary Education, 1763-1790: The Secularization of Ex-Jesuit Colleges (Philadelphia: American Philosophical Society, 1978).

47. John Porter, The Vertical Mosaic (Toronto: University of Toronto Press, 1965).

48. Machiavelli, The Prince; Sir Thomas Elyot, The Book Named the Governor; and Baldesar Castiglione, The Book of the Courtier.

49. Brian Simon, Studies in the History of Education, Vol. 1 (London: Lawrence and Wishart, 1965).

50. Harold Silver, The Concept of Popular Education (London: McGibbon & Key, 1965).

51. Jones, The Charity School Movement; Adamson, Pioneers of Modern Education; and Edward A. Fitzpatrick, LaSalle: Patron Of All Teachers (Milwaukee: Bruce, 1951).

52. Hannah More, Practical Piety, 2 vols. (London, 1818); and Sarah Trimmer, Instructional Tales (London, 1821).

53. Thomas W. Laqueur, Religion and Respectability (New Haven: Yale University Press, 1976).

54. Bernard Semmel, The Methodist Revolution (New York: Basic Books, 1973).

55. Donald H. Akenson, Irish Education Experiment (Toronto: University of Toronto Press, 1970); Alison Prentice, The School Promoters (Toronto: McClelland & Stewart, 1977); John Hurt, Education in Evolution (London: Puladin Books, 1972); and

Merle Curti, The Social Ideas of American Educators (Rev.ed.; Paterson: Littlefield, Adams, 1959).

56. Phillip McCann (Ed.), Popular Education and Socialization in the Nineteenth Century (London: Methuen, 1977); Michael B. Katz, The Irony of Early School Reform (Cambridge: Harvard University Press, 1968); and Prentice, The School Promoters.

57. George Z.F. Bereday (Ed.), Charles Merrimam's "The Making of Citizens" (New York: Teachers College, 1966).

58. Silver, Concept of Popular Education; and J.F.C. Harrison, Quest for the New Moral Order (New York: Charles Scribner's Sons, 1969).

59. For two examples for inclusion and exclusion of a religious and a racial minority, see R.L. Schnell and Patricia T. Rooke, "Intellectualism, Educational Achievement, and American Catholicism." Canadian Review of American Studies 8 (Spring 1977): 66-76; and Louis R. Harlan, Separate and Unequal (Chapel Hill: University of North Carolina Press, 1958).

60. Joel H. Spring, Education and the Rise of the Corporate State (Boston: Beacon Press, 1973); Samuel Bowles and Herbert Gintis, Schooling in Capitalist America (New York: Basic Books, 1976); and Paul C. Violas, The Training of the Urban Working Class (Chicago: Rand McNally, 1978).

BIBLIOGRAPHY

Adamson, John W. Pioneers of Modern Education in the Seventeenth Century. New York: Teachers College, 1971.

Adkins, Arthur W.H. Merit and Responsibility: A Study in Greek Values. London: Oxford University Press, 1960.

Akenson, Donald H. Irish Education Experiment: The National System of Education in the Nineteenth Century. Toronto: University of Toronto Press, 1970.

Anderson, R.D. Education in France, 1848-1870. London: Oxford University Press, 1975.

Artz, Federick B. The Development of Technical Education in France, 1500-1850. Cambridge, Mass.: M.I.T. Press, 1966.

Axtell, James. The School Upon a Hill. New Haven: Yale University Press, 1974.

Baldwin, John W. and Goldthwaite, Richard A. (eds.). Universities in Politics: Case Studies from the Late Middle Ages and Early Modern Period. Baltimore: The Johns Hopkins Press, 1972.

Banks, Oliver. Parity and Prestige in English Secondary Education. London: Routledge and Kegan Paul, 1955.

Bantock, G.H. T.S. Eliot and Education. New York: Random House, 1969

Barber, Elinor G. The Bourgeoisie in Eighteenth Century France. Princeton, N.J.: Princeton University Press, 1955.

Barclay, William. Educational Ideals in the Ancient World. London: Collins, 1959.

Barker, Sir Ernest. Traditions of Civility: Eight

51

<u>Essays</u>. Hamden, Conn.: Archon Books/Shoe
String Press, 1967.

Barker, Rodney. <u>Education and Politics, 1900-1951:
A Study of the Labour Party</u>. Oxford: Clarden
Press, 1972.

Bazeley, E.T. <u>Homer Lane and the Little Common-
wealth</u>. New York: Schocken Books, 1969.

Bendix, Reinhard. <u>Nation-Building and Citizenship:
Studies of Our Changing Social Order</u>. Garden
City, N.Y.: Doubleday Anchor Books, 1969.

Bendix, Reinhard. <u>Work and Authority in Industry:
Ideologies of Management in the Course of
Industrialization</u>. New York: Harper Torch-
books, 1963.

Bernbaum, Gerald. <u>Social Change and the Schools:
1918-1944</u>. London: Routledge and Kegan Paul,
1967.

Bettelheim, Bruno. <u>The Uses of Enchantment: The
Meaning and Importance of Fairy Tales</u>. New
York: Vintage Books, 1977.

Black, C.E. <u>The Dynamics of Modernization: A
Study in Comparative History</u>. New York:
Harper Torchbooks, 1967.

Bornstein, Diana. <u>Mirrors of Courtesy</u>. Hamden,
Conn.: Archon Books, 1975.

Brauer, George C., Jr. <u>The Education of the Gentle-
man: Theories of Gentlemanly Education in
England, 1660-1775</u>. New Haven, Conn.: College
and University Press, 1959.

Brauner, C.J. <u>American Educational Theory</u>. Englewood Cliffs, N.J.: Prentice-Hall, 1964.

Brim, Orville G., Jr. and Wheeler, Stanton.
<u>Sociolization After Childhood: Two Essays</u>.
New York: John Wiley and Sons, 1966.

Clapp, Margaret (ed.). The Modern University.
Ithaca, N.Y.: Cornell University Press, 1950.

Cochrane, Charles Norris. Christianity and Classical Culture: A Study of Thought and Action
from Augustus to Augustine. Corrected ed.
New York: Galaxy Books, 1957.

Cohen, Sol. Progressive and Urban School Reform:
The public School Association of New York,
1895-1954. New York: Teachers College, 1964.

Coveney, Peter. The Image of Childhood. Harmondsworth: Penguin Books, 1967.

Cremin, Lawrence A. American Education: The
Colonial Experience. New York: Harper & Row,
1970.

_____. The Genius of American Education. New
York: Vintage Books, 1966.

_____. The Transformation of the School: Pro-
gressivism in American Education, 1876-1957.
New York: Alfred A. Knopf, 1961.

_____. The Wonderful World of Ellwood Patterson
Cubberley: An Essay on the Histiography of
American Education. New York: Teachers Col-
lege, 1965.

_____. (ed.). Republic and the School: Horace
Mann on the Education of Free Men. New York:
Teachers College, 1957.

Cross, Barbara M. (ed.). The Educated Woman in
America: Selected Writings of Catharine
Beecher, Margaret Fuller, and M. Carey Thomas.
New York: Teachers College, 1965.

Curran, Francis X. The Churches and the Schools.
Chicago: Loyola University Press, 1954.

Bronfenbrenner, Urie. Two Worlds of Childhood:
U.S. and U.S.S.R. New York: Russel Sage
Foundation, 1970.

Brumbaugh, R.S. and N.M. Lawrence. Philosophers on Education. Boston: Houghton Mifflin, 1963.

Cable, Mary. The Little Darlings: A History of Child Rearing in America. New York: Charles Scribner's Sons, 1975.

Calam, John. Parsons and Pedagogues: The S.P.G. Adventure in American Revolution. New York: Columbia University Press, 1971.

Callahan, Raymond E. Education and the Cult of Efficiency. Chicago: University of Chicago Press, 1962.

Cassirer, Ernst. The Logic of the Humanities. New Haven: Yale University Press, 1961.

_____. The Philosophy of the Enlightenment. Boston: Beacon Press, 1955.

_____. The Question of Jean-Jacques Rousseau. Bloomington, Ind.: Midland Books, 1963.

_____. Rousseau, Kant and Goethe. New York: Harper Torchbooks, 1963.

Castle, E.B. Ancient Education and Today. Harmondsworth: Penguin Books, 1961.

_____. Educating the Good Man: Moral Education in Christian Times. New York: Collier Books, 1962.

_____. The Teacher. London: Oxford University Press, 1970.

Cheal, John E. Investment in Canadian Youth: An Analysis in Input-Output Differences Among Canadian Provincial School Systems. Toronto: Macmillan, 1963.

Curti, Merle. The Social Ideas of American Educators. Rev.ed. Paterson, N.J.: Littlefield, Adams, 1959.

Curtis, Mark H. Oxford and Cambridge in Transition, 1558-1642. Oxford: Oxford University Press, 1959.

Daly, Lowrie J. The Medieval University, 1200-1400. New York: Sheed and Ward, 1961.

deMause, Lloyd (ed.). The History of Childhood. New York: Harper Torchbooks, 1974.

Demos, John. A Little Commonwealth: Family Life in Plymouth Colony. New York: Oxford University Press, 1970.

Donohue, John W., S.J. St. Thomas Aquinas and Education. New York: Random House, 1968.

Dunkel, Harold B. Herbart and Education. New York: Random House, 1969.

_____. Herbart and Herbartianism: An Educational Chost Story. Chicago: University of Chicago Press, 1970.

Dunn, William Kailer. What Happened to Religious Education? The Decline of Religious Teaching in the Public Elementary School 1776-1861. Baltimore: Johns Hopkins Press, 1958.

Dworkin, Martin S. (ed.). Dewey on Education: Selections. New York: Teachers College, 1959.

Eaglesham, E.J.R. The Foundations of Twentieth-Century Education in England. London: Routledge and Kegan Paul, 1967.

Elson, Ruth Miller. Guardians of Tradition: American Schoolbooks of the Nineteenth Century. Lincoln: University of Nebraska Press, 1964.

Evans, Leslie W. Education in Industrial Wales, 1700-1900: A Study of the Works Schools System in Wales during the Industrial Revolution. Cardiff: Avalon Books, 1971.

Farber, Bernard. Guardians of Virtue: Salem Families in 1800. New York: Basic Books, 1972.

Farrell, Allen P. The Jesuit Code of Liberal Education: Development and Scope of the Ratio Studiorum. Milwaukee: Bruce, 1938.

Fisher, Robert T. Classical Utopian Theories of Education. New York: Bookman Associates, 1963.

Fitzpatrick, Edward A. La Salle: Patron of All Teachers. Milwaukee: Bruce, 1951.

Frankena, W.K. Three Historical Philosophies of Education. Chicago: Scott, Foresman, 1965.

Freeman, Kenneth J. Schools of Hellas. (Classics in Education, No. 38). New York: Teachers College Press, 1969.

Gallagher, Donald A. (ed.). Some Philosophers on Education: Papers Concerning the Doctrines of Augustine, Aristotle, Aquinas, and Dewey. Milwaukee: Marquette University Press, 1956.

Ganss, George. Saint Ignatius' Idea of a Jesuit University. Milwaukee: Marquette University Press, 1956.

Garforth, Francis W. (ed.). John Stuart Mill on Education. New York: Teachers College Press, 1971.

Gartner, Lloyd P. (ed.). Jewish Education in the United States: A Documentary History. New York: Teachers College Press, 1969.

Gay, Peter (ed.). John Locke on Education. New York: Teachers College, 1964.

Gillis, John R. Youth and History. New York: Academic Press, 1974.

Goldstrom, J.M. Education: Elementary Education, 1780-1900. Newton Abbott: David & Charles, 1972.

_____. The Social Content of Education, 1808-1870: A Study of the Working Class Reader in England and Ireland. Totowa, N.J.: Rowman & Littlefield, 1978.

Gordon, Michael (ed.). The American Family in Social-Historical Perspective. New York: St. Martin's Press, 1973.

Gould, Joseph E. The Chautauqun Movement. New York: State University of New York, 1961.

Greene, Maxine. The Public School and the Private Vision: A Search for America in Education and Literature. New York: Random House, 1965.

Greven, Philip. The Protestant Temperament: Patterns of Child-Rearing, Religious Experience, and the Self in Early America. New York: Alfred A. Knopf, 1977.

Gutex, Gerald Lee. Pestalozzi and Education. New York: Random House, 1968.

Haarhoff, T.J. The Stranger at the Gate: Aspects of Exclusiveness and Co-operation in Ancient Greece and Rome, with Some Reference to Modern Times. Oxford: Basic Blackwell, 1948.

Handlin, Oscar, and Mary F. Handlin. Facing Life: Youth and the Family in American History. Boston: Atlantic-Little Brown And Co., 1971.

Hans, Nicholas. New Trends in Education in the Eighteenth Century. London: Routledge and Kegan Paul, 1951.

Hansen, Allen Oscar. Liberalism and American Education in the Eighteenth Century. New York: Octagon Books, 1965.

Harlan, Louis R. Separate and Unequal. Chapel
    Hill: University of North Carolina Press,
    1958.

Harris, Robin S. A Bibliography of Higher Educa-
    tion in Canada: Supplement 1965. Toronto:
    University of Toronto Press, 1965.

_____, and Arthur Tremblay. A Bibliography of
    Higher Education in Canada. Toronto: Uni-
    versity of Toronto Press, 1960.

Harrison, John F.C. (ed.). Utopianism and Educa-
    tion: Robert Owen and the Owenites. (Classics
    in Education, No. 37.) New York: Teachers
    College Press, 1968.

Haskins, Charles H. The Rise of Universities.
    Ithaca: Cornell University Press, 1957.

_____. Studies in Mediaeval Culture. New York:
    Frederick Unger, 1958.

Hawes, Joseph M. Children in Urban Society:
    Juvenile Delinquency in Nineteenth Century
    America. New York: Oxford University Press,
    1971.

Heeney, Brian. Mission to the Middle Classes: The
    Woodard Schools, 1848-1891. London: SPCK,
    1969.

Heslep, Robert D. Thomas Jefferson and Education.
    New York: Random House, 1969.

Hofstadter, Richard and Wilson Smith (eds.).
    American Higher Education: A Documentary
    History. 2 vols. Chicago: University of
    Chicago Press, 1961.

Holl, Jack M. Juvenile Reform in the Progressive
    Era: William R. George and the Junior Repub-
    lic Movement. Ithaca: Cornell University
    Press, 1971.

Holmes, Brian. Problems in Education: A Comparative Approach. London: Routledge and Kegan Paul, 1965.

Hunt, David. Parents and Children in History: The Psychology of Family Life in Early Modern France. New York: Basic Books, 1970.

Jaeger, Werner. Early Christianity and Greek Paideia. New York: Oxford Galaxy Books, 1969.

Jarrett, James L. (ed.). The Educational Theories of the Sophists. (Classics in Education, No. 39.) New York: Teachers College Press, 1969.

Jernegan, Marcus W. Laboring and Dependent Classes in Colonial America, 1607-1783. New York: Frederick Unger, 1960.

Johnson, Clifton. Old Time Schools and School Books. New York: Dover, 1963.

Joncich, Geraldine (ed.). Psychology and the Science of Education: Selected Writings of Edward L. Thorndike. New York: Teachers College, 1962.

Jones, Richard Foster. Ancients and Moderns: A Study of the Rise of the Scientific Movement in Seventeenth Century England. 2nd ed. Berkeley: University of California Press, 1961.

_____. The Triumph of the English Language: A Survey of Opinions Concerning the Vernacular from the Introduction of Printing to the Restoration. Stanford: Stanford University Press, 1953.

Jorgenson, Lloyd P. The founding of Public Education in Wisconsin. Madison: State Historical Society of Wisconsin, 1956.

Kaestle, Carl F. The Evolution of an Urban School System: New York, 1750-1850. Cambridge: Harvard University Press, 1973.

Karier, Clarence, Paul Violas, and Joel Spring.
    Roots of Crisis: American Education in the
    Twentieth Century. Chicago: Rand McNally,
    1973.

Katz, Michael B. The People of Hamilton, Canada
    West: Family and Class in a Mid-Nineteenth
    Century City. Cambridge: Harvard University
    Press, 1975.

_____ and Paul H. Mattingly (eds.). Education
    and Social Change: Themes from Ontario's
    Past. New York: New York University Press,
    1975.

Kazamias, Andreas M. (ed.). Herbert Spencer on
    Education. (Classics in Education, No. 30).
    New York: Teachers College Press, 1966.

_____. Politics, Society and Secondary Educa-
    tion in England. Philadelphia: University of
    Pennsylvania Press, 1966.

Kett, Joseph F. Rites of Passage: Adolescence in
    America. 1790 to the Present. New York: Basic
    Books, 1977.

Kibre, Pearl. The Nations in the Mediaeval Univer-
    sities. Cambridge: Mediaeval Academy of
    America, 1948.

_____. Scholarly Privileges in the Middle Ages.
    Cambridge: Mediaeval Academy of America, 1962.

Kiefer, Monica. American Children Through Their
    Books, 1700-1835. Philadelphia: University
    of Pennsylvania Press, 1948.

Kimball, Solon T. and James E. McClellan. Educa-
    tion and the New America. New York: Random
    House, 1962.

King-Hall, Magdalen. The Story of the Nursery.
    London: Routledge and Kegan Paul, 1958.

Kitto, H.D.F. The Greeks. Harmondsworth: Penguin
    Books, 1957.

Krug, Edward A. (ed.). Charles W. Eliot and Popular Education. (Classics in Education, No. 8.) New York: Teachers College, Columbia University, 1961.

_____. The Shaping of the American High School, 1880-1920. Madison: University of Wisconsin Press, 1969. [Paperback reprint].

_____. The Shaping of the American High School, 1920-1941. Madison: University of Wisconsin Press, 1972.

Lannie, Vincent P. (ed.). Henry Barnard: American Educator. New York: Teachers College Press, 1974.

Laqueur, Thomas Walter. Religion and Respectability: Sunday Schools and Working Class Culture, 1780-1850. New Haven: Yale University Press, 1976.

Latham, Jean. Happy Families: Growing Up in the Eighteenth and Nineteenth Centuries. London: Adam & Charles Black, 1974.

Lawr, Douglas and Robert Gidney (eds.). Educating Canadians: A Documentary History of Public Education. Toronto: Van Nostrand Reinhold, 1973.

Lazerson, Marvin and W. Norton Grubb (eds.). American Education and Vocationalism: A Documentary History, 1870-1970. New York: Teachers College Press, 1974.

Leclercq, Jean O.S.B. The Love of Learning and the Desire for God: A Study of Monastic Culture. New York: Mentor Books, 1962.

Lee, Gordon C. (ed.). Crusade Against Ignorance: Thomas Jefferson on Education. New York: Teachers College, 1961.

Lilley, Irene M. Friedrich Froebel: A Selection

from his Writings. London: Cambridge University Press, 1967.

L'Orange, H.P. Art Forms and Civic Life in the Late Roman Empire. Princeton: Princeton University Press, 1972.

Lowndes, G.A. Silent Social Revolution: An Account of the Expansion of Public Education in England and Wales, 1895-1965. 2nd ed. London: Oxford University Press, 1969.

MacKinnon, Frank. The Politics of Education. Toronto: University of Toronto Press, 1960.

MacLeod, Anne Scott. A Moral Tale: Children's Fiction and American Culture, 1820-1860. Hamden, Conn.: Archon Books, 1974.

MacNaughton, K.F.C. The development of the Theory and Practice of Education in New Brunswick. ("University of New Brunswick Historical Studies" No. 1.) Fredericton: University of New Brunswick, 1947.

Mason, John E. Gentlefolk in the Making: Studies in the History of English Courtesy Literature and Related Topics from 1531 to 1744. New York: Octagon Books, 1971. Originally published in 1935 by the University of Pennsylvania Press.

Mattingly, Paul H. The Classless Profession: American Schoolmen in the Nineteenth Century. New York: New York University Press, 1975.

McCann, Phillip (ed.). Popular Education and Socialization in the Nineteenth Century. London: Methuen, 1977.

McClintock, Jean and Robert (eds.). Henry Barnard's School Architecture. New York: Teachers College Press, 1970.

McDonald, Neil and Alf Chaiton (eds.). Egerton Ryerson and His Times. Toronto: Macmillan of Canada, 1978.

62

McLachlan, James. _American Boarding Schools: A Historical Study_. New York: Charles Scribner's Sons, 1970.

McLeish, John. _Evangelical Religion and Popular Education: A Modern Interpretation_. London: Methuen & Co., 1969.

Meier, August. _Negro Thought in America, 1880-1915: Racial Ideologies in the Age of Booker T. Washington_. Ann Arbor: University of Michigan Press, 1963.

Mennel, Robert M. _Thorns and Thistles: Juvenile Delinquents in the United States, 1825-1940_. Hanover, N.H.: The University Press of New England for The University of New Hampshire, 1973.

Meyer, Adolphe E. _The Development of Education in the 20th Century_. Englewood Cliffs, N.J.: Prentice-Hall, 1949.

Middlekauf, Robert. _Ancients and Axioms: Secondary Education in Eighteenth Century New England_. ("Yale Historical Publications," Miscellany 77.) New Haven: Yale University Press, 1963.

Milton, John. _Areopagitica and On Education_. New York: Appleton-Century-Crofts, 1951.

Mohl, Raymond A. _Poverty in New York, 1783-1825. The Urban Life in American Series_. New York: Oxford University Press, 1971.

Moir, John S. _Church and State in Canada West: Three Studies in the Relation of Denominationalism and Nationalism, 1841-1867_. Toronto: University of Toronto Press, 1959.

Monroe, Walter S. _Teacher-Learning Theory and Teacher Education, 1890 to 1950_. Urbana: University of Illinois Press, 1952.

Morgan, Edmund S. _The Puritan Family: Religion_

and Domestic Relations in Seventeenth-Century New England. Rev.ed. New York: Harper Torchbooks, 1966.

Morgan, Edmund S. Virginians at Home: Family Life in the Eighteenth Century. Charlottesville, Va.: Dominion Books, 1963.

Mulcaster, Richard. Richard Mulcaster's Positions. Abridged and edited by Richard L. DeMolen. New York: Teachers College Press, 1971.

Murphy, James. Church, State and Schools in Britain, 1800-1970. London: Routledge and Kegan Paul, 1971.

_____. The Education Act 1870: Text and Commentary. Newton Abbott: David & Charles, 1972.

Musgrave, P.W. Society and Education in England since 1800. London: Methuen, 1968.

Nash, Paul (ed.). History and Education: The Educational Uses of the Past. New York: Random House, 1970.

Nettleship, R.L. The Theory of Education in Plato's Republic. London: Oxford University Press, 1935.

Newcomer, Mabel. A Century of Higher Education for American Women. New York: Harper & Bros., 1959.

Newsome, David. Godliness and Good Learning: Four Studies of a Victorian Ideal. London: John Murray, 1961.

Nietz, John. Old Textbooks. Pittsburgh: University of Pittsburgh Press, 1961.

Opie, Iona and Peter. The Lore and Language of Schoolchildren. London: Oxford University Press Paperbacks, 1967.

Orme, Nicholas. English Schools in the Middle Ages. London: Methuen, 1973.

Ornstein, Martha. The Role of Scientific Societies in the Seventeenth Century. Hamden, Conn.: Archon Books, 1963.

Owen, Robert. A New View of Society and Other Writings. Introduction by G.D.H. Cole. London: Everyman's Library, 1927.

Padberg, John W., S.J. Colleges in Controversy: The Jesuit Schools in France from Revival to Suppression, 1813-1880. Cambridge: Harvard University Press, 1969.

Passin, Herbert. Society and Education in Japan. New York: Teachers College, 1964.

Pearce, Roy Harvey. The Savages of America: A Study of the Indians and the Idea of Civilization. Rev.ed. Baltimore: Johns Hopkins Press, 1965.

Pearson, Lu Emily. Elizabethans at Home. Stanford: Stanford University Press, 1957.

Piaget, Jean (ed.). John Amos Comenius on Education. (Classics in Education, No. 33.) New York: Teachers College Press, 1967.

Pinchbeck, Ivy and Margaret Hewitt. Children in English Society. 2 vols. Toronto: University of Toronto Press, 1971-73.

Platt, Anthony M. The Child Savers: The Invention of Delinquency. Chicago: University of Chicago Press, 1969.

Pollard, Hugh M. Pioneers of Popular Education, 1760-1850. London: John Murray, 1956.

Pollitt, J.J. Art and Experience in Classical Greece. London: Cambridge University Press, 1972.

Prentice, Alison. The School Promoters: Education and Social Class in Mid-Nineteenth Century Upper Canada. Toronto: McClelland and Stewart, 1977.

Price, K. Education and Philosophical Thought. Boston: Allyn & Bacon, 1962.

Rabb, Theodore K. and Rotberg, Robert I. (eds.). The Family in History: Interdisciplinary Essays. New York: Harper Torchbooks, 1973.

Rashdall, Hastings. The Universities of Europe in the Middle Ages. 3 vols. New ed. Edited by F.M. Powicke and A.B. Emden. London: Oxford University Press, 1936.

Ravitch, Diane. The Great School Wars: New York City, 1805-1973. New York: Basic Books, 1973.

Reisner, E.H. Nationalism and Education Since 1789. New York: Macmillan, 1922.

Ringer, Fritz K. Education and Society in Modern Europe. Bloomington: Indiana University Press, 1978.

Roberts, Robert. The Classic Slum: Salford Life in the First Quarter of the Century. Harmondsworth: Penguin Books, 1973.

Rosenberg, Charles E. (ed.). The Family in History. Philadelphia: University of Pennsylvania Press, 1975.

Ross, Elizabeth Dale. The Kindergarten Crusade: The Establishment of Preschool Education in the United States. Athens: Ohio University Press, 1976.

Rubinstein, David and Simon, Brian. The Evolution of the Comprehensive School, 1926-1966. London: Routledge and Kegan Paul, 1969.

Rudolph, Frederick. The American College and University: A History. New York: Alfred A. Knopf, 1962.

Rudolph, Frederick. (ed.). Essays on Education in the Early Republic. Cambridge: Harvard University Press, 1965.

Rusk, Robert R. Doctrines of the Great Educators. 4th ed. Toronto: Macmillan, 1970.

Schachner, Nathan. The Mediaeval Universities. New York: Perpetua Books, 1962.

Schlossman, Steven L. Love and the American Delinquent: The Theory and Practice of "Progressive" Juvenile Justice, 1825-1920. Chicago: University of Chicago Press, 1977.

Schultz, Stanley K. The Culture Factory: Boston Public Schools, 1789-1860. New York: Oxford University Press, 1973.

Seeley, J.R., R.A. Sim, and E.Q. Loosley. Crestwood Heights: A Study of the Culture of Suburban Life. New York: Science Editions, 1963.

Selleck, R.J.W. English Primary Education and the Progressives, 1914-1939. London: Routledge and Kegan Paul, 1972.

Sennett, Richard. Families Against the City: Middle Class Homes of Industrial Chicago, 1872-1890. Cambridge: Harvard University Press, 1970.

Simon, Joan. The Social Origins of English Education. London: Routledge and Kegan Paul, 1970.

Sissons, C.B. Church and State in Canadian Education: An Historical Study. Toronto: Ryerson Press, 1959.

_____. Egerton Ryerson: His Life and Letters. 2 vols. Toronto: Clarke, Irwin, 1937.

Sizer, Theodore R. Secondary Schools at the Turn of the Century. New Haven: Yale University Press, 1964.

Sizer, Theodore R. (ed.). The Age of the Academies. New York: Teachers College, 1964.

Smail, William M. (ed.). Quintilian on Education. (Classics in Education, No. 28.) New York: Teachers College Press, 1966.

Spring, Joel H. Education and the Rise of the Corporate State. Boston: Beacon Press, 1973.

Stewart, W.A.C. and McCann, W.P. The Educational Innovators. Volume I: 1750-1880. Volume II: Progressive Schools, 1881-1967. By W.A.C. Stewart. London: Macmillan and Co., 1967-68.

Stone, Lawrence. The Crisis of the Aristocracy, 1558-1641. Abridged ed. New York: Oxford University Press, 1967.

_____. (ed.). Schooling and Society: Studies in the History of Education. Baltimore: Johns Hopkins University Press, 1976.

_____. (ed.). The University in Society. 2 volumes. Princeton: Princeton University Press, 1974.

Strickland, Charles E. and Charles Burgess (eds.). Health, Growth, and Heredity: G. Stanley Hall on Natural Education. New York: Teachers College, 1965.

Sturt, Mary. The Education of the People: A History of Primary Education in England and Wales in the Nineteenth Century. London: Routledge and Kegan Paul, 1967.

Sutherland, Gillian (ed.). Matthew Arnold on Education. Harmondsworth: Penguin Books, 1973.

_____. Policy-Making in Elementary Education, 1870-1895. London: Oxford University Press, 1973.

Sutherland, Neil. Children in English-Canadian Society, 1880-1920: Framing the Nineteenth

Century Consensus. Toronto: University of
Toronto Press, 1977.

Talbott, John E. *Politics of Educational Reform
in France, 1918-1940*. Princeton: Princeton
University Press, 1969.

Tholfsen, Trygve R. (ed.). *Sir James Kay-Shuttle-
worth on Popular Education*. New York:
Teachers College Press, 1974.

Thorndike, Lynn. *University Records and Life in
the Middle Ages*. New York: Columbia University Press, 1944.

Timothy, H.B. *The Early Christian Apologists and
Greek Philosophy: Exemplified by Irenaeus,
Tertullian and Clement of Alexandria*. Assen:
Van Gorcum, 1973.

Tobriner, Marian Leona, S.N.J.M. (ed.). *Vives'
Introduction to Wisdom: A Renaissance Text-
book*. (Classics in Education, No. 35). New
York: Teachers College Press, 1968.

Torrance, Thomas F. (ed.). *The School of Faith:
The Catechisms of the Reformed Church*. London:
James Clarke, 1959.

Troen, Selwyn K. *The Public and the Schools:
Shaping the St. Louis System, 1838-1920*.
Columbia: University of Missouri Press, 1975.

Tyack, David B. *The One Best System: A History of
American Urban Education*. Cambridge: Harvard
University Press, 1974.

Ulich, Robert. *The Education of Nations*. Cambridge:
Harvard University Press, 1961.

Vaughan, Michalina, and Archer, Margaret Scotford.
*Social Conflict and Educational Change in
England and France, 1789-1848*. Cambridge:
Cambridge University Press, 1971.

Vaughn, William Preston. *Schools for All: The*

Blacks and Public Education in the South,
1865-1877. Lexington: University Press of
Kentucky, 1974.

Veysey, Laurence R. The Emergence of the American
University. Chicago: University of Chicago
Press, 1965.

Walbank, F.W. The Awful Revolution: The Decline
of the Roman Empire in the West. Toronto:
University of Toronto Press, 1969.

Walsh, William. The Use of Imagination: Educational Thought and the Literary Mind. Harmondsworth: Penguin Books, 1966.

Warner, Marina. Alone of All Her Sex: The Myth
and the Cult of the Virgin Mary. London:
Quartet Books, 1978.

Webber, Thomas L. Deep Like the Rivers: Education
in the Slave Quarter Community, 1831-1865.
New York: W.W. Norton, 1978.

Welter, Rush. Popular Education and Democratic
Thought in America. New York: Columbia University Press, 1962.

Wesley, Edward B. NEA: First Hundred Years. New
York: Harper and Bros., 1957.

West, E.G. Education and the Industrial Revolution.
London: B.T. Batsford, 1975.

_____. Education and the State. 2nd ed. London:
The Institute of Economic Affairs, 1970.

Whitbread, Nanette. The Evolution of the Nursery-
Infant School: A History of Infant and Nursery
Education in Britain, 1800-1970. London:
Routledge and Kegan Paul, 1972.

Wishy, Bernard. The Child and the Republic: The
Dawn of Modern American Child Nurture. Philadelphia: University of Pennsylvania Press,
1968.

Wynne, J.P. Theories of Education. New York:
     Harper & Row, 1963.

CHAPTER 2

SOCIOLOGY OF EDUCATION

INTRODUCTION

The purpose of the following review is to
examine the development of the field of sociology
of education, to identify major or continuing
issues or controversies and distinctive modes of
inquiry within the discipline and to attempt to explain the nature and contribution of the field to
the understanding and/or advancement of education
as an enterprise and as an institution. Faced with
a task of this magnitude, one must admit at the outset the difficulty of encompassing a synthesis of
all the above facets of the field in one chapter.
Inevitably, the "product" will be a selective account which, as one of many possible alternatives,
can only be justified if the grounds of selection
are made explicit.

The content of the chapter has assumed its
particular form as various problematics have been
resolved temporarily by the taking of a series of
decisions. The referents and outcomes of the decisions will be listed briefly in the introduction
and their expansion will then form the body of the
chapter.

(i) Defining sociology of education

The sociology of education[1] is a specialized
field of study which seeks to treat the educational
systems of developed societies as social institutions. Such inquiry is undertaken at various levels. At the macrocosmic level, the focus is on the
educational system in its relations with other
institutions in the wider social structure while at
a less general level, the social structure and
functioning of the constituent educational groups
of the system--like the schools--must be studied.
At yet another level--the microcosmic level--the

concern is with the social relations of educational activities, for example, the separate culture of the school. Finally, attention must be paid to the educational consequences of factors in the external social environment of pupils, teachers and schools.[2]

Williamson[3] cautions that we should not adopt a static, perhaps reified, view of sociology of education as a "thing," merely a set of references or of solutions to problems. In fact, it is an ongoing process with a range of dimensions such as discussion and teaching, research and writing, which occurs in a variety of institutional settings. Adopting an expanded definition by juxtaposing the ideas of Floud, Halsey and Williamson has entailed other decisions. The major one was the adoption of an orientation which could be termed a tentative attempt at a "sociology" of the sociology of education, that is to say, an attempt to provide a rendering of the sociology of education's own biography.[4] The varying yet related discussions by Friedrichs and Bernbaum of the chosen orientation have provided guidelines for all the later sections of the chapter. The remaining decisions have flowed from the taking of this particular decision.

(ii)   Selecting case studies to illustrate the development of the field of sociology of education

To paraphrase Basil Bernstein,[5] sociology of education is carried out in an historical context and its problems and approaches are an expression of the context. Changes in sociological theory and in educational policies, practices and ideologies over time are the factors which affect the sociology of education in social contexts where the discipline has developed. Comparative data would seem to offer heuristic potential but theoretical and practical barriers which affect the achievement of that potential relate to lacunae in the present state of the sociology of knowledge and to a lack of detailed studies providing solid and systematic evidence on the institutionalization of sociology of education

as an academic discipline.[6] For these reasons,
the better documented cases of the emergence of
sociology of education in the United States and
England will be considered and, even so, there will
be a reliance on a certain amount of speculative
interpretation.

(iii)   Identifying aspects of sociological theory
        and educational practices and ideologies
        which have penetrated the discipline

        In spite of the "uncomfortable relation" of
sociology and education,[7] the field of education
has exercised a strong attraction for sociologists.
The previous section on the development of the
field will lay the groundwork for further discussion in this section to be illustrated by references from research.

        Contemporary sociology of education is ex-
periencing a situation which has been defined as a
paradigmatic crisis:

        ... a situation when the prevailing
        consensus within the community of
        scientists begins to break down, new
        normal science is no longer capable
        of solving the sorts of problems which
        scientists consider important, when
        established conceptual frameworks and
        methodological procedures become the
        subject of critical scrutiny.[8]

That is to say, the structural-functionalist approach and its associated positivistic empiricist
methodology (termed by some the "normative" paradigm) which has predominated in the sociology of
education is now "under attack" from a collection
of approaches which have formed a number of loose
alliances. These have been called the "interpretive" paradigm, "critical" sociology or even the
second of the "two sociologies."[9]

        The conventional or normative paradigm rests

largely on the structural-functionalist perspective. The implicit view of man is a passive one in which society, having an "out thereness" quality, acts to constrain or mould man to its purposes. Social interaction is seen as essentially rule governed. Thus, the mode of inquiry is traditional empiricism with emphases on survey techniques and questionnaire approaches, on the minimizing of investigator variables and on an element of structure, for example, role as the basic research unit.

The recent shift of focus towards "situated activities of negotiated meanings"[10] or, stated more simply, observing the content and context of interaction gets closer to how people actually experience the situation and society as a dialectical one. They seem to suggest that in making sense of his world, man is faced with the problem of constructing his social reality. Interpretations which are formulated by those interacting on a particular occasion may require reformulation during subsequent interactions. This change of focus in the interpretive paradigm to interactional contexts and their contents has implications for its methodology. The study of interaction has to be made from the standpoint of the actor. The trend is toward the construction of case studies of ongoing activities using participant observation and strategies and techniques for recording interaction. The task of the researcher is then to produce documentary interpretation of the selected interaction.

The comparing and contrasting of perspectives from the two paradigms will form the basis of the second section of the chapter. This will be accomplished by indicating characteristic features of theoretical approaches and of their expression in educational research and by raising critical questions which emerge from their use.

(iv) Estimating the contribution of the field

The critical stance adopted in the previous sections of the chapter must be carried through to

the final section. One must guard against global
pronouncements on the value of sociological inquiry
into education. For example, Bernstein emphasises
that:

> Sociologists are creatures of their
> time, and the range of approaches
> to their subject is in part a real-
> isation of the political context and
> the sociologist's relation to it.[11]

It is necessary to take into account the resonance
between implicit value positions of various sociological approaches and educational arrangements
operating when examining research questions (and
their answers) which receive attention at a particular time.

      The distinction made between education as an
institution and as an enterprise is an important
one for sociology. It raises in another form the
basic conflict of a value-free versus a value-orien-
ted sociology. The discussion in this context does
not pretend to provide an answer but it should reveal, at least, a sensitivity to the problem.

DEVELOPMENT OF THE FIELD

      The sociological study of education has a
long history in the United States reaching back
into the nineteenth century when both sociology and
the formal study of education made their appearance
in the curricula of American universities and colleges. What emerged eventually was an educational
sociology which was at one and the same time social
progressive and reform-oriented.[12] This was not
surprising in light of the changing problems facing
American society. The influx of immigrants, the
changing domestic population patterns and the industrialized nature of society were among the societal
changes. These trends intensified in the early
decades of the twentieth century and encouraged in
sociologists a concern for the "social problems"
of education. As a consequence, colleges and univer-

sities began to offer prospective teachers courses
in educational sociology; the National Society
for the Study of Educational Sociology and the Journal of Educational Sociology were established; and
approximately twenty-five textbooks on sociology
and education were published. The early work with
its moralistic and utilitarian overtones was associated with writers like Lester Ward and E.G. Payne[13]

Between the 1930s and early 1950s interest
in the field waned. Reasons adduced by those who
have examined this middle stage emphasise the marginal status of the field. Some indicators of
marginal status in terms of academic criteria are
given by Corwin.[14] For example, in 1947 Herrington
examined forty-five teachers' colleges and found
that seventy percent of the professors teaching educational sociology had majored in education and only
four percent in sociology. Of one hundred universities sampled in 1953, only eighteen percent offered a course in educational sociology. Conrad's
survey of the literature between 1940 and 1950
showed that theoretical concepts were present in
only fourteen percent of educational sociology researches reported in the American Journal of Sociology, the American Sociological Review and the
Journal of Educational Sociology. These findings
cast doubt on the competence of teachers in the
area, on the desirability of sociologists becoming
associated with education in institutions of higher
learning, and on the quality of a research literature in which emphasis was on description rather
than analysis.

Hansen's terse comment is apt:

> ... no one, or too few, cared to be
> associated with a field of suspect
> parentage and undesirable character
> ...[15]

It reinforces the previous point by directing attention to other features of sociology and education
at that time. Sociologists were themselves not
particularly secure in their status as academics of
merit. Overidentification with a less prestigious

field would not have enhanced their "image." The
content of much of the writing in educational sociology had little sociological relevance. Rather,
it consisted of polemics on the reorientation of
educational goals. The service nature of the courses provided for teacher trainees tended towards
dubious "recipes" for the solution of educational
problems met in practical situations in schools
rather than to introduce students to the dominant
ideas of sociological theory and research, integrated at the conceptual level with relevant concerns in the study of education.

Hansen[16] pursues his argument further and
concludes that the decline of the discipline of
educational sociology in the middle stage relates
ultimately to the different modes employed by sociology and education to study man and society. The
basic difficulty between the two is referred to as
the "essential hiatus" between education and sociology. Sociology is seen to imply the empirical
mode of enquiry which is

> ... dedicated to the establishment
> of verified knowledge internally
> consistent, cogent, and adequate to
> its subject. In such inquiry and
> from such theory emerge statements
> of what is, what is likely.

The mode of normative inquiry characterizes education and is

> ... dedicated to the establishment
> of imperatives for the development
> of policies, programs, and actions,
> and to the establishment of normative
> theory, that is, to an internally
> consistent and cogent body of pre-
> scription, adequate to the realiza-
> tion of desired goals and consistent
> with the valid ethic.

If indeed these distinctions are valid, it is
not difficult to see that such a hiatus provided a
formidable barrier to the development of significant

79

research and, to a large extent, accounted for sub-
standard methodology and atheoretical approaches.
The melioristic orientation of educational sociology
was not able to draw a clear distinction between
the "is" and the "ought" whereas its claim to draw
on sociology as a social science brings with it
the obligation to employ the empirical realm.

During the late 1950s and into the 60s and
70s, American society has experienced stresses
associated with factors such as urban renewal, race
relations, the war on poverty, the student protest
movements, the rise of the counter-culture, the
Vietnam war, Watergate and so on. Attention has
been focussed on sociology and sociological knowledge as essential tools to solve the problems arising out of these factors. Some indicators of the
heightened interest in sociology include the expansion of university enrolments in sociology, and of
membership of the American Sociological Association
(from 4,400 in 1955 to 15,000 in 1975), the vast
amounts of money which have been made available for
research and the improvements in the status of the
academic sociologist.[17]

In the eyes of some commentators,[18] the
changes in real and perceived status for sociology
have been reflected in its sub-discipline--the
sociology of education. Symbolic of the resurgence
of interest in education is the change of nomen-
clature to sociology of education. It is important
to note that a section of the Sociology of Education
was established by the American Sociological Association and The Sociology of Education was adopted
as an official journal of the Association.[19] The
American Educational Research Association has established a division designated as Social Context
of Education.[20] Inhering in the name change are
changes in orientation. Two examples only are cited.
Firstly, the field is now seen to be the scientific
study of an institution in the same way that sociologists study the law, religion, or medicine.
Secondly, the faction espousing establishment or
normative sociological theory, focusing on the
essentials of a cohesive, orderly society which

80

stresses the socialization function of education and which has occupied the dominant position in American sociology of education, has now to contend with a virile challenger--in Havighurst's terms[21]-- the critical sociology faction which studies control, conflict, negotiation and coercion in society. The controversy which has been engendered by these two factions has revived interest in both theory, and research and methodology, in the sociological study of education.

For Shimbori,[22] the content of the discipline has moved from the compilation of findings useful to teachers (1900-1910), to an essentialist view of education to counter the measurement movement of psychology (in the 1920s), to a sociology of educational problems, a scientific base for the community school movement, a diagnosis of youth problems (from the 30s to the 1950s), while the later 50s and onwards have seen a concentration on the objective study of education consequent upon the change of name to the sociology of education. He also delineates certain trends in the revivified sociology of education--the trend towards a policy science, closer relationships with the disciplines of economics, political science and comparative education, expanded research interest, for example, the role of higher education in the formation of elites.

To conclude, let us examine a comment made by Bressler in the 1960s:

> The sociology of education has now earned the imprimatur of respectability but only after sociologists of substantial reputation and consequence have testified by their researches that they stood prepared to rescue the study of formal education from the desuetude that had befallen it as a result of historical neglect.[23]

This passage points to two elements in any analysis of the biography of sociology of education. The

first element is personnel engaged in the enterprise and the second is the utilization of an historical perspective. The latter element is of
prime concern because it provides the overarching
framework for all the other elements in an analysis.
A partial, and in some ways distorted, view of the
state of the discipline is obtained if it is examined ahistorically. The personnel element must be
considered within an historical framework. For
example, one may generalize on intuitive grounds,
that younger sociologists would predominate in
Havighurst's critical faction in American sociology
but such a description gains explanatory power only
after the origins, attitudes, qualifications and
statuses of younger sociologists have been traced
and compared with a similar analysis for older
sociologists working at the same point in time.
There are other elements which are not so obvious
in the Bressler comment. These elements refer to
complex relationships like the theory-research nexus
in sociology, the changing dialectic between the
ideologies of the disciplines of sociology and of
education and between academic disciplines and their
social environment, the nature and degree of interaction between an institutionalized sociology of
education and extra-institutional groups such as
educational authorities or youth. These relationships have many consequences for a sociology of education: who teaches what and to whom, what gets
researched and what gets neglected, does any sociology of education knowledge (which is published
or otherwise disseminated) make any difference in
educational policy-making and should it anyway?
Information on such elements and questions is required before a rigorous "sociology" of sociology
of American education becomes available.

In England, the sociology of education as a
discipline was a post World War II development but
with its roots in the pre-war tradition of systematic interest in the role of education in relation
to fertility, social mobility, class and occupational structures pursued by demographers and others
at the London School of Economics. To this "political arithmetic" orientation in the latter part of

the 40s was added social-psychological work on the sociology of the school.[24] The organizational structure of schools, the social origins of measured intelligence and its relation to attainment and the impact of these concerns on the wider issues of manpower requirements and social capacity were dominant issues in the decade or so after the War. The class and professional position of teachers practising at different levels was one feature of the sociological analysis of the structure of schools. There was a preoccupation with studies of the class conditioning of educational chances supplemented by research into the influence of social class on educational performance and vocational aspiration. A notable lack was a systematic sociological analysis of the relation between the systems of education and the economy although Vaizey had commenced work on the allocation of economic resources to English education. Floud and Halsey[25] subsume these foci of interest under the general heading of the social determinants of educability. The impulse was towards demonstration of educational "wastage,", an understandable preoccupation in view of the provisions and manifest and latent consequences of the Education Act of 1944.

The contrast between Britain and the United States at this time with regard to the sociological study of education is quite striking. There were only two major English sociologists engaged in research and systematic teaching in the sociology of education during the period of the 1950's. They were Mrs. Jean Floud and A.H. Halsey to whom has been attributed an active role in the creation of this new field of study. There were few universities at that time with viable departments of sociology and the first master's degree in the area was not established until 1964 in the University of London's Institute of Education.

The close association of Floud and Halsey with the London School of Economics makes it no surprise that that institution became the legitimizing institution for the specialized field of the sociology of education as a subject. There were, of

83

course, other factors involved as well as personnel.
For example, a major interest at the School related
to the problems and process of industrialization,
that is in particular, to the relationships between
stratification, mobility and industrialization.
The structural-functional tradition dominant in
sociology could be applied in a weak form to the
problems of social policy and educational planning
--a legitimate area for the sociology of education.[26]
The favoured methods of demography and the social
survey restricted the selection of research problems
to those amenable to such treatment.

It was not until the sixties that the so-
called period of academic imperialism arrived. This
period was characterized by a rapid expansion in the
numbers of undergraduates taking social science
courses, in the institutionalization of the teaching
of sociology of education in colleges and institutes
of education and in the identification by approximately one quarter of the members of the British
Sociological Association of sociology of education
as a main interest.[27] The enhanced interest in and
visibility of the field of study was reflected in
the burgeoning publications of a text-book variety.
The names of other workers in the field like Musgrove, Banks, Swift, Musgrave and Taylor became
prominent and their books supplemented the reader
by Halsey, Floud and Anderson which, in the relatively short time from publication in 1961, had
achieved the status of a "classic" work.[28] The sections of the "subject" identified by these authors
remained fairly constant. If we examine Banks' 1958
book, we note typical subdivisions: background to
the field, the relation between education and the
economy and social mobility, the influence of the
family on educability, political aspects of the
control of education, the teaching profession, the
school as a formal organization and as a social
system and the relation between educators and social
change. The theoretical framework in such works was
derived largely from structural-functional theory.
These pre-occupations of content and theoretical
approach may also be traced to the research literature of the time. Swift and Acland's bibliography
appended to their review of British sociology of

education published in 1969 is a convenient and accessible source to support this view.[29]

To concentrate solely on increasing personnel--teachers and students,--publications--journals and textbooks--and research output in the sociology of education results in an over-optimistic picture of the state of the field as the 1960s drew to a close. Other aspects of importance deserve mention. The rapidity of change in the social organization of sociology of education knowledge and its distribution raised a number of difficulties. These ranged from questions concerning who taught sociology of education and to whom, and what was their competence to the question of what was taught as sociology of education?[30] It was inevitable that there should be a shortfall of teachers qualified in sociology (and, consequently, in the sociology of education) to staff the increased numbers of courses resulting from the pressure of enrolments in sociology courses in arts or social science degrees and in courses for prospective teachers in colleges and institutes of education. Less than adequately qualified staff are unlikely to be able to apply the sociological mode of thinking to education to produce suitable courses for teaching and non-teaching oriented students. Student dissatisfaction may well have arisen because the promise of the application of a sociological perspective in the analysis of education yielded few returns.

During this time, the push towards comprehensivization of secondary schooling as a means of reducing educational problems and of satisfying political and social ideologies of equality was proceeding but not without critical comment and scrutiny. The demonstration by sociologists of the presence of inequality in British education has perhaps stimulated efforts to redress the balance,[31] but without extensive explanation, they could not guarantee the success of the particular methods attempted. The result of such efforts was the development of a variety of secondary school structures or organizational styles. In addition, differentiated knowledge styles which had been a feature

85

of the tripartite system of secondary education
entrenched by the 1944 Education Act and which had
been criticized on the grounds of perpetuating inequality were found to persist in the comprehensive
school via such methods as streaming. This had the
unintended effect of perpetuating the status quo.
Sociologists were placed in the positon of de facto
advocacy of a liberal social policy which did not
give the expected effect.

The upsurge of research into the inability
of education in the United States to deal effectively with its minority groups was a further influence in Britain. Investigations into the education provided for the "Newsom" child and the raising
of the school-leaving age shifted the focus of attention from the organizational structure of schools
to the content of schooling.

As has been mentioned previously, it was
during this period that the upheavals affecting
American society and education stimulated the appearance of identifiable factions in American sociology: the establishment of the normative sociology
faction and the faction espousing critical sociology.
This dichotomy was reflected among the sociologists
with a major interest in education. The critical
faction comprised supporters of a number of theoretical approaches including neo-Marxism, symbolic-
interactionism, phenomenology and ethnomethodology.
The revived interest in these viewpoints diffused
across the Atlantic (although one must also remember
the European influence on British sociology) and
elicited a striking response in the emergent generation of young sociologists, the beneficiaries of
the "revolution" in the provision of sociology in
the preceding decade or so.

Two events stand out as markers ushering in
the era of the "new" sociology of education in
Britain. The first was the Annual Conference of
the British Sociological Association in 1970 which
had as its theme the sociology of education. As
Richard Brown states:

> The Conference, and its more per-
> manent embodiment in this volume,
> were intended to provide the oppor-
> tunity for a survey, however in-
> complete, of the present state of
> the field and an assessment of
> current work and new problems ...
> despite the considerable achieve-
> ments of the sociology of education,
> during the previous two decades
> especially, a great deal of dis-
> satisfaction with the present
> situation was expressed by those
> currently working in this field ...[32]

It is clear from this comment that the field was
subject to influences for change from without and
to pressures of discontent from within the ranks of
its own members.

The professional conference is an important
arena for the expression of controversies, of criticisms of previously taken for granted orthodoxies,
and for the expression of new directions. Apart
from the impact of individual "performances" by
charismatic figures, the rapid dissemination of ideas
amongst colleagues is fostered and publication possibilities are an accepted outcome. The selection
of papers from the 1970 Conference published in the
volume Knowledge, Education and Cultural Change was
an indicator of the strength of the movement for
renewal in the field. Papers in the "old" sociology
of education tradition received scant attention.
The collection illustrates the emergence of a critical attitude to the structural-functional and
systems frameworks, the use of alternative theoretical frameworks such as the conflict or phenomenological approaches, and the advocacy of a focus on
the content of education in an enlarged, and in
some ways redefined, sociology of education.

The second marker was the publication of two
volumes of articles in 1971. The first volume,
edited by Michael F.D. Young, is entitled Knowledge
and Control   New Directions in the Sociology of

Education while Earl Hopper has edited the second collection which is called Readings in the Theory of Educational Systems. Both volumes are mentioned because of the overlap in their selections indicating the coalescence of like ideas and their sponsors to constitute an alternative movement. The significance of the Young volume for our purpose here is the contrast it offers to typical sociology of education texts cited previously. The sections in this book bear these headings: Introduction (Knowledge and Control written by Michael Young), Curricula, Teaching and Learning as the Organization of Knowledge (includes On the Classification and Framing of Educational Knowledge by Basil Bernstein), Social Definitions of Knowledge (with an article on Classroom Knowledge by Nell Keddie) and Cognitive Styles in Comparative Perspective (with contributions by Pierre Bourdieu, Robin Horton and Ioan Davies relating to Systems of Education and Systems of Thought, African Traditional Thought and Western Science and The Management of Knowledge). Other features can also be mentioned, for example, the heavy input from writers associated with the London Institute of Education (which might be said to have replaced the London School of Economics as the legitimating agent for the sociology of education) and the strong trend towards a sociology of knowledge approach to the study of education with links to neo-Marxist ideas and phenomenology.[33]

Young expressed a two-fold aim for his book --that it should open up "alternative directions for sociological enquiry in education" and that it should "define a set of problems, which up to now, appear to have been largely neglected." The neglect would be overcome by focussing on "enquiry into the social organization of knowledge in educational institutions."[34] Young's mission[35] is to convert the reader to the view that the sociology of education and the sociology of knowledge are one and the same.

The Hopper collection is significant here also because of the views expressed by one of the contributors, A.H. Halsey--one of the foundation members of the "old" sociology of education tradition in England. He advanced the argument that this volume, a descendant of the 1961 collection Education, Economy and Society, illustrates the theoretical advance in the discipline in the ensuing decade, the sharpening of the definition of the field and the need to accept as the next crucial task for workers in the field a "programme of empirical validation."[36]

These publications, following as they did upon the Sociological Conference of 1970, created widespread interest in the area, interest which has had a polarizing effect similar to the factions reported by Havighurst. Workers in the area seem to have been disposed to align themselves with the "old" sociology of education or with the "new." In sum, the range of theoretical approaches and their associated methodologies, the airing of the controversies between the proponents of the various approaches, the variety of research questions under investigation and the accelerated production of published material attest to the vitality of the field in Britain. Many questions arise from the deflationary situation of British sociology of education. One question, for example, is the extent to which the pressure from a more competitive academic market in the seventies has "created" the press towards more publications in this field, a factor linked with career timetables. The interaction of a great complex of socio-contextual factors needs to be teased out to gain a detailed picture of the development of sociology of education as a subject and as an enterprise.

The field of sociology of education continues to evolve but the complexities of its development are beyond the scope of the present study. It is instructive to list some foci which would require systematic examination, were the review to be brought completely up to date. These foci include: (i) analysis of the courses provided by the Open University in Britain (as a way of assessing yet another legitimating institution for the field and of tracing the distribution of selected sociological

89

knowledge). In a similar way, there is a need to identify the loci of legitimation or innovation in the field in the United States; (ii) review of the nature and volume of publications in the area (to compare those which are theoretically based, to examine authors with respect to age differences, organizational affiliation, source of academic qualifications, and so on); and (iii) survey of the degree of diffusion of publications in British sociology of education or of dissemination of the "new" sociology of education by visiting British academics to North America (to gauge the current strength of the field; for in the past, the stronger influence has flowed in the reverse direction). A sociological understanding of the field of sociology of education should be stimulated by monitoring the convergent and divergent patterns and themes in these two major social contexts.

ISSUES, CONTROVERSIES AND MODES OF INQUIRY

The sociologist of education works in a field which suffers the disadvantages, as well as gaining from the advantages, of its parent discipline--sociology and of its subject of study--education. This position is succinctly stated by Hammersley and Woods in the following excerpt:

> Theoretical and methodological orientations in this field have paralleled those in sociology as a whole, though with a time-lag and refracted through particular policy concerns.[37]

The sociologist embarking on a study of education has decisions to make on the theoretical or conceptual framework he will adopt and the research methodology he will employ to aid the analysis of a particular set of data. He is necessarily drawn into the dilemmas inherent in these areas of his discipline. One fundamental given is the mutual inter-penetration of sociological theory and research, for as Rex concludes:

> Whatever the conception of science
> held by the sociologist, careful
> consideration of the methods of
> investigation proposed in terms
> of that conception showed that some
> sort of theoretical construction
> was necessary.[38]

The third influence constraining the sociologist, in addition to theory and methodology, is
external to him and is often out of his control.
This is the influence referred to by Hammersley and
Woods as "particular policy concerns." The sociologist is not free to make unilateral decisions on
the aspects of the educational institution he wishes
to study. Governmental and educational authorities
exert powerful control in myriad areas. These include the access to educational organizations, spon-
sorship and funding of certain types of research
and not others, and the origination and implementation of policies which affect not only the content
and structure of formal schooling but its underlying
philosophy and values. The policy issue raises a
major controversy highlighted by the "new" sociology
of education. Michael Young, following Seeley,
describes the debate in terms of the "taking" of
(educators') problems versus the "making" of (sociologists') problems.[39]

The three themes--theoretical orientations,
research methodology and the policy claims of edu-
cation--form the organizing foci for the remainder
of this section. Two points should be made at the
outset. These three factors have existed in dialectical relationship with one another throughout
the history of the discipline. The strength or
degree and direction of the relationship have varied
over time. Their relative separation here is an
artificial device for heuristic purposes. Secondly,
the present study serves the limited objectives of
identification and initiation of discussion: no
claim is made to provide a detailed and exhaustive
account.

THEORETICAL ORIENTATIONS

The sociologist of education has available to him theoretical orientations which range from structural functionalism to conflict theories, with variants derived from Marx or modern writers like Coser and Dahrendorf, to the array of interactionist perspectives. Opportunities are afforded for exploration of educational questions at both the macro- and micro-levels. In a similar way, a number of methods are available to be used in the investigation of research questions. While scientific inquiry in sociology may be dichotomized into two polar modes, traditional empiricism and participant observation, there is a whole spectrum of strategies inbetween. These strategies include survey and questionnaire techniques, studies of the documentary, comparative, case, sociometric, non-participant and participant observation type.[40] Thus, the worker in this field is faced by something of an embarrassment of riches. Though sociology may be described as "a weakly co-ordinated body of thought,"[41] it is prolific in approaches and methodologies which must be understood and applied appropriately in the search for sociological knowledge about education.

The notion of paradigms in sociology of education was introduced earlier. Two competing paradigms were identified: the normative and the interpretive. The interpretive paradigm is tending to develop a new orthodoxy within contemporary sociology of education although the phenomenon is more strongly evident in British sociology of education than in the North American version where, perhaps, symbolic-interactionism and neo-Marxist approaches have been the favoured revivals.

It is proposed, then, to illustrate major sociological issues and controversies by briefly outlining their main features, by providing exemplification of their use in the study of education and by raising some of the critical questions which proponents of one or other of the main orientations tend to make of their rival. One point of clarification should be made prior to the discussion. The label "new" sociology of education is somewhat misleading.[42] Taking one aspect of this point, approaches in the sociology of education are not substantively "new." Their newness derives from the circumstance that they are enjoying an upsurge from popularity and, perhaps, are being used in different combinations and for analysing different problems from the ways they have been used previously.

Structural-functionalism is a theoretical perpsective having its roots in early nineteenth century French and German thought which became dominant in American sociology in the 1950's via the writings of Talcott Parsons. Structural-functional theory views societies as systems made up of parts, each of which performs a particular function for the operation of the whole. The structure of any institution is seen as being determined by the function it performs in the society of which it forms a part.

Emile Durkheim, as the father of the normative consensus paradigm in sociology, played an important part in the development of the sociological interest in education for he held the belief that men are made moral through society and that it is the school's socialization function to aid the initiation of each child into his society.[43] Durkheim went so far as to delineate specific areas of research in which a sociologist should work. The areas were: identification of the current social facts of education and their sociological function, identification of the relationship between education and cultural change, cross cultural and comparative research in various types of educational systems, and investigations of the classroom and school as an ongoing social system.[44] These areas help to illustrate the perspective and possible methods of inquiry of structural-functionalism. Implied in this specific list is the sociological mode of thinking or of enquiry which entails the avoidance of reductionism, the explanation of social facts by other social facts, and the utilization of sociological concepts like "culture" and "social system" to frame the understanding of human group behaviour.

Empirical social research also had its origins in the nineteenth century and it became an important tradition in a number of centres in America in the 1950s, the major exponent being Paul Lazarsfeld. This tradition places great emphasis on large-scale surveys of attitudes and the variables explaining the distribution of attitudes. Towards the end of the 1950s, the traditions of structural-functionalism and empirical social research became more and more closely interpenetrated.[45]

With its holistic model of the social system, the structural-functionalist approach tends to analyse educational structures and processes in terms of their contribution to basic system requirements. Major preoccupations have been the analysis of the role of education in socialization, social selection, role allocation and social control seen from a systems perspective which is predicated on the maintenance of ongoing social equilibrium.

Talcott Parsons and W.A.L. Blyth provide classical examples of the application of the structural-functionalist tradition to the analysis of classroom interaction and of social processes in schools. Parsons' opening sentence outlining the aim of his paper encapsulates a major feature of structural-functional theory:

> ... an analysis of the elementary
> and secondary school class as a
> social system, and the relation
> of its structure to its primary
> functions in the society as an
> agency of socialization and allo-
> cation.[46]

The social system of the class is linked to the school as a social system which in turn is linked to the social system of the community in which the school is situated, and so on. The sociological investigator's task is then to examine the structure of the social system of the school class determined as it is by two functions (internalizing in pupils "the commitments and capacities for successful performance of their adult roles" and the allocation of "these human resources within the role-structure of the adult society"[47]) which have been identified by the researcher <u>prior</u> to the analysis. Blyth emphasises the normative nature of the social structure of the junior school throughout his discussion. He says, for example, that the maintenance of cohesion and control in the school depends on:

> ... the establishment of norms
> including explicit rules, on the
> use of some form of rewards and
> punishments, and on the self-
> maintaining process which schools
> as institutions engender.[48]

The school's functions of socialization and autonomy are achieved by the establishment of <u>school</u> norms. Concepts which are used in conjunction with "norm" in Blyth's structural-functional analysis are "role," "value" and "culture."

Criticisms have been made that the structural-functional approach operates with an over-integrated view of society by unduly emphasising those aspects which are thought to be the functional requirements of the social system. This produces a conservative orientation because these requirements parallel those of the "established" interests in the social structure. An over-integrated view of structure may be linked to an over-socialized concept of man, that is, man is conceived as an atomistic unit constrained and moulded by the requirements of a reified social system. It is claimed that such a view dehumanizes man and fails to support man's active role in the historical process.

Giddens also finds functionalism wanting and expresses his criticisms in terms of: the reduction of human agency to internalization of values, the failure of functionalism to treat social life as actively constituted through the doings of its members, the treatment of power as a secondary phenomenon

with norm or value as the basic feature of social
activity, the perspective's inability "to make
conceptually central the negotiated character of
norms, as open to divergent and conflicting interpretations, in relation to divergent and conflicting
interests in society."[49]

To these theoretical and conceptual criticisms must be added reservations about methodology.
While the complaint has been that British sociology
is laggard in applying rigorous methodolgies to
research problems, American sociology has been
accused of being obsessed with empiricist methods.
Any amount of statistical information may, for example, be gathered by survey or questionnaire techniques but it is difficult to make sociological
sense of a great mass of data without the tools for
analysis and interpretation made available by sociological theory. More seriously, overemphasis on
empiricist research in the sociology of education
may lead to failure to add, in a cumulative fashion,
to sociological understanding of the institution
of education. Much structural-functionalist research is termed positivist in that there is arbitrary imposition of a priori investigator categories for differentiating the data.[50] This procedure
does not take into account the complexity of social
reality or the perspectives of actors who actively
interpret and construct, at least part of, their
world. Classroom interaction researchers have recently adopted alternative theoretical and methodological frameworks to avoid the defects enumerated
above.[51]

The interactionist framework, fashioned by a
somewhat loose amalgam of the perspectives of symbolic-interactionism, phenomenology and ethnomethodology, is drawn on to cater for the wider range of
topics under investigation in contemporary sociology
of education. Here, the features and use in research
of the various perspectives are considered separately
while the criticisms given refer generally to an
interactionist approach.

The symbolic-interactionist[52] approach in

American sociology has emerged from the contributions of workers like George Herbert Mead, W.I. Thomas, William James and C.H. Cooley. It has been closely associated with the University of Chicago both in its early developments in the 1930s and 1940s and in the period of resurgence in the 1960s and onwards. The major concern of symbolic-interactionism is to understand how co-operative social behaviour is possible. It rests on three basic premises: that human beings act towards things in the light of the meanings the things have for them, that such meanings arise out of human interaction and that each person has an interpretive process by which he can deal with the meanings of the things he encounters.

The key interdependent concepts of "self," "role" and "meaning" are utilized in the investigation of the negotiations, adjustments, and mutual interpretations that take place within interactions. Mead's notion of self as process or reflexive self refers to the ability of the person to note things and to determine their significance to his line of action. In his writings, Talcott Parsons develops the view that actors act toward each other in interactions within the constraints of their roles. The actors' roles impose on them certain expectations of each other's behaviour because they occupy particular status-positions. Meaning is the way in which people actually use a term in their behaviour. Meaning and value comprise the elements of symbols. Man is stimulated to act both by the symbols and the physical stimuli in his environment. In methodological terms, the study of action requires the researcher to adopt the role of the actor so that the researcher can see the actor's world from his standpoint.

One example of a study which uses the symbolic-interactionist perspective is given. While acting in his role as a lecturer, Clark McPhail[53] experienced a walk-out by most of the members of his class. He followed up the students the same afternoon and obtained detailed reports from those who did and did not walk out. These verbatim

reports were then used to construct the sequence
of events in the lecture which had involved his
students in deflecting routine and creating new
lines of social behaviour. In fact, these data
provided an empirical record of an elementary form
of collective behaviour. McPhail was interested
in the attention participants had paid to one
another's behaviour. As a consequence of inter-
person cues, behaviours were constructed which, by
means of the reports, the investigator had access
to and could subject to empirical examination. The
examination revealed the process of symbolic-interactionism in which the participants fitted together
a routine sequence of behaviours, deflected the
sequence of behaviours so that a problematic situation was perceived to exist and finally attempted
to resolve the problematic situation by means of
walking or not walking out of the lecture.

There is no one phenomenology, rather there
are many phenomenologies.[54] Two significant strands
in the phenomenological movement have developed.
The first is the mundane or non-transcendental phenomenology of the social world (associated with
Schutz and his followers) and the second is the
existential phenomenology of Jean Paul Sartre and
Maurice Merleau-Ponty. The latter strand has been
linked with sociology of knowledge by some sociologists of education, for example, Michael F.D. Young.
The work of Alfred Schutz has been recognized as
the point of entry into phenomenological sociology
and present day phenomenologists and ethnomethod-
ologists, including Aaron Cicourel, Harold Garfinkel
and George Psathas, freely concede their debt to
Schutz.

Phenomenologists subscribe to the view that
the primary phenomenological task is to observe,
describe and reconstitute the characteristics and
inter-relations of phenomena as phenomena in the
intersubjective world of everyday life. Actual concrete experiences and meanings of men in their mundane activities are the raw data upon which the
phenomenologist reflects. From these "first order"
constructs are developed the "second order" constructs of the sociologist by which the social

phenomena are interpreted. This transformation from
first to second order constructs is possible because
of the dimensions or properties of human activity
which include consciousness, intentionality and
subjective meaning. The method of achieving description and reconstitution of the activities of
everyday life is termed the "phenomenological reduction." The sociologist must suspend or bracket
all prejudgments in order to perceive the meaning
of phenomena without distortion while attempting
to understand the processes, such as "typification,"
by which actors in their everyday world make sense
of it. Admitting the actor's "definition of the
situation" can lead to a questioning of the relationship between the categories used by the actor
to understand his world and those of the researcher.

The following definition of school might be
accepted by teachers and pupils (members in schools)
and by sociologists of education (observers in
schools).

> A school is an institution. People
> meet at specified regular intervals
> for specified purposes; they engage
> in certain kinds of activity called
> teaching, learning, play, punishment
> and the like.[55]

The question is then what can the phenomenological
perspective contribute to an understanding of the
intersubjectivity of everyday life of the school?
Much of what Esland has described as typical school
activity occurs in classrooms as part of the teaching-learning process. Attention is being paid by
phenomenologists to the relationships between teachers and pupils by means of the concept of "negotiation." Actors in the classroom situation bring to
it their unique definition of reality. In addition,
pupils and teachers share to varying degrees a
common perspective on the definition of the classroom itself. The lack of perfect congruence results
in negotiation between them in order to regulate
and routinize what happens in the classroom. It is
the variable presence of shared typifications of

reality that makes the outcome of each interaction so problematic. The studies of Stebbins[56] and Wertham[57] seek to elaborate the dimensions of negotiation identified by Geer[58] as exchange of knowledge and bargaining for control.

Stebbins explored the meaning of disorderly behaviour in the classroom as defined by teachers. By means of actual observation in classrooms and interviews with the observed teachers, Stebbins concluded that teachers have a disorderly behaviour set. The actions of teachers to avert or arrest misconduct in pupils were related to factors such as the perception of cues (pupil acts), development of identities of classroom participants (below average or poorly behaved students), and professional experience (the biographical situation of the teacher and his associated stock of knowledge at hand). The operation of the disorderly behaviour set was shown to vary with different classes taught by the same teacher.

Negotiation, as seen through the eyes of students (lower-class gang members) was the subject of Wertham's study. This investigation utilised observation and interviews with gang members over a two-year period. Accounts of classroom situations in which gang members were labelled delinquent as compared with situations in which the same students remained ordinary students were analysed. Wertham concluded that students became delinquent as a result of not accepting teacher authority. Gang members did not a priori recognise a teacher's authority as legitimate. Teachers had to prove the legitimacy of their claims and these claims were judged in terms of criteria established by these particular students.

Harold Garfinkel originated the term ethnomethodology[59] and the critique of orthodox sociology which it implies. He has been joined by others interested in this field, for example, Aaron Cicourel, Roy Turner, the late Harvey Sacks and Don Zimmerman. The abiding concern of ethnomethodology is with practical reasoning, that is, with the question of the meaning of social actions:

> ... a different sort of sociological
> enterprise is proposed in which a
> study is made of the methods by which
> people interpret and display the
> social world as having the recog-
> nisable features it appears obviously
> to have.[60]

Making sense out of any social situation generally
entails using the medium of ordinary language to
communicate an account of it to someone else. In
fact, Garfinkel considers that the making of sense
of situations and the telling of that sense are
equivalent. Thus a large part of the ethnomethod-
ologist's task is the study of account building by
members during social action because the fundamental
assumption of the ethnomethodological approach is
that the social world is essentially an ongoingly
achieved world.

Other than "account" (which subsumes the
idea that perception = explanation) another basic
concept in ethnomethodology is that of "indexi-
cality." This refers to a property of language.
Words can be understood in terms of their literal
meaning and in terms of the particular context in
which they occur. In order to "do ethnomethodology,"
the sociologist must question the previously taken-
for-granted contexts of meaning in which members'
accounts of everyday life are set while remaining
ethnomethodologically "indifferent" (in the sense
of abstaining from judging adequacy, success, value,
importance and the like). "Members" are those who
share a stock of commonsense knowledge about the
social world and a competence to apply that knowledge. Competence involves the taken-for-granted
ability to make reasonable observations and to produce sensible talk and activities.

George Payne[61] provides an example of what
ethnomethodological analysis looks like in practice.
His paper explicates the means by which members
produce and make sense of the first few utterances

of a lesson as those of a lesson, an essential step
indicative of the intersubjectivity of a particular
social world--the classroom. The "lesson" is what
it is because the teacher and pupils have shared
methods for producing it. Payne's data are ten
utterances (shared unequally by the teacher and one
student) spoken soon after the members have entered
the classroom. From these, Payne produces an analysis of the methods, cultural understandings and
machinery which may have been used in the production
of the utterances. This enables him to conclude
that such talk did, in fact, constitute a lesson.

     The recrudescence of the interactionist
framework in the United States and then in Britain,
particularly with respect to the phenomenological
and ethnomethodological components, has been a
major cause of the intensified struggle between
factions in sociology, and subsequently in sociology of education, in the late 60s and into the 70s.
The interactionist framework seemed to offer promising lines of inquiry and to foster a healthy
scepticism about the predominance of positivist
and empiricist research. But the supporters of
conventional sociology, stung by the force of the
critique, have fought back and have sought to expose the weaknesses of the interactionist or interpretive position on both theoretical and methodological grounds.[62] Because of the strong inter-
weaving of theory and methodology in the interactionist framework, criticisms are noted together.

     In that the ontological, metaphysical and
epistemological assumptions of the interactionist
perspective are in many ways incompatible with
those of other theoretical stances in sociology,
the resolution of crucial issues such as subjectivity
and objectivity are unobtainable at present. This
might suggest that there is little point in pursuing
the assertions and counter-assertions of the pro-
and anti-interactionists but one justification is
the need to develop awareness and sensitivity to
basic problems in the discipline which tend to receive more attention in complex discussions in
sources coming from the philosophy of the social

102

sciences. There is no pretence at coming to grips
with this problem; the point being made is that
the criticisms of the interactionist position which
are noted here relate back to features of its on-
tology, metaphysics and epistemology whether this
is stated in explicit terms or not.

Sharp and Green focus on the essential
idealism of the perspective which treats the external world as a subjective construction of the
actor's "constituting consciousness."[63] In other
words, the subject-object dualism is caused to disappear because of the interpretation that phenomena
only exist insofar as actors classify or identify
them as existing. These authors state their position clearly:

> We do not agree, therefore, that the
> starting point for sociological in-
> quiry should necessarily be the sub-
> jective categories of social actors
> and that social scientific concep-
> tions of social reality should merely
> be what Schutz describes as second
> order constructs, i.e. constructs of
> the constructs of the acting subject.[64]

The emphasis upon society as a network of
human meanings rejects the view that societies exhibit regularities like those in the physical world
which are then open to understanding and explanation
through the same logical procedures as those in the
natural sciences. Different methodologies, different relations between investigator and subjects
and different loci for research are required to deal
with a social reality which is "constantly in a
state of becoming rather than being."[65] Preferred
forms include participant and non-participant observation, subjects' definitions of the situation as
basic data and microcosmic level studies.[66]

A number of difficulties accrue from this
cluster of theory-related aspects of the research
methodology of interactionism. The first problem
is a familiar one--what counts as valid knowledge?

103

The positivist-empiricist tradition is an attempt to answer that question by treating sociological problems in a scientific way—accepting only propositions that are falsifiable and replicable. It is obvious that interactionist research does not subscribe to this view and cannot generate quantitative data capable of being treated in a rigorous manner. Failure to produce a substantive body of knowledge supported by systematic empirical research has earned interactionist research a reputation (not entirely undeserved) for concern with trivialities and with documentation of the obvious.

Reliance on the participation of the researcher in the gaining of his data reflects an acceptance of verstehen as generic to all social interaction and of the belief that the investigator must draw on the same sorts of resources as his 'subjects' do in making sense of the conduct which it is his aim to analyse and explain.[67] This orientation leads to a suspicion of quantitative evidence and may extend to "a rather naive outright rejection of 'positivist' methodolgical techniques."[68] There is also the problem that overt behaviours as well as their underlying social norms and rules are subject to differential interpretations. Acknowledging the commitment of the interactionist to relativism, it is difficult to see why the investigator's "account" of the research situation should be any more "real" than that of the actor. It seems that there are no answers to other questions that might be posed in this same connection; for example, have the interpretations made by either researcher or actor been subjected to social structuring and under what historical conditions have these interpretations emerged?

Two serious disadvantages may arise from the belief in the constant creation and recreation of meanings in each encounter between individuals and groups of people under observation. There may be restriction of the definition of 'social encounter' to one type in which the partners are classified as free and equal. In fact, all interactions between persons are relations of power to which parti-

cipants contribute unequally, bringing with them
unequal resources. Giddens generalizes that the
failure to recognize the centrality of power in
social life is a characteristic feature of the
interactional perspective.[69] He draws attention
to a related feature, that the perspective deals
with action as meaning rather than as praxis--"the
involvement of actors with the practical realization of interests through human activity."[70]

Secondly, investigators may fail to take
adequate account of the social constraints on human
actors. There are limits to the negotiability of
definitions in any situation which are set partly
by the asymmetries of power operating but, partly
also, by contextual structures present, that is,
social and physical resources and constraints such
as opportunities, expectations and facilities. By
not relating social interactions to social structure
the fragility of the routine of everyday life is
highly exaggerated. The potential of studies which
attempt to integrate the interactional and structural, and the micro and macro levels of analysis
has not yet been fully explored.

The sociology of knowledge perspective has
not received a great deal of attention in the sociology of education until recent times. It has had
more impact in other sub-disciplines such as the
sociology of science, of religion and of art. An
interesting development has been the bifurcation in
the application of a sociology of knowledge perspective to the "new" sociology of education. On the
one hand, sociology of knowledge concepts have been
linked with a phenomenological perspective as in
the work of British sociologists like Young, Esland
and Keddie and on the other, in the case of European
sociologists like Bourdieu or the Americans Bowles
and Gintis, with a neo-Marxist perspective. It
should be noted that Basin Bernstein's work, however,
on the classification and framing of educational
knowledge and class-based language codes and social
control, illustrates a contribution to the older
normative tradition in the sociology of education.
The remainder of the discussion will attempt to in-

dicate the social location of the sociology of
knowledge within sociology generally, to outline
some of the main ideas arising from it, and to
provide some guidelines to the contemporary application of these ideas to the sociology of education.

The roots of the sociology of knowledge[71]
are to be found in the writings of Karl Marx, Karl
Mannheim and Max Webber. The contemporary revival
of interest in the field has been influenced, also,
by the work of C. Wright Mills, Robert Merton,
Pierre Bourdieu, Alan Blum, Peter Berger and Thomas
Luckmann. The focus on knowledge per se, on the
individuals and groups who specialize in the production of knowledge, and on the social behaviour,
roles and institutions specific to the creation of
knowledge are all subsumed by the term sociology
of knowledge. More specifically, the sociology of
knowledge is concerned with a determinate relationship between knowledge and social structure. It
seeks to specify how knowledge and society inter-
penetrate, to examine the social influences on the
production and differentiation of knowledge, its
validation, distribution, and on subsequent processes of change in knowledge. Of particular interest
has been the extent to which social factors mediate
between knowledge and belief, or stated another way,
the development of ideology.

One of the reasons why sociology of knowledge
has tended previously to be marginal to the central
concerns of American and British sociology is proposed by Phillips.[72] A separation has developed
between sociologists who are interested in "science"
--the practice of knowledge and those who are concerned with "epistemology" or the theory of knowledge. We have noted already that a propensity to
try to imitate aspects of the methodology of the
natural sciences has led to an indifference to what
are seen as 'philosophical' issues. While sociologists of knowledge and science have explored the
origins of scientific ideas and their relation to
social and cultural contexts, they have failed to
consider questions of the validity and justification
of the knowledge claims involved. Some of the

criticisms of the phenomenological perspective, however, have begun to confront the problematics of this area.

Gunter Remmling's description of the parameters of the sociology of knowledge is a useful one in this context. The areas delineated have salience when the application of the sociology of knowledge perspective in the study of education is examined. Remmling says:

> The sociology aims at discovery, analysis, and description of different thought styles but the discipline is more than that, it is also a theory of the relation of ideas and reality asserting the primacy of reality and the determination of ideas by reality.[73]

Some of the core ideas associated with thought styles and the determination of ideas by reality will be noted by reference to a few leading theorists.

The Marxist position supports the contingency of the validity of thought on the social location of its producers or distributors; if the dominant view of knowledge in society is the view of the "ruling class," then all "bourgeois" knowledge is ideological and distorted for man's consciousness is determined by his social being. Class conflict is seen to be the basis of any society. In accord with this position, Marxian theory asserts the primacy of economic reality and the determination of ideas (the ideological superstructure) by this economic reality.[74] A present-day elaboration of Marxian thought is provided by Bourdieu who has developed

> a deeper awareness of the peculiar efficacy of culture in that culture is seen as structuring the system of social relations by its own functioning.[75]

The ideas of the other theorists (mentioned later) could be seen as reactions to the Marxian position.

Karl Mannheim had a non-revolutionary interpretation of the relation between class, ideology and knowledge. He did not think that the bourgeois view of reality was superior or inferior to the 'proletarian' view, but that all classes possessed limited views of reality because of their different backgrounds and social perspectives. The group with the greatest potential to see the world in a less limited way was the "socially unattached or free-floating intellectuals," hence the interest in investigating individuals and groups who produce knowledge.[76] A conceptualization tending towards a non-determinate analysis of the relationship between knowledge and social structure was posited by Max Weber. This arose out of his perception of the duality of society. For him, society comprised forms of meaningful social action and routinized structures of social relationships and thus, in contrast to Marx's interpretation, economic organization could not be said to have the primary role in any explanation of social change. Hamilton concludes:

> Hence a Weberian sociology of
> knowledge is committed to allotting
> some autonomy to ideas or knowledge,
> in the explanation of any historical
> and social reality.[77]

Berger and Luckmann[78] appear to go further than Mannheim by suggesting that all knowledge is socially constructed, that is interpreted or filtered through the culture of those acquiring the knowledge. Another important feature is that knowledge as a whole is regarded as being socially constructed. Knowledge includes common sense reality as well as academic subjects. They, in fact, suggest that sociology of knowledge must begin with the common sense view of reality rather than with the history of ideas or the study of academic forms of knowledge. A sociology of knowledge has to deal not only with the "empirical" variety of knowledge in human societies but also with the processes by which <u>any</u> body of knowledge comes to be socially established as "reality."

The claim by Michael F.D. Young that

> sociology of education is no
> longer conceived as the area
> of enquiry distinct from the
> sociology of knowledge[79]

may be overstated but it has redirected attention to questions of the social organization of knowledge in educational institutions, of the problematic nature of educational knowledge, and of the centrality of issues of control in formal education. A further consequence has been the rapid proliferation of a literature on the sociology of curriculum. These directions have stemmed more from a phenomenological sociology of knowledge.

One example of a study in the phenomenological genre is Nell Keddie's investigation[80] of the effects of teacher presupposition about pupils on the organization of curriculum knowledge in the classroom and the relation between teacher and pupil definitions of the classroom situation. Of particular interest to Keddie were categorisations of pupils made by teachers, e.g., "ideal pupil" and "failure," and categories of organization of curriculum knowledge in the classroom such that "C stream social science" was seen as something different from "A stream social science." She found that teachers appeared to have two organizing categories in defining and maintaining pupil identities--ability and social class. Influenced by implicit categorisation of types of pupils, teachers made judgments on subject content and pedagogy appropriate for children in classes streamed A, B and C. This occurred even though all members of the teaching department supported a policy in which social science was to be taught as an undifferentiated programme across the ability range. In other words, teacher definitions varied between staffroom and classroom--between teacher-teacher and teacher-pupil interaction.

Esland's article,[81] published in the same
source as Keddie's, is a conceptualization of a
model to be applied to the analysis of teaching
and learning as interrelated processes for organizing knowledge. The theoretical components of the
model are symbolic-interactionism and a phenomenological sociology of knowledge. Esland hypothe-
sises that research into the decisions of teachers
to innovate in the curriculum and pedagogical presentation must gather data at three different
levels. These are the ideological level (paradigms, vocabularies of motive, public and private
rationales), the structural and institutional context level (negotiated division of labour between
teachers and pupils), and the level of external
loci of cognitive support for teachers ("publics"
and epistemic communities). He concludes that the
use of such a model should help in the task of

> ... seeking explanations--and
> even descriptions--of the sources
> and the processes of change, and
> the continual restructuring of
> consciousness and ideation, as
> it occurs in the pupil and teacher
> career.[82]

The other branch of the trend towards incorporation of a sociology of knowledge orientation to the study of education has been linked with
neo-Marxist thought. This has come with the return
to an emphasis on the determining effects of social
systems--in particular of the capitalist system.[83]
Associated with this tendency have been the criticisms of the "romantic" reform movement in education which predicted a revolution in education
merely with a change in the conceptions teachers
hold about teaching.[84]

> Rather than actors' perspectives
> and actions being seen as emerging
> out of interaction, they are now
> seen as being the products of social

110

structural forces, either
directly, or mediated by the
cultural hegemony of the ruling
class. In those versions of
this tendency close to a neo-
Hegalian Marxist position, the
stress on the knowledge which
underlies actors' constructions
is retained, but this knowledge
is now seen as the product and
reproducer of alienation.[85]

In their study of progressive primary
schools, Sharp and Green emphasize that their research design had to include the wider structural
context as well as the constructs of the teachers
involved. To take account of the problem of power,
the "political structure of staff relationships in
the school," "the relationship between the teachers
and their pupils and the role of the teacher in the
social structuring of pupils' identities," and "the
interrelationships between teachers collectively
and their clients, in this case the parents" had
to be examined.[86] In their words:

Unlike the phenomenological, we
employ a concept of false consciousness and implicitly highlight in critical fashion the
falsity, where it is substantively
incorrect, and naivete, where it
is superficial, of the actor's
consciousness. We try to generate
explanations of structures latent
to the totality as they recognize
it and thus go beyond phenomenological description which tends to
be based squarely on the subject's
here and now.[87]

The comment by Sharp and Green reiterates
criticisms of the interactionist perspective like
idealism, subjectivism and relativism discussed
previously. Logically, these problems must also
appear in a phenomenologically informed sociology

111

of knowledge. Expanded discussions of Young's work and that of others associated with him can be found in the writings of Karabel and A.H.Halsey, Denis Lawton and Geoff Whitty.[88] As in the case of Sharp and Green, those who propose the use of a structuralist perspective in the study of education tend to include in their argument a refutation of other perspectives whether from conventional or interactionist theory and thus, at the same time, provide a defence for their own position. The movement away from a crude economic determinism in the neo-Marxist reorientation obviates one of the traditional criticisms of Marxist explanations. It remains to be seen whether structuralist studies of education will be able to maintain a balance in their consideration of the dialectical relationship between the significance for change of man's intentionality and concern with the circumstances which provide the parameters within which change may or may not take place.

To conclude, Warwick has a comment appropriate to this point and he also draws attention to possible ideological difficulties:

> It is possible that any sociological analysis will be caught in such tension, for the force of history of old structures and processes, if not sufficiently analysed can be seen to be an uncontrollable determinant of activity and meaning, holding back the attempts of man to improve his own meanings on the world. In addition, sociology is bound by the varying meanings which sociologists themselves attach to the world. An ethnocentric viewpoint based in a respect for 'science' and 'rationality' may well lead more readily to a concern for order, whereas one that is born in a respect for cultural relativism, may well lead to the problem of control.[89]

112

RESEARCH METHODOLOGY

The purpose of this section is neither to detail the design nor to assess the findings of some "representative" sample of sociological investigations into education. Rather, it is briefly to indicate a few significant features of research methodology which have had a continuing impact, or are emerging as newer trends, in the sociology of education.

One fundamental characteristic of sociology is the close association of theory and research[90]: a particular theoretical approach necessarily brings in its train one research model with its specific methods rather than another. At whichever point we start, the sequence linking theory and research seems to be that if model A of man and model A of society are hend then inquiry into the "world" will be based on research model A'', not research model B''. Thus, if support is given to the view of man as passive, constrained and moulded by the society around him, and society is seen to comprise functioning structures which maintain the entire system in equilibrium, then the "scientific" research model is the preferred form. The features of this model are "reliable definitions, order and control of materials, detached and rational behaviour by investigators"[91] and, typically, three distinct stages.[92] The first is the creative stage with identification of the problem, formulation of the hypothesis and deduction from the hypothesis. The investigator's initial hunch is the link between theory and problem. In the second stage, the research design is set up and data collected. This technical stage is concerned with reliability while the final or theoretical stage comprises analysis of data and drawing of conclusions thus returning the researcher to the theory which stimulated the original hypothesis.

The quality of the theory which generates the "sociological imagination"[93] needed for interpreting data relates directly to the quality of the research produced. The concept of the socio-

logical imagination is the key to the theory-
research nexus, for as Swift reminds us:

> It is not so much that there is
> something "out there" which is
> sociological as that we perceive
> something sociological about that
> which is "out there."[94]

Sociologists who adopt the epistemology and
objectives of the natural sciences are likely to
experience failure, according to Giddens, because
their discipline has not yet produced "an integrated
corpus of abstract laws" which can satisfy "the
criteria of acceptability of both the professional
community and the lay public."[95] By logical extension, this argument has force for the sociology
of education. That there is such conflict over
the validity of the various theoretical approaches
currently being applied to the study of education
suggests that cogent criticism of educational research is especially urgent for the future development of the field.

The application of the "scientific" model
has been favoured in sociology, and consequently
in the sociology of education, for reasons other
than "research" reasons.[96] For example, such advocacy has been politically expedient as a means
of facilitating the establishment of sociology as
a subject of university study and to enable sociology to compete with disciplines like psychology
for "academic respectability." The process has
been extended by the institutionalization of compulsory statistics and methods courses for sociology students and this also acts to define "academic" sociology. What cannot be made clear to the
bulk of students who have only a brief introduction
to the discipline is that textbook reports of
research studies using this or that method represent only a formal reporting of what actually
happened in the research. In fact, there may have
been post hoc falsification of changes in hypotheses, exclusion of some data and excessive weight-
ing on other data, or interference from peripheral
uncontrolled factors.

114

There are a number of contributing factors
to the situation referred to above but a fundamental problem is the nature of the subject-matter
with which sociology deals. Sociology explores
"whole life-situations of larger populations in
their everyday context,"[97] a very different research
problem from that faced by the psychologist with
his carefully controlled laboratory experiments.
There is a dissonance between positivist, and perhaps at times empirical, methodology and the subject-matter of sociology. Nature and society are
different; "Nature is not a human production,
society is."[98]

With the rise to prominence of the interpretive paradigm in theory, there has been a subsequent reaction against the use of the "pure
science" research model and a challenge has been
offered to the reliability of the results obtained
from studies based on the model. It has been noted
that interpretive theory emphasizes ideas like
"active man" and "socially constructed reality."
To investigate research problems from such a conceptual standpoint requires a research model other
than that described above. Thus, the relevance of
natural science methodology is brought into question. Weber's conept of verstehen underlies the
efforts to capture the perceptions of the actors
themselves by means of extensive use of the method
of participant observation. This method underlines,
also, the necessity to take into account the researcher's own perceptions and views on social
reality. In any situation, he too defines the situation and his presence affects the other participants so that they redefine and modify their behaviours. The "becoming" nature of the social
reality of any research situation lessens the feasibility of employing the "pure science" model.

The innovative trend of these criticisms in
contemporary sociology (in what has been a continuing dilemma for sociological theory and research)
lies in the vigour of the advocacy of the interpretive model and its preferred research forms and
the vehemence of the denunciation of positivist-

empiricist research. The proponents of the interpretive paradigm, especially in Britain, have been
highly critical of the prior research tradition in
the sociology of education.[99] This is another aspect of the deflationary situation in current sociology and in the sub-field of sociology of education.
What has tended to happen in the sociology of education, however, is that rhetoric or polemic has
been substituted for the advancement of carefully-
conceived alternatives based on an established research tradition. The definition of research, with
the theories and concepts that guide it, may be
broadened to the point where it is simply regarded
as being completely arbitrary and subjective.[100]
A corollary of this stance--not usually acknowledged
by its supporters--is that the interpretive theories
and concepts may thus be seen as relativistic, even
ephemeral.

A continuing dilemma in sociology associated
with the positivist conflict, and which has also
been brought into sharper relief, is the conflict
between "value free" and "value oriented" sociology.
To put the conflict in terms of its suggested resolution, Bryant points out that "new" sociology ex-
hibits a "rejection of value-freedom" and a "commitment to criticism."[101] In the sociology of
education, this has led to research in which the
values and aspirations of researchers are manifest
and in which there is an attempt to justify the arguments in favour of social change.[102]

Walker[103] looks at this issue in another
way. He traces the use of particular styles of
research on classroom interaction in America and
Britain to a variety of influences including struc-
turally different education systems, research traditions and underlying ideologies. In the United
States, Walker suggests that it is political ideologies. In the United States, Walker suggests
that it is political ideologies, having assumptions
of a strong moral commitment to liberal political
attitudes and a "democratic" conception of personality, which have affected the concept of teacher-
child relationships in school. Authoritarianism
and domination have been seen as a cause of social

problems. As a consequence, classroom observational researchers, using analysis based on the authoritarian/democratic dichotomy, have dominated the field. In Britain, on the other hand, the metaphysical orientation of research to education leads to a focus on economic thought and social structures rather than on culture and personality. For sociologists of education, the crucial concept has been social class and the main function of education the legitimization of the existing social structure. Therefore, the study of classroom interaction has not been considered a valid research activity; the greater emphasis has been given to research which moves out of the school into the home and eventually to the social class structure.

One conclusion reached by Walker is that research is a cultural product. We might generalize from this to say that sociology, in that "its images reveal as much of the culture that generated [it], as [it] does in the way of substantive findings," is also a cultural product. Thus, the "value" question is inescapably part of any examination of sociological work. Perhaps an appropriate way of concluding this section, and to foreshadow the brief discussion on policy which is to follow, is to quote A. McClung Lee:

> Crucial in evaluating any sociological effort is to find out for what kind of individual or organization. social clique ... the work was consciously put together. All sociologists write and study within one or more groups cultural contexts... Their writings are thus to be seen as significantly ... autobiographical ... They are also written for an audience with one or more social and individual purposes. In other words, probing questions about any sociological work should include knowledge by whom? for what? and for whom?[104]

117

POLICY CLAIMS IN EDUCATION

This section seeks to identify the nature of the influence of policy matters in the sociology of education, a valid concern for a review of the field which has attempted to adopt a sociology of knowledge approach. Unfortunately, the elaboration of the theme cannot be pursued in the present context.

Policy claims arise from two social locations. The first is within sociology itself--carried by its members--in this case, sociologists of education. The second is external to the discipline-- to be found in the socio-cultural milieu. The "carriers" are members of the "publics," consisting of teachers, administrators, political figures, parents, which relate to education and sociology. Although the sources are analytically distinct, the effects of policy claims as praxis--sociologists, educationists and others attempting to realize their interests--lead to "contamination" which makes disentangling consensual and competing claims a difficult task. The politics of education, an underdeveloped area for sociological inquiry, would seem to be an appropriate arena for systematic examination of this issue. We cannot disregard policy claims in sociological inquiry, however, for there is need to clarify questions of by whom, for what and for whom.

There are a number of facets to the policy issue viewing it from the perspective of the sociologist. These facets raise again the basic contradictions within sociology: normative versus interpretive approaches, objectivity versus subjectivity, value-free versus value oriented sociology. The decisions sociologists take on these issues influence their stance on policy. There is space to list only three of these varying positions towards policy: the uncommitted, the committed and the indirectly committed.

Sociologists who espouse fundamental research have decried the press towards products and immediacy of impact. There is a fear that, while policy-related research may produce results of theoretical importance, the loss of autonomy in the posing of such research questions may reduce their potential for theory. Sociologists with this view are likely to support the organization of sociology as both a mystery and a discipline, as ways of excluding public influence over their work while accepting the direction of fellow-scientists over matters such as the selection of problems, procedures and forms of reporting.[105] The inherent dilemma is the appeal for social and political action versus the detached long-term objective of scholarship and controlled development.

Halsey[106] offers a clear contrast by stating that part of the task of the sociologist is to "inform the political debate" for his expertise allows him to decide what is sociologically and politically possible. He argues further that:

> The problem of the entanglement
> of analysis with value assumptions
> is intrinsic to sociological
> study. To get it straight we must
> first distinguish the "scientific"
> from the "value" problem, to ask
> separately what is possible and
> thereby, to decide preferences and
> priorities.

In other words, he is not oversimplifying the re-lationship between sociology and politics. Rachael Sharp has adopted this position in seeking to formulate a radical educational policy after con-ducting research which has questioned the liberal democratic assumptions underlying child-centred education.[107]

Eric Hoyle[108] has disclaimed the notion that the theories of sociologists directly affect the thinking of educational policy-makers but has suggested that they are responsible for the crea-tion of climates of opinion which serve indirectly to influence policy. He has examined the contem-porary value-context of educational decision-making by distinguishing the forms and interactions of

social theory of education in Britain. The conclusion he arrived at was that the majority of
British sociologists of education may be termed
"nomothetic radicals" which implies that they employ theories which focus upon the structure of
education and attempt to be analytical and empirical. At the same time, there is a concern for
theory which is normatively oriented towards egal-
itarian social and educational change. Hoyle
states that the nomothetic radicals have presented
a clear value position which has had implications
for the types of problems defined as strategic,
for the methods employed to investigate these problems and for the use to which their findings have
been put. The findings have "helped to create the
climate of opinion which has supported policies
of expansion, comprehensivization and delayed selection."

One final example, the work of Jencks, in
the tradition of large-scale empirical research
on inequality in American education, is examined
by Christopher Hurn.[109] His article suggests that
Jencks' work should be seen as a policy research
than, as is generally held, as a major contribution
to knowledge of the effects of schools on students.
Jencks' conclusions, while not setting out definite
policies, undermine the accepted beliefs that educational reform can promote both equality and
equality of opportunity, thus helping to create
the sort of climate of public and professional
opinion favourable to the critical writings of
Bowles and Gintis, for example, which exhibit a
definite value stance.

Varying policy claims arise from sources
external to sociology and sociologists. The first
emerges from recognition of a basic assumption
which underlies policy claims; that all educational
issues have political and ideological connotations.
Education must compete with other institutions for
societal resources. Young indicates that decisions
and non-decision about priorities allotted to education are made in "contexts where there is differential access to resources, both of economic

120

support and cognitive legitimacy."[110] He illustrates this view by examining the control function
of the Schools Council in Britain which is an
extra-governmental body having powers of recommendation on such matters as educational finance,
curricula, examinations and research. The publics
represented on the Council include teachers,
teachers' unions and local educational authorities.
Young provides evidence to suggest that the Schools
Council, because of its prestige, financial resources and educational ideology defines educational
priorities, limits educational change and supports
educational research in such a way as to exert an
influence on the work of sociologists of education.[111]

It is interesting to speculate whether this
line of argument can be advanced to try to explain
the lack of influence of the ethnomethodological
approach on sociological inquiry into education in
America. Karabel and Halsey[112] offer a tentative
comment that the rise of ethnomethodology can be
linked with the counter-culture movement in American
society. The bulk of organizations for mass education, in spite of the upheavals of the sixties
and seventies, have remained within mainstream
culture. If the publics associated with education
support research dealing with "mainstream" problems, it is unlikely that the ethnomethodological
approach would attain cognitive legitimacy among
researchers in education. Karabel and Halsey point
out that critics of education have taken a politically radical position rather than one which is
culturally radical and thus, there has been a
greater use of conflict theory in the study of
American education.

The expectations held by interested publics
exert other types of policy claims on sociologists.
The ideology of equal opportunity and the assign-
ment to education of a role in social mobility
contribute to a dependency on, or an over-valuing
of, sociological research findings. These are
thought to provide "answers" to educational problems and, by extrapolation, to social problems

generally. Bernbaum notes some of the effects of
recommendations of sociologists on the British
education system including the expansion of educational facilities to provide greater opportunities
for children from lower social classes.[113] One
difficulty has been that teachers and administrators may expect immediate answers to questions
relating to policy and its implementation while
some sociologists may be only secondarily interested in the problems of applying their findings
and conclusions. In the short-term, neither group
is satisfied with the slowness of educational
change--but for different reasons. Secondly, dissatisfaction arises because of the intransigence
of problems to merely educational solutions.

In recent years, the growth of higher education and the consequent focus on the relations
of education to national power and prosperity, the
child-centred movement which has spread from the
elementary to secondary schools and stimulated a
desire for reform, and interest in the education
of socially and "culturally" deprived children have
contributed to the rapid growth of sociological
inquiry into education. According to Harp and
Richer,[114] concentrations on the educational areas
listed tends to raise certain kinds of questions.
In effect, the direction of the sociology of education is moulded by such external forces. These
authors, having surveyed North American sociology
of education research, suggest that the attempts
to balance the pressure from those outside sociology and the demands of the discipline itself have
resulted in studies limited to topics like the
selection and socialization functions of education,
the nature of school as a social institution, and
the school as a place of work to the exclusion of
topics like the content of schooling. The per-
vasiveness of the liberal-democratic ideology held
by laymen and professionals alike has insulated
certain facets of education from inquiry.

The issue of policy claims requires systematic treatment to establish the influence on the
development of the field. Claims arise within
sociology (depending how sociologists view their

122

role--as detached academics or as men of action)
and external to sociology (as interested and influential publics try to achieve their goals for
education by utilizing the contributions of sociologists); that these two sources interact with
one another is a further indication of the nature
of the field of sociology of education itself.[115]

SOCIOLOGY AND EDUCATION

A brief recapitulation of the essential
nature of sociology is given prior to embarking
on the final section of this review. Sociology
is distinguished from other disciplines which
study education by the way the sociologist approaches the explanation of social, and specifically education, phenomena. He seeks causes for
problems in the fact of people's membership of
social groups and in the ways in which these groups
are related to each other, that is, in terms of
group membership and group organization.[116] The
sociologist draws not only on the sociological
imagination to bring into focus what is obscured by
education's institutional procedures and the taken-
for-granted daily practices of its members[117] but
also on the sociological consciousness which leads
him to see through the facades of educational
structures, to recognize the other side of what is
officially respectable in schools, to be conscious
of the highly relativized state of values in
modern education, and to be alert to the dangers
of parochialism in this outlook on the human meanings embedded in educational contexts.[118] The
tools he uses for collection, analysis and interpretation of data on educational phenomena are
selected from a diversity of theoretical frameworks
and concepts and research strategies and techniques.
Thus, the sociological perspective is to be seen
as a complement to those perspectives brought to
bear on education by the disciplines of philosophy,
history and psychology. Sociology provides a means
of undertaking the detailed study of the institution of education and of its relation to various
aspects of the wider social structure. The attempt

123

to _understand_ education is systematised by the application of scientific procedures and methods.

Previous sections of the chapter have laid the groundwork for the final section which attempts to survey the perceived and potential contribution of the field to the study of education. While the examples adduced to illustrate the links between sociology and education are necessarily selective, reference will be made to the interrelated themes of education as an enterprise (an undertaking which is "central to the formation and transformation of social beings"[119]) and education as an institution ("a structure composed of the cultural elements transcribed into patterns of social action"[120]). Sociological contributions can be considered at various levels. The examples given will range from the more pragmatic to the more abstract; from issues of policy to issues of theory. This, however, is not to pose a simple dichotomy but to point to the diversity of effects on education sociological study may bring. We shall focus on two major areas which exemplify the role of sociology in education: sociology _as a component in teacher education_ and as _a source of theoretical templates_ for the analysis of the educational social order. The chapter will be concluded by a brief reference to the contribution of the sub-field of sociology of education to its parent discipline--sociology.

The discipline of sociology occupies an interesting position in that its "subject"--education--also provides many of its "clients." The notion of a value-free sociology of education is difficult to sustain. Education is an enterprise which "consumes" knowledge from a large number of sources to aid its functioning. Teachers, significant members of educational organizations, are also in Halsey's terms "applied sociologists" and their "pedagogy depends on sociology more closely than on any other science."[121] The pragmatic and theoretical facets of the sociological contribution are manifested in the teacher preparation example.

The relevance of sociology for teacher

124

education has rested on two basic assumptions, that it has utility for the classroom performance of the teacher and that it provides for the personal academic development of the teacher as student.[122] These assumptions can only be made explicit by consideration of sociological findings. Five postulates, with an outline of their supporting arguments, are listed to indicate the potential of sociological inquiry for educational practice.

Sociology identifies and elaborates characteristics of the population that encourage or prevent learning:

Studies in what might be termed the pluralistic aspects of educational disadvantage are strongly represented in the literature of sociology of education. Their large number serves to reflect the pervasive character of an ideology of equal opportunity. Most of the work undertaken in this area has been within the normative paradigm and has tended to look to factors outside the school, particularly the family, to account for the determinants of achievement.[123] It is only in recent years with interest in, for example, definitions of educational knowledge, that interpretive thought has begun to influence the conclusions of traditional research.[124]

Two trends among others are pertinent for prospective teachers. First, sociology serves to expose the particular plight of such groups in society as women, the poor, migrants, minority groups, the physically and mentally handicapped, inner city and rural inhabitants. Future teachers need to be confronted with up-to-date "hard data" to enable them to form an alternate view of the reality of the school situations which they will enter. More subtle and complex is the second trend. This is the continuing attempt to provide an understanding of "how" and "why" the administrative decisions which are made in the classroom are tied to the social class nature of inequality of educational opportunity. The great debates of the sixties and early seventies focussed on race and I.Q., genetic and environmental influences on intelligence, and the variables affecting educability. Proponents of the diversity of views espoused include Coleman, Jencks, Herrnstein, Riessman, Jensen and Moynihan.[125] A contrasting view is advanced by Nell Keddie that it is in schooling itself and the kind of life experiences it offers to children that the mechanism of distributing educational opportunity is to be found.[126] Explanations of the causes of educational inequality range from a stress on cultural differences in home background, to the need to recognize the allocatory forces acting within schools themselves, and as a third possibility, to an emphasis on the material conditions of life in different social classes.[127] Teachers are increasingly being involved in "innovation" aimed at reducing educational disadvantage --whether they understand it or not. It would seem appropriate that they are sensitized to the issues and inherent conflicts, both theoretical and pragmatic, of such action.

The sociological perspective draws attention to the importance of institutional arrangements in the causation of individual strain and specifies the structural sources of individual differences:

The important area of selection of pupils can be examined at both macro- and micro-levels. The comprehensivization of secondary schools, the classification of educational priority areas, the setting up of open plan primary and secondary schools and classrooms, direct and indirect federal government funding and control of state and non-state schools have received attention in British and American sociology of education using, in general, a structural-functional framework for analysis.[128] The relationships between the institution of education and other institutions in society have been elucidated as well as the manifest and latent functions of education.

At the more micro-level, that is focussing within schools, the consequences of experience management have been investigated. Studies by Cicourel and Kitsuse and Rosabeth Kanter are examples of the use of newer interpretive approaches.[129] In the former case, it was shown that classification of students by counsellors initiated organizational actions which resulted in the defining of potential college or non-college careers of those students. Kanter found that nursery schools, by providing a social world with the phenomenological impact of bureaucracy, produced children having a "world view" attuned to bureaucratic life. Study of this area directs the trainee teacher to the socio-contextual influences on the teacher's task. It also serves to highlight the recurrent nature of the process of appraisal by the teacher of his own pedagogy.

Sociology develops an understanding that things are not what they seem: it reveals the complex nature of the transmission of knowledge in a social context:

The new directions taken by the theory in the sociology of education have been responsible for an upsurge of interest in the knowledge area. Disturbing and challenging ideas are emerging from exploration of questions relating to the management of knowledge (what part does education play in the creation of social consciousness?), to teaching and learning as the organization of knowledge (how does knowledge come to be organized within educational institutions?), and to the concept of cultural reproduction and social reproduction (does the education system recreate the power and symbolic relationships between classes by contributing to the differentiated distribution of culture capital among those classes?).[130] These ideas posit alternative insights into the world of education and of teachers' roles within it.

Of more immediate relevance to the prospective teacher is the objectively-informed approach to school curriculum provided by sociology which reveals the day-to-day problems involved in the schooling process. The taken-for-granted worlds of subject teaching, team teaching, integrated studies and pedagogical styles become problematic

127

when made objects of sociological investigation. For example, Musgrave[131] has examined the sociological determinants impinging on the relationship between knowledge and curriculum and of the ways in which knowledge is transformed into curricula. Flude and Ahier[132] caution against the use of unexamined categories like "ability," "rationality" and "cognitive complexity" by teachers to justify their own activities. Bernstein's work on codes[133] led him to relate types of curriculum codes to differences in pedagogical strategies and school organization and to examine the crisis in pedagogy indicated by the increasing implementation of integrated rather than collection type codes. The dimensions of the social organization of knowledge in curricula have received attention by Michael Young.[134] He has suggested a schema based on two dimensions, degree of stratification and degree of specialization, which relates conceptually to Bernstein's two ideal-type curricula. Curriculum has been defined and set in its context in the micro- and macro-social arrangements termed schooling by John Eggleston.[135]. He has developed a sociology of the school curriculum which incorporates both positivist functionalist and non-positivist sociological approaches to curriculum. The continued production of theoretical and empirical work on these questions has direct implications for curriculum-makers and teachers of sociology of education in teacher education.

The results of sociological inquiry into interaction in the classroom have an implicit bearing on strategies of teaching:

An illustration is given to show how a narrowly-conceived problem of student teachers is exposed in its wider dimensions by applying a sociological perspective. Of prime importance to young teachers is the problem of discipline defined by them as class control. Geer[136] has put forward a concept of negotiation which subsumes the dimensions of exchange of knowledge and nargaining for control to explain control in the classroom. This concept would seem to offer greater heuristic possibilities than the prescriptions of many classroom management manuals. A critical phenomenological examination of the "recipe knowledge" of methods of control provided by textbooks designed for student-teacher use has been undertaken by Cooke.[137] The work of Hargreaves and others has examined deviance in school--an example of a study in the phenomeno-logical genre.[138] This style of research may be a means of introducing students to the interpre-tive view that classroom reality is socially con-structed. This implies that they may be led to consider issues of profound importance for their teaching strategies. For example, greater pupil control over structuring his own curriculum knowl-edge and of the pace of his own learning, the teacher's role as guide rather than instructor, and diminution of social distance between teacher and pupil on some of these issues.

It is important to note that the phenomeno-logical approach to classroom interaction neglects certain crucial factors. Differences in power and prestige, unequal reward structures, bureau-cratic aspects of the school as a formal organi-zation are among the factors which shape what hap-pens in classrooms because of their function as structural constraints. Writings of Talcott Par-sons, Willard Waller, M.D. Shipman, G. Bernbaum and Robert Witkin, some exemplars of the normative approach, take account of such factors.[139] In order to understand classroom interaction, then, one must include both normative and interpretive materials in sociology courses.

Teacher education curricula usually contain an educational psychology component. Study of in-teraction affords an opportunity for students to juxtapose the sociological critique and prior ap-proaches used by psychologists. Analytical findings produced by Amidon and Hough, Bales, Flanders and others have resulted in detailed data on verbal and non-verbal behaviour in classrooms and a multi-plicity of sophisticated instruments for their col-lection.[140] Sociologists have pointed out the methodological dangers in the imposition of re-searchers' categories on those of the observed

129

because inaccurate or distorted results may be obtained. The phenomenological imperatives to admit the actor's definition of the situation and to engage in "bracketing" of observer preconceptions of the actor's social world may be seen as a corrective to these perceived dangers. If the role of the contemporary classroom teacher includes that of "applied social scientist," then in order to cope with the expectations inhering in this designation, teachers require in their training an introduction to the research methodologies of both the normative and interpretive paradigms.

The discipline of sociology offers theoretical and methodological contributions to the training required by teachers for the lifetime task of reflection on the full meaning of their work as educators:

The sociology and technological changes within modern industrial society and the rapid expansion of education have given rise to an urgency about the development of theories rather than concentrating on methods in teacher education. There are fundamental dilemmas in the teacher's task. While developing his individualistic solutions to the problems of freedom versus control in the classroom, the teacher cannot ignore the effects of the stratified industrial society which continually impinge on the school. Sociology does provide an analysis of the structure and function of education in relation to society's other institutions. In process of creating a learning environment, the teacher must define his role in it vis-a-vis his particular pupils. How can he balance the demands which arise from negotiations with individuals and groups within and outside the school? How can the conflict nature of the formal school environment be revealed to the teacher while he is immersed in it? If schooling is a social process, how can the teacher take account of social phenomena like the selection of process relating to knowledge as well as pupils, the social organization and composition of pupils in the classroom, and the social control of knowledge? It needs to be remembered that there are sociological approaches which emphasize "the subtle texture of meaning which constitutes social reality."[141]

The foregoing arguments have suggested that sociology offers one route towards an understanding of the phenomenon of education seen from the teacher's perspective. The claim is made that sociological knowledge can assist the prospective teacher to develop an education "theory" to guide his teaching behaviour. The teacher who has been introduced to normative and interpretive approaches has experienced reflexive sociology in that each perspective provides a critique of the other's theory and methods. As the teacher seeks to deal with situations in the classroom, his sociological stock of knowledge should, therefore, lead him to practise a pedagogical style which takes cognizance of the complex dialectical nature of the teaching-learning process.

We turn now to the second area in which to examine the sociological contribution. Watson states it thus:

> Sociological models may be used
> as theoretical templates for the
> analysis of the social order.[142]

It has been shown previously that sociology provides a wide range of theoretical models. In general terms, the value of the application of these models is that they impose a sense of order on the complexity of the "real world" and explicate the logical processes involved in cumulating the knowledge which allows that sense of order to be achieved. More specifically, if different models are used to examine the same issue the possibility of greater understanding is enhanced as well as the subversion of absolutist claims on knowledge. Evaluation of the use of sociological templates entails an examination of both the quality of the "pattern" and the accuracy of the interpretation of "fit" between the template or pattern and the phenomena to be studied. The accomplishment of this task is beyond the limits of the present chapter.

However, selected phenomena to which theoretical models have been applied will be reviewed and then, some of the consequences of these applications will be delineated. Again, the attempt is being made to encompass theoretical and pragmatic facets of sociological inquiry in relation to education as both enterprise and institution. This review supplements the examples already provided in the second section of the chapter.

Sociological interest in the phenomenon of educational inequality has been substantial. This is the area selected by Watson himself to exemplify the application of various theoretical templates.[143] These theoretical frameworks with their differing views of society, and thus of the causes of educational inequality, can be applied to understand the practices of compensatory education which are undertaken as a solution to the problem. Watson outlines the features of the order-consensus model, the conflict model and interactionist models which enable the selection of key aspects of society through which organized redress strategies can be examined. For the order-consensus or functionalist theorist, the notion of "cultural deprivation" is used to locate the cause of educational disadvantage within families and local communities, perceiving them to lack adherence to the mainstream culture. This view leads to compensatory strategies which aim to enable deprived children to "catch up"--to become equipped with the values and competences necessary for satisfactory adjustment to mainstream culture. The concepts of "domination" and "false consciousness" are used by conflict theorists to explain disadvantage in terms of dominant and subordinate classes or groups. Educational strategies are seen to be inadequate; rather, other forms of socio-economic redress and the revitalizing of subordinate group ideologies are endorsed. Of particular concern to those with an interactional orientation is the notion of "labelling" within school settings, especially as part of classroom interaction. Interactionists tend to leave the practical proposals for obviating the regressive effects of labelling to those working in such situations.

Watson draws attention to the fact that the
models of society used by professional sociologists
are also part of citizens' commonsense images of
society and that both of these sets of models have
political implications. This means that if citizens
and sociologists espouse one or other of the models,
in order to lessen inequalities through educational
policies and strategies, they are perceived as
adopting a political stand whether they are aware
of it or not.

Phillip Robinson[144] presents his analysis
of British education and poverty by reviewing the
various strategies that have been attempted and
the variety of sociological perspectives on poverty
that have been developed over the past ten years.
These perspectives are then used not only to evaluate the achievements of compensatory policies but
to present fresh insights into the nature and in-
cidence of child poverty, the potential of a comprehensive official anti-poverty policy and the
role of the schools in the overall strategy. Concepts such as the "culture of poverty" and the
"cycle of deprivation" are traced from their genesis
to their assimilation (and perhaps distortion) in
the corpus of common-sense knowledge from whence
they are used by policy-makers and others to justify
particular strategies and decisions. From these,
Robinson moves to a consideration of "deficit" and
"difference" theories of educational deprivation.
These theories are linked to implicit models of
society and theories which locate the individual
within that society. Robinson concludes that
deficit theories tend to reflect an "order" model
whilst difference theories relate to a "conflict"
model. He then examines varying programmes with
their implicit theories and concludes:

> The hope of the 'sixties was that
> the schools would be the spearhead
> of policies of social justice,
> first comprehensive, then compen-
> satory, community and finally con-
> tinual education would rid society
> of glaring inequality. Slowly a

133

dawn is arising which sees the
school powerless in the face of
structural inequality.[145]

From this point in his analysis, Robinson is able
to suggest an alternative strategy of redress.

A third example in this area is one which
illustrates the use of theoretically-informed empirical research. Williams[146] has investigated a
casual model designed to show how teacher prophecies may transmit the effects of students' social
origins to their academic achievements. Cognitive
and normative dimensions of teacher expectations
and standardized and teacher evaluations of achievement have been included in the model. Through the
process of "estimation of the model," Williams is
able to show that teachers do not base their expectations on students' ascribed characteristics
but on the criterion of students' achievement.
However, as teacher expectations do appear to
affect the certification of school learning, this
suggests that unmeritocratic processes are present
in schools and may have consequences for later
occupational attainments. The study seems to im-
plicate schools in the inheritance of inequality
although in more subtle ways than overt social
class discrimination.

The second example is that of social control
and education. Brian Davies[146] has conducted an
intensive exploration of this theme, starting from
the premise that to understand the complex nature
of "social control," one must understand the complex nature of the "social," and this can only be
accomplished if there is a conscious juxtaposition
of a number of theoretical approaches from sociology.

Davies' method, therefore, is to utilize
within his book a number of models of man--Marxian,
Durkheimian, Meadian, Interactionist, Parsonian,
Schutzian and Ethnomethodological--and the theories
of society proposed by Marx, Durkheim and Weber to
elaborate the meaning of the "social." The origins

and development of mass education in Britain and the United States are traced to support his claim that key values or ideologies of a society are refracted through its educational system. Davies then moves on to examine the links between control and education exhibited by the original and contemporary versions of Marxian, Durkheimian and Weberian social theory--for example, for Durkheim, one major link was the necessity of imposing knowledge categories upon individuals, for Marx, the repressive State (and thus State education) which enabled class domination and surplus-value extortion, and for Weber, rationality via bureaucracy. To complete his sampling of a variety of theoretical approaches, Davies devotes a chapter to two overviews of what school is for--that is, to the work of Basil Bernstein and Pierre Bourdieu. His cryptic sub-titles to the respective sections "Bernstein: change within limits" and "Bourdieu: plus ça change ..." encapsulate the major features he draws from their views. Bernstein, following in the Durkheimian tradition, is concerned with analysis of limited changes in forms of social control and their connection with the class structure (of schools moving from tradionalism to progressivism and the changing balance between visible and invisible pedagogies) whilst Bourdieu, having synthesized elements from the thought of Durkheim and Marx, maintains that the basic principle behind the efficacy of symbols is the structured structure. Having established the groundwork, Davies' analysis carries him to the conclusion that sociology gives rise to

> a complex agenda of questions and problems for research in connection with the school and social control rather than a way of evaluating how we do it when we do.[148]

As a contrast to Davies' treatment of the theme, we can turn to an article by William Spady.[149] He seeks to explore the relation between the authority system of the school and the emergence of violence in the schools. He delineates the socialization, instructional, custody-control,

135

certification and selection functions of the school and perceives them as constraints on students. Control is defined in Weberian terms as power and authority to which Spady adds the notion of persuasion. He then analyses the nature of legitimate authority and of the structural conditions for student achievement in schools. Spady is enabled, therefore, to distinguish situations under which the legitimation of teacher authority is problematic and, consequently, to deduce the conditions under which student protest is likely to arise. This example, according to Davies, would illustrate an evaluation of how social control is "done" in schools.

It is suggested that the application of sociological templates to the educational phenomena of inequality and social control, and to others of interest to sociologists, may have at least four consequences which refer to the concepts and processes of doubt, liberation, rationality and understanding. These consequences have contributions relevant to professional sociologists and students of sociology as well as to the members of publics associated with education.

By doubt is meant the questioning of the validity of social relationships which have previously been taken for granted. The acceptance of an ideology of liberal educational reform has placed great stress on the potential of formal education for social change and this has been reflected in educational policies, for example, strategies of compensatory education and equal access to schooling. However, the frameworks and analyses of sociologists like Bowles and Gintis, Bourdieu, Robinson, Sharp and Green, Ford, Rist and others focus attention on different aspects within schools and direct critical scrutiny to the wider social context. Their findings also carry an implicit message that cautions against inflexible adherence to current knowledge. Bierstedt[150] has argued that sociology "liberates ... from the provincialisms of time, place, and circumstance." The same point is made by Berger[151] who speaks of sociology as a

136

means to extradite students from their parochialism
--their attachment to the limited context of their
own experience. Liberation is engendered because
the application of sociological templates enables
sociologists and laymen to transcend time, circumstance and particular cultural contexts because
social theory arrives at general principles charac-
terising human societies. Strategies of educational redress and forms of social control in education are able to be understood because they can
be linked back to the images of man and society
(held consciously or unconsciously) which form a
framework within which educationalists, administrators, politicians, teachers and others operate.

The encouragement of rationality arises from
sociology's attempt to stimulate scientific inquiry
into educational phenomena rather than dependence
on dogma and faith. The illumination of research
questions by theory prior to the actual investigation, noted in Williams' study on teacher prophecies, illustrates something of the nature and
function of logic and scientific method. The quality of "scientific disinterest" in sociological
inquiry, evident in Davies' analysis of social control and education, acts as a balance to the normative climate in which the educationist must necessarily work.[152]

The final consequence, that of understanding,
relates to the critical character of sociology as
a practice; the application of sociological theory
and method to the study of social institutions
facilitates the setting up of debate between sociologists and the lay members of those institutions
through whose conduct the institutions exist.[153]
For example, the concepts of sociology cannot be
understood simply by immediate experience; to
understand them requires an order of understanding
beyond the phenomenal world of direct experience.
Secondly, social reality is a multi-layered phenomenon. As subsequent layers of meaning are discovered, the perception of the whole is altered.
Thus, if people are exposed to sociological reasoning, the potential is there for the development of
different forms of understanding of educational
phenomena.

CONCLUDING COMMENT

It would seem to be appropriate to conclude this chapter by reflecting in a limited way on the contribution the sociology of education makes to sociology itself.[154] Two claims, speculative only at this stage, are made for the sociology of education in this regard. The first is that a review of the biography of the sub-field of sociological inquiry into education serves to add to the development of a serious study of the social and institutional sources of the parent enterprise, that is to say, of a sociology of sociology. And the second, that the study of the centrally important institution of education produces data which are of substantive, theoretical and methodological relevance to sociology as both enterprise and institution.

A principal preoccupation of sociology is educational--teaching sociologists are disseminators of "social knowledge, a perspective, and a methodology."[155] As Brim has commented:

> For the sociologist, the formal educational system of this country constitutes what is probably his richest and most accessible source of raw data on personality and social interaction; it only needs to be systematically minded by careful research.[156]

The contrasting findings of sociological studies into the roles of teachers and students, into curriculum, into schools as formal organizations-- that is, with other educational contexts--can add to the body of knowledge of the sociologist-cum-teacher in order for him to reflect on his role (what are my rules for the constitution of successful "teaching" or "learning"?) and to incorporate other elements into his curriculum (what does sociology of education knowledge offer to allow me to conceptualize new possibilities for making the world "real" to my students?).[157] As well, the sociologist in an academic setting may be re-

138

directed to perceive both the educational and political functions and implications of his discipline.[158]

The corpus of sociology of education can contribute to sociology in other ways: to designated sub-fields like the sociology of knowledge (for example, the intensive exploration of the contextual and situated character of taken-for-granted categories and hierarchies in the work of the "new" sociologists of education in Britain may have potential for the study of the acculturation of thought systems) or to studies·on themes which cut across sub-field boundaries (for example, the relationship between Church and State, poverty in society, pressure group activity, dilemmas of women at work, attitudes to ethnically subordinate groups) or to illustrate the shifting patterns of interest and the dangers of premature closure in sociological inquiry (for example, with the emergence of the interpretive paradigm in sociology of education in this decade previously invisible or uninteresting topics of investigation, subsumed by the twin concerns of action and knowledge,[159] have risen to prominence).

Finally, Bottomore's foreword to the Bourdieu-Passeron volume on Reproduction in Education, Society and Culture is adduced because his comments encompass both of the claims made in the opening sentences of this conclusion.[160] Bottomore firstly locates Bourdieu's research on cultural reproduction in the sociological tradition of studies concerned with the maintenance of systems of power by the transmission of culture. He then refers to the substantive, theoretical and methodological contribution of this particular work. The principal theoretical proposition is identified as

> ... every power which manages to
> impose meanings and to impose them
> as legitimate by concealing the
> power relations which are the basis
> of its force and adds its own
> specifically symbolic force to
> those power relations.

From this beginning, other propositions have been formulated, for example, those relating to "pedagogic action" which is defined as the "imposition of a cultural arbitrary by an arbitrary power." By analysing a particular system of pedagogic action (the French educational system), empirically testable propositions are shown to emerge from the theoretical propositions while at the same time the construction or modification of these latter propositions is stimulated by their confrontation with the empirical phenomenon. Extrapolation of the Bourdieu-Passeron theory of classes and dominant groups evidenced by the imposition of culture and pedagogic action leads to the positing of a concept of "symbolic violence"--a basic characteristic of a "determined social structure." Bottomore concludes that Bourdieu's whole project of continuing research has revealed new features in the analysis of social classes and political power by connecting cultural phenomena with structural characteristics in a society and has begun to show how a culture produced by certain structure, in turn, helps to maintain it.

The examples given above and in the previous section are merely suggestive of a framework for the argument which would need to be constructed in order to substantiate the claims made for the contribution of a sociology of education to both education and sociology. The fundamental difficulty in the "accomplishment" of this chapter, whether in terms of the development, the issues, controversies and modes of inquiry, or of the contribution of the field of sociology of education inheres in the nature of the discipline itself. Floud and Halsey state it thus:

> ... that of presenting an orderly
> and coherent analysis of a set of
> institutions which by their nature
> confound social-psychological and
> sociological issues, straddling as
> they do the psychological and the
> organizational structure of society.[161]

This is also by way of acknowledging the necessity

for diverse perspectives to be brought to bear on
the study of education.

1. The use of the term "sociology of education" as opposed to the term "educational sociology"
could be the subject of an extensive discussion.
I do not see this as salient for the over-all purpose of the present work. Sociology of education
has been accepted as the preferred term although
educational sociology appears when the early stages
of the development of the field receive attention.
The impression should not be given, however, that
educational sociology as a label or as an actual
orientation has not survived. For a detailed exposition of the issues see, for example, G. Jensen,
Educational Sociology (Englewood Cliffs, N.J.:
Prentice-Hall, 1965); W. Taylor, "The Sociology of
Education," in The Study of Education, ed. T.W.
Tibble (London: Routledge and Kegan Paul, 1967);
and R. Stalcup, Sociology and Education (Columbus,
Ohio: C.E. Merrill, 1968). It seems useful to
note, also, the stance adopted by Donald Swift:

> The development of the discipline
> (and hence its value in society)
> follows from a mutually stimulating
> relationship between theorizing
> and information-gathering, each of
> which is dependent upon the other
> for meaning. There is no point in
> distinguishing between the motives
> for doing research. What matters
> is the candlepower of the theories
> which illuminate the information,
> and the rigour with which it is
> collected. Consequently sociology
> and education have a great deal to
> offer each other.

From D.F. Swift, The Sociology of Education (London:
Routledge and Kegan Paul, 1969), pp. 5-6.

2. This definition of the field has been taken
from Jean Floud and A.H. Halsey, "The Sociology of
Education," Current Sociology VII (1958): 170.
The review article is, in itself, a marker in the

development of the field. It represents the earliest attempt by British sociologists of education to provide a systematic and coherent critique of their subject and it has the additional virtue of anticipating many of the issues which have arisen in the debates of the 1970s.

3. Bill Williamson, "Continuities and Discontinuities in the Sociology of Education," in Educability, Schools and Ideology, eds. M. Flude and J. Ahier (London: Croom Helm, 1974), p. 3.

4. The general idea of a "sociology" of education was taken from Robert Friedrichs, A Sociology of Sociology (New York: The Free Press, 1970). One useful section draws attention to the need to examine sociological "paradigms and the differential status of their advocates, their diffusion and subsequent modifications, the impact of a given sociocultural milieu and a given time," p. xix. A second way of conceiving of this orientation is in terms of the sociology of (sociology of education) knowledge. Bernbaum has summarized this point in the following way:

> An approach, therefore, which enquires into the origins and nature of the sociology of education will enable questions to be asked about the ways in which, and the degrees to which, sociologists concerned with education have accepted the dominant categories of educationalists and teachers. It will encourage an investigation of the extent to which the whole idea of enquiry has been dominated by the structural-functional perspectives of the parent discipline and of the consequences of any such domination. It will help us to establish the conditions and processes by which teaching and research relevant to the curricula of the sociology of education have been selected and institutionalized in educational organizations, and to explore any relationships between these develop-

ments and the careers of the personnel engaged in teaching and research.

From Gerald Bernbaum, <u>Knowledge and Ideology in the Sociology of Education</u> (London: The Macmillan Press, 1977), p. 13. An alternative conceptualization of the sociology of education as an invention, an innovation or a social science adapting to and moulded by its power context is examined in B.Y. Card, "The State of Sociology of Education in Canada - A Further Look," <u>Canadian Journal of Education</u> 1 (1976): 3-32.

5. Basil Bernstein, "Sociology and the sociology of education: a brief account," in <u>Approaches to Sociology: An Introduction to Major Trends in British Sociology</u>, ed. John Rex (London and Boston: Routledge and Kegan Paul, 1974), p. 145.

6. J. Graham Morgan, "Contextual Factors in the Rise of Academic Sociology in the United States," <u>Canadian Review of Sociology and Anthropology</u> 7 (1970): 159.

7. Donald Hansen, "The Uncomfortable Relation of Sociology and Education," in <u>On Education: Sociological Perspectives</u>, eds. D. Hansen and J. Gerstl (New York: John Wiley, 1967), pp. 3-35.

8. This Kuhnian interpretation is cited by Rachel Sharp and Anthony Green, <u>Education and Social Control: A Study in Progressive Primary Education</u> (London: Routledge and Kegan Paul, 1975), p. 1. Kuhn's notions of 'paradigm' and 'normal science' and their application to sociology are themselves subject to much controversy. These arguments cannot be entered into here but can be explored in, for example, I. Lakatos and A. Musgrave, eds., <u>Criticism and the Growth of Knowledge</u> (Cambridge: Cambridge University Press, 1970); T.J. Nossiter et al., eds. <u>Imagination and Precision in the Social Sciences</u> (London: Faber and Faber, 1972); and Christopher Bryant, "Kuhn, paradigms and sociology," <u>British Journal of Sociology</u> XXVI (1975): 354-359.

9. These terms can be attributed in the order listed to T. Wilson, "Normative and interpretive paradigms in sociology," in Understanding Everyday Life, ed. J. Douglas (Chicago: Aldine, 1970), pp. 57-79; Robert J. Havighurst, "Sociology in the Contemporary Educational Crisis," Journal of Research and Development in Education 9 (1975): 14; and Olive Banks, "The 'New' Sociology of Education," Forum for the Discussion of New Trends in Education 1 (1974): 4.

10. This Schutzian notion has more recently been expanded by Peter Berger and Thomas Luckman, The Social Construction of Reality (New York: Anchor Books, 1967).

11. Basil Bernstein, p. 157.

12. W. Brookover and D. Gottlieb, A Sociology of Education (New York: American Book Co., 1964, 2nd edition), pp. 3-4.

13. Orville Brim Jr., Sociology and the Field of Education (New York: Russell Sage Foundation, 1958), p. 9.

14. R.G. Corwin, A Sociology of Education (New York: Appleton-Century-Crofts, 1965), pp. 59-60.

15. Donald Hansen, p. 5.

16. Hansen, p. 16.

17. Robert Havighurst, pp. 13-14.

18. Cf. D. Hansen and J. Gerstl, op.cit.; Jean Floud and A.H. Halsey, op.cit.; and Neil Gross, "Some Contributions of Sociology to the Field of Education," in Sociology of Education: A Book of readings, ed. R. Pavalko (Itasca, Ill.: F.E. Peacock, 1976, 2nd edition), pp. 19-31.

19. W. Brookover, p. 10.

20. C. Wayne Gordon, ed., Uses of the Sociology of Education 73rd NSSE Yearbook, Part II (Chicago: The University of Chicago Press, 1974), p. ix.

21. Robert Havighurst, p. 14.

22. M. Shimbori, "Educational Sociology or Sociology of Education," International Review of Education XVII (1972): 6-7. Shimbori's analysis of the state of the field can be supported by examining the nature of the contributions in: the 73rd NSSE Yearbook published in 1974 referred to in footnote 20; The Journal of Research and Development in Education 9 (1975) - the whole issue is devoted to the sociology of education; C. Arnold Anderson, "Sociology of Education in a Comparative Framework," International Review of Education XVI (1970): 147-159; S. Bowles and H. Gintis, Schooling in Capitalist America (New York: Basic Books, 1976).

23. Marvin Bressler, "The Conventional Wisdom of Education and Sociology," in Sociology and Contemporary Education, ed. C.H. Page (New York: Random House, 1966, 2nd printing), p. 76.

24. Jean Floud and A.H. Halsey, pp. 166-167.

25. Floud and Halsey, p. 174.

26. Basil Bernstein, p. 149.

27. Donald Swift and Henry Acland, "The Sociology of Education in Britain, 1960-1968: a bibliographical review," Social Science Information 8 (1969): 31.

28. Cf. Frank Musgrove, The Family, education and society (London: Routledge and Kegan Paul, 1966); Olive Banks, The Sociology of Education (London: Batsford, 1968); D.F. Swift; Peter Musgrave, The Sociology of Education (London: Methuen, 1965); William Taylor, The Secondary Modern School (London: Faber and Faber, 1963); and A.H. Halsey, J. Floud and C.A. Anderson, eds., Education, Economy and Society (Glencoe, Ill.: The Free Press, 1961).

29. Donald Swift and Henry Acland, pp. 51-64.

30. A post hoc overview of these questions as they relate to the British context is given in the publication, Ivan Reid and Eileen Wormald, eds., Sociology and Teacher Education (Sociology Section of the Association of Teachers in Colleges and Departments of Education, 1974).

31. Sociologists had a considerable influence, directly or indirectly, on educational policy in various ways. For example, they served on committees producing official reports, were involved in government sponsored and funded research projects or were called upon for expert advice by politicians of ministerial rank. This issue is subjected to analysis and interpretation of such sources as the following: Gerald Bernbaum, op.cit., pp. 9-26; Michael Flude, "Sociological Accounts of Differential Educational Attainment," in Educability, Schools and Ideology, eds. M. Flude and J. Ahier, pp. 15-52; and A.H. Halsey, ed., Educational Priority, Vol. 1 (London: H.M.S.O., 1972).

32. Richard Brown, ed., Knowledge, Education and Cultural Change (London: Tavistock, 1973), p. 2.

33. Michael F.D. Young, ed., Knowledge and Control: New Directions for the Sociology of Education (London: Collier-Macmillan, 1971) and Earl Hopper, ed., Readings in the Theory of Educational Systems (London: Hutchinson, 1971).

34. M.F.D. Young, pp. 2-3.

35. The use of the term "mission" is deliberate. I am here following Roland Robertson's interpretation of the debate in sociology which has attended contemporary interest in paradigms. He expresses one consequence of this ferment as the development of deflationary sociological situations. These are situations in which:

> the concern to overthrow an existing, or to establish a new, paradigm has

147

led to a kind of sociological sectarian fundamentalism.

See Roland Robertson, "Toward the identification of the major axes of sociological analysis," in Approaches to Sociology, ed. John Rex, p. 107.

36. A.H. Halsey, "Theoretical Advance and Empirical Challenge," in Readings in the Theory of Educational Systems, ed. Earl Hopper, p. 262.

37. Martyn Hammersley and Peter Woods, eds., The Process of Schooling (London and Henley: Routledge and Kegan Paul in association with The Open University Press, 1976), p. 1.

38. John Rex, Key Problems of Sociological Theory (London: Routledge and Kegan Paul, 1961), p. 175.

39. M.F.D. Young refers to the "making" and "taking" of problems in the Introduction to his volume Knowledge and Control, p. 1. This notion is a central one in his argument. Young attacks conventional sociology of education for its over-emphasis on the issue of order at the expense of that of control. We might extend Young's version of "making" by educators and "taking" by sociologists to the situation in which educators, particularly administrators working within theor normative framework, selectively "take" sociological evidence "made" by sociologists, working in an empirical framework, to use it in "solutions" to educational problems.

40. John Eggleston has edited a collection of research papers which illustrate the use of many of these theoretical approaches and methodological strategies. See John Eggleston, ed., Contemporary Research in the Sociology of Education (London: Methuen, 1974).

41. John Eggleston, "Sociology and Sociology of Education," University of Alberta, November 1973 (Mimeo.), p. 5. In this paper, Eggleston is

reflecting the posture adopted by Basil Bernstein, pp. 145-159.

42. There is an increasing literature on this question. References which indicate the far-ranging nature of discussion of the point include: David Gorbutt, "The Sociology of Education," Education for Teaching 89 (1972): 3-11; Alvin Gouldner, For Sociology (London: Allen Lane, 1973); Frederick Erickson, "Gatekeeping and the Melting Pot," Harvard Educational Review 45 (1975): 44-70; John Eggleston, ed., Introduction, pp. 1-16; Jerome Karabel and A.H. Halsey, "The New Sociology of Ed--cation," Theory and Society 3 (1976): 529-552.

43. Donald Edgar, "Durkheim, China and the Individual in Education." Paper presented at the Sociological Association of Australia and New Zealand Annual Conference, La Trobe University, Australia, 1976 (Mimeo.), pp. 8-13.

44. Cited by W. Brookover and D. Gottlieb, p.4.

45. M. Hammersley and P. Woods, eds., p. 8.

46. Talcott Parsons, "The School Class as a Social System: Some of Its Functions in American Society," in Education, Economy and Society, eds., A. Halsey, J. Floud and C. Anderson, p. 434.

47. Ibid.

48. W.A.L. Blyth, "Social processes in junior schools," in Basic Readings in the Sociology of Education, ed. D.F. Swift (London: Routledge and Kegan Paul, 1970), p. 95.

49. Anthony Giddens, New Rules of Sociological Method (London: Hutchinson, 1976), p. 21.

50. Swift discusses these types of methodol-ogical criticisms by comparing and contrasting sociology and psychology in educational research. See Donald Swift, "Sociology and educational re-search," in Research Perspectives in Education, ed. W. Taylor (London: Routledge and Kegan Paul, 1973),

pp. 172-187.

51. For a critique of earlier approaches to the study of classroom interaction and an exposition of alternatives, see Michael Stubbs and Sara Delamont, eds., Explorations in Classroom Observation (London: John Wiley, 1976).

52. References consulted here include: A. Rose, ed., Human Behaviour and Social Processes (London: Routledge and Kegan Paul, 1962); H. Blumer, Symbolic Interactionism, Perspective and Method (Englewood Cliffs, N.J.: Prentice-Hall, 1969); G. Salaman and D. Weeks, Social Interaction (Bletchley, Bucks.: The Open University Press, 1972).

53. Clark, McPhail, "Student Walkout: A Fortuitous Examination of Elementary Collective Behaviour," in Symbolic Interaction, eds. Jerome Manis and Bernard Meltzer (Boston: Ally and Bacon, 1972, 2nd edition), pp. 208-225.

54. The diversity of phenomenologies poses problems with regard to references. For Schutzian phenomenology which is based on his interpretation of Husserl, see Alfred Schutz, Collected Papers I: The Problem of Social Reality, ed. Maurice Natanson (The Hague: Martinus Nijhoff, 1962) and The Phenomenology of the Social World, trans. Walsh and Lehrnet, with an introduction by G. Walsh (Evanston, Ill.: Northwestern University Press, 1967). Two references which present phenomenological views, in addition to those of Schutz, are S. Lyman and M. Scott, A Sociology of the Absurd (New York: Appleton-Century-Crofts, 1970); P. Filmer et.al., New Directions in Sociological Theory (London: Collier-Macmillan, 1972).

55. Geoffrey Esland, The Construction of Reality (Bletchley, Bucks.: The Open University Press, 1971), p. 20.

56. Robert Stebbins, "The Meaning of Disorderly Behaviour: Teacher Definitions of a Class-

150

room Situation," Sociology of Education 44 (1971): 217-236.

57. C. Wertham, "Delinquents in Schools," in School and Society, eds., B. Cosin et.al. (London: Routledge and Kegan Paul, 1971), pp. 39-48.

58. Blanche Geer, "Teaching," in School and Society, eds. B. Cosin et al. op.cit., pp. 3-8.

59. H. Garfinkel, Studies in Ethnomethodology (Englewood Cliffs, N.J.: Prentice-Hall, 1967). Examples of additional sources: P. Dreitzel, ed., Recent Sociology No. 2 (New York: Macmillan, 1970); P. Attewell, "Ethnomethodology since Garfinkel," Theory and Society 1 (1974): 179-210; R. Turner, ed., Ethnomethodology (Harmondsworth, Middlesex: Penguin, 1974).

60. Martyn Hammersley and Peter Woods, p. 8.

61. George Payne, "Making a lesson happen: an ethnomethodological analysis," in The Process of Schooling, eds., M. Hammersley and P. Woods, pp. 33-40.

62. The complexities of the underlying assumptions of, and open debates on, interactionist sociological perspectives can be followed in these sources inter alia: M. Natason, ed., Philosophy of the Social Sciences: A Reader (New York: Random House, 1963); D. Emmet and A. Macintyre, Sociological Theory and Philosophical Analysis (London: Macmillan, 1970); Edo Pivcevic, "Can there be a phenomenological sociology?" Sociology 6 (1972): 335-349; Bob Gidlow, "Ethnomethodology: a new name for old practices," British Journal of Sociology 23 (1972): 395-405; John Goldthorpe, "A revolution in sociology?" Sociology 7 (1973): 449-562; Scott McNall and James Johnson, "The new conservatives: ethnomethodolgists, phenomenologists and symbolic interactionists," The Insurgent Sociologist 5 (1975): 49-65; Donald Carveth, "The Disembodied Dialectic: A Psychoanalytic Critique of Sociological Relativism," Theory and Society 4 (1977): 73-102.

63. R. Sharp and A. Green, p. 21.

64. Ibid., p. 22.

65. David Gorbutt, p. 6.

66. Jerome Karabel and A.H. Halsey, pp. 542-543.

67. Anthony Giddens, p. 52.

68. Martyn Hammersley and Peter Woods, eds., p. 3.

69. Anthony Giddens, p. 53.

70. Ibid.

71. An important source book is J. Curtis and J. Petras, eds., The Sociology of Knowledge: A Reader (New York: Praeger, 1970). Useful references inter alia: Gunter Remmling, ed., Towards The Sociology of Knowledge (London: Routledge and Kegan Paul, 1972); P. Hamilton, Knowledge and Social Structure (London: Routledge and Kegan Paul, 1974); P. Berger and T. Luckmann, The Social Construction of Reality (New York: Anchor Books, 1967). C.W. Mills, "Methodological Consequences of the Sociology of Knowledge," American Journal of Sociology XVI (1940): 316-330.

72. Derek Phillips, "Epistemology and the Sociology of Knowledge: The Contribution of Mannheim, Mills, and Merton," Theory and Society 1 (1974): 59-88.

73. G. Remmling, p. 135.

74. Karl Marx and Friedrich Engels, "Concerning the Production of Consciousness," in The Sociology of Knowledge: A Reader, eds. J. Curtis and J. Petras, p. 105.

75. John Kennett, "The Sociology of Pierre Bourdieu," Educational Review 25 (1973): 238.

76. Karl Mannheim, "The Sociology of Knowledge," in The Sociology of Knowledge: A Reader, eds. J. Curtis and J. Petras, p. 123; and P. Hamilton, pp. 127-129.

77. P. Hamilton, p. 101.

78. See The Introduction, Peter Berger and Thomas Luckmann, pp. 1-18. In this section, the authors sketch in a background of ideas from nineteenth century thought - Marxian, the Nietzchean and the historicist - and then outline their "solution" to the problem of the sociology of knowledge.

79. M.F.D. Young, ed., p. 3.

80. Nell Keddie, "Classroom Knowledge," in Knowledge and Control, ed., M. Young, pp. 133-160.

81. Geoffrey Esland, "Teaching and Learning as the Organization of Knowledge," in Knowledge and Control, ed. M. Young, pp. 70-115.

82. Esland, p. 111.

83. Cf. S. Bowles and H. Gintis; Maurice Levitas, Marxist Perspectives on the Sociology of Education (London and Boston: Routledge and Kegan Paul, 1974); the Altussherian approach to the study of educational institutions in L. Altussher, "Ideology and Ideological State Apparatuses 'notes towards an investigation'," in Education: Structure and Society, ed. B. Cosin (Harmondsworth, Middlesex: Penguin in association with The Open University Press, 1972), pp. 242-280.

84. This viewpoint is discussed in the following sources inter alia: R. Sharp, "Open Schools - Closed Society: Progressive Education in Practice and the Free School Alternative," Dialogue 10 (1976): 51-69; Christopher Hurn, "Theory and Ideology in Two Traditions of Thought about School," Social Forces 54 (1976): 848-865; and David Hargreaves, "Deschoolers and New Romantics," in Educability, Schools and Ideology, eds. M. Flude

and J. Ahier, pp. 186-210.

85. M. Hammersley and P. Woods, ed., p. 2.

86. R. Sharp and A. Green, pp. 33-34.

87. Ibid., p. 35.

88. Jerome Karabel and A.H. Halsey; Denis
Lawton, Class, Culture and the Curriculum (London
and Boston: Routledge and Kegan Paul, 1975);
Geoff Whitty, "Sociology and the Problem of Radical
Educational Change," in Educability, Schools and
Ideology, eds., M. Flude and J. Ahier, pp. 112-237.

89. Dennis Warwick, "Ideologies, Integration
and Conflicts of Meaning," in Educability, Schools
and Ideology, eds., M. Flude and J. Ahier, p. 99.

90. This implies ipso facto that atheoretical
research is "poor" sociological research. Harp
and Richer subscribe to the established notion of
a complementary relationship between theory and
research in the sociology of education. See J. Harp
and S. Richer, "Sociology of Education," Review of
Educational Research 39 (1969): 671.

91. J. Eggleston, ed., pp. 2-3.

92. M. Shipman, The limitations of social
research (London: Longman, 1972), pp. 4-5.

93. C. Wright Mills, The Sociological Imagination (Harmondsworth, Middlesex: Penguin, 1970),
p. 11. Mills uses the term sociological imagination
in the following way:

> ... a quality of mind that will
> help [sociologists] to use infor-
> mation and to develop reason in
> order to achieve lucid summations
> of what is going on in the world
> and of what may be happening within
> themselves.

94. D.F. Swift, "Sociology and educational research," in Research Perspectives in Education, ed. W. Taylor, pp. 179-180.

95. A. Giddens, p. 14.

96. For a discussion of a range of reasons for the support given to the natural science research model, see inter alia: Alan Ryan, ed., The Philosophy of Social Explanation (London: Oxford University Press, 1973); R. Keat and J. Urry, Social Theory as Science (London and Boston: Routledge and Kegan Paul, 1975); P. Hammond, ed., Sociologists at Work (New York: Basic Books, 1964); R. Hinkle, Jr. and G. Hinkle, The Development of Modern Sociology (New York: Random House, 1954).

97. J. Eggleston, ed., p. 3.

98. A. Giddens, p. 15.

99. For example, Michael F.D. Young, ed.; two selections by Ioan Davies, "The Management of Knowledge: A Critique of the Use of Typologies in Educational Sociology," in Readings in the Theory of Educational Systems, ed. E. Hopper, pp. 111-138 and "Education and Social Science," New Society 345 (1969): 710-711; David Gorbutt; David Walsh, "Varieties of Positivism," in New Directions in Sociological Theory, ed. P. Filmer et.al., pp. 37-56; D. Hargreaves, S. Hester and F. Mellor, Deviance in Classrooms. (London: Routledge and Kegan Paul, 1975).

100. This is an exaggerated form of the argument which cautions that "sociologists should be on guard against oversimplifying the social process to make social action seem more determinate than it is." See S. Mennell, Sociological Theory: Uses and Unities (London: Nelson, 1974), p. 36.

101. Christopher Bryant, Sociology in Action (London: Allen and Unwin, 1976), p. 309.

102. Examples include: S. Bowles, H. Gintis

and P. Meyer, "The Long Shadow of Work: Education, The Family, and The Reproduction of the Social Division of Labour," The Insurgent Sociologist V (1975): 3-22; Julienne Ford, Social Class and the Comprehensive School (London: Routledge and Kegan Paul, 1969); S. Baratz and J. Baratz, "Early Childhood Intervention: the social science base of institutional racism," in Language in Education, ed., A. Cashdan (London: Routledge and Kegan Paul in association with The Open University Press, 1972), pp. 188-197; R. Rist, "Student social class and teacher expectation," Harvard Educational Review 40 (1970): 411-451; M.F.D. Young, "On the Politics of Educational Knowledge," Economy and Society 1 (1972): 194-215; Rachel Sharp, "Open Schools - Closed Society: Progressive Education in Practice and the Free School Alternative," Dialogue 10 (1976): 51-69.

103. R. Walker, "The Sociology of Education and Life in School Classrooms," International Review of Education XVIII (1972): 36-37.

104. A. McClung Lee, "Humanist Challenges to Positivists," The Insurgent Sociologist VI (1975): 42.

105. M. Shipman, p. 1.

106. A.H. Halsey, ed., pp. 3-4.

107. Rachel Green, pp. 51-69.

108. Eric Hoyle, "Social Theories of Education in Contemporary Britain," Social Science Information 9 (1970): 169-186.

109. Christopher Hurn, pp. 849-854.

110. M.F.D. Young, p. 194.

111. Ibid, p. 196.

112. J. Karabel and A.H. Halsey, pp. 548-549.

113. Gerald Bernbaum, p. 42.

114. John Harp and Stephen Richer, pp. 678-691.

115. For a concise illustration of this point see Rob Walker, pp. 32-41, in which Walker uses the example of research on the interaction between teacher and students within the social arena of the classroom. This is an especially useful article for the purpose of this review because a comparison is made of the British and American contexts.

116. M. Coulson and C. Riddell, Approaching Sociology (London: Routledge and Kegan Paul, 1970), p. 20. These authors provide a useful discussion of sociology as a critical discipline in their first chapter.

117. Peter Berger, Invitation to Sociology: A Humanistic Perspective (New York: Anchor Books, 1963), p. 53.

118. J. Karabel and A.H. Halsey, and M.F.D. Young.

119. R. Dale, G. Esland and M. MacDonald, eds., Schooling and Capitalism (London and Henley: Routledge and Kegan Paul in association with The Open University Press, 1976), p. 1.

120. Guy Rocher, A General Introduction to Sociology (Toronto: The Macmillan Co. of Canada, 1972), p. 311.

121. A. Halsey, "Sociology for Teachers," in Sociology and Teacher Education, eds. I. Reid and E. Wormald, p. 29. Halsey's second comment is taken from an early lecture of Professor Emile Durkheim.

122. I. Reid, "Sociology in Colleges of Education: Some Considerations," in Sociology and Teacher Education, I. Reid and E. Wormald, eds., p. 8.

157

123. See, for example, B. Bernstein, Class, Codes and Control Vol. 1 (London: Routledge and Kegan Paul, 1971); J.S. Coleman, "Academic Achievement and the Structure of Competition," Harvard Educational Review XXIX (1959: 339-351; F. Strodtbeck, "Family Integration, Values, and Achievement," in Talent and Society, eds. D. McClelland et.al. (Princeton, N.J.: Van Nostrand, 1958), pp. 135-194; and F. Katz and R. Browne, eds., Sociology of Education (Melbourne: Macmillan, 1970).

124. Cf. M. Stubbs, Language, Schools and Classrooms (London: Methuen, 1976); M. Wax and R. Wax, "Cultural Deprivation as an Educational Ideology," in The Culture of Poverty: A Critique, ed. E. Leacock (New York: Simon and Shuster, 1971), pp. 127-139; and P. Bourdieu and J.-C. Passeron, Reproduction in Education, Society and Culture (London and Beverly Hills: Sage, 1977).

125. The claims and counter-claims of the various proponents can be followed in the references cited. F. Riessman, The Culturally Deprived Child (New York: Harper and Row, 1962); the entire issue of the Harvard Educational Review 38 (1968) is concerned with equal educational opportunity and contains articles by Coleman and Moynihan A. Jensen, "How much can we boost I.Q. and scholastic achievement?" Harvard Educational Review 39 (1969): 1-123; R. Herrnstein, "I.Q.," Atlantic Monthly 28 (1971): 43-64; C. Jencks, op.cit.; G. Hodgson, "Do Schools Make a Difference?" Atlantic Monthly 231 (1973): 35-46.

126. Nell Keddie, ed., Tinker, Tailor ... The Myth of Cultural Deprivation (Harmondsworth, Middlesex: Penguin, 1973). A comment on the book's cover indicates the orientation taken by Keddie and her contributors ... "It is possible that we should regard 'cultural deprivation' as a mythology developed to mask and support a class system to which we are all, wittingly or not, committed."

127. The debate on these differing views can

be found in a series of articles in The Australian and New Zealand Journal of Sociology. The Reference lists appended to the articles are a useful source of additional information in the area. See Ancich et.al., "A descriptive bibliography of published research and writing on social stratification in Australia, 1964-1967." ANZJS 5 (1969): 48-76; D. Toomey, "What causes educational disadvantage?" ANZJS 10 (1974): 31-37; T. Knight, "Powlessness and the student role: structural determinants of school status," ANZJS 10 (1974): 112-117; R. Connell, "The causes of educational inequality: further observations," ANZJS 10 (1974): 186-191; and D. Toomey, "Educational Disadvantage and Meritocratic Schooling," ANZJS 12 (1976): 228-235.

128. Articles by Eggleston, Byrne and Williamson, Halsey in Contemporary Research in the Sociology of Education, J. Eggleston; P. Sexton, The American School (Englewood Cliffs, N.J.: Prentice-Hall, 1967), especially chapters 3 and 4; M. Bowman, "The human investment revolution in economic thought," in Education: Structure and Society, ed. B. Cosin, pp. 43-70; B. Bernstein, "Open Schools, open society?" in School and Society, eds. B. Cosin et.al. (London: Routledge and Kegan Paul, in association with The Open University Press, 1971), pp. 166-169; H. Walberg and S. Thomas, "Open Education: an operational definition and validation in Great Britain and the United States," American Educational Research Journal 9 (1972): 197-208; and in R. Pavalko, ed., the articles in chapter 2 on Social Selection: Determinants of Educational Aspiration and Attainment and in chapter 5 - Schools and the Larger Society.

129. A. Cicourel and J. Kitsuse, The Educational Decision-Makers (New York: Bobbs-Merrill, 1963); R. Kanter, "The Organization Child: Experience Management in a Nursery School." Sociology of Education 45 (1972): 186-212.

130. The first two questions are explored in chapter 9, I. Davies, "The management of knowledge:

a critique of the use of typologies in the sociology of education," pp. 267-288 and chapter 3, G. Esland, "Teaching and learning as the organization of knowledge," pp. 70-115, in Knowledge and Control, ed. M.F.D. Young. The third question is the subject of P. Bourdieu, "Cultural reproduction and social reproduction," in Knowledge, Education and Cultural Change, ed. R. Brown, pp. 71-117.

131. One example of Musgrave's writing in the area is P. Musgrave, Knowledge, Curriculum and Change (Melbourne: Melbourne University Press, 1973).

132. M. Flude and J. Ahier, eds.

133. B. Bernstein, "On the classification and framing of educational knowledge," in his book, Class, Codes and Control Vol. 1, pp. 202-230.

134. M.F.D. Young, "An approach to the study of curricula as socially organized knowledge," in Knowledge and Control, ed. M.F.D. Young, pp. 19-46.

135. J. Eggleston, The Sociology of the School Curriculum (London, Henley and Boston: Routledge and Kegan Paul, 1977).

136. B. Geer, "Teaching," in School and Society, eds. B. Cosin et.al., op.cit., pp. 3-8. An expanded discussion of negotiation can be found in W. Martin, The Negotiated Order of the School (Toronto: Macmillan Co. of Canada, 1976).

137. G. Cooke, "Toward a phenomenological approach to teaching," Paper presented at the Sociological Association of Australia and New Zealand Annual Conference, Waikato University, New Zealand, 1975 (Mimeo), pp. 1-24.

138. D. Hargreaves, S. Hester and F. Mellor. This study, the first major empirical investigation to apply labelling theory to the study of deviance in school, is one of the few sociological studies in the area. Most of the work done previously has

160

been carried out by psychologists within a clinical and psychometric perspective.

139. It is suggested that the following are particularly relevant to this point: T. Parsons, "The School Class as a Social System: Some of its Functions in American Society," in Education, Economy, and Society, eds. A. Halsey, J. Floud and C. Anderson, pp. 434-455; W. Waller, The Sociology of Teaching (London: John Wiley, 1967, 3rd reprinting); M.D. Shipman, Sociology of the School (London: Longmans, Green, 1968); G. Bernbaum, "Headmasters and schools: some preliminary findings," and R. Witkin, "Social class influence on the amount and type of positive evaluation of school lessons," both in Contemporary Research in the Sociology of Education, ed. J. Eggleston, pp. 228-244 and pp. 302-324 respectively.

140. See E. Amidon and J. Hough eds., Interaction Analysis: Theory, Research and Application (Reading, Mass.: Addison-Wesley, 1967); R. Bales and F. Strodtbeck, "Phases in group problem solving," in Ibid., pp. 98-102; N. Flanders, Analyzing Teacher Behavior (Reading, Mass.: Addison-Wesley, 1970).

141. R. Sharp and A. Green, p. 20.

142. D.R. Watson, "Sociological Theory and the Analysis of Strategies of Educational Redress," International Review of Education XXII (1976): 42.

143. Ibid., pp. 41-62. As the review in the second section of the present chapter substantially covers the same ground, reference will be made only to the applications of theoretical templates.

144. Phillip Robinson, Education and Poverty (London: Methuen, 1976).

145. Ibid., p. 98.

146. Trevor Williams, "Teacher Prophecies and the Inheritance of Inequality," Sociology of

Education 49 (1976): 223-236.

147. Brian Davies, Social Control of Education (London: Methuen, 1976).

148. Ibid., p. 175.

149. William Spady, "The Authority System of the School and Student Unrest: A Theoretical Exploration," in Uses of the Sociology of Education, ed. C. Wayne Gordon, pp. 36-77.

150. Robert Bierstedt, "Sociology and General Education," in Sociology and Contemporary Education, ed. C.H. Page, p. 41.

151. P. Berger, p. 53.

152. This comment refers back to Bressler's exposition of differences between the conventional wisdom of education and sociology to be found in his chapter, in Sociology and Contemporary Education, ed. C.H. Page, pp. 76-114.

153. This theme is explored by T. Burns, "Sociological Explanation," British Journal of Sociology XVIII (1967): 353-369.

154. The discussions by Page, Nisbet and Bressler in the volume Sociology and Contemporary Education, ed. C.H. Page, though published as early as 1963, are still very relevant to the present theme. Other sources include: G. Bernbaum, "Sociology of Education," in Education and its Disciplines, ed. R.G. Woods (London: University of London Press, 1972), pp. 91-116; and D. Hansen, "The Uncomfortable Relation of Sociology and Education," in On Education: Sociological Perspectives, eds. D. Hansen and J. Gerstl, pp. 3-35.

155. C.H. Page, "Sociology as an Educational Enterprise," in Sociology and Contemporary Education, ed. C.H. Page, p. 16.

156. O. Brim Jr., p. 7.

157. Of course, the nature and extent of "borrowing" from the sociology of education will vary according to how the sociologist sees himself--in Bressler's terms--as man of "science," "action" or "significance." See Marvin Bressler, "The Conventional Wisdom of Education and Sociology," in Sociology and Contemporary Education, ed. C.H. Page, pp. 99-101.

158. For example, discussions of political and educational factors in issues such as the possibility of transcending or transforming taken-for-granted concepts in education as a consequence of recognizing their socially constructed character or the unmasking of the influence of the imperatives of educational and social policy requirements by procedures which make nanifest the latent value assumptions and tacit theoretical presuppositions underlying various theoretical traditions of sociological inquiry can be found in Worlds Apart: Readings for a Sociology of Education, eds. J. Beck, C. Jenks, N. Keddie and M.F.D. Young (London: Collier Macmillan, 1976).

159. M. Hammersley and P. Woods, eds., p. 2.

160. P. Bourdieu and J.-C. Passeron, with a forword by Tom Bottomore, pp. v-viii.

161. J. Floud and A.H. Halsey, p. 168.

BIBLIOGRAPHY

Althusser, L. "Ideology and Ideological State Apparatuses 'notes towards an investigation'." In Education: Structure and Society, pp. 242-280. Edited by B. Cosin. Harmondsworth, Middlesex: Penguin in association with The Open University Press, 1972.

Attewell, P. "Ethnomethodology Since Garfinkel." Theory and Society 1 (1974): 179-210.

Banks, O. "The 'New' Sociology of Education." Forum for the Discussion of New Trends in Education 1 (1974): 4-7.

Beck, J., Jenks, C., Keddie, N. and Young, M.F.D., eds. Worlds Apart Readings for a Sociology of Education. London: Collier Macmillan, 1976.

Berger, P. Invitation to Sociology: A Humanistic Perspective. New York: Anchor Books, 1963.

_____, and Luckmann, T. The Social Construction of Reality. New York: Anchor Books, 1967.

Bernbaum, G. Knowledge and Ideology in the Sociology of Education. London: The Macmillan Press, 1977.

_____. "Sociology of Education." In Education and its Disciplines, pp. 91-116. Edited by R.G. Woods. London: University of London Press, 1972.

Bernstein, B. "On the Classification and Framing of Educational Knowledge." In Class, Codes and Control, pp. 202-230. B. Bernstein. London: Routledge and Kegan Paul, 1971.

_____. "Sociology and the Sociology of Education: a brief account." In Approaches to Sociology: An Introduction to Major Trends in British Sociology, pp. 145-159. Edited by

164

J. Rex. London and Boston: Routledge and
Kegan Paul, 1974.

Bierstedt, R. "Sociology and General Education."
In Sociology and Contemporary Education, pp.
40-55. Edited by C.H. Page. New York: Random
House, 1966; reprint ed., 1963.

Blumer, H. Symbolic Interactionism: Perspective
and Method. Englewood Cliffs, N.J.: Prentice-
Hall, 1969.

Blyth, W.A.L. "Social Processes in Junior Schools."
In Basic Readings in The Sociology of Educa-
tion, pp. 95-108. Edited by D.F. Swift.
London: Routledge and Kegan Paul, 1970.

Bourdieu, P. and Passeron, J.-C. Reproduction in
Education, Society and Culture. London and
Beverly Hills: Sage Publications, 1977.

Bowles, S. and Gintis, H. Schooling in Capitalist
America. New York: Basic Books, 1976.

Bressler, M. "The Conventional Wisdom of Education
and Sociology." In Sociology and Contemporary
Education, pp. 76-114. Edited by C.H. Page.
New York: Random House, 1966; reprint ed.,
1963.

Brim Jr. O. Sociology and the Field of Education.
New York: Russell Sage Foundation, 1958.

Brookover, W. and Gittlieb, D. A Sociology of Education. 2nd ed. New York: American Book
Co., 1964.

Brown, R., ed. Knowledge, Education and Cultural
Change. London: Tavistock, 1973.

Bryant, C. Sociology in Action. London: George
Allen and Unwin, 1976.

Burns, T. "Sociological Explanation." British
Journal of Sociology XVIII (1967): 353-369.

Card, B.Y. "The State of Sociology of Education in Canada - A Further Look." Canadian Journal of Education 1 (1976): 3-32.

Cicourel, A. and Kitsuse, J. The Educational Decision-Makers. New York: Bobbs-Merrill, 1963.

Corwin, R.G. A Sociology of Education. New York: Appleton-Century-Crofts, 1965.

Coulson, M. and Riddell, C. Approaching Sociology. London: Routledge and Kegan Paul, 1970.

Curtis, J. and Petras, J., eds. The Sociology of Knowledge: A Reader. New York: Praeger, 1970.

Dale, R., Esland, G. and MacDonald, M. eds. Schooling and Capitalism. London and Henley: Routledge and Kegan Paul in association with The Open University Press, 1976.

Davies, B. Social Control and Education. London: Methuen, 1976.

Dreitzel, P., ed. Recent Sociology No. 2. New York: Macmillan, 1970.

Eggleston, J. The Sociology of the School Curriculum. London, Henley and Boston: Routledge and Kegan Paul, 1977.

_____, ed. Contemporary Research in the Sociology of Education. London: Methuen, 1974.

Esland, G. The Construction of Reality. Milton Keynes: The Open University Press, 1971.

_____. "Teaching and Learning as the Organization of Knowledge." In Knowledge and Control, pp. 70-115. Edited by M.F.D. Young. London: Collier-Macmillan, 1972.

Filmer, P., Phillipson, M., Silverman, D. and

Walsh, D. New Directions in Sociological Theory. London: Collier-Macmillan, 1972.

Floud, J. and Halsey, A.H. "The Sociology of Education." Current Sociology VII (1958): 165-233.

Flude, M. and Ahier, J., eds. Educability, Schools and Ideology. London: Croom Helm, 1974.

Friedrichs, R. A Sociology of Sociology. New York: The Free Press, 1970.

Garfinkel, H. Studies in Ethnomethodology. Englewood Cliffs, N.J.: Prentice-Hall, 1967.

Geer, B. "Teaching." In School and Society, pp. 3-8. Edited by B. Cosin et al. London: Routledge and Kegan Paul, 1971.

Giddens, A. New Rules of Sociological Method. London: Hutchinson, 1976.

Gorbutt, D. "The New Sociology of Education." Education for Teaching 89 (1972): 3-11.

Gordon, C.W., ed. Uses of the Sociology of Education. 73rd N.S.S.E. Yearbook, Part II. Chicago: The University of Chicago Press, 1974.

Gross, N. "Some Contributions of Sociology to the Field of Education." In Sociology of Education: A Book of Readings, 2nd ed., pp. 19-31. Edited by R. Pavalko. Itasca, Ill.: F.E. Peacock, 1976.

Halsey, A.H. "Sociology for Teachers." In Sociology and Teacher Education, pp. 29-32. Edited by I. Reid and E. Wormald. Sociology Section of the Association of Teachers in Colleges and Departments of Education, 1974.

_____. "Theoretical Advance and Empirical Challenge." In Readings in the Theory of

Educational Systems, pp. 262-281. Edited by
E. Hopper. London: Hutchinson, 1971.

_____., ed. Educational Priority Vol I: E.P.A.
Problems and Policies. London: Her Majesty's
Stationery Office, 1972.

Hamilton, P. Knowledge and Social Structure.
London: Routledge and Kegan Paul, 1974.

Hammersley, M. and Woods, eds. The Process of
Schooling. London and Henley: Routledge and
Kegan Paul in association with The Open Uni-
versity Press, 1976.

Hansen, D. "The Uncomfortable Relation of Sociology and Education." In On Education Sociological Perspectives, pp. 3-35. Edited by
D. Hansen and J. Gerstl. New York: John
Wiley, 1967.

Hargreaves, D. "Deschoolers and New Romantics."
In Educability, Schools and Ideology, pp. 186-
210. Edited by M. Flude and J. Ahier. London:
Croom Helm, 1974.

_____., Hester, D. and Mellor, F. Deviance in
Classrooms. London: Routledge and Kegan Paul,
1975.

Harp, J. and Richer, S. "Sociology of Education."
Review of Educational Research 39 (1969):
671-694.

Havighurst, R.J. "Sociology in the Contemporary
Educational Crisis." Journal of Research and
Development in Education 9 (1975): 13-22.

Hopper, E., ed. Readings in the Theory of Educational Systems. London: Hutchinson, 1971.

Hoyle, E. "Social Theories of Education in Contemporary Britain." Social Science Information
9 (1970): 169-186.

Hurn, C. "Theory and Ideology in Two Traditions of Thought about Schools." Social Forces 54 (1976): 848-865.

Kanter, R. "The Organizational Child: Experience Management in a Nursery School." Sociology of Education 45 (1972): 186-212.

Karabel, J. and Halsey, A.H. "The New Sociology of Education." Theory and Society 3 (1976): 529-552.

Keddie, N. "Classroom Knowledge." In Knowledge and Control, pp. 113-160. Edited by M.F.D. Young. London: Collier-Macmillan, 1971.

_____., ed. Tinker, Tailor ... The Myth of Cultural Deprivation. Harmondsworth, Middlesex: Penguin, 1973.

Kennett, P. "The Sociology of Pierre Bourdieu." Educational Review 25 (1973): 237-249.

Lawton, D. Class, Culture and the Curriculum. London and Boston: Routledge and Kegan Paul, 1975.

Lee, A. "Humanist Challenges to Positivists." The Insurgent Sociologist VI (1975): 41-50.

Levitas, M. Marxist Perspectives on the Sociology of Education. London and Boston: Routledge nad Kegan Paul, 1974.

Lyman, S. and Scott, M. A Sociology of the Absurd. New York: Appleton-Century-Crofts, 1970.

McPhail, C. "Student Walkout: A Fortuitous Examination of Elementary Collective Behaviour." In Symbolic Interaction, 2nd ed. pp. 208-225. Edited by J. Manis and B. Meltzer. Boston: Allyn and Bacon, 1972.

Marx, K. and Engels, F. "Concerning the Production of Consciousness." In The Sociology of Knowl-

169

edge, pp. 97-108. Edited by J. Curtis and
J. Petras. New York: Praeger, 1970.

Mannheim, K. "The Sociology of Knowledge." In
The Sociology of Knowledge, pp. 109-130.
Edited by J. Curtis and J. Petras. New York:
Praeger, 1970.

Mennell, S. Sociological Theory: Uses and Unities. London: Nelson, 1974.

Mills, C.W. "Methodological Consequences of the
Sociology of Knowledge." American Journal of
Sociology XVI (1940): 316-330.

_____. The Sociological Imagination. Harmonds-
worth, Middlesex: Penguin, 1970.

Morgan, J.G. "Contextual Factors in the Rise of
Academic Sociology in the United States."
Canadian Review of Sociology and Anthropology
7 (1970): 159-171.

Musgrave, P. Knowledge, Curriculum and Change.
Melbourne: Melbourne University Press, 1973.

Page, C.H. "Sociology as an Educational Enterprise." In Sociology and Contemporary Education, pp. 3-39. Edited by C.H. Page. New
York: Random House, 1966; reprint ed., 1963.

_____., ed. Sociology and Contemporary Educa-
tion. New York: Random House, 1966; reprint
ed., 1963.

Parsons, T. "The School Class as a Social System:
Some of its Functions in American Society."
In Education, Economy and Society, pp. 434-
455. Edited by A.H. Halsey, J. Floud and C.A.
Anderson, Glencoe, Ill.: The Free Press,
1961.

Phillips, D. "Epistemology and the Sociology of
Knowledge: The Contribution of Mannheim,
Mills, and Merton." Theory and Society 1

(1974): 58-88.

Reid, I. "Sociology in Colleges of Education:
Some Considerations." In Sociology and Teacher Education, pp. 7-14. Edited by I. Reid
and E. Wormald. Sociology Section of the
Association of Teachers in Colleges and Departments of Education, 1974.

_____ and Wormald, E., eds. Sociology and
Teacher Education. Sociology Section of the
Association of Teachers in Colleges and De-
partments of Education, 1974.

Remmling, G., ed. Towards the Sociology of Knowledge. London: Routledge and Kegan Paul,
1973.

Rex, J. Key Problems of Sociological Theory.
London: Routledge and Kegan Paul, 1961.

Robertson, R. "Toward the identification of the
major axes of sociological analysis." In
Approaches to Sociology, pp. 107-124. Edited
by J. Rex. London and Boston: Routledge and
Kegan Paul, 1974.

Robinson, P. Education and Poverty. London:
Methuen, 1976.

Rocher, G. A General Introduction to Sociology.
Toronto: The Macmillan Co. of Canada, 1972.

Rose, A., ed. Human Behavior and Social Processes.
London: Routledge and Kegan Paul, 1962.

Salaman, G. and Weeks, D. Social Interaction.
Bletchley, Bucks.: The Open University Press,
1972.

Schutz, A. Collected Papers 1: The Problem of
Social Reality. Edited by M. Natanson. The
Hague: Martinus Nijhoff, 1962.

_____. The Phenomenology of the Social World.

Translated by G. Walsh and F. Lehrnet. Evanston, Ill.: Northwestern University Press, 1969.

Sharp, R. and Green, A. Education and Social Control: A Study in Progressive Primary Education. London: Routledge and Kegan Paul, 1975.

Shimbori, M. "Educational Sociology or Sociology of Education." International Review of Education XVIII (1972): 3-12.

Shipman, M. The Limitations of Social Research. London: Longman, 1972.

Spady, W. "The Authority System of the School and Student Unrest: A Theoretical Exploration." In Uses of the Sociology of Education, pp. 36-77. Edited by C.W. Gordon. Chicago: The University of Chicago Press, 1974.

Stebbins, R. "The Meaning of Disorderly Behavior: Teacher Definitions of a Classroom Situation." Sociology of Education 44 (1971): 217-236.

Stubbs, M. and Delamont, S., eds. Exploration in Classroom Observation. London: John Wylie, 1976.

Swift, D.F. "Sociology and Educational Research." In Research Perspectives in Education, pp. 172-187. Edited by W. Taylor. London: Routledge and Kegan Paul, 1973.

_____. The Sociology of Education. London: Routledge and Kegan Paul, 1969.

_____. and Acland, H. "The Sociology of Education in Britain, 1960-1968: A bibliographical review." Social Science Information 8 (1969): 31-64.

Taylor, W., ed. Research Perspectives in Education. London: Routledge and Kegan Paul, 1973.

Turner, R., ed. Ethnomethodology. Harmondsworth, Middlesex: Penguin, 1974.

Walker, R. "The Sociology of Education and Life in School Classrooms." International Review of Education XVIII (1972): 32-41.

Warwick, D. "Ideologies, Integration and Conflicts of Meaning." In Educability, Schools and Ideology, pp. 86-111. Edited by M. Flude and J. Ahier. London: Croom Helm, 1974.

Watson, D.R. "Sociological Theory and the Analysis of Strategies of Educational Redress." International Review of Education XXII (1976): 41-62.

Wertham, C. "Delinquents in Schools." In School and Society, pp. 39-48. Edited by B. Cosin et al. London: Routledge and Kegan Paul, 1971.

Whitty, G. "Sociology and the Problem of Radical Educational Change." In Educability, Schools and Ideology, pp. 112-237. Edited by M. Flude and J. Ahier. London: Croom Helm, 1974.

Williams, T. "Teacher Prophecies and the Inheritance of Inequality." Sociology of Education 49 (1976): 223-236.

Williamson, B. "Continuities and Discontinuities in the Sociology of Education." In Educability, Schools and Ideology, pp. 3-14. Edited by M. Flude and J. Ahier. London: Croom Helm, 1974.

Wilson, T. "Normative and interpretive paradigms in sociology." In Understanding Everyday Life, pp. 57-79. Edited by J. Douglas. Chicago: Aldine, 1970.

Young, M.F.D. "An Approach to the Study of Socially Organized Knowledge." In Knowledge and Control, pp. 19-46. Edited by M.F.D. Young. London: Collier-Macmillan, 1971.

Young, M.F.D. "On the Politics of Educational
     Knowledge." _Economy and Society_ 1 (1972):
     194-215.

_____., ed. _Knowledge and Control: New Direc-_
     tions for the Sociology of Education. London:
     Collier-Macmillan, 1971.

CHAPTER 3

PSYCHOLOGY OF EDUCATION

Concerned as it is with the study of human behaviour, it is inevitable that there develop a close association between psychology and education. The concern of this chapter is to review the nature of this association and the contribution of educational psychology to the field of education. This chapter will begin with a discussion of the definition of educational psychology and its historical development. The research methodology particular to educational psychology will be reviewed, followed by a discussion of the major trends in contemporary educational psychology.

THE DEFINITION OF EDUCATIONAL PSYCHOLOGY

Any review of the literature in the field of educational psychology, whether it be brief or extensive, contemporary or historical, reveals a lack of agreement concerning its definition. Obviously, educational psychologists agree that their field is concerned with the relationship between psychology and education,[1] but frequently, this represents the limit of their agreement. The major disagreements in attaining a more specific definition relate to the form and nature of the relationship between the two disciplines. As the definition of educational psychology is one of the major controversies in the area, its discussion must form an integral part of this chapter.

The formal relationship between psychology and education began in the latter 19th century. An early definition from this period is that given by Harris in his 1898 book, <u>Psychological Foundations of Education</u>. He states "Educational psychology deals with all phases of the action and reaction of the mind by itself or in the presence of objects, by which the mind develops or unfolds, or is arrested, or degenerates."[2] As is evident from this definition, the relationship between the two disciplines was conceived as broad and virtually all inclusive, to the degree that if one removed the qualifier, educational, from the above definition, one would be left with a definition of psychology itself. The breadth and all inclusiveness of such early definitions of educational psychology suggest the difficulty educational psychologists have faced in defining the nature and scope of their field.

There is by now a considerable body of literature which attests to the inability of educational psychologists to come to agreement concerning the nature and scope of their field. Content analyses of the numberous text books in educational psychology, at any point between 1920 and the present, have revealed the lack of agreement concerning the content, and hence, definition, of educational psychology. Cuff, in an early study of this issue, collated the chapter headings of eighteen educational psychology text books written between 1929 and 1934.[3] From these works he identified 70 topics covered by their authors. Only 26 per cent of these topics were considered important by a sample of professors of educational psychology who were asked to endorse the importance of these areas to the field. Concurring with this position, Cronbach, in a review of educational psychology published in 1950, concluded that educational psychology was in a state of disarray, and that the area was so broad ". . . no educational psychologist can be fully competent over the entire area."[4] Following a review of a number of studies involving content analyses, Ellis concluded that ". . . it is evident that educational psychology has not yet reached the point where its content has been stabilized or its value universally recognized."[5]

Efforts to formulate a median definition of educational psychology for the 1956 annual review of the area were abandoned when Tyler found little concordance concerning a basic definition among text book authors, annual reviewers, authors of journal articles or basic descriptions of the work

of educational psychologists.[6] That this position
still holds today is apparent in a perusal of educational psychology texts which have been published
over the past decade. There is still little agreement among authors concerning the content of the
field. The observation made by Archer in 1941 is
still appropriate today. "It is somewhat remarkable that we never know when we open a new text-
book of educational psychology, what subject matter it is likely to contain or how that matter is
likely to be arranged."[7] The disorganization position concerning the definition of educational psychology is still prominent today and is highlighted
in the comment by Good in his 1976 article:

> Many of us who respond to the
> label, educational psychologist,
> do not have a shared meaning of
> that label. Indeed, a survey is
> now underway within the dimension
> of educational psychology in the
> American Psychology Association to
> describe the major roles, responsi-
> bilities, and orientations of edu-
> cational psychologists.[8]

Often, those who follow the disorganization
position, refrain from defining the field in any
formal manner, preferring to use an idiosyncratic
definition which is seldom, if ever, explicated.

Another prominent approach to the definition
of educational psychology is to view the field as
the application of general psychology to the educational enterprise. In an address to the National
Educational Association convention in 1887, Pau
stated that "Educational psychology is commonly
interpreted to mean the study of general psychology
with stray observations about children's minds.[9]
The strength of this position in 1947 is mirrored
in a humorous passage by Wolfe:

> If you wish to write an education
> psychology text, start with a good
> average introductory text. Remove

the chapters which deal with the
nervous system and sense organs
and write three new chapters to
use the space. These three new
chapters will have such titles
as Learning in the Schoolroom,
Measuring Student Progress and
Social Psychology of the Schoolroom. . . .[10]

Further support for this position was added by the
1957 statement by Stroud that "An educational psychologist is by history any psychologist who de-
notes his energies to educational problems."[11] A
decade later, Warburton stated that "Educational
psychology is, in fact, general psychology applied
to human behaviour in a certain social setting."[12]
That this is a prominent view of educational psychology today is exemplified by the efforts of
Belkin and Gray to answer the question "What is
educational psychology?" They tend to conclude
that the educational psychologist is a psychologist
who applies his general area of specialization, be
it development, experimental, or social psychology
to the educational process.[13] While this position
still finds contemporary support it has generated
considerable criticism from numerous educational
psychologists.

One group of critics have attacked the latter position because of its lack of specificity
with respect to education. In 1948 the Committee
on the Function of the Division of Educational
Psychology of the American Psychological Association developed a definition characteristic of
this group of critics. The committee concluded
that:

Educational psychology is concerned
primarily with the study of human
behaviour as it is changed or directed under the social processes
of education, and secondarily, with
those studies of processes that
contribute to an increased under-

178

standing how behaviour is changed
and directed through education.[14]

Inherent in this definition is the notion that
educational psychology is a specific branch of
psychology whose concern is the study of human
behaviour and learning in relation to the educative process. Consistent with this view, Carter, in 1954, and Tyler, in 1956, defined educational psychology ". . . as that branch of psychology which deals with school learning and its
correlates."[15] In a further expansion of his
definition, Tyler proceeded to note that ". . .
an understanding of learning involves knowledge
of (a) learners, (b) learning-teaching processes
and products, and (c) teachers."[16] Perhaps one
of the most specific definitions of educational
psychology offered by proponents of this position is that of Stephens:

> Viewed as an effort to contribute
> to general knowledge, educational
> psychology is taken to be the
> study of those social mechanisms,
> particularly those mechanisms
> available to institutions, by
> which the learning mechanisms
> within the pupil are engaged.
> As an applied science, our sub-
> ject is considered to include
> the description of educational
> growth, as the dependent vari-
> able, and all the factors that
> affect it, as independent
> variables.[17]

In another statement of his position, Stephens
states that educational psychology ". . . is the
division of psychology which seeks to understand
the phenomena of educational growth, just as social
psychology is the division of psychology which
seeks to understand social phenomena."[18] As
Stephens suggests, the epitome of this position
will be achieved when theories derived in educational psychology are applied to general psy-

179

chological problems. Such a position is obviously the antithesis of the conception of educational psychology as the application of general psychological principles to the field of education.

In the past 25 years, a number of educational psychologists have argued that educational psychology must become more relevant to the goals of education, and develop its own body of theory in order to attain the position of Stephens, as described above. An early advocate of this position was Blair who, in 1949, reached the following conclusion concerning the focus of educational psychology:

> Educational psychologists still have the important and unfinished task before them of showing how theoretical psychology can contribute to the solution of practical educational problems. That is a unique and significant job which neither the general psychologist nor practical educator can do. Unless it is done by the educational psychologist, it will doubtless be left undone.[19]

One of the most quoted, and influential advocates for the development of a discrete theory of educational psychology is Ausubel who in his 1968 book defined educational psychology as that branch of psychology which ". . . is primarily concerned with the nature, conditions, outcomes, and evaluation of classroom learning." His conception of educational psychology includes not only a clear statement of what educational psychology is, but also, a statement of what it is not. Educational psychology is not ". . . an amalgam of learning theory, developmental psychology, mental hygiene, and educational and psychological measurement."[20] This latter position is in contrast to that of a number of past and contemporary theorists in the field. Expanding upon his initial definition, Ausubel states that "As an applied science, educational psychology is . . . concerned with those properties of learning that can be related to efficacious ways of _deliberately_ effecting stable cognitive changes which have social value."[21]

Among contemporary educational psychologists then, there are a number of prominent views concerning the definition of the discipline. One notable position is that the field is so disorganized that a definition is unattainable. A second position is that educational psychology is simply the application of general psychology to the educational process. A third view holds that educational psychology is a branch of psychology in its own right. More recently, a number of educational psychologists have argued that in order to maintain its position as a distinct discipline of psychology, educational psychology must become more relevant to education by developing its own body of theory. Perhaps a more moderate and encompassing position is that proposed by Carroll, and Mathis, Cotton and Sechrest.[22] These authors argue that educational psychologists should have the dual ability to develop theory concerning the educational process as well as to apply relevant theories, developed in psychological and other areas, to the process of education. As such the educational psychologist must be both a specialist and a generalist. Perhaps, as educational psychology focuses upon relevant issues in education, a more precise definition of the field will emerge.

HISTORICAL DEVELOPMENT

At the present time there exists no complete history of educational psychology, although a few brief accounts of the development of the field now exist.[23] In these accounts, as in any literature devoted to the history of the educational process, psychological or otherwise, the origins of educational psychology are sought in classical Greece. Considered of particular relevance is Aristotle and his organized laws of association as presented in De Memoria et Reminiscentra, concerned as it was with "learning, association, memory, retention, and meaningfulness of experience."[24]

Many other great scholars have been identified as founding fathers of the field of educational psychology, although in many instances the knowledge which they generated was also utilized by other disciplines. Thus, Vives (1492-1540), Bacon (1561-1626), Comenius (1592-1670), Descartes (1596-1650), Pestalozzi (1746-1827), and Herbart (1776-1841) have all been cited in association with the early history of the psychology of education.

There is generally some agreement for regarding the latter nineteenth century as a period significant to the actual development of educational psychology as a separate entity. Watson cites the experimental investigations of associationism by Galton, the published papers of Hall's investigations with children, and the study on memory by Ebbinghaus, all of which occurred in the 1880s, as "crucial aspects of educational psychology."[25] Charles, on the other hand, places the actual beginning of the field of educational psychology at a somewhat later date, citing J. McKeen Cattell's succinct statement made in 1929 on the status of the discipline of psychology:

> A history of psychology in America prior to the last fifty years would be as short as a book on the snakes in Ireland since the time of St. Patrick. In so far as psychologists are concerned America was then like heaven for there was not a damned soul around.[26]

If this then was the state of psychology, the infant educational psychology may be regarded as indeed in a fledgling state.

Of the various scholars cited for their influence on the development of the field of educational psychology as a separate entity, the names of William James, G. Stanley Hall, John Dewey, and Edward Lee Thorndike stand out.

William James, teacher, philosopher, M.D., and pioneer of the 'new' functional psychology in America[27] had a profound effect upon the development of educational psychology. His three books which are considered to have been most influential are Principles of Psychology published in two volumes in 1890, the Briefer Course--a shortened version of the Principles in text book form in 1892, and Talks to Teachers on Psychology and to Students on Some of Life's Ideals, first published in 1899.[28] Principles of Psychology is devoid of specific reference to educational applications but the implications for the educational process of chapters on such topics as memory, habit, and experience are clear. In his chapter on memory, James proposed a position intermediary between the leading positions of his day, the faculty psychology position that cultivation of powers of memory resulted in a better memory for everything, and the associationist position that memory for a given event is the result of such associative laws as frequency, recency, and vividness of association. What James suggested was that retentiveness was a general property of brain structure which varied from individual to individual and was dependent upon practising a specific brain pathway. In a series of experiments to find out whether the practice of some memory functions would aid others, he concluded that training had no influence on general retentiveness, that practice in learning one sort of material was of no value in learning other material.[29] The implications of this finding were in direct contrast to many of the current educational practices of his day with respect to studying subjects for their disciplinary value. Of direct pertinence to the practice of teaching in his day was James' Talks to Teachers, the book form of a series of public lectures which James presented to Cambridge teachers. As indicated by James in his preface, he made every attempt to shape the book so that it contained information which while psychologically sound was of practical value:

> I have found by experience that what by hearers seem least to relish is analytical technicality, and what they most care for is concrete practical application. So I have gradually weeded out the former, and left the latter unreduced; and, now that I have at last written out the lectures, they contain a minimum of what is deemed 'scientific' in psychology, and are practical and popular in the extreme.[30]

According to Baldwin, these works of James "were the first books to make serious inroads on the scholastic faculty psychology, . . . and to bring modern psychology into the schoolroom and apply it to the everyday problems of the aim of education."[31] James' educational contributions were intricately bound up with his psychology. The educational theories and practices he proposed were based on his psychology, that of the functional point of view. Accordingly, education was viewed as the means whereby the child was assisted in the development of his native resources to equip him for a life in society. James is regarded as the first educator to hold this viewpoint.[32] Despite his success in affecting educational practice by making avoidable practical concrete applications of psychology to teachers, the suggestion has been made that James influence was less than it might have been. He established no "school" of psychology and had almost no doctoral students. Those who came to study psychology with him at Harvard were thus forced at a point in their studies to seek the Ph.D. degree elsewhere. Amongst these students was Edward L. Thorndike who, a short period of time later, was to play an important role in the rapid growth of the field of educational spychology.[33]

G. Stanley Hall's name is perhaps better known today for his association with the child study movement, publication of his 1883 study, The Contents of Children's Minds on Entering School being regarded as the force which introduced that movement.[34] However, as indicated by Boring in his brief discussion of the history of educational psychology, Hall had "a great deal to do" with early happenings in that field.[35] Hall's psychology was based on a major premise, "a general psychonomic law" which was an adaption to psychology of the concepts of biological evolution and physical recapitulation. The mind was seen as developing through a series of stages, generally corresponding to those through which it was believed early man had progressed. Each stage was regarded as a stimulus to the next. This principle underlay Hall's theory of child development and led to his child psychology being described as ". . . a kind of nature study of children's minds."[36]

A student, but certainly no follower of James,[37] Hall's association with education is believed to have begun with a Sunday morning lecture series in Boston on current educational programs. It was in Boston too that Hall first introduced the questionnaire method to discover the contents of children's minds, and papers reporting the results of these questionnaires soon followed. A multitude of studies involving questionnaires evolved on such widely ranging topics as anger on dolls to moral and religious experiences. The technique had become a fad and as a result of its widespread and indiscriminant use, became criticized for its lack of reliability, validity and conclusions, at which point Hall developed other interests.[38] His introduction of this method of study had resulted, however, in a psychology of a more experimental measurable type

185

than that current at the time. During this period, Hall had become president of Clark University, and his period of tenure was distinguished not only by the increased recognition of the importance of child study and a more scientific research but also by the creation in 1889 of a department of pedagogy, a term "almost synonymous" with educational psychology at that institution. This department was the forerunner of many such departments in the years that followed. Credit to Hall must also be given for the founding of a new journal, the Pedagogical Seminary (today known as the Journal of Genetic Psychology) which although originating as the vehicle for the publication of material arising from the new observational approach to education, became an outlet for scientific research relating to practical educational problems.

The man most frequently referred to as the father of modern educational psychology is Edward L. Thorndike who has been described as the first man deserving of the title "educational psychologist."[39] A student of James at Harvard, the later, of James McKeen Cattell at Columbia, Thorndike's early research was with animals. Prior to Thorndike, there had been some study of the psychology of learning, but this tended to be sporadic and unsystematic. It was Thorndike who first systematized the study of learning with his quantitative experiments on animal learning, completed for his doctoral dissertation in 1898. It is this much cited research of cats in the puzzle box which resulted in the Law of Effect, a fundamental aspect of Thorndike's theory of Connectionism, concerning the relationship between stimulus and response. According to the Law of Effect, learned behaviour was seen as dependent on the success or failure attached to the experience of the organism. This new principle operated in addition to the Law of Exercise, already accepted in his day.

In 1899, Columbia University took over the New York College for the Training of Teachers,

186

renaming it Teachers College. Shortly afterwards, Thorndike was made instructor in Psychology,[40] and on Cattell's recommendation switched from studies on animals to those involving humans. As earlier, he maintained the same research focus: the nature of learning and the conditions which affected it. Thorndike remained at Teachers College until his retirement in 1940, influencing generations of students and the whole field of educational psychology. The stature of the discipline at Teachers College was such that in 1917, educational psychology became a requirement for all candidates seeking the doctoral degree.[41]

One of the most significant aspects of Thorndike's contributions to education was his dedication to research rigor. He was concerned with the quantitative evaluation of research and held that educational procedures should be based not upon opinion, but on the results of such research. In Educational Psychology, published in 1903, he stated: "We conquer the facts of nature when we observe and experiment upon them. When we measure them we have made them our servants."[42] In 1918, he made his now famous statement "What ever exists at all exists in some amount. To know it thoroughly involves knowing its quantity as well as its quality."[43] In 1921, his belief that quantitative research could effect human kind for the better was again visible "In proportion as it becomes definite and exact, this knowledge of educational products and educational purposes must become quantitative, taking the form of measurements."[44] In 1904, he published the first non-mathematical book on statistics, An Introduction to the Theory of Mental and Social Measurements,[45] and for the first time a theoretical exposition and statistical handbook was available in the new area of social science measurement. This book was only one of the many publications produced by Thorndike during his lifetime. His early research was reported in Elements of Psychology in 1905,[46] and his three volumes of Educational Psychology published in 1913[47] included among other material his work on individual

187

differences, transfer of training, intelligence testing, and quantified research methods. Before 1931, Thorndike was cited as having a bibliography of some 250 items.[48] These publications were not only confined to experimental and empirical work, but also related to more practical aspects of his discipline. This is evident in such publications as the Psychology of Algebra in 1923, the Thorndike Arithmetics in 1924 and the Teachers' Word Book of 20,000 words in 1931.[49]

Thorndike's influence has been vast. Its extent can be gauged by the fact that it is only recently that his principles of learning have begun to be refuted.[50] His research and theories on the nature of learning and the learning process were influential in changing the school curriculum from one, where the training of potential faculties point of view placed responsibility for learning on the child, to one, where the responsibility for learning was placed on the school to structure the educational experience so that it would produce the most efficient learning.[51] Thorndike emphasized the individual uniqueness of each child. He established the legitimacy of quantitative research and introduced it as a source of decision making in education. He firmly established the influence of educational psychology and provided a hope that through it could be solved the educational problems of the day, a hope that has been held with some varying degree of optimism to this time.

Another influential educational psychologist of that early era was Charles Judd. A student of Wundt under whom he obtained his degree in 1896, Judd returned to America where he became interested in education and educational research. At Yale he gave courses in psychology for teachers and during this period published Genetic Psychology for Teachers[52] in which he attempted to show how learning was a process of social inheritance. In 1909, he accepted the position of Director of the School of Education, a position which he held for some thirty years.

During this period, he was involved in "four lines of scientific work in the special field of education."53 Of these four areas of interest, that for which Judd is most noted, is his analysis of reading. He developed a method for the photographic study of eye movements which was employed to modify procedures for teaching reading so as to give training in silent, and later, remedial reading. Judd's other interest areas were the psychology of high school education which he addressed in Education as Cultivation of the Higher Mental Processes,54 the psychology of arithmetical processes or number consciousness, and the formulation of a social psychological base for education.

In the minds of many, no discussion of the early development of educational psychology would be complete without reference to John Dewey. It is true that John Dewey took his Ph.D. with Hall at Clark and was president of the American Psychological Association in 1899. However, the fact that he engaged in little research and that his psychological writings are embedded in his other contributions, has disguised the extent of his contribution to educational psychology.55 His position on the need for educational procedures to be placed on sound psychological theories was apparent in his presidential address to the American Psychological Association. In this address he maintained that the greatest obstacle to educational reform was the persistence of an outmoded psychological creed which prevented the introduction of a new educational psychology and teaching practices to awaken interests and impulses.56 Like Thorndike, Dewey's psychology was child centered and the educational theories he later promoted in his more philosophical writings reflected this.

During this period when educational psychology was forming for itself a distinct area, a parallel development was occurring in the realm of testing. This movement began in England with Galton who has been regarded as one of the

189

originators of educational research in that
country. Galton's interest in psychometrics arose
from his investigations into the inheritance of
ability in man. His systematic inquiry of inheritability necessitated its classification according to a standard scale. Galton's solution
to this problem was to apply the normal distribution curve to psychological data, estimating
the number of persons in each grade of ability in
the population. Further contributions of Galton
included the development of tests, rating scales
and questionnaires, as well as two important advances in the history of statistics, the method
of ranks and the method of correlation.[57] In
America, further development in the area of
testing continued during the 1890s mainly as a
result of the investigations of J. McKeen Cattell
into the relationship between "mental tests" and
academic ability. Tests at this time were not
organized into scales but functioned as separate
entities and the inappropriateness of these
tests as intellectual measures was not understood.
The testing movement reached respectability with
the work of Alfred Binet in France, "who" in
response for a request to develop a test to identify subnormal children for educational purposes,
was responsible with Theodore Simon for the development of the first scale to measure intellectual ability.[58] His scale "a metrical scale,"
was based on a variety of tests to tap mental
capacity and contained age norms which later became known as mental ages. Through the testing
movement, educational psychology was supplied
with one of its most basic tools and this "in
combination with the work of Thorndike in the
field of measurement" introduced an era of test
development and measurement. By the end of the
1920s then, "there existed a rather distinct area
of psychology concerned with human development,
child growth, the psychology of learning and the
development of educational statistics and measurement."

Consideration of the development of any
discipline warrants not only attention to those

190

individuals significant in its evolution, but also to those events important to its establishment as a separate entity. Among such events are courses in educational psychology, development of university study in the field, and its literature.

During the 1800s courses in psychology as applied to education began to make their appearance. In 1839, a course in "Mental Philosophy" was offered in the normal school at Lexington in what was apparently the first ever course in educational psychology. In 1863, the normal school at Osmego offered a course in "child study" and in 1886 Iowa University offered a course in mental philosophy in its "normal department." In 1886, an educational psychology course, "applied psychology" was offered by the Department of Pedagogics at the University of Indiana.[59] At that time, as now, the perennial problem of the diversity of course content was prevalent and this is reflected in the varying names of the courses.

As education became established as a legitimate area of higher learning, chairs of education were established. The first such chair was established at the State University of Iowa in 1873.[60] The first department of education, "the Department of Science and Art of Teaching" was established at the University of Michigan in 1879. This was followed in 1881 by a Department of Pedagogy at the University of Washington in 1881 and shortly afterwards by similar departments at the University of North Carolina, and John Hopkins in 1884. Teachers College of Columbia University was established in 1888, and the school of education at the University of Chicago in 1900.[61] A similar development in educational history occurred on the other side of the Atlantic. The first chair of education was established in Scotland in 1876, while the first English chair was established at Manchester in 1899.[62] The specific data which marks the establishment of a department of "Educational Psychology" is unknown, but one of the earliest reported is that of the

191

University of Nebraska which in 1901 (or 1902) reported the establishment of a College of Education with a list of departments including "Educational Psychology."[63]

Two journals were established early in the history of the area. One of these, Pedagogical Seminary, established by G. S. Hall has already been mentioned. The other, the Journal of Educational Psychology was established in 1910. the lead article in the first issue, "Contributions of Psychology to Education" was written by E. L. Thorndike. This journal was aimed at providing a broad coverage of the interest areas of its clientele and included all the areas of general psychology as well as, among other topics, problems of mental development, heredity, intellectual differences, measurement of mental capacities, psychology of mental tests and problems of hygiene. For many years, it served not only to acquaint its readers with the latest research in the field but also as a source of scholarly reviews and discussion of contentions issues or pressing concerns in the area. In 1963, publication of theoretical, non-empirical papers in educational psychology was transferred to a new journal, the Educational Psychologist (originally the newsletter of Division 15, the Division of Educational Psychology of the American Psychological Association), and the Journal of Educational Psychology has since then concentrated on reports of empirical research.

The subject areas of interest to educational psychologists in the early years of this century are still of interest today. As may be expected there have been some additions to the field, notably in that area concerned with the social facets of the child's behaviour. The prime areas of concern still continue to be human development, child growth, learning, and the study of individual differences. Obviously, each of these areas has expanded enormously over the years to the point where each could be studied in its own right. This development combined with

192

the advent of new schools of psychology, psychoanalysis, behaviourism, and the Gestalt psychology, has tended to further fractionate an already divided discipline.

In developing as a discipline, educational
psychology has gone through stormy times. A common theme often raised concerns about the subject
matter to be taught. In 1926, Watson suggested
that the subject matter might be selected in
four ways, through ". . . the judgment of a man
skilled in psychological research," through
". . . the evaluation of subject matter in the
light of its contribution to professional success," through ". . . job-analyses" or through
eliciting the opinions of "a group of experienced
teachers, supervisors and administrators."[64] In
1936, Cuff again raising the same question, won-
dered whether students were regurgitating "relatively useless and stereotyped content" which
they could relegate "to a mental ash heap." He
proceeded to state that ". . . as a matter of
professional self respect, psychologists should
attempt to determine what psychology is of the
most worth in the training of teachers."[65]
During this period and later, many comparisons
and careful analyses of text books were conducted.
All of these revealed a considerable lack of
agreement as to what should constitute the subject matter of educational psychology.[66] In one
study of text books, topics which were treated
by one author were entirely omitted by others.[67]

Not only was there concern over the content of educational psychology during this period
but also concern over its function. In 1948,
Brownell commented that it would be difficult to
prove that classroom teaching was any better than
it was 30 years previously despite a better understanding of psychology and exposure of teachers
to discipline through university courses.[68] Con-
bach in his introduction to the 1950 annual review of Psychology, commented that "the Planning
Board notes that the field has declined in prestige" and "the present studies are limited and

integrative thinking is distinctly lacking."[69]
Educational Psychology had lost its momentum and
there were continuing exhortations for it to re-
establish itself as a discipline.[70] The disarray
during the 1950s was such that the possibility of
including educational psychology under the umbrel-
la of clinical psychology was considered.[71]

Demands for a more scientific education,
resulting in response to scientific and technological advances in the 1950s in Russia, resulted
in the re-establishment of Educational Psychology
as a meaningful discipline during the 1960s.
Educational research funds were now available and
psychology had access to these. This was a period of affluence which was reflected in the large-
scale research efforts which began to emerge.
Membership of educational psychologists in the
American Psychologist Association rose from 525
in 1959 to a membership in the vicinity of 4,000
today.[72]

Concern over many long standing problems
remains[73] and it is widely recognized that there
is a long way to go in understanding and controlling learning processes and the variables that
affect them. However, educational psychology has
come a long way since the turn of the century
when material for texts was so scarce that James
could state: "Educational psychology, I think
there are about six weeks of it."[74]

RESEARCH METHODOLOGY IN EDUCATIONAL PSYCHOLOGY

As was discussed in the Definition section
of this chapter, one prominent view of educational
psychology is that it is simply the application
of general psychology to the educational process.
This position has come under considerable criticism in recent years on purely methodological
grounds. Such criticism has emanated from three
prominent groups, psychologists, educational
psychologists and humanistic psychologists. Psychologists argue that they are concerned with the

194

derivation of general laws of human behaviour, which may or may not have significance in education. As a result, they are justly irritated and often horrified by the premature application, and over-generalization of their findings to the process of education.[75] In contrast, educational psychologists are becoming increasingly convinced that the general research of the psychologists has little relevance to educational psychology.[76] Humanistic psychologists are perhaps even more militant, believing that it is inappropriate to apply the methods of science to the study of human behaviour. Their position is that a distinctive social scientific method must be developed, which will take into account the complexity of persons and their interactions with their environment.[77]

In general, there are three reasons why psychologists view their theories as having only incidental value for education at the present time. Firstly, they argue that their goal is to discover general laws of human behaviour, which may be relevant to education following extension and experimental testing in the educational setting.[78] Secondly, many psychologists are of the opinion that applications of their laws is premature in the sense that there is still considerable research to be accomplished prior to any application of their theories.[79] Finally, because of a concern for scientific control, the majority of psychological experiments are carried out in laboratory settings, which often possess little external validity. This latter concern has provoked Broufenbrenner to comment that ". . . much of developmental psychology is the <u>science of the strange behaviour of children in strange situations with strange adults for the briefest periods of time</u>."[80]

After initial and perhaps naive hopes that many of the basic laws of human behaviour derived by psychologists would find immediate and direct application in the field of education, educational psychologists have become increasingly disillu-

sioned with the idea over the past quarter century. Essentially, educational psychologists
have come to question the relevance of the majority of basic psychological research in relation
to the issues which face them in the educational
forum.[81] The primary argument is that the basic
controlled and often brief laboratory studies,
which form the basis of most psychological
theories, lack external validity for the educational setting. The external validity of an
experiment is the degree to which its results can
be generalized to different populations, environments and tasks.[82] Typical of this view of many
contemporary educational psychologists is the
following comment by Gagne and Rohwer:

> Remoteness of applicability to
> instruction, we note with some
> regret, characterizes many studies
> of human learning, retention, and
> transfer, appearing in the most
> prestigious of psychological
> journals. The findings of many
> studies of human learning pres-
> ently cannot be applied directly
> to instructional design for two
> major reasons: (a) the conditions
> under which the learning is in-
> vestigated . . . are often unrep-
> resentative of conditions under
> which most human learning occurs;
> and (b) the tasks set for the
> learner . . . appear to cover a
> range from the merely peculiar
> to the downright esoteric.[83]

In a similar view Elmgren noted that "experimental learning psychologists" had "almost completely neglected the study of children's learning
in the school situation" in contrast to the extensive work done on "learning problems with rats in
labyrinths, guinea-pigs, primates, and so forth."[84]
Thus, as Mitchell points out "the challenge that
speaks (and sometimes shrieks) of 'relevance' can
be rejected, ignored, controverted, rationalized,

or redefined in less objectionable terms, but it still exists and must be contended with in one way or another."[85]

While many educational psychologists are of the opinion that basic psychological research has its place and may be of value in generating ideas for educational research, most humanistic psychologists are in complete disagreement with such a premise.[86] Hampden-Turner states the humanist position very aptly:

> I believe that the mystique in which social science tries to envelope itself is actually a sign of failure. I regard it as one of those false shirt fronts liable at any moment to roll up under the wearer's chin. We need to question whether a science about human beings should be incomprehensible to human beings, for it seems unlikely that an incomprehensible social science can help human beings to heal, nurture, and enlighten one another.[87]

Thus, the majority of humanistic psychologists see the need for a truly unique psychological method appropriate to the study of man.[88] Such a methodology would deal with the process of growth as human beings in all their complexities interact with an equally complex environment. That this is the problem of educational psychology is highlighted by Mitchell when he states that research problems should be conceptualized "within the framework of person-environment interaction systems" and in "multivariate terms that accurately reflect the complexity of both personological and environmental domains."[89]

There has, then, been a growing realization that both the theories and the methods of general psychology are of little direct value in the eval-

uation and development of educational procedures.
Concomitantly there has been considerable attention in the literature in the past decade to the
issue of what is an appropriate methodological
stance for educational psychologists. Three
approaches to this question have emerged: (a)
the models approach; (b) the methods approach;
and (c) the systems or ecological approach.

Those following the models approach have
attempted to categorize the various research dispositions available with some consideration of the
relative merits of each in relation to the concerns of educational psychology. Perhaps the
simplest such categorization is that of Glass who
discusses the relative merits of elucidatory and
evaluative inquiry in education.[90] Elucidatory
research is equated to the basic scientific
approach, the short comings of which have been
discussed earlier. Evaluative research "involves
obtaining information to judge the worth of a
program, product, or procedure."[91] Glass is of
the opinion that, because of the rapid rate of
change in the technology of education, the evaluative approach is the most appropriate at present.

Next in complexity are the triadic classi-
fications presented by Ausubel, and de Bie.[92]
Ausubel's system involves: "(a) basic-science
research, (b) extrapolated research in the basic
sciences, and (c) research at an applied level."[93]
While Ausubel does not deny the importance of
each of these types of research for progress in
education, he is most concerned that the limitations of each be clearly understood. He is of
the opinion that as one moves from basic to applied research relevance is gained at the expense
of rigor. However, if one elects in favour of
rigor the inability to generalize findings to
education must be accepted. The system proposed
by de Bie differs somewhat from that proposed by
Ausubel. De Bie proposes three types of research
strategy: free basic research; problem-focused
research; and applied research.[94] Basic research
is seen as having primarily a theoretical aim,

while applied research has as its primary aim the solution of a social problem. De Bie sets problem-focused research between these two approaches in the sense that it is directed toward theory building and the solution of a social problem.

The final example of the models approach is that outlined by Gage.[95] He has suggested a six level, basic-applied continuum of research. The levels he proposes are: "Basic scientific investigation, content indifferent; basic scientific investigation, content relevant; investigations of educationally oriented problems; classroom experimentations; field testing; and installation program."[96] A careful review of the systems proposed by Glass, Ausubel and de Bie suggests that each of their categories can be subsumed under the system proposed by Gage. Of his proposal system Gage concludes that:

> As a paradigm of the innovation-installation process, the foregoing analysis represents an idealized conception that has probably been followed in this exact form only rarely. Yet it does portray the kind of division of labour that exists in our society, only if in an unorganized haphazard way. The research worker who fits himself in this paradigm should at least have a conception of where he fits in the total enterprise of educational research.[97]

As has also been pointed out by Gage, each of these levels of research interact with each other. Where a given educational psychologist's research endeavours lie with respect to this continuum will be determined jointly by his mandate and the particular problem with which he is presently concerned. It is perhaps safe to conclude that most if not all "basic scientific investigation, content indifferent" can be left to those in sub-

199

tantiative areas of psychology. Give that each of the remaining levels of educational research are of equal importance to progress in education it is important that societal agencies responsible for educational research realize this fact and foster each accordingly.[98] Obviously educational psychology must concentrate on basic applied research.[99] However, the longevity and complexity of such applied research will require a change in attitude on the part of those institutions supporting such research.

A second group of educational psychologists recognizing the complexity of basic applied educational research have endeavoured to extend the methods of basic research to fit the needs of the applied situation. Many psychologists are of the belief that applied research by its very nature is synonymous with mediocre and often careless research. Unfortunately some applied researchers have used the vicissitudes of the applied setting as an excuse for loose and often meaningless research. However, given the imperative work of those concerned with developing rigorous research methods for applied studies mediocre research concerning applied problems can no longer be condoned.

Obviously, where feasible, basic applied research should employ the true experimental methods of basic research. There are numerous books and articles outlining the methods of basic research. For those who are not familiar with the methods of basic research the overviews presented by McLean and Wiggins are excellent introductions to this domain.[100] McLean presents a most readable discussion of three types of research in educational psychology, the status study, the planned experiment, and evaluative research. His discussion of measurement, validity, and reliability in relation to these three modes of research is thorough and throughout his discussion he provides reference to more extensive discussions of these concerns. Wiggins on the other hand provides a concise discussion of the problems

200

of controlling extraneous variables in true experiments. He discusses extraneous variation due
to experimenter, subject manipulation, and measurement variables, and presents four modes by
which each type of variation may be controlled.
Even a cursory reading of the chapters by McLean
and Wiggins convinces the reader of the sheer complexity of carrying out true experiments in the
educational setting. While such a venture is possible it requires considerable ingenuity and public relations to achieve. No doubt these latter
two factors account for the propensity of many
psychologists, educational and otherwise, to remain steadfastly in their laboratories doing in-
consequential research.

Central to the basic research paradigm in
the social sciences is the control of extraneous
variables by random sampling is very difficult to
achieve.[101] Recently a number of quasi-experimental methods have been proposed, which provide for
the control of extraneous variation by methods
other than random sampling. For a full review of
these methods the reader should consult Blalock,
Campbell and Stanley, Bracht and Glass, Shulman,
and Snow.[102] These authors present the methodology required to accomplish internal and external
validity of an experiment where random sampling is
not possible. Campbell and Stanley have presented
sixteen designs with an evaluation of the degree
to which each controls certain threats to internal
and external validity.[103] Bracht and Glass,
Shulman, and Snow have extended upon the methodology presented by Campbell and Stanley in the
direction of presenting designs which control for
the external validity or representativeness of
true experimental and quasi-experimental designs.

Akin to the issue of random sampling in
basic applied research is the concern surrounding
the sheer complexity of many applied problems.
Cronbach has echoed the sentiments of a number
of educational psychologists when he noted:

More complex designs are needed

so that educational theory can
recognize the interaction between
materials of instruction, form
of presentation, frequency and
method of evaluation, and individual differences.[104]

Thoresen has proposed a systems approach to the
solution of the complexities of applied research
in counseling, which may be of equal relevance in
the field of educational psychology.[105] A similar
approach to that of Thoresen has been advocated
and employed by Kalos and Lundgren.[106]

A similar but far more extensive approach
to the complexity of basic applied research in
education is the ecological approach proposed by
Bronfenbrenner.[107] He introduces his paper as
follows:

This is a presumptuous paper. It
makes bold to call into question
prevailing approaches to educational
research, and to propose a new
perspective in method, theory, and
substance.[108]

Presumptuous perhaps, but in our estimation it
must become required reading for all psychologists,
and especially educational psychologists. In
order to delimit the complexity of many applied
settings Bronfenbrenner employs terminology adapted from Brim to describe the ecological structure
of the educational environment.[109] He depicts the
educational environment as a micro-system, a meso-
system, and exo-system, and finally as a macro-
system. As one moves through these four systems
the factors impinging on the educational environment become more and more involved and complex.
Bronfenbrenner, then, discusses each of these
systems in turn developing from his discussion a
set of twenty propositions concerning research
strategies. Where possible he employs current
research to illustrate the implementation of each
of his propositions. He concludes his discussion

by presenting a set of proposed studies which exemplify the implementation of his propositions. It would be presumptuous indeed to attempt to summarize Bronfenbrenner's paper here. We can only urge that readers sample his excellent discussion for themselves.

While appropriate methodology is one important requisite for basic applied research, the statistical methods to be employed in these designs are of equal importance. Blalock, and to a lesser degree, Campbell and Stanley, have presented the statistical procedures which relate to their proposed designs.[110] The more recent methods proposed by Bronfenbrenner, Kalos and Lundgren, and Thoresen are not accompanied by a discussion of the statistical methods appropriate to them.[111] However, it is important to note that statistical methods are available for these more complex designs. An extensive and yet succinct discussion of current developments in the field of statistics is presented by Tatsuoka.[112] In the first section of his chapter he acquaints his readers with the major books and computer programs available, which relate to multi-variate methods. Next he gives a brief overview of recent advances in Stepwise Multiple Regression, Cannononical Correlational Analysis, Clustering Methods, Multiple Comparisons, Correlational and Repeated Measures Analyses, and Pattz Analysis. The final segment of his chapter is devoted to a description of research studies which employ these methods. No doubt the interested reader can with some effort integrate the methodological proposals of Bronfenbrenner, Campbell and Stanley, Kalos and Lundgren, and Thoresen with the statistical models reviewed by Tatsuoka. However, it would no doubt facilitate research advances if a work integrating these newer methods with their statistical counterparts were available.

As has been noted earlier, the three dominant areas in educational psychology have been developmental theory, the study of individual differences, and learning theory. In the next

203

section of this chapter, current trends in each of these areas are discussed and some of the major issues posed. Recently, some educational psychologists have been concerned with the development of interactional theories to interrelate and advance previous research concerning both individual differences and learning theory. A further group of educational psychologists have been concerned to counteract the dehumanizing effect of the experimental attitude to educational psychology by the introduction of more humanistic approaches. A discussion of interactional models and humanistic approaches is also included in the following section.

DEVELOPMENTAL THEORY AND EDUCATION

The influence of developmental theories on the field of educational psychology has always been recognized. That this has been particularly so during the last decade is due to the increasing involvement of psychologists in programs of educational intervention, such as early childhood and compensatory education. As a result of this involvement, large numbers of educational psychologists have begun studying questions and problems relating to the deliberate enhancement of intellectual development. Among those developmentalists whose theories have been investigated are Havighurst with his sequence of developmental tasks to be mastered at each stage of development,[113] and Gesell with his descriptions of typical kinds of behaviour at each age level, and his theory that development and behaviour at all age levels, including the teen years, are governed by maturational forces. Gesell's influence on educational practice has been considerable due to the prominence of the research and publication of the Gesell Institute and the Gesell Institute Readiness Tests.[114] Despite strong criticisms of Gesell's work, particularly his theory that maturation is all powerful, he has continued to exert considerable influence on the philosophy and practices of some educational systems.[115]

Of all the developmental psychologists who have contributed to the field of education, undoubtedly the most influential is Jean Piaget who has achieved a unique status as an authority on the development of children. In fifty years of studying children, he has contributed literature related to their intellectual, moral and perceptual development, publishing many books and articles in the process.[116] His theories have been endorsed, interpreted, applied and elaborated by many psychologists and educators,[117] particularly so during the current decade when a shift in emphasis in early intervention programs refocused the concern of such programs on cognitive rather than socio-emotional development. His influence is visible in self-paced discovery methods, in activity methods in learning, and in the idea of "readiness" for formal teaching methods. A number of Follow Through Programs[118] are based on Piaget's ideas which are increasingly reflected in curricula areas, such as the SCAS: The Science Curriculum Achievement Study.[119]

The current popularity of the theory has in no way diminished the debates about its validity or relevance,[120] although the focus of these debates has changed over the years. The Piagetian model of development is concerned with the acquisition of competencies and has attempted to depict the course in which these structures are built up, and to state which components are first and prerequisite for later elaborations or stages. Stages are believed invariant, that is sequenced in a certain order, with the earlier less difficult and thus obtainable before later stages. The higher the stage, the higher the structural organization, and the better able the individual to analyze problems and integrate diverse considerations. The goal of education, following this model, is to stimulate development step by step through stages.

Early research of Piaget's theory sought to validate his findings and consisted of elaborate replication of his observations, using representative samples across a variety of cultures. Although differences in development rate have been found in some cultures, these are generally regarded as resulting from the interaction between development and experience, and it is now widely agreed that the research evidence supports the general idea of the universality of cognitive stages.[121] Of more recent concern is the meaningful definition of a stage. Recent research by Bower[122] and Pavey Hill[123] suggest the presence, in younger age children, of operations expected of children of a later age. Studies by Brainerd,[124] Siegel,[125] and Wang, Resnick and Boozer,[126] have reported the presence of sequential rather than convergent relations for within stage operations. A recent review of a larger number of studies based on Piagetian theory by Brown and Desforges[127] led the authors to doubt the integrity and hence utility of stages as defined by Piaget. Pointing out that in order to have utility, a stage must have "a substantial degree of homogeneity with the behaviors of most children for the greater part of the stage," the authors document the surprising lack of such homogeneity in many Piagetian studies.[128] They argue against the idea that this degree of variance can be accounted for by the Piagetian "horizontal decalage" or the spread and generalization of operations which make up that stage. There appears no doubt that empirical research on Piagetian operations is seriously questioning the validity of Piaget's definitions of the operations present in specific stages. However, this does not mean that the findings of such research cannot be utilized for instructional purposes. One promising line of investigation is suggested by the finding that certain within operation tasks appear to be sequential rather than concurrent as previously theorized. Should future research continue to support this finding, then it will have direct relevance to curriculum development.

If the first wave of research generated by Piagetian theory was concerned with establishing the legitimacy of his observations, the second,

206

and still current, wave has been concerned with
the possibility of accelerating the cognitive
stages that he postulated, and thus increasing
the level of intelligence of the child. Two of
these cognitive stages, "concrete operations" at
around age seven, and "formal operations" at the
onset of adolescence, occur normally during the
child's contact with the school. Since these
cognitive stages are believed to indicate qualitative changes in the forms of thinking available
to the child, educational psychologists have been
concerned to investigate the possibility of their
acceleration through direct instruction. To date,
research has concentrated almost exclusively on
the possibility of training concrete operational
thinking, and except for an occasional isolated
study, research concerned with training the thinking associated with formal operations still awaits
investigation.

The endeavours of educational psychologists
to accelerate the development of cognitive structures has not been supported by Piaget who has
ventured the opinion that although "accelerated"
children may reach a certain point faster, their
intellectual development will not be as great as
that of children who proceed at their own pace.[129]
In a specific discussion of the development of
mathematical concepts he stated: "When adults
try to impose mathematical concepts on a child
prematurely, his learning is merely verbal; true
understanding of them comes only with his own
mental growth."[130] Similar arguments against
specific training and in favour of general experience have been advanced by other psychologists
of Piagetian persuasion.[131] As previously stated,
the Piagetian position claims that developmental
behaviour change is irreversible, general over a
field of responses, sequential and hierarchical.
Early attempts to train Piagetian concepts such as
conservation[132] failed to meet these development
criteria, although following their training ses-
sions children were often able to give the immediate post test response required.[133] Two recent
articles reviewing conservation studies present

more positive findings of the possibility of training cognitive functions.[134] There is now evidence that training programs can induce conserving responses in both the short and long term, and that once trained, these responses appear no more susceptible to counter-suggestion in the trained conserver than they are in the natural conserver.[135] The extent to which conserving responses will generalize to dimensions on which no training was offered is still debatable. Generally, specific transfer has been obtained, when different materials but the same conservation dimension have been used. When transfer to dimensions on which no training has occurred has been tested for, a less stable though not necessarily pessimistic picture has emerged.[136] Although the literature related to the training of Piagetian logical operational skills is dominated by the studies on conservation, the induction of general and multiplicative classification skills, and class intrusion relations have also been investigated with varying degrees of success.[137]   In total, there now exists considerable evidence that it is possible to establish instructional programs to train a number of Piagetian logical concepts. What the effect of such training will be cannot be truly evaluated in the short term, but only over time. It has yet to be seen whether these attempts at concept training result in the goal of higher intellectual performance or just faster acquisition of intellectual performance with no change in ultimate capacity.

Despite the volume of Piagetian inspired research in the literature and its current status as a curriculum guide in education, actual research of Piaget's theory is still in its infancy and educational practice is dependent on the individual attempts of teachers and curriculum developers rather than on empirical research for the translation of Piagetian constructs into instructional strategies.[138]

Part of the problem in evaluating and assessing the practical implications of Piaget's theory is that much more information is required about the important processes that lie at its heart than is available at the present time. Insufficient knowledge of "stage structures" "equilibration dynamics" and the limits of "decalage" prevent the implementation of instructional procedures to stimulate development at appropriate, let alone "optimal" times. Piaget's recent writings have been described as more theoretical and less child centred than was previously the case,[139] a situation that is not conducive to the theory clarifications that are presently required.

Although the evidence is growing that Piagetian logical concepts are amenable to direct instructional programs, this information represents but the first step in the planning of a Piagetian based curriculum. Many methods have been used to effect success in training but as yet little is known about the relative effectiveness of the various strategies employed.[140] A thorough analysis of present instructional strategies in the conservation literature has been suggested as one means of illuminating present knowledge of effective instructional techniques. The importance of planning systematic, rigorous research with both short term and longitudinal monitoring of training gains is regarded as essential if the nature of the functional relationships within developments, operations and stages is to be explicated. The extension of training procedures to investigate the strategies applicable to the more complex developmental operations must also be undertaken, in particular the facilitation of structures necessary for formal thought.[141]

Some efforts have been made to translate Piagetian theory into classroom practice, but the primary task of applying Piagetian principles to the classroom still awaits accomplishment. While the delay in the extension of Piagetian principles to the classroom in a scientific manner is due partly to the time involved in completing meaningful longitudinal research, it is also the result

of the seeming disinterest of Piagetian theorists
in operationalizing their theoretical postulates
in a manner that permits their application to a
modern classroom. A notable exception is the work
of Kamii in the area of the preschool.[142] Though
limited, the present state of knowledge does permit
some suggestions regarding educational applications
of Piaget's theory. The research of Brainerd in
identifying developmental sequences in mathematics
suggests a need to reorient curriculum in this
discipline with instruction in ordinal number concepts preceding those in cardinal numbers.[143]
Learning might be enhanced by prudently extending
the curriculum those training procedures and programs already identified as effective. To most
researchers, however, the wisest application of
Piaget's theory lies in the provision of a multi
level curriculum with multi training strategies
so that children with multi levelled intellectual
structures may be permitted to interact in ways
which could facilitate progressive structural
transformations.[144] In practice, this position
seems general and little removed from that pertaining in the English system as described by Elkird
on that advocated by the Piagetians themselves.

In summary, Piaget has provided us with the
only comprehensive theory of intellectual development of any stature, and for this reason his ideas
will continue to hold a unique place in the field
of educational psychology for some time to come.
Currently, a number of basic theoretical issues
prevent the direct application of his theory to the
classroom setting. Present research suggests that
even if some of his assumptions are disproven, the
resultant findings still have direct application
to educational instruction. Ideally, his theory
holds promise as a basis for intellectual assessment,[145] classroom instruction, and curriculum
planning but much research remains to be accomplished before the promise of the theory can be
fulfilled.

INDIVIDUAL DIFFERENCES AND EDUCATION

Educational psychologists have long recognized the importance of individual differences in scholastic ability. The turn of the century saw several eminent psychologists striving to develop a brief, general measure of ability with little success. Binet and his co-worker Simon developed the first such scale in 1905. After evaluating the usefulness of this scale with twenty-seven persons Decroly and Degand reported as follows:

> Despite some faults and flaws, we are persuaded that these tests can already render service in waking classifications of pupils for a school or classes in special training. . . Thus we advocate their immediate use from the beginning of the school year to reduce trials that are harmful to both students and their teachers.[146]

From this pioneering work, the measurement of individual differences for diagnostic purposes received its initial impetus. It has prospered to this day. A parallel and equally important form of measurement is directed toward the evaluation of student progress. Related to the identification of students differing from the norm, is the design and provision of special programs to meet their needs. In an effort to provide the reader with some knowledge of these areas the most relevant, current strategies and issues will be discussed under the following headings: Diagnostic Assessment; Student Evaluation; and Special Education.[147]

Diagnostic Assessment. The intelligence scale developed by Binet and Simon was quickly adapted for North American use by Terman and his colleagues at Stanford University. The Stanford-Binet test found wide use until 1950, by which time educational psychologists developed instruments designed to correct two of the major drawbacks inherent in the Stanford-Binet test. The need for a more specific diagnostic index than a single score of intellectual ability led to the development of multi-faceted intelligence tests and a range of specific ability tests. The desire to provide diagnostic assessment for all students led to the development of group tests. A persistent problem to the present is the general nature of both general and specific ability tests. For example, most reading tests can predict or identify reading difficulties, but do not provide any clear identification of the skills requiring remediation nor prediction of required remedial procedures. It is imperative that researchers in this area change their emphasis from diagnostic testing to prognostic testing. It is no longer sufficient to identify general deficits. An extensive research program is needed to (1) identify those specific deficits which underly an individual's inability to achieve; (2) develop assessment devices to measure such specific deficits; and (3) develop instructional procedures to remediate these specific individual deficits.

Until recently the primary statistical model employed in the identification of individual differences was the normative model.[148] Under this model the individual's score on a given test was compared to the distribution of scores for a large sample of his peers. Based upon the properties of the normal curve describing the distribution of scores for the sample, his score could then be expressed as a percentile. Thus, if his score were at the tenth percentile ninety percent of the population could be predicted to attain scores higher than his. Using this model those requiring special educational programs could be identified. In the past decade, however, educational psychologists have been more concerned to identify an individual's level of performance on a given task in relation to instructional activities. Hence, there has been a dramatic shift away from norm-referenced tests and toward criterion-referenced tests.[149] The principal objective of the criterion-referenced test is to evaluate "what" the individual can do rather than to compare his ability to his peers. The mastery learning model and many of the newer remedial models have stimulated the need for criterion-referenced tests. Wedman has provided a brief but informative paper describing some of the principal psychometric differences between norm-referenced and criterion-referenced tests.[150] A more extensive discussion of the evaluation models that have been applied to criterion-referenced testing as it is employed in mastery learning is provided by Meskauskas.[151] It is probable that a shift in emphasis from the normative model to the criterion model by developers of diagnostic instruments would result in greater precision in this domain. Obviously, a mastery model of remediation would be a prerequisite or corequisite of such a shift.

Student Evaluation. As in the area of diagnostic assessment the traditional model in student evaluation has been the normative model.[152] For most teachers student evaluation occurs in the context of the group of students with whom they are presently concerned. Thus, the scores of an individual student are either formally or informally compared to the distribution of performance scores for the group of whom he is a member. Popular forms of evaluation are the multiple choice test, the short answer test and the essay test. A central concern among psychometric specialists has been the desire to maintain objectivity in each of these methods, while maintaining high standards of validity and reliability. There are available numerous discussions elucidating the strategies available to the test constructor for attaining high levels of objectivity even in essay style tests.[153]

When student performance is compared to an external reference group such as a sample of his North American age or grade peers, then a standard achievement test is employed. Although some school districts have developed their own achievement tests, the majority of such tests have been

213

developed by University groups or under the auspices of commercial test publishers. Standard achievement tests were initially derived for research purposes, often to evaluate the effects of specific instructional programs. As such they were frequently derived on relatively small, geographically biased samples. In the context of their initial purposes these were not serious limitations. In the past decade these tests have been employed for intra- and inter-school comparisons, and at times national comparisons. If there is a need for this type of comparative evaluation, then standardized achievement tests will have to be developed which are equal to the task. Such tests will need to tap a broader range of elements within the particular achievement domain, and they will require larger reference samples representative of the various geographical and demographic domains across which they are to be used.[154]

Special Education. On the basis of general intellectual ability, approximately 82% of school children (66% normal, 16% academically talented) do not have individual differences of sufficient note to warrant special educational provisions.[155] A number of authors have discussed methods of providing for individual differences within this group of students.[156] The remaining 18% of students require, and in most school systems receive, some form of special education. Students in this latter group are frequently classified into one of four major subgroups. A large proportion (approximately 10%) are classified as "educably retarded" on the basis of general measures of intellectual ability. Similar, a number of other students are considered "gifted" (approximately 3%). The remaining 5% are typically referred to as the "learning disabled" on the basis of either specific or general deficits which impede their school progress. Since the early 1960s, a further group of students, the disadvantaged, have also been considered to require special education.[157] The modes of special education provided for each

214

of these groups have taken the form of specific organizational arrangements within a school system and/or the provision of special instructional methods.

Until recently, the most popular administrative provision for the educably retarded has been placement in a special class.[158] Typically, such classes are small in number (6-16), taught by teachers who are specialists in the field, and contain instructional programs and media appropriate to that population. A second, but perhaps less popular, strategy is to retain retarded students within regular ability grouped classrooms.[159] As might be expected, there are those school districts that favour a partial model under which retarded students attend special classes for the basic skill subjects and regular classes for all other subjects. This latter approach is often favoured because it tends to accommodate both the academic and social needs of the retarded. During later grades, most school districts now provide a work-study program designed to facilitate the transition of retarded individuals from the school to the community.[160] Regardless of the administrative structure, there are now a considerable number of behavioural programs available for use with the retarded. These programs focus on numerous areas including self-help skills, behavioural management and basic academic skills. In that these programs have been successful, they have shifted the emphasis in the education of the retarded from a custodial approach to a training for independence model.[161]

Traditionally, the majority of research in the area of learning disabilities has focused upon their etiology. In these studies learning disabilities have been conceptualized as neurological dysfunctions, perceptual motor dysfunctions or psycholinguistic dysfunctions. In their paper, Hobbs and Lahey concluded that there is little support for the notion that meaningful treatment programs can be derived from these traditional etiologically based positions. They suggest that

215

the more appropriate alternative is the derivation
of treatment strategies based upon the behavioural
model. A number of reviews including their own
support this latter contention.[162] The postulates
of stimulus response learning have contributed to
the development of precise management strategies
for special education teachers, peer tutoring programs, and a variety of skill acquisition programs
in reading, writing and mathematics. Students
with learning disabilities are subject to the same
administrative groupings as the educably retarded.
Often, in large urban areas, highly specialized
classes are available for specific types of learning disabled children. There is at present a
growing trend to retain learning disabled children
in regular classrooms, providing for their needs
by the implementation of increasingly efficient
special programs.

Despite considerable progress in the development of educational approaches for the edu-
cable retarded and the learning disabled, considerable research remains to be accomplished.
Studies to date comparing the relative efficacy
of the various administrative structures available
for the management of these students has been
equivocal.[163] Middle range research continues to
dominate this area which requires better designed,
longitudinal studies with a broader range of outcome measures. A second concern in this area is
the establishment of efficient transition procedures which facilitate the return of special
students to the regular classroom where appropriate.
Too often these students are left or encouraged to
remain in the "protection" of the special class
while procedures for regular evaluation and
transitions await development and evaluation.[164]

As Vernon, Adamson and Vernon have noted,
a typical attitude to the gifted is that they are
already advantaged, and thus require no special
provisions. They go on to demonstrate "that many
of them [gifted] do have difficulties, and that
conventional schooling may turn them into poor
learners and waste their talents."[165] Despite
this pessimistic observation, most school districts

216

have endeavoured to make some provision for the gifted. Three administrative approaches are popular: acceleration; partial or full special class groupings; and enrichment.[166] Previous research in this area has failed to isolate the most appropriate mode of managing the gifted child and prevailing economic priorities give little hope that such research will be accomplished in the immediate future. However, if appropriate provision is to be made for these children, research in this area is imperative.

Current social, political, and economic factors have stimulated increased attention and research on the disadvantaged over the past twenty years. Passow, and Austin and his colleagues, have provided comprehensive reviews of the various models of compensatory education for the disadvantaged and the research pertaining to these models. While the majority of intervention in this area has focused on the early childhood years, programs have been evaluated for target groups ranging from infancy to adulthood. Most programs have resulted in short term gains for their recipients that have tended to disappear over time. Austin and his colleagues have argued that such results have occurred because of the relative brevity of these programs. They stress that long-lasting gains will only accrue as a result of long term intervention. Passow is in agreement with this point and in addition is critical of the limitations of the variables which have been selected for evaluation of current programs.[167]

LEARNING THEORY AND EDUCATION

Perhaps the most obvious point of common interest for psychologists and educators alike is the area of learning. Psychologists have studied the phenomena related to learning for nearly a century with apparent cycles of optimism and pessimism concerning the applicability of their theories to the field of education.[168] While to the uninitiated the process of learning in humans may

217

seem simple and straightforward, such simplicity is quickly replaced by confusion upon even a cursory review of the numerous treatises on learning theory. Most authors agree that learning can be defined as any relatively permanent change in behaviour which occurs as a result of experience.[169] However, as Kimble has pointed out, any more specific and theoretical definition is usually based upon the theory which spawned it and as a result is open to considerable disagreement among learning theorists.[170]

The complexity and lack of agreement among learning theories is further exemplified by the plethora of polar concepts in the field. A partial list of these polar concepts is: operant-respondent conditioning; connectionist-cognitive theories; receptive-discovery learning; and rote-meaningful verbal learning. Against such seeming disorganization it quickly becomes obvious that a taxonomy of learning is required. One of the first such taxonomies was that proposed by Spence in 1953.[171] A revised version of this taxonomy was presented by him in 1959, which included the following major categories of learning: conditioning; selective learning; serial learning; skills learning; symbolic learning; and social learning.[172] Perhaps the most meaningful and useful taxonomy is that derived by Gagne.[173] In his taxonomy Gagne discusses eight types of learning, which are hierarchically ordered, as follows: signal learning; stimulus-response learning; chaining; verbal association; discrimination learning; concept learning; rule learning; and problem solving. Ball has presented a similar taxonomy to that of Gagne with some additional categories. While Ball's presentation is most lucid and informative, his additional categories can be subsumed within Gagne's system.[174]

In addition to providing some structure to an otherwise confusing field the use of a taxonomic approach permits the fusion of two major groups of learning theory. Traditionally learning theorists have viewed as either connectionists (S-R theorists) or cognitive theorists. Gagne's taxonomy allows these two positions to be considered together in proper perspective. When the current literature is categorized in this fashion it becomes apparent that there has been an important shift in the interests of learning theorists interested in the phenomena of human learning. In 1959 Spence noted that learning theorists knew far more about serial learning and stimulus-response learning than the higher and more complex forms of learning.[175] In the last decade, however, theorists have moved to the study of the more complex forms of learning.[176] This change in emphasis is an important one for the field of educational psychology. Instead of conceptualizing the complex learning which occurs in the classroom in terms of simple S-R learning theories, such learning can now be conceptualized in terms of the more complex cognitive theories, which are presently being evolved. An example of this potential is illustrated by the excellent review paper by Clark.[177] He has reviewed some 250 studies on concept attainment in an effort to derive a set of teaching prescriptions for the classroom. A major focus for contemporary educational psychologists will be applied research of the higher order learning theories in education.

It is important at this point to review the various postulates of learning theory and their implications for education. Gagne's taxonomy of learning will be used to impose order upon this review. As each type of learning is discussed the critical components of that form of learning will be outlined followed by a consideration of its impact on education.[178] It should be stressed that such an organization will not satisfy all readers, however, the taxonomic approach to learning is relatively new and no doubt better taxonomies can and will be derived.

Signal Learning (Type 1). Traditionally, this form of learning has been referred to as classical or respondent conditioning.[179] Hall defines this form of learning as follows: "A

219

stimulus that does not initially elicit a particular response will do so after that stimulus
has been followed closely and consistently by a
stimulus that does elicit the response."[180]
Typically when a puff of air is presented to the
human eye the person will blink. If this sequence
is preceeded by a tone over a number of trials
the person will blink when the tone is presented
alone.

For signal learning to occur, the necessary
internal condition, that is, the condition which
must be present in the learner, is the possession
of a natural reflex. Other than reflexive motor
behaviours the other major category of such responses is emotional behaviour such as fear, anger
and pleasure. There are two external conditions,
that is conditions in the environment, necessary
for signal learning to occur. First, the signal
stimulus and the natural stimulus must occur in
close proximity to each other; one half second
has been found to yield optimal conditioning.
Second, there must be repeated pairings over a
number of trials. Generally there is an inverse
relationship between the intensity of the natural
response and the number of trials.[181]

The educational implications of this form
of learning are perhaps rather minimal. However,
most human phobic behaviour has been conceptualized
as being classically conditioned. Thus, if reading
aloud is repeatedly followed by harsh words, which
in turn produce a fear response, then reading
aloud may become a signal stimulus for fear. Such
signal stimuli often generalize rapidly, thus in
the above example all school subjects may produce
a fear response. If this form of generalization
occurs the person may be said to have a school
phobia. Other school related fears have been conceptualized to occur in a similar fashion, the
most notable of which is test anxiety. One form
of conventional management of such fears, systematic desensitization, was formulated using the
classical conditioning paradigm. Other methods
of dealing with school related anxiety have been

discussed by McKeachie.[182]

Stimulus-Response Learning (Type 2). This
form of learning was initially investigated by
Thorndike.[183] His postulates were later studied
and extended by Skinner, who argued that this
form of learning could account for most if not all
forms of human behaviour.[184] Skinner refers to
this mode of learning as operant conditioning,
while numerous others label it instrumental learning.[185] Thorndike's initial formulation was that
if a response to a stimulus is followed closely by
a reinforcing event, then the bond between that
stimulus and response will be strengthened. A
second important principle is that of practice,
that is, the more frequently this latter sequence
of events occurs the stronger the bond between
stimulus and response will become.

The most important internal condition in
this type of learning is the presence of a set of
events in the learner's environment which are reinforcing. Using good circular logic, proponents
of this form of learning define a reinforcing
event as any occurrence which increases responding. For most humans there is a range of primary
reinforcers, usually consummatory responses, which
by association lead to a sequence of secondary
reinforcers, such as money, praise, and so forth.
There are three external conditions which are important to this form of learning. As previously
stated, the response must be followed by a reinforcing event in order for its probability of
occurrence to be increased. A second important
component is the temporal relationship between
the operant and its reinforcement. It is necessary
that there be a close temporal relationship between
the behaviour and the reinforcer. Finally, the
stimulus-behaviour-reinforcement sequence must be
repeated several times in order for learning to
obtain.

The interaction between the three external
components necessary for stimulus response learning

221

to occur is referred to as a schedule of reinforcement. When the behaviour is followed repeatedly by the reinforcing event, it is said to be on a continuous reinforcement schedule. Most behaviours, however, are acquired under a partial reinforcement schedule, of which there are two major types. A ratio schedule occurs when the reinforcement follows a certain number of responses, and an interval schedule obtains when reinforcement occurs after a given time interval. Ratio and interval schedules may be either fixed or varied. For example, most legislative bodies operate on a relatively fixed interval schedule, passing most laws just prior to a recess. In contrast, most husbands reinforce their wives for excellent meals by doing the dishes on a varied ratio schedule (often a very slim schedule). Behaviours on a continuous schedule extinguish very quickly, while behaviours reinforced on a varied, partial, schedule extinguish very slowly.

The educational influence of stimulus response learning theory has been considered. As noted earlier this has occurred primarily because of the applications suggested and made by Thorndike and Skinner, and their students.[186] The major applications have been in the following areas: (1) behaviour modification; (2) mastery learning; (3) programmed instruction; and (4) achievement motivation. Developments in these four areas will be briefly reviewed in order to acquaint the reader with the impact that stimulus response learning theory has had on education.

Behaviour modification is the application of the principles, derived by stimulus response learning theorists, to the process of changing human behaviour. Recently, part I of the 72nd yearbook of the National Society for the Study of Education was devoted to the topic of Behaviour Modification in Education.[187] This volume contains numerous excellent articles on the application of behaviour modification to teacher training, special education, and standard classroom situations. While behaviour modifiers were initially concerned to ameliorate discipline problems in the classroom, more recent applications have been directed toward incrementing academic behaviours. Essentially, behaviour modification involves identifying a target behaviour, a number of words to be read, or mathematics problems to be successfully completed, and then arranging a schedule of reinforcement to consequate this behaviour. Often a token economy is employed, under which students earn tokens or points for emitting target behaviours. Certain numbers of tokens may then be used to purchase tangible reinforcers or privileges.[188] As Anderson has pointed out, token systems are most often useful when the target population is "disadvantaged, retarded, disturbed, or very young." In most normal classroom situations social reinforcement, for example praise, is the most usual and effective form of reinforcement.[189] Lipe and Jung have provided a very complete and insightful review of the use of incentives in educational settings.[190]

A concomitant educational application of stimulus-response learning theory to education has been the development of the personalized system of instruction (PSI) system. Fred S. Keller initiated this field with his now classic article, "Good-Bye Teacher . . ."[191] Initially applied to college courses such as introductory psychology, statistics and physics this method has now been extended to numerous other college courses and school subjects.[192] In recent years the PSI movement has converged with educational models proposed by Carroll and Bloom.[193] The current and more popular term for this method of education is mastery learning.[194] The essential components of mastery learning were summarized by Block and Burne as follows:

1. A set of course objects are prespecified, which students will be expected to master at a specified level;

2. The course is broken down into a number of smaller learning units;

3. Each unit is taught for mastery - all students are first exposed to a unit in standard

223

fashion and are then tested for mastery of the
unit's objectives;

4. Those who fail to master a given unit
are exposed to additional instruction and testing
until they attain mastery;

5. Student performance is evaluated by
means of individual performance (number of units
mastered) and not in comparison to the norm.[195]

Mastery learning has already been exposed to considerable classroom evaluation and has also created
a number of controversial issues. The research and
issues relating to this model are well documented
in the works of Bloom, Block and Burns, Robin, and
Ryan.[196]

The third, and perhaps equally controversial
application of stimulus-response learning theory to
education is in the area of programmed instruction.
This technology has been applied in the preparation
of textual material, material for teaching machines,
and more recently programs for computer assisted
instruction. Like mastery learning the material
to be learned is broken down into a sequence of
small units and the student is required to respond
to the material, and then, he is able to compare
his response to the correct response (a reinforcing
event). Most contemporary programs also employ
social reinforcement, that is the student is informed that he has made a good response. Space does
not permit extensive discussion of programmed instruction, however, the issue and research have
been reviewed by a number of authors.[197]

The final aspect of education to which
stimulus response learning theory has been applied
is student motivation. While Skinner's variant of
stimulus response theory argues that reinforcement
is necessary and sufficient to produce desired
behaviour, Hull and Spence have advanced a model
of stimulus response learning which stresses both
reinforcement and learned predispositions.[198]
Using essentially the Hull-Spence model of stimulus
response learning David C. McClelland set out to

224

describe, and later to modify an important component of school learning, the student's need for
achievement. McClelland found that students high
in need achievement took moderate risks, desired
and used feedback, and preferred to be responsible
for their own behaviour. McClelland then demonstrated that using a variety of strategies, an individual's need achievement could be increased, and
that this in turn increased his actual achievement.
A number of educational psychologists have attempted to apply McClelland's model in the school setting
with generally varied but positive effects.[199]

Chaining (Type 3). As Gagne has pointed out
it is rare in human behaviour for a single isolated
response to occur. More frequently the individual
performs a series of responses, in which a chain
of stimulus response sequence is involved. Gagne
uses chaining to refer to a chain of motor responses, such as driving a golf ball or drawing a
square. He conceptualizes that a sequence of motor
chains may be combined to form a motor skill, such
as playing golf or drawing. Obviously the acquisition of motor chains is most important when one
learns to write. The internal condition requisite
for chaining is knowledge of each stimulus response
link in the chain to be learned.[200]

Four external conditions are important in
this form of learning. First, a procedure must be
employed to facilitate the learner's performance
of the individual stimulus response links in the
order in which they occur in the chain. One method
employed to produce a chain of responses is to work
backward through the individual links. This method
is referred to as the "progressive part" method and
has the advantage of always allowing reinforcement
in the form of completing the chain successfully.
Another method often used is prompting in which
external cues (usually verbal) are employed to re-
instate the links in their proper order. Contiguity is also an important external condition, in
that "the chain must be executed in close time succession if the chain is to be established."[201]

Third, the chain must be repeated until it is
smooth, in order to prevent forgetting. Finally,
it is important that the terminal link leads to
reinforcement. If this condition is not met, the
individual's ability to perform the chain is
quickly lost.

The acquisition of motor chains, and in turn,
motor skills, may not seem immediately relevant in
educational activities. However, such learning is
important at various stages in the individual's
academic life. During pre-school and in the early
grades the child is called upon to acquire an increasingly complex set of self care skills. As
noted above, writing is a motor activity of utmost
importance to the individual's progress. Numerous
laboratory, art and technical courses require the
acquisition of complex chains of motor behaviour.
It is perhaps important to note that while the
skills themselves are non-verbal their acquisition
can be facilitated by verbal cues.

Verbal Association (Type 4). Often referred
to as pair-associate or serial learning this form
of learning involves verbal chaining. For example
in naming an object the following sequence may be
conceived to occur: (1) the object is presented
(stimulus); (2) the individual observes the object
(response); (3) the object's characteristics are
evaluated (stimulus); and (4) the individual names
the object (response). In learning a piece of prose
or poetry, the chain of verbal associations will be
far more lengthy and complex. Two internal conditions are important in verbal associative learning.
First, each link in the chain must have been previously acquired. Second, the individual must have
learned the necessary "coding" or mediating responses. Mediating responses may be pictures, words,
or visual and auditory images.

There appears to be several external conditions important to verbal associate learning. As
in chaining, the verbal units must be presented in
their proper sequence and the learner must actively
make the responses required by the chain. External

cues facilitating the ordering of the units, such as mnemonics or poetic meter, facilitate acquisition. When long sequences are to be learned the "progressive part" method will facilitate learning. Feedback is necessary so that the learner can confirm whether his responses are correct or not. Finally, practice and good discrimination of component units are important in order to offset proactive and retroactive interference from other material.[202]

As Mandler has noted verbal association learning although initially considered "as a verbal analogue of simple conditioning, has developed into a much more complex situation."[203] He has provided a brief but important overview of some of the issues related to the process of verbal associative learning.[204] Gagne and Rohwer note a number of references which support the notion that a multiprocess theory is necessary to explain this type of learning.[205] An important aspect of verbal associative learning is the mode of encoding employed by the learner. Currently, there is a considerable debate concerning the relative merits of imagery and verbal encoding in verbal associative learning.[206] The outcome of this debate will be important to educational strategies employed to facilitate verbal associative learning.

Another current debate is the distinction between rote and meaningful verbal learning.[207] Ausubel has argued that most verbal learning in the school is not rote but rather meaningful. That is, individuals are rarely called upon to learn passages of material verbatim, but rather the ideas or meaning within the passage. Thus, meaningful learning of a passage is more rapid, leads to better recall, and is rarely subject to interference. These phenomena occur because the ideas contained in the material are subsumed into an existing cognitive structure. While Gagne suggests that meaningful verbal learning may be explained as a form of verbal associative learning, it is perhaps better to consider it as a type of rule or principle learning.[208]

Discrimination Learning (Type 5). This form
of learning involves the acquisition of the capacity
to make different responses to individual members
of a class of items. As Gagne points out, this form
of learning is very basic and for the most part is
considered to have occurred before the child enters
school. As internal conditions for this type of
learning the individual must have previously acquired in isolation the individual chains within
the class, and the initial stimulus and final response in each chain must have been learned as dis-
criminated stimulus response connections. Three
external conditions are important in this form of
learning. The learner must be prompted to rehearse
each chain, repetition is required as the number of
class members increases, and confirmation must follow
correct responding.[209] The importance of prompting,
mediational strategies, and variety in facilitating
discrimination learning have been considered by a
number of authors.[210] While this form of learning
is important in pre-school programs it is probably
of minimal importance in regular school curricula.

Concept Learning (Type 6). Once the individual is able to discriminate between elements
within a class, concept learning can take place.
In concept learning, the individual develops the
ability to respond in a single way to a class of
objects, which extends beyond those elements of the
class that have been experienced. Thus, once the
concept of a table has been learned the individual
can react to novel occurrences of that concept without further learning. Gagne distinguishes between
concrete and abstract concepts and uses the term
concept learning to refer to the acquisition of
concrete concepts. Concrete concepts are those
which can be learned by observation, that is, the
members of the class are tangible.

As an internal condition for concept learning, the individual must have learned a set of
verbal chains representative of members of the
class, and be able to discriminate members from
non-members. The external conditions for concept

228

learning are primarily embodied in a set of verbal instructions. First, previously learned representatives of the class are presented in close proximity using the question "What is it?" Then novel examples of the class are presented followed by the same question. In both of the previous steps confirmation of correct responding is important. As a final step concept acquisition may be verified by presenting further novel examples of class members. Once the concept has been learned further repetition does not appear necessary. As Gagne has noted, this form of learning is most important because it frees the individual from the control of specific stimuli. Concepts are an essential aspect of human reading, communication, and thinking, all of which are performed without reference to external stimuli.[211]

As would be expected the shift from stimulus response to cognitive conceptions of human learning has fostered a number of theories and related research on concept learning. Klausmeier, Ghatala and Frayer conceptualize the acquisition of concepts to occur at four distinct levels. They propose that concepts may be acquired at the concrete, identity, classificatory and formal levels. Having defined these levels they then discuss completed and proposed research on the acquisition of given concepts at each of these levels.[212] Clark, after an extensive review of previous research on concept acquisition, has proposed an instructional sequence for teaching concepts.[213] While this area of research is exciting, it still awaits applied evaluation and will no doubt undergo considerable revision as the results of research are obtained.

Rule Learning (Type 7). Once a set of concrete concepts has been acquired, the learner is able to learn abstract concepts and rules. Abstract concepts are also referred to as defined concepts in that they relate two or more concrete concepts. Similarly, rules express the relationship between two or more concepts. Gagne has argued that abstract concepts and rules are acquired

229

under the same conditions. The central position of rule learning in contemporary learning theory is amply demonstrated in the following comment by Gagne: ". . . rules are probably the major organizing factor, and quite possibly the primary one, in intellectual functioning. The Ss⟶R connection, once proposed as the unit of mental organization, has now been virtually replaced by the rule in the theoretical formulations of most psychologists."[214]

An essential internal condition for rule learning is prior knowledge of those concepts inherent to the rule. The external conditions, which facilitate rule learning, are contained in a sequence of verbal instructions. First, a general statement is made concerning the performance expected once learning has occurred. This is seen to signal to the individual when learning has occurred and thus act as a reinforcing event. Next, the component concepts making up the rule are reviewed, followed in close proximity by a statement of the rule. Finally, the learner is asked to demonstrate the rule. Gagne stresses an important distinction between demonstration and statement of the rule. Meaningful learning, in the sense that Ausubel uses the term, can only be inferred when the learner is able to demonstrate a rule. Once the learner can demonstrate the rule, further repetition of the instructional sequence does not appear to be necessary.[215]

A major concern of learning theorists at the present time is understanding the process by which individuals organize and use rules. There have been a number of theoretical formulations developed to describe how humans organize and employ the rules which govern their behaviour. Overviews of some of these theories are provided by Ausubel, Broadbent, and Mandler.[216] Concomitant with studies of cognitive process are theories concerning the acquisition of rules. Both of these areas of study have and will continue to have important ramifications for educational practice.

Educational psychologists have been most active in applying theoretical findings concerning rule acquisition to instructional paradigms. Gagne has outlined the general instructional sequence which is most often employed in rule learning as follows:

Step 1: Inform the learner about the form of the performance to be expected when learning is completed.

Step 2: Question the learner in a way that requires the restatement (recall) of the previously learned concepts that make up the rule.

Step 3: Use verbal statements (cues) that will lead the learner to put the rule together, as a chain of concepts, in the proper order.

Step 4: By means of a question, ask the learner to "demonstrate" one or more concepts of the rule.

Step 5: (Optional, but useful for later instruction): By a suitable question, require the leader to make a verbal statement of the rule.[217]

This outline illustrates many of the issues being examined and discussed by educational psychologists at present. Areas currently being investigated are pre-instructional strategies, the importance of prompts and questions in instruction, the mode of organizing instruction, and the importance of overt responding during rule acquisition.

Pre-instructional strategies which have been examined are pretests, behavioural objectives, and advanced organizers. Stemming from different theories of rule organization and acquisition, each of these strategies is postulated to acquaint the learner with the nature of what is to be learned. Arising from the work of Bloom in 1956 there has

231

developed a considerable literature on behavioural objectives.[218] Gagne and Briggs have provided a brief but informative chapter on technical issues related to the development of behavioural or performance objectives.[219] Overviews of research pertaining to behavioural objectives have been provided by Duchartel and Merrill, and Wittrock and Lumsdaine.[220] Hartley and Davies have provided a comprehensive review of the research pertaining to pretests, behavioural objectives, overviews, and advanced organizers.[221] Most authors conclude that a more complex theory is required which will assimilate the interaction between individual differences in learners, type of pre-instructional devise, and type of material to be learned.[222] Such a theory is required to explain the present, conflicting results concerning the facilitatory effects of pre-instructional methods.

Inherent in Gagne's instructional model is the use of prompts and questions to facilitate the process of rule acquisition. Gagne and Rohwer have provided a brief overview of some of the research on prompting in concept and rule learning.[223] The importance of questions in rule acquisition has been studied intensively by Frase and his colleagues.[224] Current research on questions and instruction are reviewed by Frase, Gall, and Wittrock and Lumsdaine.[225] Wittrock and Lumsdaine conclude their brief review as follows:

> . . . most of the research on adjunct questions has contributed to an understanding of the attentional processes in the learning of factual information. In research or adjunct questions, additional studies of encoding and meaningful processing of themes, concepts, and complex organizations are needed.[226]

An essential component of Gagne's taxonomy of learning theories is the notion that the learner must have acquired subordinate performances prior to mastery of material at a higher level of learning. This thesis has led him to propose that a

232

hierarchy of learning must be developed in order to teach a given principle or set of principles. Gagne and his colleagues have developed whole sequences of hierarchies necessary for instruction in a variety of subjects, such as mathematics. They have also reported a number of studies evaluating the importance of learning hierarchies in instruction.[227] Recently Gagne's work on learning hierarchies has been critically reviewed by White.[228] He has concluded that certain methodological flaws must be corrected before the importance of learning hierarchies can be evaluated fully.

Before leaving this section on rule learning it is important to discuss modeling, a very important form of learning that can be related to rule learning. Ball in his extension of Gagne's taxonomy described modeling or social learning as an independent form of learning.[229] However, as Baldwin has pointed out, Bandura, the major investigator of modeling, has tended to describe it in cognitive terms.[230] The sequence of steps in modeling has sufficient similarity to those outlined earlier to suggest that modeling is a form of rule learning.[231] Baldwin has provided an excellent review of social learning.[232] Wittrock and Lumisdaine have provided a brief review of recent studies on modeling and instruction.[233]

Problem Solving (Type 8). This mode of learning occurs whenever the individual must juxtapose a sequence of known rules to solve a novel problem. Learning accrues, in that the individual acquires a higher order rule. The newly acquired rule immediately generalizes to that class of problems related to the novel problem. The internal condition necessary for problem solving is knowledge of those rules which are relevant to the problem. The important external condition for learning during problem solving is the juxtaposition of previously acquired rules in the correct sequence. This latter phenomena may be facilitated by questions and instructions, which cue the learner

233

toward the appropriate solution.[234]

The major form of instructional strategy related to problem solving is discovery learning. Ausubel has provided a brief overview of the rationale and research pertaining to discovery learning.[235] A major debate in the literature concerns the relative merits of receptive as opposed to discovery learning.[236] Both modes of learning involve the acquisition of rules, receptive learning under the conditions of rule learning, and discovery learning under the conditions of problem solving. When achievement is the major outcome variable research has tended to favour receptive learning. However, learning by discovery probably has the advantage of developing rules pertinent to independent thinking, which are important once the individual has completed his formal education. For example, are scientists trained under discovery learning more productive than those trained by receptive methods. Thus, while the short term advantage may favour receptive learning this may not hold in the long term.

Another phenomenon related to problem solving is creativity. Ball has tended to isolate creativity as a separate form of learning, while most other authors identify it as a specific form of problem solving.[237] Using a systems approach Ripple has attempted to develop a model of creative behaviour. Based upon this model he postulates methods by which creativity may be facilitated in students.[238] Research on creativity is in its infancy, no doubt further research on this important facility will have important implications for educational practice in areas such as art and creative writing.

The preceding discussion of learning theory and education raises a number of general issues. From the perspective of Gagne's taxonomy of learning it seems counterproductive to maintain any sharp distinction between so-called learning and cognitive theories. They are both learning theories that explain different forms of human learning. There

234

seems no need to reinterpret reinforcement theory
in cognitive terms, nor for that matter is it important to explain all learning in reinforcement
terms.[239] It is obvious that most school learning
is complex in nature, and that contemporary cognitive theories offer more meaningful explanations
of this type of learning. Educational psychologists have an important task before them. Further
studies are urgently needed to evaluate the utility
of current cognitive theories in the applied setting.

A second concern relates to Gagne's taxonomy
itself. Can the taxonomy, in its present form,
incorporate all the variants of learning of which
humans are capable? For example, Gagne and Briggs
have provided a preliminary discussion concerning
the acquisition of intellectual skills, cognitive
strategies, information, motor skills and attitudes
as these forms of learning relate to the taxonomy.[240]
If indeed these varied forms of learning and the
theories which explain them do not fit into the
present taxonomy then it must be revised. Such a
taxonomy is most important in providing organization
in an otherwise confusing area. By reference to
the taxonomy educators can quickly determine the
most appropriate strategy for instruction in a given
area.

The final issue has already been alluded to
in the previous discussion. It should be self
evident by now that there does not exist a unique
mode of learning for all abilities for all individuals. This observation would suggest that a complex inter-actional theory is required to predict
the most appropriate learning strategy for a given
individual, who is attempting to learn a specific
ability. Until recently educational psychologists
had done little to develop such inter-actional
theories. However, in the past decade a number of
these theories have emerged. They will be the focus
of the following section.

INTERACTIONAL THEORIES AND EDUCATION

Current research on curiousity has suggested that there is an optimal level of complexity, which individuals find interesting. Interest declines rapidly as the individual is beset by increasing levels of complexity.[241] This basic phenomenon explains perhaps the desire of most psychologists to study relatively simple aspects of human behaviour. However, an increasing number of educational psychologists have come to the realization that they must deal with the complex interaction between differences in individuals and modes of instruction if they are to answer the concerns of contemporary educators.[242] Traditionally, psychologists have tended to follow two distinct approaches in their research endeavours. One group have used the experimental method, controlling for individual differences by randomization procedures, and examining the effects of treatments on one or more outcome measures. The remaining approach has been to examine the inter-relationships between a number of person characteristics organizing them into constellations of traits or aptitudes. Cronbach in 1957 wrote an important article describing in detail these two approaches and calling for their integration.[243] That his concern went unheeded for a considerable period of time is demonstrated by the fact that he wrote a similar more forceful article in 1975.[244] However, since the mid-1960s educational psychologists have begun to study the complex interaction between individual differences and different instructional modes. Commonly, these studies are referred to as aptitude treatment interaction (ATI) studies. In order to acquaint the reader with some of the issues in this area the remaining discussion will be organized under the following headings: Aptitude Treatment Interaction Models; Methodological Issues in Interactional Research; and Educational Implications of Interactional Models.[245]

Aptitude Treatment Interaction Models. Essentially all of the ATI models view learning as a

function of two factors, aptitudes and treatments.
In early research aptitudes were viewed rather
narrowly as the individual's scores on scholastic
aptitude tests and general ability tests. Researchers soon saw the need to broaden this meaning, leading some to adopt the term attribute, and
others, the term trait.[246] The term trait probably
holds the broadest meaning and has a long history
of use in personality research. Recently, Cronbach
and Snow have defined an aptitude as "any characteristic of a person that forecasts his probability
of success under a given treatment."[247] Snow pre-
fers the term aptitude, arguing that the terms
trait and attribute suggest a pursuivance in the
characteristics being described.[248] In our view
researches in this area will continue to employ the
three terms interchangably. In current research
aptitudes tend to refer to a broad domain of personal characteristics, including demographic measures, scores on specific and general aptitude tests,
scores on a wide range of personality measures, and
a variety of measures of cognitive abilities and
styles. The term treatments also symbolizes a diverse range of instructional variables, such as the
inductive-deductive dimension, the degree of structure, the type of instruction and so forth. Many
of the recent studies, investigating aptitude treatment interactions have been reviewed by Berliner
and Cahen, and Snow.[249]

While many of the aptitude treatment interaction studies have been atheoretical in nature,
some researchers have developed theoretical models
depicting the expected interaction between specific
aptitudes and treatments. One such model is that
developed by Bloom, which depicts an interaction
between student characteristics and instruction.
Student characteristics refer to the cognitive entry
behaviours and the affective entry characteristics
brought to the learning task by the student. Bloom
employs the term quality of instruction as the
measure related to the learning task. Quality of
instruction is defined as "the degree to which the
presentation, explanation, and ordering of elements
of the task to be learned approach the optimum for

a given learner."[250] Bloom employs in his research the following outcome measures: level and type of achievement; rate of learning; and affective outcomes. He has reported an extensive number of studies bearing upon the relationship between student characteristics, instruction, and learning outcomes.[251]

A second theory based line of research has been stimulated by the work of David Hunt. He uses as his paradigm the Lewinian formula, which states that behaviour is a function of the characteristics of the person and the environment. Applying this paradigm to the classroom "the Behaviour (learning) would be seen as jointly determined by P (kind of student) and E (way of teaching."[252] Hunt has proposed that such a model must be (1) interactive; (2) account for developmental change; (3) account for the reciprocity of the relationship between the person and the environment; and (4) practically oriented. Based upon these concerns he has proposed a "developmental matching model." Hunt describes this model as follows:

> From a developmental view, conceptual level can be considered in terms of increasing conceptual complexity, increasing interpersonal maturity, and increasing understanding of oneself and others. The sequence of stages . . . can be telegraphically summarized as proceeding from an immature, unsocialized stage (A) to a dependent, conforming stage (B) to an independent, self-reliant stage (C). . . . For the Stage A person to progress to Stage B, he must understand and incorporate the cultural rules. Since rules are learned best when they are clearly defined, the matched environment to foster development to Stage B is a clear, consistent, highly structured one. Following

238

> similar logic, the matched en-
> vironment for progression from
> Stage B to Stage C is moderately
> structured with encouragement
> for self-expression and autonomy.[253]

This model, then, predicts a set of relationships between certain characteristics of learners and the instructional environment. In a recent article, Hunt has discussed some of the research pertaining to his developmental matching model.[254]

Current aptitude treatment interaction models are certainly preferable to those unidimensional models, which focus upon either aptitudes or modes of instruction. However, several authors have argued that the bidimensional aptitude treatment models are insufficient to account for all the variance in the relationship between individuals and their acquisition of skills. A number of authors have stressed the importance of environmental factors in this equation.[255] Walberg has proposed the following multiplicative model to describe the contribution aptitude (A) environment (E) and instruction (I) to learning (L):

$$L_h = b_1(A_i) + b_2(E_j) + b_3(I_k) +$$

$$b_4(A_i E_j) + b_5(A_i I_k) + b_6(E_j I_k) +$$

$$b_7(A_i E_j I_k) \quad 256 \ (1)$$

In this equation b refers to a regression weight expressing the relative importance of each factor in the learning outcome. Other authors have argued that the nature of the specific task being acquired also interacts with aptitudes and instruction to determine the outcome of learning.[257] If the equation proposed by Walberg is extended to accommodate the task (T) dimension the complexity of this area of research is truly exemplified. The revised formula would be:

$$L_h = b_1(A_i(+ b_2(E_j) + b_3(I_k) + b_4(T_m) +$$

$$b_5(A_iE_j) + b_6(A_iI_k) + b_7(A_iT_m) +$$

$$b_8(E_jI_k) + b_9(E_jT_m) + b_{10}(I_kT_m)$$

$$+ b_{11}(A_iE_jI_k) + b_{12}(A_iE_jT_m) +$$

$$b_{13}(A_iI_kT_m) + b_{14}(E_jI_kT_m) +$$

$$b_{15}(A_iE_jI_kT_m) \quad (2)$$

At least conceptually a formula of this complexity seems warranted in the sense that individuals with different aptitudes may indeed require different modes of instruction for different tasks in different environments $(A_iE_jI_kT_m)$. Only subsequent research will demonstrate whether such a complex model is necessary.

Methodological Issues in Interactive Research
The principal methodological concern related to interactive research is whether in fact there exist appropriate statistical models to accommodate the complexity inherent in the various interactional models.[258] The review of multivariate statistical procedures by Tatsuoka suggests that available methods are sufficient to the complexity posed by the interactive models.[259] Multivariate Analysis of Variance can be used in planned experiments involving several measures of learning outcome and multiple independent variables such as aptitude, instructional, environmental, and task dimensions. Path Analysis could be employed to evaluate predicted weights for the factors in formula 2.

Perhaps a more pertinent methodological issue relates to the selection of appropriate strategies for deriving the true weights and components in the conceptualized model. Should one follow the example set by Hunt and thoroughly exhaust research in one small segment of the full model?[260] A major risk here is that when entered into the more complex equation the limited number of variables studied intensely in isolation may interact with other variables in the full model in a quite different manner than when they were studied alone. The logistics and complexity of the full model virtually rule out any purely empirical attempt to provide the model with real values. To date most large scale empirical studies manipulating multi-aptitude and treatment variables have been rather disappointing.[261] Snow suggested that the majority of researchers have opted for middle-range instructional experiments, that is, "short-term experiments with a few controlled instructional variables aimed at testing fairly simple propositions."[262] Cronbach and Snow concluded that such studies have failed to lead either to theoretical advances or practical utility.[263] Most authors agree that research in this area is desperately in need of a theory, which would depict both the essential variables and their mode of interaction.[264] As Berliner and Cahen have noted theoretical leads will come from many sources and those developing such theories will have to "sift through the psychological literature carefully."[265] No doubt the theory building and evaluation process will occupy the energy of a number of educational psychologists in the years to come.

Educational Implications of Interactional Models. Several educators and psychologists have argued that once the full interactional model is attained, it will suggest the need for an individualized educational system. In true conservative spirit the spectre of such a system has raised a number of real and imaginary objections, concerning the envisaged cost, reorganization, and hence, the feasibility of such a system.[266] To some degree, however, the technology of a system of this nature is developing far more rapidly than the theoretical propositions necessary for its full activation. Developments such as computer assisted instruction, flexible modular programming, and the open school approach await theoretical development of interactional models to make them fully efficient. Further, it is most likely that once the interactional

241

model is fully understood, it will predict only a limited range of instructional models for the majority. The minority can then be offered efficient programs to develop their aptitudes and/or change their environments so that they develop the skills of the majority. Alternatively, they can be offered more efficient programs of instruction appropriate to their own characteristics, environments and tasks to be learned.

HUMANISTIC APPROACHES TO EDUCATION

Modern humanistic psychology grew out of a discontent with the deterministic views of man's behaviour as presented by Freudian psychoanalysis and behaviourism. Similarly, a growing discontent with "traditional" educational practices: over-emphasis on cognitive learning and prescriptively structured models of classroom education, led to a concern in education for more affective and personal kinds of learning. This concern found expression in the movement for "humanistic" education. The most influential spokesman for the application of the principles of humanistic psychology in the field of education has been Carl Rogers,[267] although discussion of the educational application of psychological principles under this model has been sufficiently wide to include an article on "Behavioural Humanism,"[268] and to permit quotation of B.F. Skinner's research as a source of evidence for use of a humanistic model.[269]

The central theme of the humanistic approach to learning is that it is "person centred." According to Rogers, education changes from a prescribed teacher-oriented activity to a free, pupil-oriented enterprise when the individual and his growth directed motivation are respected, when interpersonal conditions for growth are established, and when appropriate resources for pupil growth are provided.[270] The role of the teacher is of prime importance. In humanistic education the teacher is the facilitator who sets a climate for learning.[271] Once established, the provision of this climate is undertaken by the learners themselves and self discipline towards goals is accepted by the learner as his responsibility. Under this model, the learning emphasis is on the process of learning rather than the content, with the student working towards self chosen direction and self initiated learning, goals considered more relevant and more pervasive as a preparation for life than traditional practices.[272]

As might be anticipated, the introduction of a model presenting recommendations in such contrast to traditional practice, has resulted in considerable opposition. Rogers has been criticized for his recommendations regarding the necessity of changing both the vertical and horizontal power structure within the classroom, the school and the school district through the medium of basic encounter groups. Opposition has been directed at his downgrading of the "teacher" role and upgrading the "facilitator" role and also at the utility of the flurry of "humanizing" techniques which have evolved to "liberate" the student: open classrooms in which students are free to spend their time as they wish, elimination of teacher assigned grades in an effort to provoke a more relaxed, learning oriented classroom, introduction of more affect into classrooms to balance heavily cognitively oriented curricula, and the substitution of a variety of teaching methods for the traditional lecture or teacher-led discussion.[273] The effect of such criticism has in no way inhibited the growth of affective education but rather seems to have served to stimulate clarification of humanistic principles and hence, growth in application of the model.[274]

Although to Rogers must go credit for the extension of humanistic principles to education, he himself has not chosen to become involved in the research so necessary to identify the important elements in the model. The leader in this area has been David Aspy who has both developed and researched a systematic method of training teachers to facilitate learning in their students. Extending the client centred-human relations model of

243

training[275] into the school setting, Aspy developed a technology for training teachers to focus on both their own modes of interpersonal interaction and on the growth oriented responses of their students. This was accomplished through the development of a hierarchy of single skills which are first mastered independently and then integrated. The skills include empathy, positive regard and congruence. In mastering each skill, teachers learn to measure the skill as exhibited in their own teaching activities, develop a cognitive awareness of the skill, and then through practice and feedback become highly effective in its use. A feature of the model is its orientation toward classroom behaviour within the present model of education.[276]

Concomitant with the growth of this model has been the research of its feasibility. Classrooms where "facilitative conditions" have been present have been shown to relate significantly to greater gains in reading achievement,[277] grade point average,[278] cognitive growth,[279] and to a diffusion of liking and trust in the classroom, in turn related to improved utilization of abilities by the student and greater confidence in himself.[280] More recently, the results of a larger body of studies conducted at the elementary and secondary levels have been released by Aspy and his colleagues.[281] The results of this later research confirm the correlation between the provision of facilitative conditions and academic achievement and indicate that the condition most conducive to learning occurs when teachers with high levels of interpersonal skills are supported by principals who themselves exhibit high levels of the skills. The provision of facilitative conditions by teachers has also been related to fewer discipline problems, lower absenteeism, improvement in I.Q. scores and problem solving, and has been found unaffected by geographic location of class, social composition or race of teacher.

The humanistic models proposed by Rogers and Aspy are but two of many proposed in the last decade. Recently, John P. Miller[282] has grouped a number of these models under a taxonomy based upon their orientation and degree of structure provided.

244

Seventeen affective teaching models have been grouped into four categories: (1) developmental models, (2) self-concept models, (3) sensitivity and group orientation models, and (4) conscious-expansion models, according to the principal focus of the model within the general framework of personal integration. The models selected were chosen not only for their theoretical base and clear rationale but also because of their applicability to the classroom situation. Perhaps one of the most notable features of Miller's work is his explication of a statement so often made by the humanists but so often misinterpreted - that there is no best way of teaching that is applicable in all situations. Miller has given structure and meaning to this often made statement and though his work has yet to be evaluated, it offers new hope for identifying important process and outcome variables in humanistic education. Certainly, it is proof of the existence of alternative, more humanistic models of teaching than were previously acceptable and adds credence to a recent claim by Carl Rogers that "We are a current to be reckoned with in American education."283 Educational psychology has had a lengthy and wide ranging association with the field of education. Depending upon the orientation of psychology itself, this association has been at various times, useful to the practice of educators. At present, there are several major reorientations occurring in psychology. In the area of developmental psychology, the propositions of Piaget are stimulating the growth of a theory of cognitive development. A taxonomy of learning theories is developing which permits stimulus response learning theories and cognitive theories to co-exist. A major effect of this taxonomy has been to refocus research on studies concerning the acquisition of cognitive abilities. Another major reorientation stems from a growing realization that complex interactional theories must be developed to predict human behaviour. As these areas of research become more established, they will no doubt influence future educational practice. Educational psychologists will have the exciting and challenging task of establishing the validity of these theories as they apply to education.

FOOTNOTES

1. David C. Berliner and N.L. Gage, "The Psychology of Teaching Methods," in N.L. Gage (Ed.), The Psychology of Teaching Methods, 75th Yearbook of the NSSE (Chicago: University of Chicago Press, 1976), pp. 1-5.

2. W.T. Harris, Psychological Foundations of Education (New York: Appleton, 1898), p. 14.

3. N.B. Cuff, "What should be included in educational psychology?" Journal of Educational Psychology 26 (1935): 689-694.

4. L.J. Cronbach, "Educational Psychology," Annual Review of Psychology 1 (1950): 235.

5. R.S. Ellis, Educational Psychology: A Problem Approach (Princeton, N.J.: Van Nostrand, 1951), p. 6.

6. Fred T. Tyler, "Educational Psychology," Annual Review of Psychology 7 (1956): 283-284.

7. R.L. Archer, "Educational Psychology, American and British: Some Points of Comparison," British Journal of Educational Psychology 11 (1941): 128.

8. Thomas L. Good, "The Teaching of Educational Psychology: Some Reactions and Questions," Contemporary Educational Psychology 1 (1976): 132.

9. Cited in Don C. Charles, "A Historical Overview of Educational Psychology," Contemporary Educational Psychology 1 (1976): 79.

10. Dael Wolfle, "The Sensible Organization of Courses in Psychology," American Psychologist 2 (1947): 437-455.

11. J.B. Stroud, "Educational Psychology," Annual Review of Psychology 2 (1951): 281.

12. F.W. Warburton, "Educational Psychology," Annual Review of Psychology 13 (1962): 371.

13. Gary S. Belkin and Jerry L. Gray, Educational Psychology: An Introduction (Dubuque, Iowa: Wm. C. Brown, 1977), pp. 3-25.

14. Victor H. Noll, John E. Horrocks and G. Lester Anderson, "The Function of the Division of Educational Psychology of the American Psychological Association: A Committee Report," Journal of Educational Psychology 40 (1949): 361-370.

15. Harold D. Carter, "Educational Psychology," Annual Review of Psychology 4 (1954): 387; Tyler, Educational, p. 285.

16. Tyler, Educational, p. 285.

17. J.M. Stephens, "Educational Psychology," Annual Review of Psychology 10 (1959): 110.

18. J.M. Stephens, Educational Psychology (Rev.Edn.) (New York: Holt, 1956), pp. 10-11.

19. Glen M. Blair, "The Content of Educational Psychology," Journal of Educational Psychology 40 (1949): 274. Other proponents of this position are: Myron H. Dembo and Stephen B. Hillman, "An Instructional Model Approach to Educational Psychology," Contemporary Educational Psychology 1 (1976): 116-123; Robert Glaser, "Educational Psychology and Education," American Psychologists 28 (1973): 557-566; D. Kallos and U.P. Lundgren, "Educational Psychology: Its Scope and Limits," British Journal of Educational Psychology 45 (1975): 111-121; Herbert J. Walberg, "Models for Optimizing and Individualizing School Learning," Interchange 2 (1971): 15-27; and Robert I. Watson, "A Brief History of Educational Psychology," Psychological Record 11 (1961): 209-242.

20. David P. Ausubel, Educational Psychology: A Cognitive View (New York: Holt, Rinehart and Winston, 1968), p. vii.

21. Ibid., p. 8.

22. John B. Carroll, "The Place of Educational Psychology in the Study of Education," in John Walton and James L. Kuethe (Eds.), The Discipline of Education (Madison: University of Wisconsin Press, 1963), pp. 101-119; B. Claude Mathis, John W. Cotton and Lee Sechrest, Psychological Foundations of Education Learning and Teaching (New York: Academic Press, 1970).

23. Edwin G. Boring, A History of Experimental Psychology (New York: Appleton Century Crofts, 1957), pp. 567-570; Don C. Charles, p. 76-88; R.E. Grinder, "The Growth of Educational Psychology as reflected in the history of Division 15," Educational Psychologist 4 (1967): 12-35; and R.I. Watson, pp. 209-242.

24. Charles, p. 76.

25. R.I. Watson, p. 213.

26. Cited in Charles, p. 78.

27. Boring, p. 508.

28. William James, The Principles of Psychology, 2 Vols. (New York: Holt, 1892); Textbook of Psychology: Briefer Course (New York: Holt, 1892); and Talks to Teachers on Psychology and to Students on Some of Life's Ideals (New York: Dover, 1962).

29. James, Principles, pp. 643-689.

30. James, Talks, preface v.

31. Bird T. Baldwin, "William James' Contribution to Education," Journal of Educational Psychology 2 (1911): 369-382.

32. Ibid., p. 375.

33. Geraldine Joncich, The Sane Positivist:

A Biography of Edward L. Thorndike (Middleton, Connecticut: Wesleyan University Press, 1968): 95.

34. Dorothy E. Bradbury, "The Contribution of the Child Study Movement to Child Psychology," Psychological Bulletin 34 (1937): 21.

35. Boring, p. 567.

36. Bradbury, p. 27.

37. A discussion of some aspects of the relationship between Hall and eminent psychologists of that period is found in Joncich, pp. 241-244.

38. Bradbury, pp. 22-27; Boring, 567-569.

39. R.I. Watson, p. 222.

40. Joncich, pp. 171-176.

41. Ibid., p. 463.

42. Edward L. Thorndike, Educational Psychology (New York: Lemcke & Buechner, 1903): 164.

43. Edward L. Thorndike, "The Nature, Purposes and General Methods of Educational Products," National Society for the Study of Education, 17th Yearbook. Part II, The Measurement of Educational Products (Chicago: The Society, University of Chicago Press, 1918): 16.

44. Cited in Joncich, p. 282.

45. Edward L. Thorndike, An Introduction to the Theory of Mental and Social Measurements (New York: Science Press, 1904).

46. Edward L. Thorndike, Elements of Psychology (New York: Seiler, 1905).

47. Thorndike, Educational.

48. Cited in Boring, p. 580.

49. Information on these texts and other practical aspects of Thorndike's work is to be found in Joncich, pp. 383-408.

50. Wilbert J. McKeachie, "Instructional Psychology," Annual Review of Psychology 25 (1974): 186.

51. Charles, p. 82.

52. Charles H. Judd, Genetic Psychology for Teachers (New York: Appleton, 1903).

53. Carl Murchison, History of Psychology in Autobiography, II (New York: Russell and Russell): 228-233.

54. Charles H. Judd, Education as Cultivation of the Higher Mental Processes (New York: Mc-Millan, 1936).

55. R.I. Watson, p. 217.

56. John Dewey, "President's Address," The Psychological Review 7 (1900): 105-124.

57. L.S. Hearnshaw, A Short History of British Psychology, 1840-1950 (London: Methuen, 1964): 56-66.

58. Alfred Binet and Theodore Simon, "Upon the necessity of establishing a scientific diagnosis of inferior states of intelligence," L'Annee Psychologigue 11 (1905): 163-191. Also in Alfred Binet and Theodore Simon, The Development of Intelligence in Children (Baltimore: Williams and Wilkins, 1916).

59. Charles, pp. 77.

60. E.P. Cubberley, History of Education (Boston: Houghton Mifflin, 1920).

61. R.I. Watson, p. 220.

62. Hearnshaw, p. 255.

63. Charles, p. 85.

64. Goodwin, B. Watson, "What Shall be Taught in Educational Psychology," Journal of Educational Psychology 27 (1926): 578-579.

65. Cuff, p. 689.

66. Details of these inconsistencies are to be found in studies by Dean A. Worcester, "The Wide Diversities of Practice in First Courses in Educational Psychology," Journal of Educational Psychology 18 (1927): 11-17; Cuff, pp. 689-694; Glenn M. Blair, "The Vocabulary of Educational Psychology," Journal of Educational Psychology, 32 (1941): 365-371; Blair, The Content, pp. 267-274.

67. Blair, p. 271.

68. W.A. Brownell, "Learning Theory and Educational Practice," Journal of Educational Research 41 (1948): 481-497.

69. Cronbach, p. 235.

70. Lee J. Cronbach, "Revitalize or Reorganize," Newsletter of the Division of Educational Psychology (1949): 4-5; Guy T. Buswell, "Educational Theory and Psychology of Learning," Journal of Educational Psychology 47 (1956): 175-184.

71. Charles, p. 86.

72. Grinder, p. 15.

73. For a review of a current approach to theory and research, the reader should consult Glaser, p. 557-566.

74. Murchison, Vol. II, pp. 225-226.

75. Urie Bronfenbrenner, "The Experimental

Ecology of Education," Teachers College Record
78 (1976): 158; E.R. Hilgard, Theories of Learning (New York: Appleton Century Crofts, 1948),
pp. 357-358; and Kenneth W. Spence, "The Relation
of Learning Theory to the Technology of Education,"
Harvard Educational Review 29 (1959): 84-95.

76. Cronbach, pp. 241-242; John K.G. Elmgren,
"Educational Psychology," Annual Review of Psy-
chology 3 (1952): 381; Robert M. Gagne and
William D. Rohwer, Jr., "Instructional Psychology,"
Annual Review of Psychology 20 (1969): 381;
Robert Glaser and Lauren B. Resnick, "Instructional
Psychology," Annual Review of Psychology 23 (1972):
208; Kallos and Lundgren, p. 111-121; McKeachie,
pp. 186-187; and Lee S. Shulman, "Reconstruction
of Educational Research," Review of Educational
Research 40 (1970): 371-396.

77. Charles Hampden-Turner, Radical Man
(Cambridge, Mass.: Schenkman, 1970), p. 1-17; and
David R. Evans and Margaret T. Hearn, "The Growth
of Humanistic Psychology: A Review Essay," Journal
of Educational Thought 11 (1977): 73-74.

78. Hilgard, pp. 357-358.

79. Spence, pp. 84-95.

80. Bronfenbrenner, p. 158.

81. Elmgren, p. 381; Gagne and Rohwer, p. 381;
Gene V. Glass, "The Wisdom of Scientific Inquiry on
Education," Journal of Research in Science Teach-
ing 9 (1972): 3-18; Kallos and Lundgren, pp. 111-
121; and James V. Mitchell, Jr., "Education's
Challenge to Psychology: The Prediction of Behavior
from Person-Environment Interactions," Review of
Educational Research 39 (1969): 695.

82. Glenn H. Bracht and Gene V. Glass, "The
External Validity of Experiments," American Educational Research Journal 5 (1958): 437-474;
Shulman, pp. 376-383; and James A. Wiggins, "Hypothesis Validity and Experimental Laboratory

Methods," in Hubert M. Blalock, Jr., and Ann B. Blalock (Eds.), Methodology in Social Research (New York: McGraw-Hill, 1968), pp. 390-427.

83. Gagne and Rohwer, p. 381.

84. Elmgren, p. 381.

85. Mitchell, p. 695.

86. Evans and Hearn, pp. 73-74.

87. Hampden-Turner, p. 7.

88. Hampden-Turner, pp. 1-17; Sidney M. Jourard, The Transparent Self, 2nd ed (New York: Van Nostrand, 1971), pp. 8-21; Abraham H. Maslow, Toward a Psychology of Being, 2nd ed. (New York: Van Nostrand, 1968), pp. 215-222; and John Rowan, Ordinary Ecstacy Humanistic Psychology in Action (London: Routledge and Kegan Paul, 1976), pp. 173-186.

89. Mitchell, p. 698.

90. Glass, pp. 3-18.

91. Ibid., p. 4.

92. Ausubel, pp. 16-20; and Pierre de Bie, "Problem-focused Research," in UNESCO Main Trends of Research in the Social and Human Sciences. Part One: Social Sciences (Paris: Mouton, 1970), pp. 578-644.

93. Ausubel, p. 16.

94. de Bie, pp. 590-591. The problem-oriented research model discussed by de Bie is very similar to the notion of a linking science advocated by Robert Glaser, "Cognitive Psychology and Instructional Design," in David Klahr (ed.), Cognition and Instruction (New York: Wiley, 1976), pp. 303-315.

95. N.L. Gage, "Paradigms for Research on

Teaching," in N.L. Gage (Ed.), <u>Handbook of Research on Teaching</u> (Chicago: Rand McNally, 1963), pp. 97-99.

96. Ibid., p. 98.

97. Ibid., p. 98.

98. This concern has been echoed by numerous other educational psychologists such as Ausubel, p. 18; Bronfenbrenner, p. 157; and Warburton, pp. 371-373.

99. The term basic applied research is used to delineate research, which is directed toward practical ends, but which is just as basic for its domain as research in the pure science. See Ausubel, pp. 14-20.

100. Leslie D. McLean, "Research Methodology in Educational Psychology," in Joel R. Davitz and Samuel Ball (Eds.), <u>Psychology of the Educational Process</u> (New York: McGraw-Hill, 1970), pp. 575-616; and Wiggins, pp. 390-427.

101. McLean, pp. 586-588.

102. Hubert M. Blalock, Jr., <u>Casual Inferences in Non experimental Research</u> (Chapel Hill: University of North Carolina Press, 1964); Donald T. Campbell and Julian C. Stanley, "Experimental and Quasi-Experimental Designs for Research on Teaching," in N.L. Gage (Ed.), <u>Handbook of Research on Teaching</u> (Chicago: Rand McNally, 1963), pp. 171-246; Bracht and Glass, pp. 437-474; Shulman, pp. 371-396; and Richard E. Snow, "Representative and Quasi-Representative Designs for Research on Teaching," <u>Review of Educational Research</u> 44 (1974): 265-291.

103. They summarize their work in three tables, Campbell and Stanley, pp. 178, 210 and 226.

104. Cronbach, p. 242; see also Ausubel, p. 19; Kallos and Lundgren, pp. 11-121; and Mitchell, pp. 695-699.

105. Carl E. Thoresen, "Relevance and Research in Counselling," Review of Educational Research 39 (1969): 275-278.

106. Kallos and Lundgren, pp. 117-119.

107. Bronfenbrenner, pp. 157-204.

108. Ibid., p. 157.

109. O.G. Brim, "Macro-structural Influences on Child Development and the Need for Childhood Social Indicators," American Journal of Ortho-psychiatry 45 (1975): 516-524.

110. Blalock, pp. 28-181; and Campbell and Stanley, pp. 171-246.

111. Bronfenbrenner, pp. 158-204; Kallos and Lundgren, pp. 117-119; and Thoresen, pp. 275-278.

112. Maurice M. Tatsuoka, "Multivariate Analysis in Educational Research," Review of Research in Education 1 (1973): 273-319.

113. Robert Havighurst, Developmental Tasks and Education (New York: Longmans, Green, 1952).

114. Frances Ilg and Louise Bates Ames, The Gesell Institute's Child Behaviour (New York: Dell, 1955). For a description of the Gesell Institute's Readiness Tests see Frances Ilg and Louise Bates Ames, School Readiness (New York: Harper and Row, 1965).

115. For criticisms of the methodology used by the Gesell Institute see Robert F. Biehler, Psychology Applied to Teaching (Boston: Houghton Mifflin, 1971): 73-76.

116. For example, Jean Piaget, The Origins of Intelligence in Children (New York: International Universities Press, 1952); "Piaget's Theory in P. H. Mussen (Ed.), Carmichael's Manual of Child Psy-

chology (New York: John Wiley and Sons, 1970):
70-732; Jean Piaget and Barbel Inhelder, The
Growth of Logical Thinking from Childhood to
Adolescence (New York: Basic Books, 1958); The
Psychology of the Child, trans. Helen Weaver (New
York: Basic Books, 1973). See also Ruth L. Ault,
Children's Cognitive Development (New York: Ox-
ford University Press, 1977) for a non-technical
presentation of Piaget's Theory, and J.H. Flavell,
The Developmental Psychology of Jean Piaget
(Princeton, New Jersey: Van Nostrand, 1963) for
a comprehensive interpretation.

117. Amongst these may be found Ausubel,
Educational; Daniel E. Berlyne, Structure and
Direction in Thinking (New York: Wiley, 1965),
Jerome S. Bruner, Toward A Theory of Instruction
(Cambridge, Mass.: Harvard University Press,
1966). Lawrence Kohlberg, "Stages of Moral De-
velopment as a Basis for Moral Education," in C.
Beck, E. Sullivan, and D. Crittendon (Eds.), Moral
Education (Toronto: University of Toronto Press,
1971): 23-92.

118. For primary grade "graduates" of Head
Start programs.

119. See C.K. Kamii, "An Application of
Piaget's Theory to the Conceptualization of a Pre-
school Curriculum," in R.K. Parker (Ed.), The Pre-
School in Action: Exploring Early Childhood Pro-
grams (Boston: Allyn and Bacon, 1972): 91-131;
_____ and N.L. Radin, "A Framework for a Pre-
school Curriculum Based on Some Piagetian Concepts,"
Journal of Creative Behavior 1 (1967): 314-324;
C. Stendler-Lavatelli, Piaget's Theory Applied to an
Early Childhood Curriculum (Boston: American
Science and Engineering, 1970); H. Sonquist, C.K.
Kamii, and L. Derman, "Applying Some Piagetian Con-
cepts in the Classroom for the Disadvantaged,"
Young Children 22 (1967): 231-245.

120. Some critics have argued that Piaget's
theory has no relevance for instruction. For discussion of this argument see S. Engelman, "Does

the Piagetian approach imply instruction?" in D. R. Green, M.P. Ford and G.B. Flamer (Eds.), Measurement and Piaget (New York: McGraw-Hill, 1971): 118-147.

121. For arguments for and against the universality of cognitive stages see P.T. Ashton, "Cross-cultural Piagetian Research: an experimental perspective," Harvard Educational Review 45 (1975): 475-506; G. Jahoda, "A Cross-Cultural Perspective in Psychology," The Advancement of Science 72 (1970): 57-70.

122. T.G. Bower, Development in Infancy (San Francisco: Freeman, 1974).

123. R.M. Povey and E. Hill, "Can Preschool Children Form Concepts?" Educational Research 17 (1972): 180-192.

124. C.J. Brainerd, "The Origins of Number Concepts," Scientific American 228 (1973): 101-109.

125. L.S. Siegel, "The Sequence of Development of Certain Number Concepts in Preschool Children," Developmental Psychology 5 (1971): 357-361.

126. M.C. Wang, L.B. Resnick, and R.F. Boozer, "The Sequence of Development of Some Early Mathematics Behavior," Child Development 42 (1971): 1767-1778.

127. G. Brown and C. Desforges, "Piagetian Psychology and Education: Time for Revision," British Journal of Educational Psychology 47 (1977): 7-17.

128. Ibid., p.9.

129. Piaget has called the acceleration question the "American Question," stating this question is asked every time he visits America, and only there. Further discussion of Piaget's views regarding acceleration may be found in D. Elkind,

258

"Giant in the Nursery - Jean Piaget," New York Times Magazine, May 26 (1968): 25-80.

130. Jean Piaget, "How Children Form Mathematical Concepts," Scientific American 189 (1953): 74-79.

131. L. Kohlberg, "Early Education: A Cognitive:Developmental View," Child Development 39 (1968): 1013-1062; H. Furth, Piaget For Teachers (Englewood Cliffs, New Jersey: Prentice-Hall, 1970).

132. The conserving child can reason that transformations in irrelevant parameters of a substance (e.g. position, shape) do not change relevant parameters (number, mass, volume etc.) of that substance.

133. Flavell, p. 377; Kohlberg, p. 1031.

134. R. Glaser and L.B. Resnick, pp. 207-276; C.J. Brainerd and T.W. Allen, "Experimental Induction of the Conservation of "First Order" Quantitative Invariants," Psychological Bulletin 75 (1971): 128-144.

135. Glaser and Resnick, p. 235.

136. Ibid., p. 235.

137. Reviews by Glaser and Resnick, pp. 236-240; H.J. Klausmeier and F.H. Hooper, "Conceptual Development and Instruction" in Review of Research in Education 2 (1974): 28-31.

138. The informal relationship between British education and the theories of Jean Piaget is discussed in D.E. Elkind, D. Hetzel, and J. Coe, "Piaget and British Primary Education," Educational Psychologist 11 (1974): 1-10.

139. Klausmeier and Hooper, p. 32.

140. Brainerd and Allen, pp. 139-141; Glaser and Resnick, p. 236.

141. Brainerd and Allen, pp. 139-143; Klaus-meier and Hooper, p. 33; S. Strauss, "Learning Theories of Gagne and Piaget: Implications for Curriculum Development," Teachers College Record 74 (1972): pp. 99.

142. For explication of a Piagetian based curriculum stressing both socio-emotional and cognitive objectives see Kamii, In Application, pp. 91-131.

143. C.J. Brainerd, "Mathematical and Behavioral Foundations of Number," Journal of General Psychology 88 (1973): 221-281.

144. Glaser and Resnick, p. 227; Klausmeier and Hooper, p. 33; Strauss, pp. 100-102.

145. Reportedly, the universities of Geneva and Montreal have been engaged for some time in developing scales of reasoning based on Piaget's theory. In the event that such scales do represent a reliable estimate of qualitative reasoning, they appear to offer more in terms of diagnosis and intervention than conventional intelligence tests.

146. S.O. Decroly and J. Degand, "Les tests de Binet et Simon pour la mesure de l'intelligence: contribution critique," Archive de Psycholigie 6 (1907): 130, cited in T.H. Wolf, Alfred Binet (Chicago: University of Chicago Press, 1973), p. 188.

147. For a comprehensive overview of the field of educational assessment the reader is referred to J.S. Ahmann and M.D. Glock, Evaluating Pupil Growth, 5th Edn. (Boston: Allyn and Bacon, 1975); and F.G. Brown, Principles of Educational and Psychological Testing, 2nd. Ed. (New York: Holt, Rinehart and Winston, 1976).

148. Ahmann and Glock, pp. 193-219.

149. S. Henrysson, "The criterion-referenced test: Its meaning and difficulties" in H.F. Crombag

and D.N. Degruijter, Contemporary Issues in Educational Testing (The Hague: Moulton, 1974), pp.
101-107; J.A. Meskauskas, "Evaluation Models for
Criterion-Referenced Testing: Views Regarding
Mastery and Standard-Setting," Review of Educational Research 46 (1976): 133-158; and I. Wedman,
"On the evaluation of criterion-referenced tests,"
in Crombag and Degruijter, pp. 108-118.

150. Wedman, pp. 108-118.

151. Meskauskas, pp. 133-158.

152. The above arguments concerning criterion-
referenced testing applies equally well to student
evaluation especially when it occurs in the context
of the mastery learning paradigm.

153. Ahmann and Glock, pp. 67-192.

154. For a more detailed discussion of some
of the issues related to evaluative testing see
Brown, pp. 457-468; and Ausubel, pp. 565-589.

155. R. Craig, W. Mehrens, and H. Clarizio,
Contemporary Educational Psychology (New York:
Wiley, 1975): 292-294.

156. Ausubel, pp. 259-265; W.C. Becker,
"Applications of Behavior Principles in Typical
Classrooms" in Thoreson, Behavior, pp. 77-106;
and Craig, Mehrens and Clarizio, pp. 279-292.

157. G. Austin, D. Preston, W. Stewart, E.
Baldwin, G. Riggins and K.M. Salyer, "Some Perspectives on Compensatory Education and Inequality,"
Contemporary Educational Psychology 2 (1977): 311-
320; and A.H. Passow, "Compensatory Instructional
Intervention," Review of Research in Education 2
(1974): 145-175.

158. M. Reynolds, "A Framework for Considering
Some Issues in Special Education," Exceptional
Children 20 (1969): p. 368.

159. Ausubel, p. 267.

160. Craig, Mehrens and Clarizio, pp. 292-293.

161. S.W. Bijon, "Behavior Modification in Teaching the Retarded Child," in Thoresen, pp. 259-290; E.M. Hanley, "Review of Research Involving Applied Behavior Analysis in the Classroom," Review of Educational Research 40 (1970): 597-625; and S.A. Hobbs and B.B. Lahey, "The Behavioral Approach to Learning Disabled Children," Journal of Clinical Child Psychology (1977): 10-14.

162. H.L. Cohen, "Behavior Modification and Socially Deviant Youth," in Thoresen, pp. 291-314; Hanley, pp. 597-625; Hobbs and Lahey, pp. 10-14; O.I. Lovaas and R.L. Koegel, "Behavior Modification with Autistic Children," in Thoresen, pp. 230-258; and A. W. Statts, "Behavior Analysis and Token Reinforcement in Educational Behavior Modification and Curriculum Research," in Thoresen, pp. 195-229.

163. Craig, Mehrens and Clarizio, pp. 292-293.

164. S.R. Forness, "A Transition Model for Placement of Handicapped Children in Regular and Special Classes," Contemporary Educational Psychology 2 (1977): 37-49.

165. P.E. Vernon, G. Adamson and D.F. Vernon, The Psychology of Education of Gifted Children (London: Methuen, 1977), p. 1.

166. Ausubel, pp. 265-267; Craig, Mehrens and Clarizio, pp. 293-295; and Vernon, Adamson and Vernon, pp. 138-196.

167. Austin et al., pp. 311-320; and Passow, pp. 145-175.

168. Perhaps the earliest psychological study of learning was that by H. Ebbinhaus, Uber das Gedachtuis in 1885, which was translated as Memory: A Contribution to Experimental Psychology (New York: Teachers College, Columbia University, 1913).

Periods of optimism are exemplified by the application of the theories of B.F. Skinner, The Technology of Teaching (New York: Appleton-Century-Crofts, 1968) and E.L. Thorndike, Educational Psychology: Vol. II, The Psychology of Learning (New York: Teachers College, Columbia University, 1913). Periods of pessimism are exemplified by the comments of K.W. Spence, The Relation, pp. 84-95.

169. B.S. Bloom, "Testing Cognitive Ability and Achievement," in N.L. Gage (Ed.), Handbook of Research on Teaching (Chicago: Rand McNally, 1963), p. 386; B.C. Mathis, J.W. Cotton and L. Sechrest, Psychological Foundations of Teaching (New York: Academic Press, 1970), p. 48; and G.A. Kimble, Hilgard and Marquis' Conditioning and Learning, 2nd Ed. (New York: Appleton-Century-Crofts, 1961).

170. For discussion of this point see Kimble, pp. 1-13.

171. K.W. Spence, "Resume of Symposium," The Symposium on Psychology of Learning Basic to Military Training Problems (Washington, D.C.: Research and Development Board, 1953).

172. Spence, p. 93.

173. R.M. Gagne, The Conditions of Learning (New York: Holt, Rinehart and Winston, 1965); _____, The Conditions of Learning, 2nd Edn. (New York: Holt, Rinehart and Winston, 1970).

174. S. Ball, "Learning and Teaching," in Davitz and Ball, pp. 5-59.

175. Spence, pp. 84-95.

176. G. Mandler, "Verbal Learning," in G. Mandler, P. Musson, N. Kogan, and M.A. Wallach, New Directions in Psychology III (New York: Holt, Rinehart and Winston, 1967), pp. 1-50; M.C. Wittrock and A.A. Lumsdaine, "Instructional Psychology," Annual Review of Psychology 28 (1977): 417-418.

177. D.C. Clark, "Teaching Concepts in the Classroom: A Set of Teaching Prescriptions Derived from Experimental Research," _Journal of Educational Psychology_ 62 (June, 1971): 253-278.

178. For those readers interested in a more extensive discussion of learning theory and education the following are recommended: Ball, _Learning_, pp. 5-59; Gagne, _The Conditions 2nd Edn._, pp. 36-236; and Mathis et al., _Psychological_, pp. 47-216.

179. An extensive discussion of classical conditioning is presented in Kimble, pp. 44-108.

180. J.W. Hall, "Psychological Foundations," in D.W. Allen and E. Seifman (Eds.), _The Teacher's Handbook_ (Glenview, Ill.: Scott Foresman, 1971), p. 585.

181. Gagne, pp. 36-38, 95-104.

182. McKeachie, pp. 164-165.

183. E.L. Thorndike, _Animal Intelligence_ (New York: McMillan, 1911).

184. B.F. Skinner, _Behavior of Organisms_ (New York: Appleton-Century-Crofts, 1938); _____, _Science and Human Behavior_ (New York: McMillan, 1953); _____, _The Technology_; and _____, _Verbal Behavior_ (New York: Appleton-Century-Crofts, 1957).

185. For a more extensive discussion of instrumental conditioning, see _Kimble, Hilgard and Marquis' Conditioning and Learning_.

186. Skinner, _The Technology_; and Thorndike, _Educational_.

187. C.E. Thoresen (Ed.), _Behavior Modification in Education, 72 Yearbook of the NSSE_ (Chicago: University of Chicago Press, 1973).

188. Greater detail of such programs can be obtained by refering to the numerous books and manuals in this area, such as J.T. Neisworth, S.L. Deno, and J.R. Jenkins, Student Motivation and Classroom Management: A Behavioristic Approach (Newark, Delaware: Behavior Technics, Inc., 1969); for a review of token systems in the classroom see K.D. O'Leary and R. Drabman, "Token reinforcement programs in the classroom: A Review," Psychological Bulletin 75 (1971): 379-399.

189. R.C. Anderson, "Educational Psychology," Annual Review of Psychology 18 (1967): 145-148.

190. D. Lipe and S.M. Jung, "Manipulating Incentive to Enhance School Learning," Review of Educational Research 41 (1971): 249-280.

191. F.S. Keller, "Good-Bye Teacher. . . .," Journal of Applied Behavior Analysis 1 (1968): 79-89.

192. D.R. Evans, "A Systematized Introduction to Behavior Therapy Training," Journal of Behavior Therapy and Experimental Psychiatry 7 (1976): 23-26; J.A. Kulik, C. Kulik, and K. Carmichael, "The Keller Plan in Science Teaching," Science 183 February, 1974): 379-383. J.S. McMichael and J.R. Corey, "Contingency Management in an Introductory Psychology Course Produces Better Learning," Journal of Applied Behavior Analysis 2 (1969): 79-83; and W.C. Sheppard and H.G. MacDermot, "Design and Evaluation of a Programmed Course in Introductory Psychology," Journal of Applied Behavior Analysis 3 (1970): 5-11. Excellent reviews of the PSI Movement are provided by A.L. Robin, "Behavioral Instruction in the College Classroom," Review of Educational Research 46 (1976): 313-354; and B.A. Ryan, PSI, Keller's Personalized System of Instruction: An Appraisal (Washington, D.C.: American Psychological Association, 1974).

193. B.S. Bloom, Human Characteristics and School Learning (New York: McGraw-Hill, 1976); and J.B. Carroll, "A model for School Learning,"

Teachers College Record 64 (1963): 723-733.

194. J.H. Block and R.B. Burns, "Mastery Learning," Review of Research in Education 4 (1976): 3-49.

195. Block and Burns, p. 12.

196. Bloom, Human; Block and Burns, pp. 3-49; Robin, 313-354; and Ryan, pp. 1-30.

197. E.B. Fry, Teaching Machines and Programmed Instruction: An Introduction (New York: McGraw-Hill, 1963); R.M. Gagne, "Learning and Instructional Sequence," Review of Research in Education 1 (1973): 12-15; J. Hartley, "Programmed Instruction 1954-1974: A Review," Programmed Learning and Educational Technology II (1974): 278-291; J.G. Holland, "Teaching Machines: An Application of Principles from the Laboratory," Journal of Experimental Analysis of Behavior 3 (1960): 275-287, 292; G.O.M. Leith, "Teaching by Machinery: A Review of Research," Educational Research 5 (1963): 187-199; A. Mackie, "Programmed Learning - A Developing Technique," Programmed Learning and Educational Technology 12 (1975): 220-228; C.S. Morrill, "Teaching Machines: A Review," Psychological Bulletin 58 (1961): 363-375; and E.A. Peel, "Some Psychological Principles Underlying Programmed Learning," Educational Research 5 (1963): 183-186.

198. C.L. Hull, Principles of Behavior (New York: Appleton-Century-Crofts, 1943); and K.W. Spence, Behavior Theory and Conditioning (New Haven, Conn.: Yale University Press, 1956).

199. A.S. Alschuler, D. Tabor and J. McIntyre, Teaching Achievement Motivation (Middletown, Conn.: Education Ventures Inc., 1970); R. deCharms, Can Motives of Low Income Black Children be Changed, (St. Louis, Mo.: Washington University, 1969); D.R. Evans, M.T. Hearn and W.W. Swirner, "Need Achievement Training with Grade Nine Students," Canadian Journal of Behavioral Science 7 (1975):

54-59; D.A. Kolb, "Achievement Motivation Training for Underachieving Highschool Boys," Journal of Personality and Social Psychology 2 (1965): 783-792; and D.C. McClelland, "What is the Effect of Achievement Motivation Training in the Schools?" Teachers College Record 74 (1972): 129-145.

200. Gagne, The Conditions, 2nd Ed., pp. 123-135; R.M. Gagne and L.J. Briggs, Principles of Instructional Design (New York: Holt, Rinehart and Winston, 1974), pp. 38-39, 66-68.

201. Gagne, The Conditions, 2nd Edn., p. 130.

202. Ibid., p. 134-154.

203. Mandler, pp. 28-39.

204. Ibid., pp. 28-39.

205. Gagne and Rohwer, pp. 404-405.

206. Wittrock and Lumsdaine, pp. 429-434.

207. Ausubel, pp. 37-123.

208. Gagne, pp. 147-150.

209. Ibid., pp. 157-171.

210. R.C. Anderson, "Control of Student Mediating Processes during Verbal Learning and Instruction," Review of Educational Research 40 (1970): 349-369; _____, Educational, pp. 131-139; and Gagne and Rohwer, p. 395.

211. Gagne, pp. 171-188.

212. H.J. Klausmeier, E.S. Ghatala and D.A. Frayer, Conceptual Learning and Development: A Cognitive View (New York: Academic Press, 1974).

213. Clark, Teaching, pp. 253-278.

214. Gagne, pp. 190-191.

215. Ibid., pp. 195-213.

216. Ausubel, pp. 37-359; D.E. Broadbent, "Cognitive Psychology and Education," British Journal of Educational Psychology 45 (1975): 162-176; and Mandler, pp. 8-30.

217. Gagne, pp. 203.

218. B.S. Bloom (Ed.), Taxonomy of Educational Objectives, Handbook: Cognitive Domain (New York: David McKay, 1956).

219. Gagne and Briggs, pp. 75-97.

220. P.C. Duchastel and P.F. Merrill, "The Effects of Behavioral Objectives on Learning: A Review of Empirical Studies," Review of Educational Research 43 (1973): 53-69. Wittrock and Lumsdaine, pp. 421-422.

221. J. Hartley and I.K. Davies, "Preinstructional Strategies: The Role of Pretests, Behavioral Objectives, Overviews, and Advanced Organizers," Review of Educational Research 46 (1976): 239-265.

222. Duchastel and Merrill, p. 66; Hartley and Davies, p. 256; and Wittrock and Davies, p. 422.

223. Gagne and Rohwer, pp. 395-397.

224. L.T. Frase, "Structural Analysis of the Knowledge that Results from Thinking about Text," Journal of Educational Psychology Monograph 60 (December 1969): 1-16.

225. Frase, pp. 1-16; M.D. Gall, "The Use of Questions in Teaching," Review of Educational Research 40 (1970): 707-721; Gagne, Learning, pp. 15-18; and Wittrock and Lumsdaine, pp. 419-421.

226. Wittrock and Lumsdaine, p. 421.

227. Gagne, The Conditions, 2nd Edn., pp. 203-

210; Gagne, _Learning_, pp. 21-25.

228. R.T. White, "Research into Learning Hierarchies," _Review of Educational Research_ 43 (1973):
361-375.

229. Ball, pp. 20-24.

230. A.L. Baldwin, "Social Learning," _Review
of Research in Education_ 1 (1973): 37.

231. Ibid., pp. 38-39.

232. Ibid., pp. 34-57.

233. Wittrock and Lumsdaine, pp. 437-438.

234. Gagne, _The Conditions, 2nd Edn._, pp. 214-
236.

235. Ausubel, pp. 467-504.

236. KcKeachie, pp. 180-181.

237. Ball, Learning, pp. 47-48; Gagne, pp. 227-
229; Ausubel, pp. 533-562.

238. R.E. Ripple, "Communication, Education
and Creativity," _Contemporary Educational Psychol-
ogy_ 2 (1977): 219-231.

239. Wittrock and Lumsdaine, pp. 426-427.

240. Gagne and Briggs, pp. 35-71.

241. D.R. Evans, "Conceptual Complexity and
Epistemic Behaviour," _Canadian Journal of Psychol-
ogy_ 24 (1970): 249-260.

242. Kallos and Lundgren, pp. 111-121; and
Mitchell, pp. 695-721.

243. L.T. Cronbach, "The Two Disciplines of
Scientific Psychology," _American Psychologist_ 12
(1957): 671-684.

244. L.J. Cronbach, "Beyond the Two Disciplines of Scientific Psychology," American Psychologist 30 (1975): 116-127.

245. For more comprehensive reviews of this area the reader should refer to the following: D.C. Berliner and L.S. Cohen, "Trait-Treatment Interaction and Learning," Review of Research in Education 1 (1973): 58-94; Bloom, Human, pp. 1-273; D.E. Hunt, "Person-Environment Interaction: A Challenge Found Wanting Before it was Tried," Review of Educational Research 45 (1975): 209-230; Mitchel, Education's, pp. 695-721; R.E. Snow, "Research on Aptitude for Learning: A Progress Report," Review of Research in Education 4 (1976): 50-105; and H.J. Walberg, Models, 15-27.

246. Berliner and Cohen, pp. 59.

247. L.J. Cronbach and R.E. Snow, Aptitudes and Instructional Methods: A Handbook for Research on Interactions (New York: Irvington, in press), p. 6.

248. Snow, p. 52.

249. Berliner and Cohen, pp. 69-85; and Snow, pp. 54-99.

250. Bloom, p. 111.

251. Ibid., pp. 1-265.

252. Hunt, p. 217.

253. Ibid., pp. 222-223.

254. Ibid., pp. 209-230.

255. Bronfenbrenner, pp. 157-204; Kallos and Lundgren, pp. 111-121; and Walberg, pp. 15-27.

256. Walberg, p. 22.

257. Berliner and Cohen, p. 59.

258. Ibid., pp. 64-66.

259. Tatsuoka, pp. 273-319.

260. Hunt, pp. 209-230.

261. Glaser and Resnick, pp. 242-244; and McKeachie, p. 167.

262. Snow, p. 51.

263. Cronbach and Snow, in press.

264. Berliner and Cohen, pp. 66-69; Snow, pp. 51-54; and Wittrock and Lumsdaine, p. 437.

265. Berliner and Cohen, p. 67.

266. Hunt, pp. 210-216.

267. For a discussion of the application of humanistic principles to public school, under-graduate and graduate education, see Carl R. Rogers, Freedom to Learn (Columbus, Ohio: Charles E. Merrill, 1969).

268. Carl E. Thoresen, "Behavioral Humanism," in Carl E. Thoresen, Behavior, pp. 385-421.

269. Carl Rogers, "Comment on Brown and Tedeschi's Article," Journal of Humanistic Psychology 12 (1972): 19.

270. Rogers, Freedom, pp. 10-97.

271. Rogers has described the teacher as one "who is sufficiently secure within and secure in relationship to others that he or she experiences an essential trust in the capacity of others to think for themselves, to learn for themselves." Carl Rogers, "Beyond the Watershed: And Where Now," Educational Leadership 34 (1977): p. 626.

272. Rogers, Beyond, p. 627.

273. William Bridges, "Thoughts on Humanistic Education, or, Is Teaching a Dirty Word," Journal of Humanistic Psychology 13 (1973): 5-13; H. Franzwa, "Limitations in Applying Humanistic Psychology in the Classroom," Today's Speech 21 (1973): 31-36; Robert C. Brown, Jr. and James T. Redeschi, "Graduate Education in Psychology: A Comment on Rogers' Passionate Statement," Journal of Humanistic Psychology 12 (1972): 1-15.

274. Charles M. Rossiter, "Maxims for Humanizing Education," Journal of Humanistic Psychology 16 (1976): 75-80.

275. Human Relations training was developed by Robert R. Carkhuff as a method of training health professionals in the facilitative conditions identified by Carl Rogers. See, Helping and Human Relations: A primer for Lay and Professional Helpers, Vol. 1, Selection and Training, Vol. 11, Practice and Research (New York: Holt, Rinehart and Winston, 1969).

276. David Aspy, Toward a Technology for Humanizing Education (Champaign, Illinois: Research Press, 1972).

277. D.N. Aspy and W. Hadlock, "The Effect of Empathy, Warmth and Genuineness on Elementary Students' Reading Achievement," reviewed in C.B. Truax and R.R. Carkhuff, Toward Effective Counselling and Psychotherapy (Chicago: Aldine, 1967): pp. 116-117.

278. K. Pierce, "An Investigation of Grade-point Average and Therapeutic Process Variables," reviewed in R.R. Carkhuff and G.B. Bereson, Beyond Counseling and Therapy (New York: Holt, Rinehart and Winston, 1967):

279. David Aspy, Toward, pp. 40-46, 59-66.

280. R. Schmuck, "Some Aspects of Classroom Social Climate," Psychology in the Schools 3 (1966): 59-65.

281. D.N. Aspy and F.N. Roebuck, "From Humane Ideas to Humane Technology and Back Again Many Times," Education 95 (1974): 163-171; _____ et al., Interim Reports 1, 2, 3, 4 (Monroe, Louisiana: National Consortium for Humanizing Education, 1974). A brief summary of these findings is available in Rogers, Beyond, pp. 627-628.

282. John P. Miller, Humanizing the Classroom (New York: Praeger, 1976).

283. Rogers, Beyond, p. 624.

BIBLIOGRAPHY

Ahmann, J.S. and Glock, M.D. Evaluating Pupil Growth. Boston: Allyn and Bacon, 1975.

Allen, D.W. and Seifman, E. The Teacher's Handbook. Glenview, Ill.: Scott Foresman, 1971.

Alschuler, A.S., Tabor, D. and McIntyre, J. Teaching Achievement Motivation. Middletown, Conn.: Educational Ventures Inc., 1970.

Anderson, R.C. "Educational Psychology." Annual Review of Psychology 18 (1967): 129-164.

Anderson, R.C. "Control of Student Mediating Processes during Verbal Learning and Instruction." Review of Educational Research 40 (1970): 349-369.

Aspy, D. Toward a Technology for Humanizing Behavior. Champaign, Illinois: Research Press, 1972.

Ault, R.L. Children's Cognitive Development. New York: Oxford University Press, 1977.

Austin, G., Preston, D., Stewart, W., Baldwin, E., Riggins, G., and Salyer, K.M. "Some Perspectives on Compensatory Education and Inequality." Contemporary Educational Psychology 2 (1977): 311-320.

Ausubel, D.P. Educational Psychology: A Cognitive View. New York: Holt, Rinehart and Winston, 1968.

Baldwin, A.L. "Social Learning." Review of Research in Education 1 (1973): 34-57.

Belkin, G.S. and Gray, J.L. Educational Psychology: An Introduction. Dubuque, Iowa: Wm. C. Brown, 1977.

Berliner, D.C. and Cahen, L.S. "Trait-Treatment

Interaction and Learning." Review of Research
in Education 1 (1973): 58-94.

Blalock, H.M. Causal Inferences in Nonexperimental
Research. New York: Norton, 1964.

Blalock, H.M. and Blalock, A.B. Methodology in
Social Research. New York: McGraw-Hill, 1968.

Block, J.H. and Burns, R.B. "Mastery Learning."
Review of Research in Education 4 (1976): 3-49.

Bloom, B.S. Human Characteristics and School Learning. New York: McGraw-Hill, 1976.

Bracht, G.H. and Glass, G.V. "The External Validity
of Experiments." American Educational Research
Journal 5 (1968): 437-474.

Brainerd, C.J. "Mathematical and Behavioral
Foundations of Number." Journal of General
Psychology 88 (1973): 221-281.

Brainerd, C.J. and Allen, T.W. "Experimental Induc-
tions of the Conservation of 'First Order'
Quantitative Invariants." Psychological Bulletin 75 (1971): 128-144.

Broadbent, D.E. "Cognitive Psychology and Education." British Journal of Educational Psychology 45 (1975): 162-176.

Bronfenbrenner, U. "The Experimental Ecology of
Education." Teachers' College Record 78 (1976):
157-204.

Brown, F.G. Principles of Educational and Psychological Testing. New York: Holt, Rinehart and
Winston, 1976.

Brown, G. and Desforges, C. "Piagetian Psychology
and Education: Time for Revision." British
Journal of Educational Psychology 47 (1977):
1-17.

Bruner, J. Toward a Theory of Instruction. Cambridge, Mass.: Harvard University Press, 1966.

Carroll, J.B. "The Place of Educational Psychology in the Study of Education," in The Disciplines of Education, edited by J. Walton and J. Kuethe. Madison: The University of Wisconsin Press, 1963.

Charles, D.C. "A Historical Overview of Educational Psychology." Contemporary Educational Psychology 1 (1976): 76-88.

Clark, D.C. "Teaching Concepts in the Classroom: A Set of Teaching Prescriptions Derived from Experimental Research." Journal of Educational Psychology 62 (1971): 253-278.

Craig, R., Mehrens, W. and Clarizio, H. Contemporary Educational Psychology. New York. Wiley, 1975.

Cronbach, L.J. "Beyond the Two Disciplines of Scientific Psychology." American Psychologist 30 (1975): 116-127.

Cronbach, L.T. and Snow, R.E. Aptitudes and Instructional Methods: A Handbook for Research on Interactions. New York: Irvington, in press.

Davitz, J.R. and Ball, S. Psychology of Educational Process. New York: McGraw-Hill, 1970.

De Bie, P. "Problem-focused Research" in Main Trends of Research in the Social and Human Sciences, Part 1: Social Sciences, edited by UNESCO. Paris: Mouton, 1970.

Duchastel, P.C. and Merrill, P.F. "The Effects of Behavioural Objectives on Learning: A Review of Empirical Studies." Review of Educational Research 43 (1973): 53-69.

Evans, D.R. and Hearn, M.T. "The Growth of Humanistic Psychology." Journal of Educational
Thought 11 (1977): 64-76.

Evans, D.R., Hearn, M.T. and Swirner, W.W. "Need
Achievement Training with Grade-nine students."
Canadian Journal of Behavioral Science 7 (1975):
54-59.

Flavell, J.H. The Developmental Psychology of
Jean Piaget. Princeton, New Jersey: Van Nostrand, 1963.

Forness, S.R. "A Transition Model for Placement of
Handicapped Children in Regular and Special
Classes." Contemporary Educational Psychology
2 (1977): 37-49.

Fry, E.B. Teaching Machines and Programmed Instruction: An Introduction. New York: McGraw-Hill,
1963.

Gage, N.L. Handbook of Research on Teaching.
Chicago: Rand McNally, 1963.

Gage, N.L. The Psychology of Teaching Methods, 75th
Yearbook of the NSSE. Chicago: University of
Chicago Press, 1976.

Gagne, R.M. The Conditions of Learning, 2nd Edn.
New York: Holt, Rinehart and Winston, 1970.

Gagne, R.M. "Learning and Instructional Sequence."
Review of Research in Education 1 (1973): 3-33.

Gagne, R.M. and Briggs, L.J. Principles of Instructional Design. New York: Holt, Rinehart and
Winston, 1974.

Gagne, R.M. and Rohwer, W.D. "Instructional Psychology." Annual Review of Psychology 20
(1969): 381-418.

Gall, M.D. "The Use of Questions in Teaching."
Review of Educational Research 40 (1970): 707-721.

Glaser, R. and Resnick, L.B. "Instructional Psychology." Annual Review of Psychology 23 (1972): 207-276.

Glass, G.V. "The Wisdom of Scientific Inquiry on Education." Journal of Research in Science Teaching 9 (1972): 3-18.

Green, D.R., Ford, M.P. and Flamer, G.B. Measurement and Piaget. New York: McGraw-Hill, 1971.

Grinder, R.E. "The Growth of Education Psychology as Reflected in the History of Division 15." Educational Psychologist 4 (1967): 13, 15, 16, 23, 27, 30, 31, 35.

Hanley, E.M. "Review of Research Involving Applied Behavior Analysis in the Classroom." Review of Educational Research 40 (1970): 597-625.

Hartley, J. "Programmed Instruction 1954-1974: A Review." Programmed Learning and Educational Technology 11 (1974): 278-291.

Hartley, J. and Davies, I.K. "Preinstructional Strategies: The Role of Pretests, Behavioral Objectives, Overviews, and Advanced Organizers." Review of Educational Research 46 (1976): 239-265.

Hobbs, S.A. and Lahey, B.B. "The Behavioral Approach to 'Learning Disabled' Children." Journal of Clinical Child Psychology 6 (1977): 10-14.

Hunt, D.E. "Person-Environment Interaction: A Challenge Found Wanting Before it was Tried." Review of Educational Research 45 (1975): 209-230.

Kimble, G.A. Hilgard and Marquis' Conditioning and Learning, 2nd Edn. New York: Appleton-Century-Crofts, 1961.

Klausmeier, H.J., Ghatala, E.S. and Frayer, D.A.

Conceptual Learning and Development: A Cognitive View. New York: Academic Press, 1974.

Kulik, J.A., Kulik, C. and Carmichael, K. "The Keller Plan in Science Teaching." Science 183 (1974): 379-383.

Lipe, D. and Jung, S.M. "Manipulating Incentives to Enhance School Learning." Review of Educational Research 41 (1971): 249-280.

Mackie, A. "Programmed Learning - A Developing Technique." Programmed Learning and Educational Technology 12 (1975): 220-278.

Mandler, G. "Verbal Learning" in New Directions in Psychology III, edited by G. Mandler, N. Kogan and M.A. Wallach. New York: Holt, Rinehart and Winston, 1967.

Mathis, B.C., Cotton, J.W. and Sechrest, L. Psychological Foundations of Teaching. New York: Academic Press, 1970.

McClelland, D.C. "What is the Effect of Achievement Motivation Training in the Schools?" Teachers College Record 74 (1972): 129-145.

McKeachie, W.J. "Instructional Psychology." Annual Review of Psychology 25 (1974): 161-193.

Meskauskas, J.A. "Evaluation Models for Criterion-Referenced Testing: Views Regarding Mastery and Standard-Setting." Review of Educational Research 46 (1976): 133-158.

Miller, J.P. Humanizing the Classroom. New York: Praeger, 1976.

Morris, B. "The Contribution of Psychology to the Study of Education" in The Study of Education, edited by J.W. Tibble. London: Routledge and Kegan Paul, 1966.

Murphy, G. Historical Introduction to Modern

Psychology. New York: Harcourt, Brace and World, 1949.

Neisworth, J.T., Deno, S.L. and Jenkins, J.R. Student Motivation and Classroom Management: A Behavioristic Approach. Newark, Delaware: Behavior Technics, Inc., 1969.

O'Leary, K.D. and Drabman, R. "Token Reinforcement Programs in the Classroom: A Review." Psychological Bulletin 75 (1971): 379-399.

Passow, A.H. "Compensatory Instructional Intervention." Review of Research in Education 2 (1974): 145-175.

Piaget, J. The Origins of Intelligence in Children. New York: International Universities Press, 1952.

Piaget, J. "Piaget's Theory." In Carmichael's Manual of Child Psychology, edited by P.H. Mussen. New York: Wiley, 1970.

Piaget, J. and Inhelder, B. The Growth of Logical Thinking from Childhood to Adolescence. New York: Basic Books, 1958.

Ripple, R.E. "Communication, Education, and Creativity." Contemporary Educational Psychology 2 (1977): 219-231.

Robin, A.L. "Behavioral Instruction in the College Classroom." Review of Educational Research 46 (1976): 313-354.

Rogers, C. Freedom to Learn. Columbus, Ohio: Charles E. Merrill, 1969.

Rogers, C. "Beyond the Watershed: And Where Now?" Educational Leadership 34 (1977): 623-631.

Ryan, B.A. PSI Keller's Personalized System of Instruction: An Appraisal. Washington, D.C. American Psychological Association, 1974.

Shulman, L.S. "Reconstruction of Educational Research." Review of Educational Research 40 (1970): 371-396.

Skinner, B.F. The Technology of Teaching. New York: Appleton-Century-Crofts, 1968.

Smedslund, J. "Educational Psychology." Annual Review of Psychology 15 (1964): 251-276.

Snow, R.E. "Representative and Quasi-representative Designs for Research on Teaching." Review of Educational Research 44 (1974): 265-291.

Snow, R.E. "Research on Aptitude for Learning: A Progress Report." Review of Research in Education 4 (1976): 50-105.

Spence, K.W. "The Relation of Learning Theory to the Technology of Education." Harvard Educational Review 29 (1959): 84-95.

Tatsuoka, M.M. "Multivariate Analysis in Educational Research." Review of Research in Education 1 (1973): 273-319.

Thoresen, C.E. Behavior Modification in Education, 72nd Yearbook of the NSSE. Chicago: University of Chicago Press, 1973.

Vernon, P.E., Adamson, G. and Vernon, D.F. The Psychology and Education of Gifted Children. London: Methuen, 1977.

Walberg, H.J. "Models for Optimizing and Individualizing School Learning." Interchange 2 (1971): 15-27.

Watson, R.I. "A Brief History of Educational Psychology." Psychological Record II (1961): 209-242.

Webb, E.J., Campbell, D.T., Schwartz, R.D. and Sechrest, L. Unobtrusive Measures: Nonreactive Research in the Social Sciences. Chicago:

Rand McNally, 1966.

White, R.T. "Research into Learning Hierarchies."
    Review of Educational Research 43 (1973): 361-
    375.

Wittrock, M.C. and Lumsdaine, A.A. "Instructional
    Psychology." Annual Review of Psychology 28
    (1977): 417-459.

CHAPTER 4

PHILOSOPHY OF EDUCATION

INTRODUCTION

Education is a normative activity. It is always characterized by what ought to be done and by what is best done. The commitment to educate is itself a choice which, though very generally taken for granted, may be given up. The choice is, as R.S. Peters points out, like the choice for reform at least in that it is directed to the betterment of whoever is the subject of this kind of activity. Those who educate necessarily intend positive changes which ought to be pursued or which are best achieved. Thus, to educate is to have in mind aims and goals of study and learning, and it is to choose to act in fulfillment of these. The normative nature of education is further constituted of judgments about what curriculum should be followed, to whom it should be taught, and how it should be taught to those who are its beneficiaries. Without such judgments education does not occur. Educational judgments draw heavily on the scientific study of education--on the study of cognition, learning, evaluation, organization, etc.; but in every case of educational conduct, aims, principles, standards and rules give point and structure. It is the normative character of education which gives rise to the philosophical study of education. In every setting of aim, in every assumption of principle, in every choice of technique and in every application of standard, it is compelling to ask why. Philosophy of education is the activity of understanding and clarifying the formal and conceptual elements of the kinds of answer which constitute justification. It is analysis of the concepts and the arguments central to the cultural enterprise of education. It is, then, a theoretical activity, the justification of which rests in the practice of educating persons. Philosophical study is reflexive. It is the disciplined examination of educational thinking, of

283

all educational thinking, including (after empirical explanation, justification, and examination of the form and axioms of justification) philosophical criticism of educational theory. This chapter is itself a critical examination of the point and adequacy of the philosophical study of education.

The traditional view of philosophy is of a rational contemplation of ultimate principles. While science deals with facts, and mathematics with numbers, philosophy is widely believed to deal systematically with fundamental principles and axiomatic assumptions of a non-material reality and human character--principles and assumptions which explain what can be known and what ought to be valued. This perception of philosophy is reflected in several general tendencies: expecting that philosophical statements will be esoteric and impractical; believing that philosophical argument is largely beyond the intellectual motivation of most people; loosely describing any statement of assumptions, rationale, or non-scientific explanation as philosophical; and uncritically regarding "philosophical" accounts with either great deference or great disdain. "A philosophy" is commonly thought to deal with the whole of reality and consequently with the holes in common sense and scientific explanation. The philosopher is commonly acknowledged to be the expert on reason and argument as the basis of his special insight of the fundamental and the whole. The philosopher is expected to be the wise man, or more literally the lover of wisdom, who by the exercise of reason is (thought to be) able to make clear the ideational nature of the reality behind and beyond the physical and social reality. Philosophy is traditionally identified by the serious and sustained effort to answer the questions of being, human nature, mind, knowledge and language, beauty, morality and social order, and related questions of logic, truth, perception, induction, memory and identity, God, free will, beauty, society, and so on.

However, the modern development of distinctive, and apparently independent, disciplines of thought in the physical and social sciences has subsequently diminished the philosophical range of epistemological authority, and has resulted in serious uncertainty about the role and warrant of philosophical claims. The diffusion of the authority of reason through many areas and kinds of expertise requires of each that it establish its authority. The task is particularly difficult for the deposed "queen of the sciences." Deposition suggests lack of authority and encourages little consideration of the legitimacy of a limited and unique authority for former monarchs. The task for philosophy has been to identify the criteria of warrant for philosophical claims and by that to identify its particular contribution to human understanding.

Philosophy of education has the same responsibility despite its point of distinction related to the conduct of education by public schooling. The need for a broadly accepted critical theory of education, created by national commitment to public schooling, sustained philosophy of education as a distinctive field of inquiry and study long after the arousal of public uncertainty with philosophical claims per se.[1] This odity lies behind a not so common but telling belief that philosophers of education relentlessly hold a traditional view of philosophy as the primary and formational discipline of education. The belief is supported by the fact that some educators still conceive philosophy of education as the theory of education. A major task of this chapter is to correct this mistaken belief by showing what philosophy of education is, what kind of claim it makes, on what warrant, and to what end.

HISTORICAL COMMENT: PHILOSOPHY AND EDUCATION

The tradition of philosophy of education is distinguished from the tradition of general

285

philosophy by its constant orientation to the practise of instruction and its comparative lack of destructive scepticism. Philosophy of education is identified by the questions of philosophy in general as they relate to and arise out of the practical conduct of the cultural and social enterprise of initiating persons into disciplined modes of thought and action. The recognition of philosophy of education as a professionally distinctive scholarly activity, however, is relatively recent. Through much of the philosophical history of the western world education was not of distinctive philosophical interest in itself. Though philosophical instruction was a continuing engagement through this history, the general enterprise of education was the focus of philosophical attention mainly as a function of social philosophy. Plato turned his attention to education as the instrument of implementation and maintenance of the ideal state. For Augustine education became a focal interest in the context of restoring the community of God. John Locke attended to the education of the landed gentry as the class of men responsible for government of private-property rights, which he took to be the principle function of government. Rousseau turned to education as the means of assuring the individual stability of gentlemen in the face of revolutionary social change. Mill also saw education as the development of human character, in his case in fulfillment of the social ideal of the greatest happiness for the greatest number. Throughout this history of philosophical consideration, education is of significance as an instrument of social ends. Particular philosophers discussed education largely as instructional process deriving its point and form from their metaphysical and epistemological theories.[2] Because of its conceptual connection with behavioral and cognitive training, it is unlikely that the relevance of education as an instrument of social ends will be ignored in social and political philosophy. However, through the 19th century and the early part of the 20th century a significant change occurred in the philosophical attention to education. During this period

286

education was increasingly viewed as a social end in itself.

Following on Rousseau's interest in the training of women and his attention to the educational conditions of individual understanding and character in the context of a pessimistic analysis of social and political order, the philosophical interests of Pestalozzi, Froebel, Herbart, and Herbert Spencer were marked by the recognition of education as the cognitive and intellectual development of the individual.[3] These men variously sought to explicate the pattern and stages of development, the complex relationship of motor, cognitive and social development, the achievement of abstract reasoning and a generative intellect, and the fulfillment of individual conditions of self-generalization--intellectual, social, and aesthetic. Education as development was more and more recognized as a right of persons, as a responsibility of the state, and as the foundation of democratic social organization. This shift in focus from the instrumental to the intrinsic value of education is the origin of philosophy of education as a distinctive field of scholarly study. The work of John Dewey clearly established an educational perspective in philosophical scholarship. With Dewey the study of education informed metaphysical, epistemological, and social theory. As he put it,

> The educational point of view
> enables one to envisage the
> philosophic problems where they
> arise and thrive, where they
> are at home, and where acceptance
> or rejection makes a difference
> in practice.[4]

This variation in philosophical focus is clearly related to the rise of modern science, the growth of industrialization, the development of psychology, and the subsequent movement to common and compulsory schooling. Dewey transformed the philosophical study of education by his radical criticism of traditional views of man, society, and schooling. While recognizing that education is socialization, he maintained that the development and exercise of intelligence is the active element of social formation. Thus education as the dynamic, open engagement of human intelligence with all aspects of individual environment is the basis of the re-formation of society and the point of schooling. Education is both the means and end. The outcome of Dewey's understanding of education was not only the new perspective on schooling as child-centered, interest oriented, and experiential. Dewey transformed as well the philosophical study of education. The transformation is well expressed in C.D. Hardie's claim that ". . . it is misleading to say that education must have a sound philosophical foundation . . . rather the reverse is true."[5] The traditional forms of philosophical realism and philosophical idealism began to reshape in the study of education around the fundamental elements of the process and achievement of education--around the facts of individual growth, the exercise of intelligence, the integration of man and his world, and the transformation of knowledge. In consequence of this radical perspective the practice of philosophy of education took two general and related directions. The most significant was the explication of Deweyan philosophy and its application to public schooling. The most dominant was the comparative study of philosophies of education.

With the infusion of Dewey's views into the practice of public schooling and the development of curriculum theory, philosophy of education was established as a central component of the professional conduct of schooling. The preparation of teachers in philosophical understanding became more imperative and increasingly a function of institutions of teacher education. At the same time the dynamic criticism of philosophical inquiry counteracted the professional tendency to identify philosophy of education with Deweyan educational theory. And while experimentalism (the general term for educational theory derived from Dewey's philosophy) remained significant in professional educational thinking, the professional study of philosophy of education was dominated by a "comparative" approach. Philosophical study of education in North America was mainly the systematic, but indeterminant, study of realist, idealist, experimentalist (and later "existentialist") schools of thought on reality, man, knowledge, value, and derived statements of educational objective, curriculum, teaching manner, and discipline, etc.[6] However, the critical spirit of philosophy which prevented myopic attention to Deweyan philosophy alone was not adequate to the prevention of anything more than a passive engagement of teachers in philosophical analysis. Whole sets of metaphysical, epistemological, and axiological theories were taken as the basis for the rationalization of education in public schooling.[7] Given the practical challenge to educate, it was important to be clear about the philosophical assumptions on which one's educational theory rests; but it was more important to develop a theory efficient to the practice of education. The failure to maintain an attitude of philosophical skepticism and an active philosophical criticism at all levels of theorizing is not uncommon in professional disciplines and not unheard of in academic disciplines. The post-Deweyan period of the philosophical study of education in the English-speaking world generally suffered this failure. Professional teachers were in the position of being well-informed of the philosophical "schools" of education but largely unable to make a philosophical "choice" between them. Philosophical study of education itself seemed to lack an epistemology. Not only did some philosophers of education begin to recognize that educational theory was only loosely related to the philosophical assumptions from which it was supposed to be logically derived, they also recognized that professional educators generally had not been provided a critical basis for assessing the "philosophical" alternatives before them. The decision for a realist or an idealist or a pragmatist philosophy depended less on the application of philosophical criticism than

289

it did on the core assumptions about man and
learning which the educator or teacher in training
held in advance of the "philosophical" consideration. The heavy choice for the pragmatic orientation of experimentalism reflected more the North
American inclination to social reform and "personal
fulfillment" than it did a critical consideration
of Deweyan epistemology and metaphysics. The
Deweyan epistemology of active inquiry had been
inadvertently forfeited in the philosophical study
of education for the arbitrariness of personal
persuasion. And though some educators still speak
of the need for the educator to have "a personal"
philosophy of education, few contemporary philosophers of education make the claim. Contemporary
philosophy of education is marked by the implications of two fundamental distinctions. (1) "Having
a philosophy" does not necessitate thinking philosophically any more than "having a theory" necessi-
tates theoretical study. One may direct his conduct of education by, for example, the exercise of
intelligent regard for an accepted set of principles and guidelines for education without having
in any way contributed to the development of these.
The point of philosophy of education is not the
transmission of philosophies but the active engagement of philosophical inquiry. Philosophy of education is a mode of thinking, not a moulding of
thought. (2) Theory of education is not identical
with philosophy of education. Any set of principles which is seriously intended to give direction to the conduct of education must take account
of empirical conditions established by the experiential and scientific study of teaching and learning. It must also make and justify a choice of
objectives and a prescription of standards to be
met. The contribution of philosophy to educational
theory is the clarification of the conceptual
structure within which the normative and the empirical elements are presented, and criticism of
the logic of the theory.

The significance of these distinctions for
the conduct of education is the genuine philosophical study of education and, therewith, a more

290

effective study of teaching practice. The in-
adequacy of thinking in terms of "having a philosophy of education" is well represented by Reginald
Archambault's criticism of modern theories of education:

> . . . in attempting to deal with
> all problems of education through
> a cluster of broad principles
> loosely organized, the theoretical
> statements, although apparently
> consistent, are in fact vacuous,
> for they permit no clear applica-
> tions to practice or even to the
> broadest policy making.[8]

Educational theory is now commonly recognized as a
general and distinctive category of theory. It is
not merely, nor principally, a philosophical product; and it is not modelled on the form of scientific theory. Educational theory in general will
at least necessarily reflect assumptions about many
of the problems characteristically the focus of
philosophical inquiry and is always, then, philosophically engaging. Any theoretical ordering of
objectives, curriculum, teaching manner, institutional means of instruction, and elements thereof,
will contain implicit or explicit views of the
nature of the world and of man's relation to other
components of reality, and of the conditions and
limits of knowing and valuing. Further, such
theories of education will make scientific claims
about specific components such as learning,
measurement, interaction, and social structure.
Finally, theories of education will make carefully
related recommendations for the conduct of education. Dewey's experimentalism, Skinner's behaviourism, Neil's exposition of free schools, and
Illich's proposals for deschooling, are widely
recognized examples of educational theories inclusive of all these elements. Such theories are
properly called theories of education. Other educational theories are directed to understanding
education and do not necessarily contain or intend
recommendations for change and conduct. Historical,

psychological, and sociological theories of childhood, learning, socialization, and curriculum are
clear examples of educational theories which may
become part of theories of education but which in
themselves do not recommend for the conduct of
education. Philosophy of education relates to
educational theory of both kinds by the clarification of meaning and the critique of argument.
It contributes conceptual and rational criticism
to theory of curriculum, theory of teaching,
theory of moral education, etc.; and the soundness
of specific theories of education and of educational theory in general depends on this kind of
analysis.

PHILOSOPHICAL ANALYSIS AND EDUCATION

Contemporary philosophy is most commonly
identified with analysis of language and argument.
Philosophers often refer to this activity variously
as linguistic analysis, conceptual analysis, and
ordinary language analysis. The point of philosophical analysis is to adequately address the
fundamental questions of reality, knowledge, and
value. And though by its efforts traditional
philosophical inquiry generated the wide range of
vigorous scientific study of nature, man, and culture (including the sciences of language), philosophy is now widely recognized to be analysis of
the dynamic, creative center of intelligent life--
critical clarification of our conceptualizing,
formulation of our reasoning, and exposition of
our choosing. It focuses, then, on the inter-
relationship of meaning, argument, and possibility
as it is embodied in language. The peculiarity of
philosophy is as John Passmore put it, "critical
discussion of critical discussion."[9] The specific
focus of attention taken by Bertrand Russell,
Ludwig Wittgenstein, G.E. Moore, J.L. Austin, P.F.
Strawson, Gilbert Ryle, and F. Waismann, during
the first half of this century, was analysis of
ordinary language. Russell sought initially to
reformulate ordinary language into the set of
simple logical constructs by which the atomic facts

of reality may be directly described. Wittgenstein later became attentive to the "faults" of ordinary language--its vague and incomplete correspondence to reality and its imprecise and ambiguous meaning. He undertook to clarify the complex and dynamic conceptualization of reality implicit in ordinary language. The logic of "reality" was no more or less than the rules of the multiple "language games" of human discourse. We follow one set of rules in talking of empirical reality, another set in making normative claims, another set in acting, and so on. J.L. Austin, Gilbert Ryle and others, extended our systematic understanding of the dynamic ordering of reality and possibility we make in ordinary discourse.10

These philosophers recognized that the analysis of our speaking must be reflexive, for the identification of "philosophical problems" to be "resolved" is itself a distinctive language game.11 We speak of knowledge as something we may discover and have while the rule of ascription we sometimes follow relates to doing; we speak of mind as an entity inhabiting a body (like a ghost in a machine, as Ryle put it) when the rule of recognition is intelligent disposition; we speak of the "essence of things", and of the precise meaning of concepts, when our rules of use allow us vagueness, ambiguity, and emotive force. We claim that statements are necessarily true or false when we ordinarily make promises and pledges which are performative and not descriptive. In general the analytic revolution in philosophy is the recognition that philosophical problems formulated on the basis of misunderstanding how language works and by displacing ordinary discourse are "dissolved" by careful analysis of language and discourse.

The view of philosophical inquiry as the analysis of language by which meaning and reason are clarified was effectively introduced to philosophy of education by D.J. O'Connor with the publication in 1957 of An Introduction to the Philosophy of Education. Declaring that "the

293

traditional philosophers promised more than they were able to deliver,"[12] O'Connor argued that given the criteria of verification we ordinarily apply to the claims and theories of science and mathematics, we cannot establish a body of positive philosophical knowledge. He attempted to show that the metaphysical and evaluational claims of philosophers of education up to this point were non-philosophical and often misleading. O'Connor concluded his analysis of speculative philosophy with a caution and a challenge:

> . . . The present state of philosophical knowledge and its past history cannot encourage us to look on philosophy as more than a laborious piecemeal effort to criticize and clarify the foundations of our beliefs. Such successes as philosophers can claim have all been of this kind. And this means that in the present condition of human knowledge we cannot hope for more from philosophy than occasional and fragmentary glimpses of enlightenment along with a reasonable confidence that its continuous practice will keep our minds free of nonsense. But this is something very valuable that only philosophers can give us.[13]

The philosopher of education properly examines claims about education by clarifying how words are ordinarily used, what are the main or central senses of a word, what words are ambiguous or vague, and what is necessary to warrant claims of educational fact and value. O'Connor showed that the proprietary of speaking of educational theory itself depended upon recognizing the varied uses of the word "theory".[14] "Theory" is used sometimes to refer to a more or less organized and unified conceptual framework of inquiry as in mathematics

(e.g. the theory of numbers) and in philosophy
(e.g. the theory of value). The term is used more
vaguely to distinguish practice or conduct from
the collection of ideas and rules which are understood to control a practice. Theory of social work,
theory of education, theory of classroom discipline, are examples of our speaking of theory in
the sense of the general conceptual background of
an activity or enterprise. We also ordinarily use
the term theory in its scientific sense, i.e. to
refer to sets of logically related laws and confirmed hypotheses which explain some range of empirical reality. The word "theory" clearly functions differently in each sense, and reference to
educational theory can be misleading insofar as we
do not pay careful attention to how it is used.
Whereas scientific theory functions generally to
describe, explain, and predict, educational theory
functions, according to O'Connor, to direct, guide,
recommend, and justify practice, and within this
context to describe empirical conditions of practice. Some educational theory of the social
sciences purports to make only empirical claims
about educational components and generally fits
O'Connor's category of scientific theory; however
much of what is widely recognized as educational
theory is, as noted earlier, normative and stands
as a correction of O'Connor's claim that "the word
'theory' as it is used in educational context is
generally a courtesy title."[15]

Philosophy of education as the critical
analysis of educational concepts and arguments
(more generally, of educational theory) has come
to dominate the field since O'Connor's publication.
Israel Scheffler exemplified the redirection of
philosophical study of education to the clarification of basic concepts and modes of understanding
by his analysis of language games common to theory
and practice of education, e.g. definition, slogan,
and metaphor. Scheffler undertook to analyze these
kinds of statements as they "are employed in
typical circumstances" in order to present appropriate "strategies of logical appraisal."[16] His
clear and thorough analysis of the ordinary employ-

ment of definitions has been widely directive for educational theorizing. The distinctions and inter-relationships of descriptive, stipulative, and programmatic definitions, as shown by Scheffler, have standardized the use and appraisal of definitions by education theorists in general. Further, this work effectively "dissolved" the problem of "the definition of education." Given the different functions of stipulative definitions (to clarify the normal reference of a term), and programmatic definitions (to promote programs of action), it is clear that there can be no definition which meets the demands for, or expectation of, the definition of education.[17] Similarly, the use of slogans and metaphors can no longer be unselfconscious or uncritical in the professional study of education. Slogans function both literally and practically to advance a general educational view with teachers and parents. The sloganistic assertion "we teach children, not subjects" when taken literally, i.e. as a "fact" about good education, has compelled great numbers of persons to attend to the child--what he wants to do and what he feels about his doing it. But when taken literally it can be judged to have positive effect only because it carries with it a "hidden curriculum." The statement does not itself make literal sense since it seems to say that we teach children though there isn't anything we try to get them to learn. The slogan, like any slogan, serves to direct the actions of uncritical appraisers to fulfill the intent of a particular educational theory, in this case the intent of child-centred education. As happened with programs of this intention, the slogans one uses to gain support of the uninformed and of the relatively uncritical allow for the haphazard development of programs, often unsuccessful and sometimes arbitrarily competitive of their appeal to the educational public.

Both slogans and metaphors, according to Scheffler, function like programmatic definitions in education to advance the effects of a particular theory or program of instruction. Metaphors, unlike slogans, are a fundamental component of

theoretical and policy development. Metaphors
are used in education as elsewhere to reflect
apparently significant analogies. Learning is
often understood as growth; teaching is sometimes
understood as shaping or moulding; schooling is
expected to have a product; and education is said
to have aim. Though metaphors, like analogies,
are necessary in conceptualizing and directing
social goals and effort, they can mislead. (The
parent expects the child to naturally flower, as
does the plant, with the right nutrients patiently
provided; or the teacher expects the child to
passively take the form he intends by his curriculum as does the clay in the potter's hands).
Scheffler's examination of our ordinary use of
analogy has clarified several criteria of use for
educational metaphors. The metaphor marks some
contextually significant analogy; its limitations
in that context are recognizable; its significance
is testable in the different contexts to which it
may be applied.[18]

Analysis of the common education metaphor
of 'aim' by R.S. Peters affected educational theorizing by compelling attention to the issue of
goals of education. Peters in his publication
Authority, Responsibility and Education[19] showed
that this issue was "dissolvable", i.e. that it
was a non-issue. This was established by his
analysis of the concept <u>education</u>. The word "education" as ordinarily used marks a positive appraisal of what is learned, just as "reform" marks a
positive appraisal of intended change. To speak
of persons as educated is to make a positive
appraisal of what they have learned and of their
understanding. The fact that we disagree on what
learning is worthwhile does not change the fact
that we ordinarily apply the criterion of worth in
speaking of education. Consequently it is mistaken
to speak of education as though it were a neutral
concept, or a neutral process. What we judge
worthwhile learning, i.e. what understanding we
value, is the substance of one of the rules of use
we apply in speaking of education. Thus disputes
about aims, i.e. about what general achievements

297

should finally be made by the formal institution of learning, are not disputes about ends extrinsic to education but rather disputes about what learning, what achievement, is necessary for education. The general achievement to be made is part of our judgment that education is occurring or that a particular process is educational, just as the achievement made is part of our judgment that a person is educated. As Peters later notes, aiming in its literal sense is part of the activity of hitting a target of some sort, and this conceptual fact clarifies its metaphorical use in education.

> When the term 'aim' is used more
> figuratively it has the same
> suggestion of the concentration
> of attention on something which
> is the focus of an activity . . .
> to ask for an aim is to ask for
> a more precise specification of
> what an action or activity is.[20]

The _purpose_ or the _motive_ of an action is different in that it is extrinsic. We may ask what is the purpose of teaching a people to read and expect to hear that the purpose is their conversion, or their employability, etc. . . We do not ask what is the purpose or what is the goal of their education, however, because 'education' "implies the transmission of what is of ultimate value." To ask this would be like "asking about the purpose of the good life." Education does not logically require some end beyond itself in order to be understood; it is an end in itself. Peters explains disputes about the aims of education as more accurately disputes about the normative feature built into _education_ which is extracted in the disputation as though it were the extrinsic motive or end of education. It is this conceptual confusion that gives rise to the theoretical issue (or philosophical problem) of what goals education should serve. What Peters has shown is that consideration of the genuine difference of belief over what is worthwhile learning has been displaced by conceptual confusion with the unsoluable problem of the "goals" of education.

Related to this particular confusion of intrinsic aim and extrinsic goal is confusion of the
normative use of 'education' and the derivative
descriptive use. With the institution of formal
systems of instruction such as public schooling,
the justifying purpose and goal of which is the
education of persons, there develops a tendency
to identify the system in terms of the goal. Consequently we sometimes speak of school systems and
education systems as though they were synonymous,
and readily refer to "years of education" (years
of schooling), "level of education" (level of
schooling), "kind of education" (kind of schooling,
e.g., academic, vocational, classical). Quite
clearly, however, "education" and "schooling" are
not synonymous terms. There is no conceptual of-
fense in Ivan Illich's claim that the achievement
of education in western culture requires deschooling. More generally we ordinarily speak of some
persons as "self-educated," and of "educational
experiences," with the implication that understanding in these cases is achieved informally, and
without schooling. Because systems of instruction
such as public schooling necessarily attempt to
bring about learning, but not necessarily worthwhile learning, the apparent synonymity is reflected in the descriptive use of "education" to refer
neutrally to schooling and other systems of instruction. Confusion of the descriptive use of
"education" with the central normative use results
in the expectation that some worth be achieved by
education and, then, that education be given
direction by the setting of goals. The descriptive use reflects the task or process sense of
"education" and obliviates the basic achievement
or product sense of "education." Education, as
Peters argued, is only understood if it is recognized as entailing achievement as well as process.
We ordinarily speak of the educated person, of
being educated, and of educational achievement,
and clearly expect that these are the point and
the outcome of educational systems, of educational
enterprise. When these are not the point then we

do not speak of formal systems of learning as
educational but as indoctrinary. To refer to a
formal system of learning as education without
implying a positive appraisal of the curriculum,
i.e. to use "education" descriptively, is to describe a system of instruction as valued by someone
presently or in the past, i.e. as education (normative use) for someone.

PHILOSOPHICAL CLAIM AND WARRANT

         As a result of the early work of analytic
philosophers, philosophy of education is now generally characterized by conceptual analysis reflecting the loose distinction made in ordinary
discourse between empirical, normative, and analytic or conceptual claims. Reflection on critical
discourse exposes a distinction in the ways we
ordinarily settle disputes about the claims we
make. Disputes or uncertainty about what we understand to be matters of fact are settled by getting
the facts. Disputes about what are understood to
be matters of value are settled finally by agreement on norms, rules, and principles. Disputes
about what are taken to be matters of logic and
meaning are settled by proofs and clarification.
We ordinarily mark claims as empirical, normative,
or conceptual in terms of the kind of verification
we take to be appropriate. That we are often un-
relieved of this dispute follows from uncertainty
as to what kind of verification is appropriate (as
is often the case with moral and religious claims),
or from lack of conviction in the adequacy of the
grounds offered as verifying. The distinction is
clear enough, however, to identify what constitutes the nature of philosophical claim and warrant. Though the philosopher will rely on empirical claims and will enter the fray of normative
dispute, what distinguishes his work is the attempt
to achieve logical and conceptual clarification.
His contribution to educational theory is the
critical elucidation of the conceptual order and
patterns of reasoning which constitute the "logical
geography" of the cultural enterprise of education.

The distinctive function of philosophy of education is not to determine goals for schooling or to construct systems of education. It is rather to critically analyse and correct the logical fit of educational claims, theories, and practices with the conceptual and rational foundations of that enterprise. Philosophical analysis is indeterminate with regard to what the goals of schooling ought to be, with regard to what subjects ought to be taught, and with regard to how the learner ought to be taught. Conceptual clarification and rational criticism are clearly distinct from ethical and prudential judgment. Though philosophical analysis is able to show us what are the conceptual and rational conditions of ethical and prudential thinking, it cannot adjudicate the ultimately subjective choice of values on which normative elements of education rest. Neither, it seems, can philosophy finally adjudicate our cultural conception--our "choice"--of education. That conceptual ordering rests deep within the cultural heritage of western man and is no less a matter of interest to the study of culture generally than it is specifically of philosophical interest. The postulation of ethical theory and of educational theory is no more the task of the philosopher than it is the task of any intelligent, critical member of the cultural traditions within which ethics and education are conceived. This task, it seems, is not fundamentally conceptual, but normative. In both ethics and education the role of philosophy is the clarification of the conceptualization of our values and our enterprises by the analysis of our most accessible embodiment of conceptional order--our discourse, i.e. our language and reason. In his effort to critically appraise the logical fit of educational claim and argument to the conceptual order within which it arises and in his recognition that all claims are subject to such analysis, the philosopher serves both the maintenance of culture and its disclosure. More specifically (and more precariously) the philosopher of education serves both the maintenance of education and its disclosure.

Philosophical clarification of educational
language does not presuppose a neat correspondence
of conceptual order with natural and social reality. The critical task of clarification is not,
then, ultimately directed merely to precision of
meaning. Conceptual analysis is aimed at clarification of precision, ambiguity, vagueness, and
mutation in our cultural conceptualization of education. Where language embodies relatively precise conceptualization, as, for example, with the
concepts discipline and teaching, clarification
of the meaning criteria enables correction and control of argument and theory. Where ambiguity con-
fuses and misleads as with the concepts interests
and thinking elucidation of rules governing word
use facilitates understanding and sound reason.
Recognition of the vagueness of terms such as
"worth," "appreciation" and "discovery" prevents
simplistic consideration and easy acceptance of
educational ideas and pedagogical proposals put in
these terms. Philosophical analysis of the language of education has the general benefit of increasing the consciousness of both theorist and
professional of the "distinctive form that human
reason takes in the practice of education."[21] It
is particularly important in the preparation of
teachers that they achieve both understanding and
competence of educational judgment. Conceptual
clarity is a condition of this competence, and is
especially so for teachers who undertake to manipulate the conditions of public schooling for the
educational benefit of children and youth. James
McClellan states this general benefit more point-
edly:

> . . . to encourage teachers and
> administrators to study philosophy
> of education is to make it more
> likely that they will come to see
> education as a philosophically
> complex idea . . . . the alter-
> native is that schooling will come
> to be seen as an end in itself or
> that education will come to be
> identified (behavioristically) as

302

training which serves the
dominant classes in the society.[22]

McClellan goes on to advise that the study of
philosophy of education "forget the system" (i.e.
public schooling) and inquire directly into the
meaning of terms central to education, and only
when the basic concepts are understood, determine
how schooling can be used to educate. The advice
reflects the development of philosophical analysis
of education. Contemporary philosophy of education
has readily participated in the analysis of epistemological and ethical concepts undertaken by
philosophers generally (e.g. mind, knowledge,
proof, evidence, value, rights, rules, equality,
authority, etc.). And on this basis philosophers
of education have undertaken the systematic analysis of the concepts central to education, and to
which philosophers generally have not attended,
e.g. education, teaching, learning, discipline,
creativity, and so on.

PHILOSOPHICAL METHOD

Achieving clarification of the conceptual
order foundational to education and thereby a
more sophisticated, dynamic perspective of the
educational enterprise for both theorist and practitioner, depends upon the exercise of techniques
of inquiry within the distinctive procedural conditions just described. Philosophical inquiry is
rather uncommon and many have difficulty recognizing it or crediting it. Critical consciousness
of conceptual order and systematic analysis of it
on the part of professional educators is, consequently, dependent on formal and demanding instruction in teacher-preparation programs. The general
lack of this consciousness and discipline of
thought is itself a telling comment on the adequacy of our formal educational systems. The problem arises in significant part because of the difficulty in succinctly stating the methodological
procedures of philosophical inquiry.

303

The general methodological statement above
indicates the objectives, the subject matter and
focus, the contribution, and the limitations of
philosophy of education. Within the context of
this understanding philosophical procedure may be
identified and illustrated. Philosophical inquiry
is characterized by inductive, deductive, analogi-
cal, and intuitive reasoning. In this regard it
is not distinctive from scientific inquiry or
literary analysis. Though its distinctive focus
is conceptual order and reason, philosophy is not
merely deductive. In part, L.A. Reid is correct
in his assertion that "philosophy, once it starts,
has no stopping-place."[23] Reid speaks here in
defence of metaphysics, i.e. philosophical proposals regarding the nature of matter, life, mind,
God, values, etc. Clearly, such proposal is not
exclusively philosophical in that it requires no
special competencies not characteristic of the
intelligent, critical scholar. And it certainly
cannot be claimed that philosophers necessarily
acquire by their profession the speculative imagination required by metaphysics. Reid's claim is
correct with regard to the variety of statements
philosophers analyze. Metaphysical, ethical,
aesthetic, scientific, mathematical, practical, as
well as conceptual statements, are all subject to
philosophical analysis. His statement is also
correct--and this is the point being emphasized
here--with regard to the modes of reason the philosopher employs. As Clive Beck has put it,
"Philosophy is typically concerned with abstract
questions, with questions at some remove from
specific experiences; therefore, it must develop
strategies of cogitation."[24] The most characteristic of these strategies are the analytic techniques of distinguishing central and peripheral
word uses, elucidating the rules of use with examples and counter-examples, describing the use of
analogous terms and related terms, identifying
ambiguity and showing vagueness, clarifying the
public criteria or conceptual logic by which language use is accountable, clarifying conditions of
sound argument and showing logical fallacy, and
finally by relating the outcome of such analysis

to the specific claim, or uncertainty, or error,
or argument regarding which the need for clarification arose. The "situation" out of which the
need for philosophical analysis arises may be the
presentation of a particular educational theory,
the making of specific claims regarding education,
or the employment of a pattern of argument in the
practice of teaching.

These analytical techniques are common to
philosophy though by no means exhaustive of philosophical inquiry.[25] The significance of them is
reflected in the unlikelihood of work which does
not depend on them being critically regarded as
philosophical. They mark a work as philosophical.
Other procedures philosophers employ, whether of
scientific, or metaphysical, or normative inquiry,
may be more or less significant in the conduct of
philosophical inquiry depending on the achievement
of conceptual and logical clarification. The
arousal of public interest in a philosophical work
may often be its normative or metaphysical issue,
but philosophical work, as Brian Crittenden puts
it, "attends particularly to such questions as
internal consistency, justification, characteristic
forms of argument, and the pattern of logical relationships among the central concepts of the system."[26] John Passmore has remarked on the distinction between "speculative" and "critical" philosophy in terms of the commitment of philosophers in
general to the critical analysis of their normative
and metaphysical claims.

> Philosophy, like science, is
> neither pure speculation nor
> pure criticism; it is specu-
> lation controlled by criticism.
> Recent philosophy . . . is
> quite as speculative as it ever
> was, although not about the
> "transcendental." The difference
> between sage and philosopher is
> not that the sage is imaginative
> and the philosopher unimaginative;
> it is that the philosopher submits

305

his speculations to the discipline
of close criticism.[27]

It is the achievement of conceptual clarification which has recognizable and effective philosophical impact on educational theory and practice.
Critical consciousness of the conceptual order of
education enables educators to order and conduct
the enterprise by educational judgment and not
merely in terms of the established contingencies
of institutional structure and convention.

PHILOSOPHY FOR TEACHERS

Philosophy is principally, then, an activity.
It is the special activity of critical thinking
about meaning--about the conceptual, logical, and
normative structuring of reality which is embedded
in, and gives point to, our language and conduct.
Philosophy of education is the activity of critical
thinking about the language and public conduct of
the educational enterprise.

The study of philosophy of education by professional teachers is not based on an expectation
that they should be professional philosophers as
well. The expectation is that the teacher be
philosophically able in the intelligent conduct of
education. As Glenn Langford indicates, formal
education is a "purposive, self-conscious, practical activity,"[28] for which teachers take major
responsibility. The responsibility is unavoidably
complex and its successful fulfillment is necessarily sophisticated. The complexity of judgment
outlined in the Introduction to this chapter is a
description of the practice of educating others.
The suggestion that such judgment is theoretical
and therefore not part of the responsibility of
the classroom teacher implicitly prescribes a non-
professional role for teachers, and allows for the
exclusive focus of schooling on otherwise non-
educational functions such as socialization, social
and economic placement, and institutional self-
maintenance. In her analysis of educational policy

306

and policy-making, Donna Kerr correctly claims
that:

> . . . the quality of our making
> and implementing of educational
> policies depends, in large
> measure, upon the quality of our
> individual maps of the conceptual
> and normative terrain of educa-
> tional policy.[29]

Those who have difficulty descriptively relating
the notion of 'educational policy' to the daily
conduct of classroom instruction may substitute
the notion of 'educational judgment' to recognize
the implication of Kerr's claim for those classroom
teachers who are committed to the education of
their students.

Students of education who are, or who intend
to become, certified professional teachers find
that their conduct of education in the classroom
requires clarity of understanding and accuracy of
reasoning in order to avoid, for example, the confusion of 'authoritative instruction' with 'author-
itarian instruction.' Philosophical sensitivity
and skill enable the teacher to recognize the
centrality of discipline to education and the
limited justification of the use of punishment in
school management. Remarking and relating consideration of what children are interested in to
consideration of what is in their interest and to
what is in the public interest is essential to the
educational direction of each child's study. In
general the rational conduct of schooling and the
fair treatment of students are requisite to the
professional commitment to educate; and these conditions account for the pursuit of philosophical
skill and understanding on the part of teachers.

KNOWLEDGE AND THE CURRICULUM

The philosophical study of education has
appropriately sought clarification of the complex

307

educational conditions of learning, teaching, and classroom management. The direction, manner, and setting of formal instruction are major normative issues in the enterprise of education. The handling of these issues is consequently subject to confusion, misjudgment, and manipulation in the social control and conduct of compulsory public schooling. Fundamental to these issues is the determination of what constitutes educational study. The selection of curriculum subjects for public schools is crucial in fulfilling the expectation that schools educate and not indoctrinate, or merely train, our children and youth. Consequently, philosophy of education is centrally concerned with the question of what study assures the student's achievement of critical skill, understanding, and judgment, and with the embedded question of what constitutes knowledge.

What does it mean to know? Philosophers have long distinguished between procedural knowledge--knowing how to do something, and propositional knowledge--knowing that such and such is the case. Upon reflection we recognize that we allow, conceptually, for persons to have procedural knowledge without having related propositional knowledge and, it seems, vice versa. I may know how to play the guitar and not be able to explain how the guitar works or by what principles and rules I make music on it. On the other hand I may rationally understand the instrument and the production of music on it and by all accounts be acknowledged as unable to play it. It seems likely of course, that if I have either kind of knowledge the other is more accessible to me than it is to someone who has neither kind. To know how is to have developed a skill by practice which can be executed at will. (The ambiguity of "know how" reflects the distinction noted above between propositional and procedural knowledge. I may know how the machine works but not know how to operate it; and you may know how to operate the machine but not know how it works. The locution "know how" is contextually ambiguous. However, unless the context makes clear that what is claimed is propo-

308

sitional knowledge, we readily take the claim to
be one of executive skill.) Now there is little
doubt that both kinds of knowledge are necessary
to being educated. Understanding requires skills
of disciplined thought--reasoning and inquiry entail the practice of complex sets of skills.

The major philosophical dispute in curriculum determination is the nature of theoretical
knowledge--knowledge that. The most commonly held
position is that propositional knowledge is justified true belief. That is, in claiming or attri-
buting such knowledge it seems there is necessarily
a condition of belief, of truth, and of truth-
supportive grounds. Clearly we take it as illogi-
cal to say we know that X though X is false. Our
concept of knowledge is, in part, that we can only
correctly claim to know that which is true. And
when we find that what we had taken to be true is
not, we clearly acknowledge this condition by dis-
claiming that we ever knew what we had earlier
claimed to know. We accommodate the condition by
saying that we thought we knew that X when we
didn't. That we confidently believed that X,
accounts for our making the mistaken knowledge
claim. Further, it seems contradictory to say "I
know that it is raining outside but I do not believe it is." Belief, confidence, or being sure
of the proposition seems upon reflection to be a
necessary condition of knowledge.[30] Finally, knowing that such and such is true is distinguished
from mere true belief by the condition of justification. One must have adequate evidence for the
truth of what he claims, to be said to know it.
Consequently, what you claim to know must be share-
able--others may also come to know it by the same
evidential consideration. Without the condition
of evidence we can make no distinction between true
belief and knowledge.

However, for a number of reasons the evidence condition is ineffective. First, if what is
taken as evidence must itself be shown to be true
we seem to fall into an infinite regress. Either
there are some things which can be known non-

evidentially and with certainty (in which case
there is a distinction between knowledge and evidential belief), or we cannot be certain of knowing
anything. Secondly, as a matter of fact we speak
of knowing what is true in a number of areas where
the notion of evidence is not unequivocally applicable. In mathematics what is required for propositional knowledge is proof, not evidence. In
the area of moral deliberation what is required
of those who claim to know is a good case for a
claim.[31] Some of our reasons in this case will be
evidential, but part of our reasoning must necessarily be a matter of moral principle or rule.
Thirdly, some of our propositional knowledge claims
seem to be conditional only on one's being in a
position to know. One's knowing such things as
his own name, or that he is in pain, or that he
feels sad, is not conditional on his having evidence for his name, or his pain, or his feeling.
One can imagine circumstances, as A.J. Ayer points
out, where we would attribute knowledge to another
on the grounds that the other has the right to be
sure.[32] For these several reasons philosophers
now tend to a more comprehensive view of the conditions of knowledge as justified true belief. To
have propositional knowledge, then, is necessarily
to believe a proposition, which is true, on the
basis of appropriate and adequate grounds for its
truth, or in some cases with the right to be sure
of its truth. We will return to this view later
in this chapter in order to examine the justification of curriculum content. The curriculum implications of this view of knowledge must first be
made clear.

The curriculum theory of Paul Hirst is fully
representative of the philosophical implications
of this view of knowledge. Given that education
is the development of disciplined and generative
understanding, then it is centrally the acquisition
of fundamental forms of knowledge.

> To be without any knowledge at all
> is to be without mind in any sig-
> nificant sense . . .. to fail to

310

acquire knowledge of a certain
fundamental kind, is to fail to
achieve rational mind in that
significant respect. Not all
knowledge is of equal importance
in the development of rationality,
of course, yet the fundamental
relationship between knowledge
and the development of mind is of
central educational significance.[33]

As the previous analysis of the nature of
knowledge makes clear, there are distinguished
within the range of epistemic claims we make several distinct types of rational judgment. These
distinct types represent the different relationships that hold between concepts, facts, and
values. Each interrelated group of concepts and
the logical operations by which meaningful propositions are generated within each are marked by
distinctive tests for truth according to which
propositions are validated. There are, according
to Hirst's analysis, seven kinds of true propositions: empirical, mathematical, moral, religious,
those of literature and the arts, those of history
and the social sciences, and philosophical. Just
as the examination of the knowledge claims we
actually make seems to substantiate the view that
knowledge is justified true belief, so also,
according to Hirst, does analysis of the range of
rational propositions in public discourse reduce
all such claims to these seven irreducible and
nonhierarchical forms of knowledge.

Allowing for the possible development of
new and different forms of human reason, Hirst
asserts that

. . . Nevertheless we can pick
out those concepts and principles
which are necessary and fundamental to anything we could at
present call understanding. The
ultimacy of these elements (of
intelligibility and reason) is

311

there and they mark out the
limits of anything we can
intelligibly conceive.[34]

Clearly, then, the educational curriculum of the
schools, however it is constructed into subjects
of study, must assure the broad intellectual development of persons across these forms of knowledge. This full initiation into modes of rational
thought, though not equivalent to general education
(which additionally includes at least physical
education and practical education), constitutes,
according to Hirst, the liberal education necessary
to the student's critical understanding of human
experience as we fundamentally conceive and validate it. Hirst goes some distance to show that
these seven forms of rational belief are distinctly
characterized by public tests for truth and are
thereby forms of knowledge. It is this latter
criterion which constitutes critical instruction
into any of these forms as educational, and critical instruction in all of them as liberating.
Hirst contends that this concept of liberal education is "of an education based fairly and squarely
on the nature of knowledge itself, a concept central to the discussion of education at any level."[35]

     It is characteristic of philosophical en-
quiry that it questions the most fundamental claims
of a public discourse. In this case, there are at
least two matters to be disputed. Hirst's notion
of a liberal education depends on his claim that
the fundamental forms of rational belief which he
identifies are necessarily marked by distinctive
tests for truth, and on the theory of knowledge as
justified true belief. A brief consideration of
the first matter and an extensive consideration of
the second will serve to correct Hirst's claims.

     Hirst's theory of forms of knowledge entails
that some systems of rational belief (i.e. the
irreducible forms) are definitive of truth. We
cannot speak of true claims apart from the truth
tests of these forms of belief. Thomas Green has
recently provided good grounds for rejecting this

formulation of the truth. For example, we may suppose that a specific object is specifically located on the moon's surface knowing that the statement is true or false. If we discover the object at the specified location we will have, according to Green, discovered a truth. If we discover that there is no such object at the location, we will also have discovered a truth. In either case we discover a truth that had been unknown or undiscovered. The truth of any such proposition is true independently of our discovery of it and independent of our evidence for it. Truth does not change with our evidence. It is not relative to the evidence that we have. If it were then we would be in the absurd position of having to say that the earth was recently flat (400 years ago) and is now spherical.[36]

From this we may conclude that the forms of rational belief which Hirst posits as definitive of true propositions are correctly taken by us as our organizations of warranted belief, and only honorifically taken as forms of knowledge. Whatever is truth, it is truth independently of our conceptual organization and postulation of evidence. Green carries his analysis a bit further to note that what is reasonable for a particular person to believe is not a function of truth, nor of the evidence available to mankind in general, but is a function of the evidence available to that person. The substance of the evidence available to me may be evidence for the truth of the proposition Q, while the substance of evidence available to me at another time may be adequate to falsify Q. In both cases it is quite possible to correctly judge that my belief is reasonable. Reasonable belief is a condition of having adequate evidence and being sure. Or as Green puts it, though it is not possible to know what is false, it may be reasonable to believe what is false. Green makes the obvious connection with teaching as an educational activity. Such activity is aimed at transmitting what is reasonable for persons to believe on the basis of the evidence and experience available to them and which is supported by the burden

313

of evidence available to mankind at large.[37]
Quite convincingly Green draws the curricular implication that teaching is too narrowly viewed as
a transmission of knowledge. The education of
persons has to do with the broad areas of belief
such as aesthetic, moral, political, and religious
as well as with mathematics and science. As Green
has shown, much of these are more adequately viewed
as matters of belief, not knowledge. "The primary
philosophical category for teaching (then) becomes
not knowledge but reasonable belief."[38] The
curriculum content of schooling is here recognized
to be a function not of irreducible epistemological
forms, but of what people judge it is reasonable
for them to believe. As Green puts it, this "is
the project any man embarks upon when he sets out
to think."[39]

It should not surprise us that what are now
recognized by some as fundamental tests of truth
have not always been recognized as such (consider
the "rise" of modern science itself, the recent
development of quantum theory, the developing interests in the disciplines of Eastern mysticism);
or are not now recognized by all (consider the
increasing acceptance of astrological claim, the
widespread commitment to the literal truth of "inspired" sacred writings, and the assertion of subjective truth in phenomenological inquiry). The
"necessary" constitution of an educational curriculum is not only open to change as Hirst acknowl-
edges, it is always an open matter, appropriately
(though not always actually) subject to negotiation. Intelligent consideration of what is reasonable to believe, of what kinds of inquiry do actually liberate one from ignorance, and especially
of fashionable ignorance, does not necessarily
conform to the standard (and somewhat vague) tests
of truth posited by Hirst.

As there is a major objection to the claim
of necessary forms of testing rational belief,
there may be grounds as yet largely unexamined for
questioning the claim that knowledge is justified
true belief. There is reason for holding that

314

knowledge is logically independent of belief, and consequently for holding that knowledge is the foundation of educational curriculum and that reasonable belief is one objective of such a curriculum.

Knowledge and belief, according to Zeno Vendler,[40] are logically distinct types such that one may be in possession of knowledge without belief. J.L. Austin had earlier pointed to the fact that we challenge knowledge claims and belief claims differently. The challenge to a knowledge claim is "How do you know?"; and to a belief claim it is "Why do you believe?" When our challenge is successful in the first case we say "You do not know." In the second case we do not say that you do not believe but that you do not have adequate reason for your belief.[41] To take the class of appropriate answers to both "How do you know?" and "Why do you believe?" as providing evidence for the same sort of thing is to ignore the logic of the questions. Though we request evidence for the truth of the proposition you believe in asking why you believe it we do not request evidence for the known in asking how you know it. In asking "How do you know?" we request evidence that you know; whereas, in asking, "Why do you believe?" we do not request evidence that you believe. "How do you know?" requests the way of your knowing, the "route" by which you came to know. The point of the question and the force of the answer is to determine that you know. "Why do you believe?", however, requests evidence for what you believe and not evidence that you believe it. We enquire into your knowing just because knowing that p entails p. Inquiring into whether or not you know, rather than into whether or not p, conforms with the logic of knowing. If it is the case that you know then it is the case that p. Establishing that p, however, does not establish that you know it. In the case of your believing that p, requesting evidence for the truth of p rather than requesting evidence that you believe it, conforms with the logic of belief. Since your believing that p does not entail p you can mistakenly believe that p; and establishing that you believe it tells

us nothing regarding the truth of the claim that
p. Requesting your evidence for the truth of the
claim that p serves us in two ways. We may evaluate the reasonableness of the belief that p, i.e.
we may be reasonably convinced that p; and, we
may evaluate the reasonableness of your believing
it.

More telling than this is Vendler's analysis
of our use of the terms "know" and "believe".
According to Vendler the content of our belief is
something like a picture of reality--a conjecture,
or representation, or interpretation of reality;
whereas the contents of our knowledge is reality
itself. We ordinarily speak of knowing things
which it makes no sense to speak of believing.
For example, we speak of knowing the painting, of
knowing that face, of knowing wines, of knowing
geography, and so on, but we do not speak of believing the painting, believing that face, believing wines, etc. The reason for this is that the
face, wines, and geography are not conjectures of
what is real which I may judge to be true or false,
correct or incorrect, i.e. which I may believe or
doubt. These things are instances of the reality
I experience, am familiar with, and know.

This distinction between conjectures of
reality and reality itself helps explain the fact
that though we do not claim both to know and to
believe the facts or the outcome, we do claim both
to know stories, statements, opinions, and theories
and to believe stories, statements, opinions, and
theories. Knowing the story and believing the
story are logically distinct just in terms of what
is known and believed. In the case of believing
the story, the story is a representation or a
"picture" of reality which I believe. I believe
what the story says. In the case of knowing the
story, the story is something (i.e. a thing, a
part of reality) I am familiar with. I know the
story (in other words, I know what the story is).
Facts and outcomes, unlike stories and theories,
are not representations of reality which we believe or do not believe; they are instances of
reality which we know or do not know. Knowing the

facts is like knowing the story in that the object
of knowing in each case is an instance of reality.
Knowing the facts is different from knowing the
story only in that I can on the basis of knowing
the story also believe the story, i.e. believe the
representation of reality which is the story. The
facts are instances of reality and cannot be believed (though, of course, statements of facts, or
his "facts" are representations and may be believed). In brief, according to Vendler:

> Forming a belief, like painting
> a picture, or imagining something,
> is a human act, which can be
> recommended . . . praised or cen-
> sured . . . Knowing something is
> not the kind of thing a man can
> choose to do . . . . knowledge is
> like seeing what there is in
> reality.[42]

There are at least two objects of knowing
which do not so readily exhibit this difference
between knowledge and belief: reasons and explanations. We speak of both knowing the reason (the
explanation) and believing the reason (the explanation). The reason and the explanation are like
facts in that they are reality itself and can be
known. When we speak of believing "the" reason,
or "the" explanation, we can only mean we believe
the reason given, or the explanation provided.
"I believe the explanation" means I believe the
explanation he provided, i.e. I believe his explanation. Clearly, knowing the reason for his
behaviour is quite distinct from knowing the reason
he gave for his behaviour. In the first case I
know why he behaved as he did and it does not make
sense to speak of my believing the reason. In the
second case I know what he said regarding his behaviour and I may or may not believe it.

The grammatical differences between "know"
and "believe" substantiate the claim that belief
is not a condition of knowledge; they indicate
that we know and believe quite different things.

317

Note that whereas we speak of knowing that he lost
the watch, knowing who lost the watch, knowing when
he lost it, knowing where he lost it, and knowing
what he lost, we speak only of believing that he
lost it. This difference does not always hold,
however, for we may say "I believe what he said"
as well as "I know what he said." In this case
(as in other cases like it where both "know" and
"believe" operate, such as knowing Jane and believing Jane, or knowing the theory and believing
the theory, or knowing his testimony and believing
his testimony), "know" and "believe" operate differently so that while my believing what he said
is conditional on my knowing what he said, my knowing what he said is obviously not conditional on
my believing what he said. The fact that "believe"
can take only one of these objects (i.e. what, but
not who, how, how to, when, where, why), and the
fact that my knowing what he said is quite independent of my believing what he said, together
strongly support the claim that we know and believe
quite different things.

Believe what is limited to taking as object
the sort of things which can be the object of
belief: statements, assertions, theories, doctrines, etc., all of which are of human authorship.
Knowing what marks a nominalization, which "believe" cannot take, and which enables "know" to
take anything (any thing), any instance of reality,
as its object--facts, relations, events, including
utterances, statements, predictions, and doctrines.[43] What following "believe," on the other
hand, is a contraction of that which and not a
nominalization. Knowing what he said is knowing
that he said that p--an instance of reality itself.
Believing what he said is believing that which he
said; more definitely, it is believing that p
which he said--i.e. his interpretation of "picture"
of reality.

This difference in objects of "know" and
"believe" readily accounts for familiar cases of
subject familiarity where it makes sense to speak
of knowing the face, the game, the definition,

318

French, Edmonton, but not of believing the face,
the game, the definition, French, Edmonton. These
cases are not unlike the cases of knowing but not
believing the facts, the explanation, and the
results. This distinction between knowledge and
belief also accounts for the more problematic cases
of knowing Jane and not believing her, knowing the
theory and not believing the theory, knowing the
doctrine and not believing the doctrine, knowing
the prediction and not believing the prediction.
Some of the things I can know straightforwardly
are not objects of belief: the face, the facts,
what he lost. Other things I can know appear also
to be the objects of belief: Jane, the theory, the
doctrine, etc. However, in these cases as in the
case of knowing and believing what he said, I know
and believe quite different things:

I know what he said   - I know that he said
                                 that p.
I believe what he said.   - I believe that p which
                                 he said.

I know Jane.   - I know her.
I believe Jane.   - I believe her story,
                                 or her word.

I know the theory.   - I know that the theory
                                 states such and
                                 such.
I believe the theory.   - I believe that such
                                 and such, which is
                                 the theory.

The clinching argument for this position is
Vendler's analysis of subjective and objective
nouns. Nouns like suggestion, prediction, statement, confession, testimony, excuse, belief, opinion, assumption, view, theory, and suspicion,
derive from illocutionary verbs or verbs expressing
mental states. These are subjective nouns; they
refer to the issue of human thought and speech:
beliefs, assumptions, statements, confessions, etc.
Nouns like fact, cause, result, outcome, and case,
refer to the things, events, relations, etc. which

are "there" to be found, located, or discovered and which do not belong to anybody.[44] These are objective nouns. The significant difference between objective and subjective nouns is that they behave differently with respect to "know" and "believe." Subjective nouns follow either "know" or "believe," but with quite different results. Believing his suggestion is knowing what his suggestion is without necessarily believing it. Objective nouns naturally follow "know" but cannot follow "believe" at all. They refer to aspects of the objective domain, of reality--the fact that he suggested that p, the facts of the crime, the cause of the explosion, the results of the experiment, the explanation of the phenomenon, the outcome of the election, the upshot of the debate, etc. The openness of know and the complete restriction on believe regarding objective nouns is easily recognized.

Since what we know is not that which we believe, the difference between knowledge and belief is not being certain in the one case and uncertain in the other, or having conclusive evidence or less conclusive evidence. For, in this case, "know" and "believe" must necessarily take the same things as object. Any knowledge claim may differ from a particular belief claim in terms of the certainty we fell. The possibility remains, however, that we may be certain about our belief that q as well as about our knowing that p (e.g. my knowledge of Jane is such that I am certain of the truth of my belief that she will come). Being certain is not a characteristic of knowledge only; we may also be certain in our beliefs. Neither does conclusiveness of evidence distinguish a belief as knowledge. On the contrary, since evidence is that "through which we see" something else, that which "points to" or indicates something further, having evidence characterizes rational belief. Knowledge is of things experienced, recognized, discovered. That which our experiences suggest, to which our discoveries point, i.e. our "pictures" of reality, are what we believe. The concept of evidence is logically related to belief in that having evidence which supports a particular

320

claim is knowing some things on the basis of which
we believe the claim.

Finally, if I claim to know that p and it
comes out that p is not the case, then clearly I
did not know. I was mistaken in my claim. There
is no more to be said than that I was wrong. I
can be both certain and mistaken in my claim to
know that p. How, then, do I know that p if I can
be certain about what is false? The fact of the
matter is that I know the truth, reality itself,
which cannot be said to be true or false. Reality
is "there"; it can no more be false than can the
facts or the truth. When we speak, as we might,
of the facts reported in a paper as false, or of
the reality of Nicholas and Alexandra as false or
of the truths of science as false, we are not
speaking of false facts or false reality or false
truths but of false "facts" or false "reality" or
false "truths." Consider my knowing that the table
is set. I know reality itself, the case, truth:
i.e. the set table. However, the set table is not
true. What is true or false is my claim "the table
is set." But I do not claim to know "the table is
set" in claiming to know that the table is set; I
claim to know the set table, so to speak. The
reality of the set table is not true or false just
as the reality of my knowing it is not true or
false. Claims, statements, testimonies, beliefs,
etc. are the sort of thing which is true or false;
and as we have seen, this is the sort of thing we
believe. Objective nouns, as already suggested,
do not take the adjective false. Thus, "true" in
true statement is interpreted differently than it
is in true result. A true statement is a statement
which is not false. A true result, on the other
hand, is a result that is not alleged; it is truly
(really) the result.[45] (That "true" has various
senses should not surprise us given that true North
contrasts with magnetic North and not false North,
and that true fish contrasts not with false fish
but with fish that does not have all the essential
characteristics of being fish.) It makes no more
sense to argue that because what I know cannot be
false it must be true than it does to argue that
because the reading on my compass is not of true

321

North it must be false. What I know, e.g. the
result of the experiment, is true in the sense that
it is the result and not an alleged result. Now
whereas the result and my knowing it are neither
true nor false, "The result is X" and "I know the
result" are statements of mine which are true or
false and which you may believe or disbelieve.

How do I know? I know by experiencing,
recognizing, discovering, understanding, being
acquainted with, being familiar with things, facts,
events, actions, relations, processes, results,
techniques, utterances, persons, theories, stories,
subject matters, words, concepts, arguments, laws,
and principles. And knowing this sort of thing
by acquaintance, experience, recognition, etc., is
basic to my believing statements, theories, doctrines, opinions, and predictions. I know that p
because I experience p (I recognize p, I understand
p, I am acquainted with p); I believe that q, on
the other hand, because I have evidence for the
truth of q.

If knowing is not believing and knowledge
is not justified true belief then Hirst's theory
of the relationship of knowledge and curriculum
is mistaken. However, it is not mistaken in quite
the way that Green's analysis suggests. Green concluded that teaching has primarily to do with the
transmission of rational belief. We are now in a
position to see the error of this notion and to
affirm our intuitive understanding of teaching as
the transmission of knowledge, and at the same
time to correct Hirst's theory of the curriculum
for liberal education.

Teaching (in its generic sense) is acting
with the intention that another learn or master
something in a way appropriate to its meaning, i.e.
that he come to know it, believe it, be able to do
it, regularly do it, be it, and so on. We learn
facts, concepts, definitions, rules, principles,
arguments, stories, theories, doctrines, beliefs,
etc. We also learn procedures, techniques, skills,
etc.; and we learn attitudes, habits, preferences,
and so on. Now, it is important to note that any

322

particular instance of all of these categories
is something real, something "there" to be recognized, discovered, understood, etc. That is, any
of these particulars is something which can be
known. I can know that snakes shed their skins,
that an isobar is such and such, the principle of
equality, the doctrines of Roman Catholicism, how
to swim, what smoking is, what generosity is, and
so on. I can know, in effect, anything which is
in principle expressible in propositional form.
I can learn any such particular in that I can know
it--recognize it, understand it, be familiar with
it, and so on. And the teacher can intend that
the learner master any such particular in the sense
that he know it. Not everything which is propositional in form is the object of belief. Definitions, rules, etc., are not themselves objects
of belief. However, claims, theories, interpretations, beliefs, and so on can be the objects of
belief. Any particular of this limited category
can be learned in that it can be believed; and
the teacher can intend that the learner master
any such particular in the sense that he believe
it. Clearly, then, teaching is conceptually related to an epistemological category which is
inclusive of and not exhausted by the category of
belief. That is, the encompassing epistemological
category of what may be taught is that of knowledge, not belief.

We have seen that some of those things which
can be known can be believed. That is, they can
be mastered in the sense that one makes them the
object of his commitment. Now, others of these
things which can be known can be executed as well.
For example, I can know the procedure and be able
to follow it, I can know the technique and be able
to employ it, and I can know the skill and be able
to perform it. To say I know the technique is to
say, at least, that I know how it is done, i.e.
that I can recognize it when it is employed and/or
that I am familiar with it and can describe it to
you. I can know that doing what Jones is doing
constitutes employing that technique and/or that
the technique is that of heating raw gas until the
butane can be drawn off. When we say that we

intend someone learn the skill, procedure, etc., we usually mean that he is to learn how to employ it, follow it, perform it, etc., that he be able to execute it, that he come to know how to do it. Sometimes, we intend that someone learn the skill, procedure, and so on, intending that he both become familiar with the skill, know how it is done, and that he become able to execute it, i.e. that he know how to do it.

It is clear that learning an ability and learning a belief are both logically dependent upon the learner's acquisition of knowledge. In the first case the learner must know that the ability which is to be learned consists of doing such and such; in the second case he must know the proposition to which he is committing himself. Clearly, my learning how to swim logically requires that I recognize what swimming is, and my learning that Louis Riel was a traitor logically requires that I understand the proposition that Louis Riel was a traitor. Of course, I may acquire this knowledge, i.e. this recognition or this understanding, in acquiring the ability and the belief, but it is logically prior in that I cannot master the skill or the belief without acquiring this knowledge and yet I may acquire this knowledge without acquiring the skill or the belief. The relationship of teaching and knowledge is reflected, again, in the intended learning of dispositions. Acquiring a habit, or an attitude, or a tendency, requires learning the prerequisite skills and beliefs. And to this extent teaching is always concerned with the learner's acquisition of knowledge. It is not surprising, then, that teaching is thought of as the transmission of knowledge. Clearly the transmission of beliefs, skills, attitudes, and habits proceeds on the basis of the learner's acquisition of knowledge.

The most important aspect of this relationship is the fact that teaching which is directed to the learner's believing something proceeds on the basis of the learner's acquisition of the

requisite knowledge. What is minimally required
for the learner to commit himself to the truth of
a proposition is that he know the proposition.
Consider teaching students the claim that the conviction of Louis Riel as a traitor was an unfortu-
nate miscarriage of justice. Fulfillment of the
intention that the students come to believe this
claim, that they commit themselves to the truth of
this claim, logically requires that they first
understand the claim. As well, teaching students
Newton's third law of motion (i.e. for every force
there is an equal and opposite force) with the
intention that they come to believe it requires
that one teach them the law, i.e. that they first
understand the law. The learner must know a proposition in order to commit himself to the truth of
it. Consider teaching someone the postulates of
Euclidean geometry. Teaching the postulates with
the intention that the student take them as true
statements about the world requires familiarizing
the student with the postulates. That is, acting
with the intention that the student come to hold
the postulates as true requires presenting them to
the student in such a way that he understands them,
i.e. knows them. The character of this relationship between knowledge and belief allows us to
teach exclusively for knowledge and understanding,
or to teach inclusively for rational belief as
well. Teaching the learner the postulates of
Euclidean geometry with the intention that he know
them is quite distinct from teaching the postulates
with the intention that he believe them. The difference is one of substantive content marked by the
intention. If the intention is that the student
understand the postulates, that he know them, then
what is being taught is different than what is
being taught when the intention is that the student
take the postulates as true statements about the
world. What is taught in the first case is an
aspect of reality, something "there" to be understood and familiarized--i.e. Euclid's postulation
of the basic character of spatial relations. The
subject matter in this case is a formal system, a
part of a discipline of inquiry, mathematics, which
is to be examined and understood. What is taught

in the second case is a postulation of the nature
of spatial relations as a true postulation of that
nature which is to be understood and believed. In
the case of teaching a student the proof of a theorem of Euclidean geometry, a teacher intending that
the student understand the proof will instruct with
the relevant definitions and postulates, and go
through the proof of the theorem for the student
so that the student sees the point of the proof,
i.e. the theorem. In this case the proof is something "there", one part of a body of knowledge to
be examined and understood. That the student does
or does not take the point of the proof as a true
statement about the world is not important. The
intention is that he understand the proof. A
teacher, however, may intend that the student believe the theorem (i.e. take it as a true statement
about the world). If his intention is that the
student believe the theorem, the teacher may present the relevant definitions and postulates and
go through the proof so that the student sees the
point of the proof and takes it as a true proposition about the world. In this case what is
taught is a proposition to be believed, to be taken
as a true representation of what is "there."

Consider the case of teaching a student the
theory that spiral nebulae are galaxies of stars
like our own galaxy. Teaching him the theory with
the intention that he know it requires presenting
the theory and the evidence for it such that the
student understands the theory, the evidence, and
the appropriateness of the evidence for the theory.
In this case the theory and the evidence for it is
part of the body of knowledge which is worthwhile
knowing. In the case of teaching the theory with
the intention that it be believed, the theory is
a true representation of the universe to be believed. Finally, consider teaching students the
claim that effective operation of a federal system
of government requires that the federal government
retain complete authority in such jurisdictions as
justice, finance, defence, trade, transportation,
and immigration, though it may give some or all
authority to regional governments in other juris-

326

dictions such as health, regional development, agriculture, fisheries, and so on. One may teach the claim intending the learner to be acquainted with it as a claim about the nature of federalism by presenting the claim to the learner with the reasons given to support it so that the learner is adequately familiar with the claim. One may teach the claim, however, with the intention that the learner believe it for these reasons, by presenting the claim as a true statement about the nature of federalism and by presenting the reasons for the claim such that the learner takes the claim as true on the basis of reasons given for it.

Teaching, knowing, and believing are related such that teaching someone with the intention that he believe that p on the basis of his having the proper backing for p is conditional on the learner's knowing a complex variety of things which, if not known by the learner, must be taught him. That is, since believing what is judged to be true on the basis of having the justification for the belief is conditional on knowing the proposition to be believed, the concepts employed in expressing it, and the reasons or evidence on which it is based, teaching someone with the intention that he believe the proposition on this basis is conditional on his coming to know the proposition, its meaning, the grounds for it, and the nature of the conclusiveness of the grounds. Consequently, coming to know and understand systems or forms by which a variety of beliefs is warranted may be itself the point of instruction and the only outcome. <u>Teaching, then, which is directed to learners' acquisition of belief on the basis of adequate and proper grounds entails the learner's acquisition of knowledge and the learner's initiation into relevant forms of inquiry and conceptualization. But the transmission of knowledge and the introduction of learners to bodies of knowledge does not entail the learners' acquisition of beliefs.</u> Of course, we very often believe what we recognize there are good grounds for believing, but this outcome is not definitive of either teaching or the relationship of <u>teaching</u> and <u>knowing</u>.

On the basis of this analysis we can clearly recognize that the curriculum of a liberal education is much more open and dynamic than Hirst suggests; and that it is so because it has to do primarily with knowledge, and not with belief as Green suggests. A liberal education is one in which persons become familiar with and competent in an optimal number of the multiple conceptual and methodological systems by which humanity orders and explores reality. These include systems of communication, computation, inquiry, social order, and cultural belief, which we may come to know well independently of what we reasonably believe. Of course what we come to know will usually affect our beliefs in one way or another. It is for this reason that we take so much interest in what our children and youth come to know. Hirst's seven forms of knowledge adequately represent the manner and limits of advanced western culture; they do not thereby exhaust the possible systems of disciplined study, inquiry, and belief which we may come to know and want our children to know. What in our judgement constitutes an optimal number and kind of conceptual and methodological systems to be studied in the education of persons is itself a matter of disciplined study which we may seek to become critically familiar with. Understanding and competence in philosophy of education is part of this disciplined study. Critical familiarity with the place of philosophy of education in the development of curriculum is itself the specific knowledge which this chapter is meant to impart. Philosophy is recognized as a disciplined method of attending to conceptual and logical structure. The practice of it is valuable to us, not because it is necessary to rational belief, but because it is effective in clarifying uncertainties, correcting errors, and resolving issues.

FOOTNOTES

1. James E. McLellan, Philosophy of Education (Englewood Cliffs, N.J.: Prentice-Hall,
1976), p. 9f.

2. Plato, Republic; Augustine, The Teacher
(De Magistro); John Locke, Second Treatise of
Civil Government and Some Thoughts Concerning Edu-
cation; Jean-Jacques Rousseau, Emile; J.S. Mill,
On Liberty and Utilitarianism.

3. Heinrich Pestalozzi, How Gertrude Teaches
Her Children; Friedrick Froebel, The Education of
Man; Johann Herbart, The Science of Education and
Outlines of Educational Doctrine; Herbert Spencer,
Education: Intellectual, Moral and Physical.

This historical comment relies on "History of
Philosophy of Education" in The Encyclopedia of
Philosophy (Macmillan & The Free Press, 1967) by
Kingsley Price.

4. John Dewey, Democracy and Education (New
York: The Free Press, 1966, publ. 1916), p. 328.

5. C.D. Hardie, "The Philosophy of Education
in a New Key," in Selected Readings in the Philosophy of Education, ed. Joe Park (New York: Macmillan Co., 1964, 2nd printing), p. 589.

6. The 41st and 54th Yearbooks (Part I) of
the National Society for the Study of Education
(NSSE), Philosophies of Education (1942) and Modern Philosophies and Education (1955) are wholly
devoted to the comparative exposition of educational implications of prevalent philosophical
"schools."

7. The strong tendency to engage teachers in
this comparative study of philosophical systems,
often called the "isms approach" to teaching
philosophy of education, is illustrated by the
textbooks often used. See, for examples: Robert
R. Rusk, Philosophical Bases of Education (London:

University of London Press, 1928); Joe Park
(ed.), Selected Readings in the Philosophy of
Education (New York: Macmillan, 1958); Van
Cleve Morris, Philosophy and the American School
(Boston: Houghton Mifflin, 1961); Philip H.
Phenix, Philosophies of Education (New York:
John Wiley & Sons, 1961); H.W. Burns and C.J.
Brauner (eds.), Philosophy and Education (New
York: Ronald Press Co., 1962); F. Bruce Rosen,
Philosophic Systems and Education (Columbus,
Ohio: Charles E. Merrill Publishing, 1968).

8. Reginald J. Archambault, Philosophical
Analysis and Education (London: Routledge and
Kegan Paul, 1965), "Introduction", p. 3.

9. John Passmore, "Philosophy," The Encyclopedia of Philosophy (Macmillan and The Free
Press, 1967), Vol. 6, p. 221.

10. J.O. Urmson, Philosophical Analysis
(Oxford: Clarendon Press, 1956), is a clear and
reliable introduction to philosophy as the analy-
sis of language. The central primary works are:
Bertrand Russell, Our Knowledge of the External
World (London: Allen & Unwin, 1914); Ludwig
Wittgenstein, Philosophical Investigations (Oxford:
Basil Blackwell, 1968); G.E. Moore, "A Defence
of Common Sense," Philosophical Papers (London:
Allen & Unwin, 1959); J.L. Austin, "A Plea for
Excuses," Philosophical Papers (Oxford: Claren-
don Press, 1961) and How To Do Things With Words
(New York: Oxford University Press, 1965); P.F.
Strawson, "On Referring," Mind, Vol. LIX, No. 235
(July 1950), reprinted in Robert R. Ammerman (ed.)
Classics of Analytic Philosophy (New York:
McGraw-Hill, 1965); Gilbert Ryle, The Concept of
Mind (Penguin Books, 1963); F. Waismann, "How I
See Philosophy," H.D. Lewis (ed.), Contemporary
British Philosophy (Third Series) (London:
Allen & Unwin, 1956).

11. John Yolton, Metaphysical Analysis
(Toronto: University of Toronto Press, 1967),
p. 196.

12. D.J. O'Connor, <u>An Introduction to the Philosophy of Education</u> (London: Routledge & Kegan Paul, 1957), p. 17.

13. Ibid, p. 45.

14. Ibid, Chapter 5.

15. Ibid, p. 110.

16. Israel Scheffler, <u>The Language of Education</u> (Springfield, Ill.: Charles C. Thomas, Publisher, 1960), p. 10.

17. Ibid, p. 22.

18. Ibid, pp. 47-52.

19. R.S. Peters, "Must an Educator Have an Aim?" Chapter 7 of <u>Authority, Responsibility, and Education</u> (New York: Atherton Press, 1966).

20. R.S. Peters, <u>Ethics and Education</u> (London: Allen & Unwin, 1966), p. 28.

21. McClellan, op.cit., p. 4.

22. Ibid, p. 10.

23. L.A. Reid, <u>Philosophy and Education</u> (New York: Random House, 1965), p. 14.

24. Clive Beck, <u>Educational Philosophy and Theory</u> (Boston: Little, Brown & Co., 1974), p. 288.

25. Ibid, p. 285f.

26. Brian Crittenden, <u>Education and Social Ideals</u> (Don Mills, Ont.: Longman Canada Ltd., 1973), p. XIV.

27. Passmore, op.cit., p. 218.

28. Glen Langford, "The Concept of Education," in <u>New Essays in the Philosophy of Education</u>

eds. Glen Langford and D.J. O'Connor (London: Routledge and Kegan Paul, 1973), p. 4.

29. Donna H. Kerr, Educational Policy: Analysis, Structure, and Justification (New York: David McKay Co., 1976), p. iii.

30. Edmund L. Gettier, "Is Justified True Belief Knowledge?" in Knowledge and Belief, ed. A. Phillips Griffiths (London: Oxford University Press, 1967), pp. 144-146.

31. Israel Scheffler, Conditions of Knowledge (Chicago: Scott, Foresman and Co., 1965), p. 58f.

32. A.J. Ayer, The Problem of Knowledge (Penguin Books, 1956), pp. 31-35.

33. Paul Hirst, Knowledge and the Curriculum (London: Routledge and Kegan Paul, 1974), p. 24.

34. Ibid, p. 93.

35. Ibid, p. 30.

36. Thomas F. Green, The Activities of Teaching (New York: McGraw-Hill, 1971), pp. 95-96.

37. Ibid, pp. 102-103.

38. Ibid, p. 105.

39. Ibid, p. 106.

40. Zeno Vendler, "On What One Knows," in Res Cogitans (Ithaca, N.Y.: Cornell University Press, 1972), Chapter V.

41. Much of the following analysis of knowledge and belief is part of my unpublished Ph.D. dissertation and some of it was presented in an unpublished paper to the Canadian Society of the Study of Education, Edmonton, June 1975. John L. McNeill, Teaching, Knowing and Believing (Unpublished Ph.D. dissertation, The University of

Calgary, 1972); and "The Relationship of Knowledge and Belief," paper delivered at The Canadian Society of the Study of Education, Edmonton, June 1975.

42. Vendler, op.cit., p. 116f.

43. Vendler provides a detailed analysis of the wh-nominalization and the relative clause construction. Ibid, Chapter V.

44. Ibid, p. 114.

45. Ibid, p. 112.

BIBLIOGRAPHY

Alston, W.P. Philosophy of Language. Englewood
    Cliffs, N.J.: Prentice-Hall, 1964.

Archambault, R.J. (ed.). Philosophical Analysis
    and Education. London: Routledge and Kegan
    Paul, 1965.

Austin, J.L. Philosophical Papers. Oxford:
    Clarendon Press, 1961.

Ayer, A.J. The Problem of Knowledge. Penguin
    Books, 1956.

Ayer, A.J. et al. The Revolution in Philosophy.
    London: Macmillan, 1967.

Beck, Clive. Educational Philosophy and Theory.
    Boston: Little, Brown & Co., 1974.

Belth, Marc. The New World of Education. Boston:
    Allyn and Bacon, 1970.

Brauner, C.J. and Burns, H.W. Problems in Educa-
    tion and Philosophy. Englewood Cliffs, N.J.:
    Prentice-Hall, 1965.

Brent, Allen. Philosophical Foundations for the
    Curriculum. London: George Allen & Unwin,
    1978.

Chazan, B. and Soltis, J.F. (eds.). Moral Educa-
    tion. New York: Teachers College Press,
    1973.

Chisholm, R.M. Theory of Knowledge. Englewood
    Cliffs, N.J.: Prentice-Hall, 1966.

Crittenden, Brian. Education and Social Ideals.
    Don Mills, Ont.: Longman Canada Ltd., 1973.

Curtis, B. and Mays, W. (eds.). Phenomenology and
    Education. London: Methuen, 1978.

334

Dearden, R.F. The Philosophy of Primary Education
    London: Routledge and Kegan Paul, 1968.

Dewey, John. Democracy and Education. New York:
    The Free Press, 1966.

Doyle, J.F. (ed.). Educational Judgements.
    London: Routledge and Kegan Paul, 1973.

Frankena, W.J. Philosophy of Education. New
    York: Macmillan, 1965.

Goldstone, Peter J. "Philosophical Analysis and
    the Revolution." Proceedings of the Philos-
    ophy of Education Society, 1970.

Green, Thomas F. The Activities of Teaching.
    New York: McGraw-Hill, 1971.

Griffiths, A.P. (ed.). Knowledge and Belief.
    Oxford: University Press, 1967.

Hardie, C.D. Truth and Fallacy in Educational
    Theory. New York: Teachers College, Colum-
    bia University, 1962.

Hedley, W.E. Freedom, Inquiry, and Language.
    Scranton, Penn.: International Textbook
    Company, 1968.

Hirst, Paul H. Knowledge and the Curriculum.
    London: Routledge and Kegan Paul, 1974.

Hirst, P.H. and Peters, R.S. The Logic of Educa-
    tion. London: Routledge and Kegan Paul,
    1970.

Hollins, T.H.B. (ed.). Aims in Education. Man-
    chester: University Press, 1964.

Kazepides, A.C. "On the Nature of Philosophical
    Questions and the Function of Philosophy in
    Education." Proceedings of the Philosophy of
    Education Society, 1970.

335

Kerr, Donna H. Educational Policy: Analysis, Structure, and Justification. New York: David McKay Co., 1976.

Komisar, B. Paul. "Teaching: Act and Enterprise." In Concepts of Teaching. Edited by C.J.B. Macmillan and Thomas W. Nelson. Chicago: Rand McNally, 1968.

Komisar, B.P. and Macmillan, C.B.J. (eds.). Psychological Concepts in Education. Chicago: Rand McNally, 1967.

Langford, Glenn. "The Concept of Education." In New Essays in the Philosophy of Education. Edited by Glenn Langford and D.J. O'Connor. London: Routledge and Kegan Paul, 1973.

Langford, Glenn. Philosophy and Education. London: Macmillan, 1968.

Lloyd, D.I. (ed.). Philosophy and the Teacher. London: Routledge and Kegan Paul, 1976.

Martin, Jane R. Explaining, Understanding, and Teaching. New York: McGraw-Hill, 1970.

Martin, Jane R. (ed.). Readings in the Philosophy of Education: A Study of Curriculum. Rockleigh, N.J.: Allyn and Bacon, 1970.

McNeill, John L. "Recognizing Teaching and Some Related Acts." Proceedings of the Philosophy of Education Society, 1975.

_____. "Justified True Belief." Proceedings of the Philosophy of Education Society, 1976.

National Society for the Study of Education. Philosophies of Education. Forty-first Yearbook, Part I, 1942.

National Society for the Study of Education. Modern Philosophies and Education. Fifty-fourth Yearbook, Part I, 1955.

O'Connor, D.J. An Introduction to the Philosophy of Education. London: Routledge and Kegan Paul, 1957.

Oakeshott, Michael. "Political Education." In Philosophy and Education. Edited by Israel Scheffler. Boston: Allyn and Bacon, 1966.

Pai, Young. Teaching, Learning, and the Mind. Boston: Houghton Mifflin, 1973.

Peters, R.S. Ethics and Education. London: George Allen and Unwin, 1966.

Peters, R.S. (ed.). The Concept of Education. London: Routledge and Kegan Paul, 1967.

Peters, R.S. (ed.). The Philosophy of Education. Oxford University Press, 1973.

Phenix, Philip H. Realms of Meaning. New York: McGraw-Hill, 1964.

Pratte, Richard. Ideology and Education. New York: David McKay Co., 1977.

Price, Kingsley. Education and Philosophical Thought. Boston: Allyn and Bacon, 1962.

Reid, L.A. Philosophy and Education. New York: Random House, 1965.

Ryle, Gilbert. The Concept of Mind. Penguin Books, 1963.

Scheffler, Israel. Conditions of Knowledge. Chicago: Scott, Foresman and Co., 1965.

_____. The Language of Education. Springfield, Ill.: Charles C. Thomas, 1960.

Schofield, Harry. The Philosophy of Education. London: Allen and Unwin, 1972.

Snook, I.A. Indoctrination and Education.

337

Soltis, J.F. <u>An Introduction to the Analysis of Educational Concepts</u> (2nd edition). Don Mills, Ontario: Addison-Wesley, 1978.

Urmson, J.O. <u>Philosophical Analysis.</u> Oxford: Clarendon Press, 1956.

Vandenberg, Donald (ed.). <u>Theory of Knowledge and Problems of Education.</u> Chicago: University of Illinois Press, 1969.

White, J.P. <u>Towards a Compulsory Curriculum.</u> London: Routledge and Kegan Paul, 1973.

Wilson, John. <u>Philosophy: Thinking About Meaning.</u> London: Heinemann Educational Books, 1968.

_____. <u>Language and the Pursuit of Truth.</u> Cambridge University Press, 1969.

Wilson, John, Williams, Norman, Sugarman, Barry. <u>Introduction to Moral Education.</u> Penguin Books, 1967.

Wilson, P.S. <u>Interest and Discipline in Education.</u> London: Routledge and Kegan Paul, 1971.

Woods, R.J. and Barrow, R. <u>An Introduction to Philosophy of Education.</u> London: Methuen, 1975.

CHAPTER 5

EDUCATIONAL THEORY

The area of education called curriculum and instruction straddles the line between educational theory and educational practice. A study of this area must take into account that it is through the activities of curriculum and instruction specialists that the discipline of education, studied and taught in universities and colleges, encounters the profession of education practiced by teachers in the school systems of Canada. Standing at the interface of the academic discipline and the profession, the curriculum and instruction specialist must be an eclectic fellow with feet planted firmly on both sides of the line. An overemphasis on educational theory or on educational practice will inevitably produce imbalance, and the resulting tumble will benefit neither educational theorists nor practitioners. However, a steady balance can be maintained provided that the curriculum specialist has a knowledge of what is taught in the schools and the structure of the body of knowledge behind it, of instructional methods used in the schools, and of the psychological principles underlying them. Yet even a grasp of what is happening in the schools and of how disciplines and theory are developing will not guarantee that, from the vantage point they occupy, curriculum and instruction specialists will be able to transmute the raw material of educational theory into the usable products of curriculum and instructional methods. There is no philosopher's stone.

Yet transmute they do. The curriculum and instruction specialist's task is to take what is known about educational needs, about learners and about learning processes, and create effective and relevant courses of study matched with suitable instructional methods, inventing what is not already extant. Often this complex task is compounded by the job of training teachers. Appearances to the contrary though, success is not magical.

339

Straddling the line between theory and practice along with the curriculum and instruction specialist are sets of procedures which allow the more or less systematic application of theory to practical needs. When using these procedures in order to create effective curriculum and suitable instruction, curriculum specialists are carrying out curriculum development, their stock in trade.

Most of this chapter is about curriculum development. It treats curriculum development as a sound scientific method which fulfils the twin functions of determining what should be taught in the schools, and the way in which it should be taught. Determining the content of curriculum, some might argue, is not really the province of curriculum and instruction specialists but rather of government and public bodies. Nonetheless, it is essential that curriculum and instruction specialists should be aware of what trends are determining provincial curriculum policy, and should be able to justify what they develop in terms of the needs of the society they serve. After curriculum determination, the chapter turns to the development of courses and units of instruction, activities collectively referred to as instructional development. The distinction between curriculum determination and instructional development is not always an easy one to make.[1] For the purposes of scrutiny, however, the two will be treated as two phases of the same process. The chapter continues with an examination of contributions typically made to curriculum and to instructional theory by curriculum and instruction specialists through their research, and concludes with a discussion of the importance of the area in the training of teachers.

So far, we have talked rather glibly about "curriculum", "instruction" and "educational theory". Definitions of these terms are needed. By curriculum is meant a set of planned experiences offered to learners in an institutional setting so that they meet the needs of a society, a policy, a value system or some other such determinant of

340

educational objectives.[2] For the most part, these institutions of formal education are under the direction of those who determine the curriculum. In Canada, this control is often quite loose, with curriculum committees in the provincial departments of education providing general curriculum guidelines, and with local boards, schools and teachers filling out the body of what is taught. Following from this, instruction can be defined as those strategies, activities and resources selected or created to help the learners meet the needs of the curriculum. Here there are two main emphases: those methods and resources aimed at transmitting information to the learners; and those whose main intention is to allow learners to apply and assimilate skills and concepts through their own activity and initiative. The overall effect of successful instruction is that learners will be able to perform in the ways that the curriculum specifies, and to fulfil the roles assigned them by society.

Educational theory refers to a body of knowledge about learners, learning and the content that is to be learned, that allows us to develop instruction for particular curricula and learners.[3] Part of this theory comes from educational psychology. The basis for most curriculum decisions has to be what we know about how the intended learners will learn what we have to teach them. This in itself means that curriculum developers need to know the various theories of how people learn, the effects of human development on cognitive processes, and how to assess those characteristics such as aptitudes, motivation and cognitive style, that are known to influence learning. In addition, the curriculum developer must either know the structure of the body of knowledge for which the curriculum is to be built, or must have a knowledge of methods enabling the derivation of that structure. Curriculum specialists either work in their own area of expertise, such as one of the academic subject areas traditionally taught in school, or they may find themselves dealing with content they know little or nothing about. In the former case, they are their own subject-matter specialists; in the latter case, they either have to rely on the advice of someone else who is an expert in the subject area, or they need skills to analyse the subject-matter for themselves. In either event, there is no such thing as pure curriculum development. It always has to be applied to subject matter.

CURRICULUM DEVELOPMENT: THE SCIENTIFIC METHOD

The application of educational theory to a particular instructional setting for the purpose of building curriculum hinges upon another important factor. This is the set of procedures which, along with the curriculum and instruction specialist, bridges the gap between theory and practice. The actual procedures that curriculum specialists employ to convert theory into practice vary according to the task in hand. Yet beneath any specific set of procedures lies a belief shared by all curriculum developers that a curriculum needs to be carefully planned and that this planning must take a scientific, problem-solving approach.[4] Planning "defines, directs and co-ordinates what the pupil is intended to learn, gives direction and purpose to teaching, provides it with justification and gives it order and coherence."[5] The scientific method allows this planning to be done in such a way that the problems to be solved are clearly identified and are accurately described, and that alternative solutions are tried out and rigorously evaluated.

The methodology of curriculum development has not always been scientific in this sense. Up until the curriculum reforms of the 1920s and 30s the prescription of courses of study and instructional methods had been at best largely based upon the judgment of individual educators, and at worst arbitrary and irrelevant. In his book Curriculum Development, Koopman[6] makes a good case for the contention that rational educational planning grew out of the need to revise the curriculum itself.

342

Prior to the 1920s, change in education occurred
slowly if it occurred at all, and curriculum was
a static affair. However, the momentous social
change wrought in society by the first world war,
and advances made in knowledge of how people learn,
inspired considerable re-evaluation of the role
of school in society as well as of classroom practice. Indeed, Koopman suggests that the origins
of the scientific approach to curriculum development lay in the need for schools to adapt to the
needs of a newly affluent and industrialized
society. The need for reform led to the invention
and adoption of procedures whereby reform could be
carried out.

The wheels of curriculum reform were greased
by other developments both within and outside education. Not least among these were the writings
and activities of John Dewey.[7] Dewey's greatest
contributions at this point in the history of curriculum development were his attempts to break
down the barriers between the school and the world
outside, and his belief that learners should be
active participants in the learning process. Here
were the beginnings of child-centred education.
Some curriculum reformers were quick to seize upon
statements to the effect that education was not a
preparation for life but rather life itself as
justification for shifting the emphasis of what
was taught in school from an academic to a pragmatic orientation based upon social needs. Others,
inspired by the idea of learners as active participants in learning rather than vessels to be
filled with knowledge, looked to reform of classroom methods to accommodate the learner and to
accompany the revised curriculum.

Reform in both the content and the way in
which the curriculum was implemented was spurred
further by research in learning. While the contributions of people such as Thorndike[8] were many
and diverse, two conclusions drawn by researchers
exemplify the impact of learning psychology on the
curriculum.[9] The first of these is that learners
forget things rather rapidly if they are not given

343

the chance to practice and to apply them at subsequent times. If a course of studies were such
that at a particular point a student knew he had
"done physics", and would have no more instruction
in it or chance to apply it, then he would rapidly
forget what he had learned. The second example
has to do with the greater understanding of the
transfer of learning from one set of circumstances
to another. If a student can learn how to calculate area and volume in a physics course, then he
will be able to transfer this ability to problems
set by a mathematics teacher. The implications of
this for curriculum and instructional methods were
quite profound. In the first instance, it was no
longer possible for a subject to be completely
learned. In the second instance, the watertight
barriers between traditional bodies of knowledge
began to appear artificial and even unnecessary.[10]

The work of the curriculum reformers of the
1920s and 30s has been described sufficiently often
that it need not be summarized here.[11] What is
important to trace is the evolution of that set of
procedures which would become the scientific method
of curriculum development. As early as 1918, we
find Bobbitt writing the following:

> Human life, however varied, consists
> of specific activities. Education
> that prepares for life is one that
> prepares definitely and adequately
> for these specific activities. How-
> ever numerous and diverse they may
> be for any social class, they can be
> discovered. This requires only
> that we go out into the world of
> affairs and discover the particulars
> of which these affairs consist ...
> These will be the objectives of the
> curriculum ... The curriculum will
> then be that series of experiences
> which children and youth must have
> by way of attaining these objectives.[12]

What is important here is threefold. First, the

curriculum is based on a pragmatic orientation to education. What is taught in the schools should prepare students to carry out the specific activities that life and society require of them. Second, these activities can be identified. Third, they can be stated in terms of objectives for directing classroom activity. Thus, in embryonic form, we find a "skills for living" philosophy of curriculum. We see a recommendation that curricular decisions be based on needs assessment. We find objectives derived from the needs assessment determining what experiences and activities the child is to undergo.

Harold Rugg, writing in 1927, develops these principles further:

> There are three definite jobs involved in the task (of curriculum-making):
> First: the determination of fundamental objectives, the great purposes of the curriculum as a whole and of its several components.
> Second: the selection of activities and other materials of instruction, choice of content, readings, exercises, excursions, topics for open-forum discussions, manual activities, health and recreational programs.
> Third: the discovery of the most effective organizations of materials and their experimental placement in the grades of public schools.[13]

This statement does two things. It makes more specific what was implicit in what Bobbitt said, particularly as far as activities and materials of instruction are concerned. In this, many of the decision-making processes followed by present-day instructional developers are anticipated. More striking, though, is the suggestion that the materials should be tried out in the schools on

an experimental basis so that, presumably, they
could be revised or abandoned depending on their
effectiveness. This points straight to the heart
of the scientific method, gathering data, and to
the fourth ingredient of curriculum development,
evaluation.

In Bobbitt's and Rugg's ideas lies the key
to the dependence of the scientific method of
curriculum development on curriculum revision. If
a curriculum is to be directed towards society,
towards the "affairs of the world", rather than
towards academic subjects, and if it is to be
child-centred, then it must take as its starting
points society and the child's preparation for
entering it, not an academic discipline. For such
a curriculum to be successful, information has to
be gathered about what society needs, and what
type of person the child is. It is in the gathering of this information, transforming it into
specifications for instruction, and the testing
and validating of the information through instruction, that the scientific method is crucial. Hypotheses are built from the information that is
made available by the analysis of the needs and
the learners. Decisions are made and tested. The
shifts in the curriculum in the early decades of
this century towards closing the gap between education and life, and towards a closer alignment
with the needs and characteristics of children
were exactly what it took to make this kind of
analysis and hypothesis-testing necessary. Never
before had educators started out to design curriculum from a position of such uncertainty. If life
itself was to be the stuff of the curriculum, and
the developing child its client, then curriculum
developers needed to do all in their power to find
out as much as they could about life and children
at the outset of their task.

The four major steps of curriculum development received their most eloquent articulation in
a small book by Ralph Tyler published in 1949 entitled Basic Principles of Curriculum and Instruction.[14] Tyler examines the area by asking four

questions, each of which corresponds to one of the four steps. What educational purposes should the school seek to attain? This, of course, requires some sort of needs assessment to be carried out. How can learning experiences be selected which are likely to be useful in attaining these objectives? In answers to this question is to be found the practical link between curriculum and instruction furnished by what we know about learning, learners and the subject matter to be learned. How can learning experiences be organized for effective instruction? To answer this question we need to look no further than the principles and procedures of instructional development. How can the effectiveness of learning experiences be evaluated? Implicit here is the practice of field-testing and revision of new curriculum, and the belief that even the most scientifically developed curriculum should not be assumed to be foolproof.

Tyler's contribution to curriculum and instruction was, and continues to be, influential. Subsequent curriculum developers still base what they do on answers to the four questions he asked. A great flurry of activity was set off by the launching of Sputnik I by the Russians in the early fifties. This event was taken as evidence that America was lacking in scientists and technologists, and the schools were expected to provide them. The curriculum reforms of the fifties in both Canada and the United States were characterized by an increased emphasis on the sciences in schools and universities.[15]

Parallel to this shift in emphasis in the curriculum was a similar trend in the methodology of education. Technology and science became more visible as tools of education as well as matters to be studied. Behavioral psychology produced programmed instruction and "programmable" teaching machines.[16] Advances in electronic communication produced remarkable developments in educational broadcasting and media. But more important were the principles, not just the tools of technology which began to permeate educational planning and

development.[17] So important was this tendency that
it is now unwise to discuss the scientific method
in curriculum development without mentioning the
contribution made to it by educational technology.

Educational Technology

The field of educational technology traces
its roots back to the realm of educational media
and audio-visual communication. It has, however,
completely outgrown its original purpose of developing multi-sensory instructional resources.
At first, the greatest contribution of technology
to education lay in its success at producing and
distributing a great number of alternative ways of
conveying subject matter to learners. Technology
provided education with the same kinds of things
it provided industry: variety and flexibility of
production techniques with subsequently a great
deal of choice for consumers. Just as in industry,
however, variety and choice in education created
all manner of problems not only in the design and
production of curriculum materials, but also in
getting the right instruction to the right learners
when they needed it.[18] In 1965, Charles Hoban
wrote that the most important problem facing educators was "not learning, but the management of
learning."[19] By this he meant not classroom administrative procedures, but organizing a rich and
varied curriculum so that the right resources could
be brought to bear as they were needed.

The realization that variety and flexibility
can only be profitable in education if an increased
emphasis is placed on planning and management led
to a great deal of soul-searching and wheel-spin-
ning in the educational technology field. At the
centre of this activity was a committee set up by
the Association for Educational Communication and
Technology, the professional organization of educational technologists, to look into the problem
of defining the field.[20] The report that emerged
took as its starting point Galbraith's definition
of technology given in The New Industrial State,

348

as the "systematic application of scientific and
other organized knowledge to practical tasks."[21]
At the same time, a Commission on Instructional
Technology of the United States Congress was preparing another report, published in 1970 with the
title To Improve Learning. Here a similar and
more thorough definition of educational technology
was given:

> Instructional technology is more
> than the sum of its parts. It is
> a systematic way of designing,
> carrying out and evaluating the
> total process of learning and
> teaching in terms of specific
> objectives, based on research in
> human learning and communication
> and employing a combination of
> human and non-human resources to
> bring about more effective instruc-
> tion.[22]

It is apparent that educational technologists are saying more or less what curriculum
developers have been saying all the time. The two
areas have converged and educational technologists
are squarely in the business of curriculum development. But that is not the end of the story, for
educational technology has contributed two important things to "classical" curriculum development.
These have to do with the nature of the process
itself and with the concept of "system".

If educational technologists differ from
curriculum developers of the Tyler school, it is
in their greater emphasis on the procedures of
development themselves. In a sense, the educational technologist is a more "pure" curriculum
developer in that traditionally any subject matter
has been grist to the mill. Educational technologists tend therefore to rely on others for information on subject matter and to concentrate more
on the development, production and testing of curriculum and resources. As a result, curriculum
development procedures, particularly those concerned

349

with the development of instructional activities
and materials, have been refined for the curriculum
developer to a point where science does as much as
it possibly can, especially in the testing and revision of curriculum, and "art" fits snugly alongside. An educational technologist who claims to
develop curriculum entirely by the scientific
method is not being totally honest. He plays hunches just like anyone else. Yet this notwithstand-
ing, the educational technologist has developed
applied research to a fine art, has, in other words,
produced a carefully honed set of research and
development tools for use in the practical world of
education rather than the research laboratory.

The sceond contribution of educational
technology to curriculum development has its origins in the old-style, multi-media technology. In
creating curriculum based on a large number of different resource and modes of delivery, the educational technologist was developing more complex instructional systems than had hitherto existed. A
system, after all, is simply an integrated whole
made up of various different parts.[23] But the more
parts there are, as in a curriculum that uses many
different resources, strategies and activities, the
more complicated it becomes to organize and to manage the system. To help them develop and implement
such systems, educational technologists turned to
systems analysis in order to make sure that all the
bits and pieces of the curriculum they developed fit
together in effective and meaningful ways. The
techniques of sytems analysis applied to educational
planning need not concern us here,[24] but it is important to note that in what follows in the discussion of instructional development, a "systems
approach" to curriculum planning is implied.

The contribution of educational technology
to curriculum and instruction lies in an emphasis
on the management of learning, in the refinement of
scientific development procedures, and in the perception of successful instruction as something
through which the many different things that are
found in the classroom, such as resources, activ-

ities, methods, teachers and students, are pulled together into an efficient and effective instructional system. Galbraith's definition of technology now takes on a clearer meaning for curriculum and instruction specialists. Carefully tuned development procedures assure the "systematic application" of educational theory, and the "practical tasks" can be taken as the setting up and smooth running of instructional systems.

It is now time to look more carefully at those procedures enabling the curriculum and instruction specialist to apply educational theory to practice and to develop successful curriculum. There are many sets of procedures and models of the curriculum development process and all of them can trace their origins to the thinking of Tyler and others in the thirties and forties. For our purposes, the procedures proposed by Taba are a reasonable place to begin the discussion.[25] The steps she proposes are: diagnosis of needs, formulation of objectives, selection of content, organization of content, selection of learning experiences, organization of learning experiences, determination of what to evaluate and of the ways or means of doing it. One important point that Taba makes is that the outcomes of education can be stated on different levels. At their broadest, stated educational outcomes have to do with the purpose and role of education in society. Such outcomes might be: the preservation of culture, the provision of a skilled workforce, and so on. On the more specific level, outcomes are expressed as objectives which describe what the students will be able to do, will know and will feel as a result of a particular instructional activity. By and large, the broad desired outcomes of education direct decisions as to the kind of things that should be taught in the schools, or guide curriculum determination. The more specific educational objectives guide the development of units of instruction.

CURRICULUM DETERMINATION

Deciding what goes into a curriculum can be a tricky business. The curriculum developer has to decide what it is that society needs from the schools, and what it is that students need to know in order to be useful and well-adjusted members of that society. This difficult task is complicated by the pressure that is brought to bear on those who determine curriculum by political, religious and community pressure groups.[26] Yet in spite of this, curriculum usually betrays reasonably clear philosophical orientations and value systems which purport to represent the direction a given society has chosen to take. An obvious example of this has already been mentioned briefly, and that was the shift in emphasis to more science and technology in the 1950s for reasons of a government policy with marked nationalist tendencies. Another more current example is the movement "back to the basics" where public opinion and public criticism have pressed for a change in the general orientation of curriculum, even if they have not completely changed classroom practice. There are, though, several more general and often conflicting perceptions of how the schools should be contributing to society. It is important to look at some of these because the selection of one over another as a basis for curriculum building within a province, school district or school affects the whole way in which the curriculum and instruction specialist converts the needs of learners into learning experiences.

Just about every writer on curriculum has addressed the question of what schools should contribute to society. Many say the same things, and some make unique suggestions which may or may not be useful. From all of these, it is possible to identify six fundamentally different orientations that a curriculum can take. In discussing these, it will be necessary to look at what each implies about the nature of man, and also at what a curriculum based on each orientation might be. For convenience, these six orientations have been

352

labelled subject matter, personal development, culture, social adjustment, employment, and adaptability.

Subject Matter

The subject matter orientation to the curriculum is by far the most traditional, evolving as the disciplines of knowledge themselves evolve.[27] In this particular orientation, it is assumed that subjects such as mathematics, physics, latin, english and so on have qualities that make them distinct and unique. Curriculum specialists who hold to this position maintain that society needs people who are rational, in the classical sense, and knowledgeable. Persons who are products of this kind of curriculum possess knowledge of facts and have been trained to think by means of the disciplines of knowledge. One learns latin to develop the mind. A person useful to society is therefore one who has a great storehouse of knowledge and who thinks logically.

The curriculum to produce such a person would take as its starting point the traditional areas of academic study. It would place less emphasis on developing individual personal qualities and on training the student to be a useful and well-adjusted member of society. It is assumed that these qualities would follow from broad knowledge and rational thinking. For example, King and Bromwell[28] assert that the intellect has the prime claim upon the curriculum. They justify this by stating that man is a "symbolizer", a creature who regulates action by reason and through knowledge. They also claim that the intellectual orientation is the most general. A trained intellect has a wider potential applicability than, say, a trained ability in a particular skill.

Personal Development

The idea that the curriculum should allow all individuals to develop to their fullest potential

353

can be traced back to Dewey[29] and has its practical
beginnings in child-centred education. In each and
every one of us there are potential abilities and
interests which have to be developed if we are to
be useful and contributing members of society.
Self-realization can be achieved if the curriculum
is carefully balanced. At bottom is the realization
that everyone is different and that these differences can only be productive if developed to the
full. This can only be done by letting each individual have a say in the direction that his or her
education takes. Rather than making every learner
subordinate to a body of knowledge that has to be
learned in a disciplined and uniform manner, the
content now becomes subservient to the needs and
interests of each individual person. For example,
Cremin[30] discusses the humanizing of knowledge so
that it can be popularized, and Brunin[31] claims
that, suitably organized, a body of knowledge can
be taught to people of any intellectual level.
Only a fully realized, satisfied person can serve
society well, and once a person has achieved their
full potential in intellectual and moral matters,
and has enjoyed the satisfaction that these achievements bring, other skills will be more easily
acquired.

A curriculum for personal development is
characterized by two main things. The first of
these is a rooting in developmental psychology. A
child goes through certain stages of development,
each of which is characterized by certain intellectual abilities and limitations.[32] The matter to be
studied in the classroom and the way in which the
child is to study it are determined by the developmental stage of the child, and by the need to lead
the child into the next stage.[33] The second is
the realization that the child is sometimes the best
judge of both what should be learned and of how to
learn it. The didactic methods, often implicit in
a structured discipline of knowledge, are less
visible. The child is left more on his own to
discover phenomena, solutions to problems and even
content. The child is largely responsible for the
unfolding of his own inner capacities.[34]

Culture

A third approach to curriculum is based upon
the conception of man as a humanist educated from
the great repositories of knowledge that mankind
has stored up since the beginning of history. For
adherents to this orientation, the purpose of education is to pass on mankind's cultural heritage
from one generation to the next. Students grow up
to be well-read and well-rounded individuals whose
contribution to society lies in their wisdom (rather
than in their knowledge) and their learning from the
past. There is implicit in this a belief in an
eternal and absolute truth which was discovered by
earlier generations and is still worth knowing.

The curriculum based upon this orientation
would involve a study of history, philosophy and
great literature. In its application, it has become known as a "liberal arts" education, with vocational and professional subjects relegated to training. This stress on intellect and culture, both
linked to the past, underlies, for example, the
thinking behind the well-known Harvard Report on
General Education which stressed the need for a
"working system of truths which relied on both
reason and experience" developed and handed on to
us by antiquity as standards for civilization.[35]

These three orientations to the curriculum
take as their starting points ideas and bodies of
knowledge outside the precinct of modern society--
academic disciplines, the study of which is largely
an end in itself; the individual person, rather
than the social being; and a cultural heritage
whose roots go back to antiquity. The second three
orientations to the curriculum are rooted in the
nature of modern society itself.

Social Adjustment

A society is a product of an evolutionary
process, and in this sense social demands on the
curriculum are just as much a product of the past

as cultural demands are. However, there is a difference. Curricula that stress the need for schools
to produce people who fit and function comfortably
in society stress also the need to educate for
modern society. Typical of this approach to curriculum is the discussion by Smith, Stanley and
Shores which begins with a study of the impact of
cultural roots and cultural change on the curriculum, but then leads immediately into an examination
of such sociological questions as the impact of
science and technology on culture, the influences
of changes in community life on society, social
stratification, changes in family life and changes
in occupation and employment.[36] The curriculum
emerges as something that allows the schools to
prepare students to face and overcome the problems
of society rooted in these questions. For Smith,
Stanley and Shores, the curriculum must aim to help
youngsters understand society in a realistic rather
than an idealistic way. It should provide them with
the abilities necessary for the solution of social
conflicts, and should itself be free of class bias.

Another frequently encountered approach to
the same set of social concerns contends that the
socially well-adjusted person is a good ethical
citizen raised in the traditions of democracy. Education for citizenship goes back, again, to the
classical world. But in today's schools, it is
entirely modern. The curriculum based on this
social-political orientation to society's needs
goes far beyond courses in government and political
science. Ideally, the principles and practices of
democracy are embodied in everything the child does
and studies, from fairytales to great literature,
from local geography to anthropology.

While this approach to the curriculum might
seem doctrinaire, its importance should not be
overlooked in times when governments are more and
more asserting authority over educational policy
and are determining the direction curriculum takes.[37]
Underlying this is the growing dependence of school
systems on provincial funding and an increasing
accountability of educators to the public, through

356

government, for what they do. Little by little, schools are beginning to reflect the political orientations of the governments who fund them, and the social biases of the public to whom they are accountable.

Employment

People leaving school have to find jobs. They have to do this to earn a living and also to make a contribution to the society that has footed the bill for their education. It seems reasonable to expect schools to produce people who are usefully employable. Typical is the emphasis Broudy, Smith and Burnett place upon the "applicative use of schooling". Here, students are taught what can be applied to the practical tasks of a society:

> Our technological civilization depends on the application of knowledge to particular problems of practice rather than on its replicative use. Mathematics and physics applied to problems of mechanics give us the profession of engineering, that in turn solves the problems of transportation, construction, mechanical toasters and space probes.[38]

Schools, then, should not be teaching in a vacuum, but within a context of practicality. A curriculum would either teach pure mathematics through engineering, the argument being that if a student can calculate stresses exerted on the supports of a bridge, he can also multiply and calculate square roots. Or a curriculum would teach skills enabling students to apply knowledge alongside the knowledge itself. It is easier for engineers to get jobs than pure mathematicians.[39]

This is only one way of looking at the job orientation to curriculum. Other writers maintain that schools should only teach subjects that will

357

enable a student to get a job, and forget the fundamental disciplines altogether. The school should provide the student with what Conant calls "marketable skills".[40] In this way, the student would not have to go through the intermediate and time-consuming step of converting theory into practice. This is something of an extreme position, and it can be argued that an exclusive preoccupation with job training in the curriculum is both foolish and undemocratic: foolish because an understanding of basic principles is necessary for the completion of even the most menial task; undemocratic because it does not permit the individual the freedom of choice to move from one kind of employment to another that a broader, more liberal education would permit.[41]

Adaptability

The last orientation to the curriculum is one of the least frequently encountered, perhaps because its roots lie outside education. Critics of education have frequently argued that knowledge and social needs are changing so rapidly that anything we teach in school today will be out of date even before the student graduates. Leader among thinkers adhering to this position is Toffler, whose book Future Shock[42] enjoyed influence and prestige as a top best-seller. Toffler argues that schools should be providing students with "cope-ability" rather than capability. In this way, people would be trained not in specific static skills and knowledge, but in ways that would enable them to adapt to changes in society and thus avoid "future shock" caused by the rapid and often incomprehensible evolution of society and technology.

Toffler was not particularly prescriptive about what a curriculum designed from this premise would look like. Presumably it would involve a study of social trends, and the development of open-mindedness. A socially aware and flexible person would emerge who would be well-adjusted enough to shift with change rather than resist it or be overcome by it. Stuart Chase[43] is more specific on this

358

point. Exploring the future from a scientific standpoint, he sees a future curriculum based on furnishing learners with a desire to know, an impulse to question, the search for data, the demand for verification, the respect for logic, the awareness of premises, and the evaluation of consequences. This looks remarkably like the scientific method itself, and suggests that "future shock" [44] can be combatted by logical, scientific inquiry. It is also interesting to note in this connection the enormous increase in interest in continuing education. It seems that people from all trades and professions are becoming more aware of their need for continual re-training to keep up with changes in their areas of expertise, and also that people in general feel a need just to keep in touch, though courses, with developments in society in general. [45]

It is important to realize that none of the proponents of the six orientations to the curriculum maintain the exclusivity of their preference. No-one would argue that if people are rational they do not need to be trained to get jobs, or that if they are well-rounded and satisfied individuals they do not have to get along with other people in a democratic society. What the orientations show is preference for a certain emphasis. Most curriculum theorists would argue the claim of a particular orientation to be of prime importance, the others following naturally from it. Those who support the subject-matter orientation would argue that if a person is first of all trained in the academic subjects, then the discipline his intellect receives will stand him in good stead when it comes to treating with his fellow man, to dealing with the future and to getting a job. Supporters of the job-training approach would maintain that a person with money in his pocket and food in his belly will be a better individual, socially well-adjusted, more humanistic and more rational. [46] What is usually found in curriculum guides are statements that emanate from a variety of the six orientations. For example, the following occur in the Alberta curriculum guide for secondary school science[47] under the heading "Objectives for secondary school science":

"To promote an understanding of the role that science has had in the development of societies." Here is an objective derived from a belief in the importance of science to our cultural heritage.

"To develop a critical understanding of those current social problems which have a significant scientific component in terms of their cause and/or their solution: a. depletion of natural resources, b. pollution of water and air ..." This shows a different approach squarely situated in a "social adjustment" orientation to curriculum.

"To promote assimilation of scientific knowledge." Now we see science treated as an academic discipline whose study is an end in itself.

"To develop attitudes, interests, values, appreciations and adjustments similar to those exhibited by scientists at work." This time, science is a means to an end, that end being the personal development of the students.

"To contribute to the development of vocational knowledge and skill." This objective stresses preparation for a job.

So it is that in any curriculum guide taken at random from any province's department of education, a variety of objectives for the schools occurs which covers a large number, if not all of the orientations to curriculum. This is not a bad thing, for it provides students with a many-faceted approach to schooling which prepares them for the many demands society will make of them when they graduate.

The curriculum and instruction specialist has to deal with the various orientations to the curriculum under two sets of circumstances. In some instances, it is they who help determine what it is that society needs from the schools. In

Canada, it is common for curriculum developers to sit on provincial curriculum committees attached to departments of education in order to determine the general direction that a curriculum should take. However, as organs of government, curriculum committees are accountable to the public and canvas public opinion through lay members. The curriculum and instruction specialist's role at this early stage of curriculum development is to make sure that the curriculum reflects the true needs of society and not the particular feelings of a pressure group or of the committee itself. The curriculum specialist, with less of an axe to grind, is the learners' watchdog, and must assure that what is offered to the learner is balanced fare and not ideologically or socially lopsided.

The curriculum specialist is involved at the next stage of the development process as well. With particular orientations as given, general objectives are converted into the more specific objectives of the curriculum guide. Here the curriculum developer functions as well as a subject-matter specialist and determines what particular pieces of content and discipline-related skills are to be taught in school. From the general objectives for science in Alberta stated above come the following objectives for high-school biology, labelled according to the various orientations to the curriculum:

Subject matter. "Understands the processes by which plants and animals function."

Personal development. "Develop an understanding of the need for using a critical, quantitative approach when looking at biological data."

Social adjustment and adaptability. "Examine the dependence of man on his natural environment, the ways in which man is causing problems by upsetting the balance of nature, and ways by which man can live in greater harmony with nature."

Employment. "Learn through project and

361

laboratory work the ways in which biologists carry out the field and laboratory research." "Develop proficiency in the use of laboratory instruments."

A third stage occurs when these more specific objectives are focussed even more tightly on learning activities for the three high-school grades, the texts to be used, the experiments to be carried out, and so on. The curriculum specialist combines knowledge of subject matter with a knowledge of resources to prescribe core curricular activities. So in grade eleven in Alberta, the biology student studies the subject matter of environmental biology, including such topics as biogeochemical cycles, the structure of ecosystems and biological succession; develops the skills of a biologist through field work and the presentation of a report; and becomes more aware of the relationships between biology and society by studying topics such as population growth, pollution, and their political, social and economic implications.

The basic orientations to the curriculum remain, in modified form, right down to the level of the classroom activities that the students work through. Whether or not the students do in fact carry out what the curriculum guides suggest is another matter. But it is not really a relevant point of argument. The local determination of curriculum, whether at the school board level, at the school or even in the individual classroom will follow more or less the same path from philosophy to activity, with a curriculum specialist playing more or less the same roles as at the provincial level. At all levels of curriculum determination, the curriculum and instruction specialist's job is to decide what society really needs the school to do, to draw up general and specific objectives for the schools that are congruent with these basic orientations, and to select general areas of subject matter and general kinds of activity that will allow the objectives to be met.

Up until this point, the curriculum developer has covered the first three points in Taba's pro-

362

cedure, and has edged into the fourth. Society's needs have been diagnosed, objectives have been formulated, broad areas of content have been selected, and some content organization has been undertaken. It is now time to turn to the second phase of curriculum development which we have identified as the development and evaluation of units of instruction. This corresponds to the rest of Taba's procedure: selection of learning experiences, organization of learning experiences, and determining what to evaluate and how to do it.

INSTRUCTIONAL DEVELOPMENT

While curriculum determination starts with the needs of society and ends with some specification of content, instructional development is a procedure that leads from a determined body of curriculum to classroom activities, strategies and resources with which the learner will come into contact. Within the instructional development process lies the crucial point at which what we know about learning, the learners and the content is applied to the tasks that need to be carried out in order for the objectives identified during curriculum determination to be achieved. Since this "systematic application of knowledge to tasks" is central to the new orientation of educational technology, it is little wonder that educational technologists above all others have been preoccupied with inventing models of the instructional development process, and with their application to the design of instructional resources and strategies. It is helpful to study the curriculum and instruction specialist's role in instructional development by breaking it down into three phases. In this we are following the lead of Nord[48] who divided instructional development into input, process and output stages. If we regard the instructional development process as a problem-solving one, as Rowntree does[49], then Nord's three phases make more sense. Decisions concerning the selection of resources and methods to solve particular instructional problems must be based on information that is available

rather than on hunches. The whole procedure may
then be systematic in the technological sense and
the product an integrated and effective instructional system. The "input" to the decision-making
process is therefore information gathered about the
needs and the learners through careful analysis.
Despite the "process" phase, this information guides
the application of our knowledge of educational
theory, cognitive processes and the nature of curriculum content so that useful "output", a system
of instructional strategies and resources, can be
created.

Within each of these three broad phases, instructional developers have identified series of
sub-steps. While these vary in name from model to
model, a generalized model of instructional development can be derived from them.[50]

```
INPUT     1.  identify needs
          2.  analyze learners
          3.  state goals
          4.  analyze tasks
PROCESS   5.  state objectives
          6.  design instructional system
                  a.  methods
                  b.  materials
                  c.  activities
OUTPUT    7.  produce any materials, guides,
                  manuals, etc.
          8.  field-test and revise as
                  necessary
          9.  implement
```

What follows looks at the three major phases of
instructional development and at some of the sub-
steps of each phase.

Input

The instructional development process, like
curriculum determination, begins with an analysis
of needs. In this case though the starting point
is not the needs of society that schools are

expected to meet, but the needs of the curriculum itself. There is a difference of degree, instructional needs being far narrower and more sharply focussed on a particular problem area than the curricular needs of society. Kaufman has defined a need as "the measurable discrepancy between where we are now and where we should be in terms of outcomes or results".[51] For the developer, "where we should be" is usually implicit or stated in the broad objectives and guidelines written by those determining what the curriculum should be, and stated in curriculum guides. They only need further interpretation to become prescriptive. "Where we are now" is for the developer to find out.

Developers begin by making sure that they understand what is meant by the general guidelines for the curriculum that are handed down. Above, we discussed how the curriculum specialist is involved at three levels of curriculum determination: the selection of particular orientations required by contemporary social needs; the conversion of these into general objectives for each area of study; and determining, in very broad terms, how these might be operationalized in classroom activities. The instructional developer must take these as a starting point, and cannot come up with effective instructional systems unless the general objectives, the curriculum outlines and the philosophical bases for them are thoroughly understood.

The second half of needs assessment, "where we are now", requires the developer to examine what it is that the learners know in the particular area of the curriculum, and also what is already in the schools that will help the learners get to where they have to go. It is important to know what the learner can do, knows and feels about a particular area.[52] A need is identified when the developer finds out, by diagnostic testing of aptitudes, abilities and knowledge[53], that the learners do not have the required capabilities, knowledge and feelings about a part of the curriculum.

Needs are descriptive. The developer next

has to make them prescriptive so that a line of
action to meet the needs can be chosen. This particular specification is called a goal. If, for
example, the developer finds out that there is a
discrepancy, measured on an achievement test, between what learners know about "the processes by
which plants and animals function" and the objectives stated in the Alberta high-school biology
curriculum guide, then a need has been identified.
It becomes the goal of the developer that, after
instruction, the learners will be able to demonstrate in some prescribed way that they know the
processes by which plants and animals function. A
goal then is a statement in general terms of what
learners will learn and also of how they will demonstrate they have learned it.

Once the developer has identified a goal,
this determines the direction of all subsequent
activity. But before a start can be made on the
design and development of the instructional system
proper, the developer needs one further set of
information. This has to do with the specific tasks
the learners will have to be able to perform if they
are to become capable of doing and knowing what the
goal says they should. Task analysis provides this
information.

It is a common mistake to think of task
analysis as having to do exclusively with psycho-
motor skills. Task analysis provides the developer
with information on how the developer is to perform
in the cognitive and affective as well as in the
psycho-motor domains.[54] If the instructional goal
requires that certain information be processed and
remembered in a certain way, or that a particular
attitude be developed towards the subject matter,
then the developer must find this out now. A preoccupation with the analysis of skills has led to
the neglect of the affective domain in a lot of
instruction. The result has often been that students may well have learned, but that they have
learned reluctantly or that they have even developed
a hostile attitude towards the subject. If this
happens, then learning runs the risk of becoming an

366

end in itself and is of little use to the learner as a functioning member of society.

Task analysis will produce a list of all the things that the learner must do, know and feel in order to attain the instructional goal. It is done in a variety of ways: through observation of someone performing a particular task, and noting down everything that happens; by analyzing experimentally the organization of concepts in a particular conceptual domain through various techniques of structural analysis[55]; through discussing with trial learners why they like or dislike certain parts of the "tasks" they have to perform. Whatever the technique--and this depends largely on the nature of the instructional goal, though it is likely that even in psycho-motor tasks there is also a cognitive and an affective component--task analysis is a scientific, quasi-experimental procedure which provides data derived empirically. This point needs stressing. If the instructional developer relies entirely on hunches at this stage, then he is on very shaky ground.

Process

The first part of the process whereby goals generate instruction requires the developer to state specific instructional objectives. These objectives, sometimes called enabling objectives, are means to an end and correspond to the steps into which the activities necessary to attain the goal have been decomposed by task analysis. If the developer has performed a satisfactory task analysis, then the writing of instructional objectives should be relatively simple. If, for example, one of the tasks that the learner must be able to perform on the way to achieving the goal of understanding the processes by which plants and animals function is comprehension of cell division through mitosis, then an objective can be stated to the effect that the student will be able to demonstrate an understanding of mitosis. This appears all too easy. However, the objective is not complete in

367

this form.

An instructional objective must include not just a statement of what the student is to do, know or feel, but also a statement of how this ability, knowledge or feeling is to be demonstrated and under what conditions.[56] This immediately leads back to what the developer knows about the learners, and complicates the picture somewhat. For example, younger children, should they be required to learn about mitosis, would be less able to demonstrate their knowledge in a written scientific paper than older children. Older children of low verbal ability would be less able to than children of higher verbal ability. In both of these cases, the objective requiring learners to demonstrate their knowledge through a written paper would be inappropriate because a learner's performance would rely more on verbal ability than on knowledge of mitosis. So the first step in the "process" phase on instructional development is to apply knowledge of the learners to the formulation of suitable objectives.

Once enabling objectives have been written for all of the tasks identified in the task analysis, the developer can turn attention to the pivotal and most difficult task of applying knowledge about learning processes and the learners to developing instruction that will enable the attainment of the instructional objectives. The transition from learning theory to instructional theory, and from instructional theory to instructional practice is not easy to make, and there is no single way of doing it. We will examine several of the options that researchers have made available to the curriculum developer.

Of the learning theorists who have thought seriously about developing instruction, Robert Gagne has probably had the greatest impact on the instructional development process. Gagne's influential book, The Conditions of Learning[57] put forward a behavioural theory of learning based upon hierarchies of skills and abilities, each a prerequisite for performance at the next level. Eight types of learning are named. They cover all possible types of learner behaviour from signal and stimulus-response learning to rule learning and problem-solving.[58] Each level in the hierarchy of learning types has associated with it the "conditions of learning" which must be present in the environment for the student to be successful in learning the particular behaviour. For example, for concept learning to take place, the following conditions have to be present: stimulus objects have to be presented simultaneously or in close succession; instructions must lead learners to identify as instances of the concept examples not previously experienced; reinforcement and contiguity must be present. Gagne's theory of learning is therefore characterized by a behavioural orientation, a hierarchical sequence of learning types and a set of conditions for each type of learning.

Gagne has used learning hierarchies to set up instructional development procedures. The most thorough exposition of this is to be found in Principles of Instructional Design which he wrote with Leslie Briggs.[59] This book begins by identifying five major types of learning outcomes: intellectual skills, cognitive strategies, verbal information, motor skills and attitudes. Learning hierarchies can be developed for objectives that fall within any of these areas. One example given by Gagne and Briggs concerns dividing groups of objects into halves and thirds. At the lowest level of this hierarchy is the ability to identify one object of a set. Next in complexity comes the apportioning of objects to subsets; then the construction of subsets by pairing. Only after this comes the "intellectual skill" of demonstrating halves and thirds of sets as two and three equal subsets.

The developer determines which of Gagne's eight types of learning are necessary for the objective to be attained. In so doing, the developer also identifies the prerequisite abilities that must lead up to the terminal behaviour and the conditions that must exist at each step in order for learning

369

to take place. With Gagne's approach, once the developer has identified the level of the behaviour specified by the objective, and the hierarchy of skills necessary for its attainment, the instructional activity and the environment within which it is to occur are largely predetermined. It should be clear, though, that objectives must be clearly defined and a thorough task analysis completed before this is possible.

A second way of classifying types of learning, also in a sense hierarchical, is offered in the Taxonomy of Educational Objectives by Bloom and his collaborators.[60] While this approach is less prescriptive for the instructional developer, it does offer some guidance in the classification of learning outcomes and implies a variety of strategies for their successful completion. Bloom's approach is again behavioural. It divides learning into two (rather than Gagne and Briggs' five) domains: the cognitive and the affective. Objectives are classified within these two domains in order of the complexity of the behaviours a learner must perform to attain them. These categories are well enough known, so they will not be discussed here.[61]

While the taxonomy does not contain any direct prescriptions for instruction, the minute accuracy with which it allows the developer to classify objectives and behaviours is very useful. Once a developer knows precisely the kind of skill or ability that the learner has to acquire, it is much easier to select instructional activities. An objective requiring comprehension of mitosis could be attained through lecture, demonstration and reading. An objective at the "analysis" level would most likely require some experimentation and observation by the learners. In addition, Bloom presents ways of evaluating the attainment of each type of objective by the learner, and this is of value for the testing of instructional activities and systems.[62]

Moving from learning theories rooted in

behaviourism to others based on a knowledge of human development and cognitive processing, we find other educational theorists and researchers who have contributed to curriculum development. Not least among these is Jerome Bruner, whose theory of instruction is based upon the notion that effective education consists of "providing aids and dialogues for translating experience into more powerful systems of notation and ordering."63 Bruner bases this claim on research of his own and of others into human development, which has demonstrated the successive development of three symbol systems as a child grows up.64 First, in the enactive mode, we know and represent our world through the actions we perform on it and it performs on us; through the iconic mode, we know it by pictorial represenations and images; through the symbolic mode, we know it through languages. Bruner's statement about the role of education therefore comes to mean that instructional activities should be designed to help the learner transform what has been learned from actions and images into linguistic forms. Language is a powerful system of notation because it allows much easier manipulation of phenomena than actions and images. It permits speculation and hypothesis-building.

However, Bruner also introduces the notion of "economy" into his theory of instruction. While language may be a more powerful way of representing something, it is not always the most economical. For example, while a verbal description of Archimedes' principle may be more powerful because it applies to all possible situations, a diagram showing what happens when something is placed into a container full of water is more economical because it requires less time and effort to understand. Seeing and feeling what happens when you get into a bath is more meaningful yet. Power, economy and mode of representation are all interrelated.65

For instructional developers, the choice of a mode of representation for instruction depends upon how the needs of power and economy are to be balanced, and on just how the learner is to interiorize and manipulate information and experiences. This in turn depends on the structure of the content and on the learner's abilities. With a good task analysis and learner analysis, these two considerations present no problems to the instructional developer. The objectives, too, should give some idea of the level of representational abstraction required of the learner after instruction. If the input into the instructional development process is clear, then Bruner's theory of instruction, sketchy though it be, will aid considerably in the design of resources and activities. It also has the advantage of being learner-centred, evolving from what is known about how a child's system of representation develops.

Our final example is taken from among recent efforts to develop instructional theories from the way learners process information rather than from the behaviours they are expected to perform or from their symbolizing systems. The work of Lauren Resnick in the development of mathematics curriculum for young children demonstrates how an information-processing approach to instructional task analysis and development differs from the behavioural and Brunerian approaches:

> Information-processing analyses
> are clearly distinguished from
> behaviorist ones by their explicit
> attempts to describe internal
> processing. They differ from the
> cognitivist Gestalt and Piagetian
> positions in their attempts to des-
> cribe the actual flow of performance
> --to translate "restructuring" or
> "logical operations" into temporally
> organized sequences of actions.[66]

This approach is characterized, then, by an interest in internal cognitive processes rather than with overt behaviours, and with the converting of what we know about the translation of experience, in the Brunerian sense, into instructional events. The mathematics activities developed by Resnick and her associates are based upon the mental operations involved in counting and computation, and the way the "data" generated at each mental step is stored and manipulated in memory.[67]

A more prescriptive approach to instruction is offered by researchers who have developed techniques for "mapping" cognitive processes and cognitive structure. One of the most interesting of these is the "cognitive objective". Using procedures similar to Resnick's, "Cognitive objectives are developed by analyzing the psychological processes and structures that are sufficient to produce needed behaviours."[68] The analysis of psychological processes, whether it is empirical or rationally based, produces a flow-chart or some other diagram showing a sequence of cognitive operations leading up to a terminal behaviour. The analysis of structures produces a network of propositions about concepts the learner must acquire, their proximity to other concepts, and the nature of the relationships between them.[69]

With either, or both, before him, the instructional developer is in possession of blueprints for instruction based upon how the learner will deal with any information that is present. These blueprints will indicate what concepts have to be acquired, in what sequence and arrangement, and how they should be related to each other in the instructional materials and activities. The diagnosis of weaknesses in the instructional system is also helped by the isolation of many discreet steps the learner goes through when processing information, which, as testing occurs, allows the pinpointing of problem areas.

There are, of course, many other places the instructional developer can look for guidance in the application learning theory to instructional practice. Summaries of areas of research abound in which learning principles and guidelines for instructional design are offered.[70] The danger with many of these is that, like all summaries, they tend to be general and may not apply precisely to the developer's task of the moment. This means that however scientific and systematic the developer has been up to this point, there is always a need to evaluate the output so as to verify that the decisions that have been taken are indeed the right ones.

Output

The "process" phase of instructional development produces written specifications for instructional materials and activities. The developer now has to prepare these for use with the learners. This will mean the production of any instructional materials that are needed and the preparation of teachers to use them and to carry out the activities and strategies. Before the instruction can be implemented in the classroom, however, it has to be tried out with a sample of the intended learners with a view to revision should problems appear.

It is during the field-testing of new instructional materials, methods and systems that the developer becomes involved in the research phase of curriculum development. Unlike "pure" research though, conditions are often created so that the environment in which the instruction is tested resembles as closely as possible a real classroom setting. A representative sample of intended learners works through the materials and activities. Data are collected. It is important for the developer to realize at this time that it is the effectiveness of the instruction that is being evaluated and not the ability of the learners. The developer needs to collect data not just on student performance, which is valuable for diagnosing difficult areas and for spotting misleading or confusing information. The developer also needs to gather information on what the students like and dislike about what they are doing, and to find out by simple observation at what points they appear bored, interested, anxious or amused. In addition, data should be gathered regularly throughout instruction, not just at the end.[71]

374

The information produced by field-testing serves as input to a second round of the development process. The decisions made the first time around are confirmed, altered or rejected on the basis of this new information. New decisions are made and converted into instructional strategies and materials as before. The modified system is tested again and the whole process repeated. A decision the developer has to make is when to stop the develop-test-revise cycle. Usually, changes made after the first go-round are quite major, and less substantial changes are required at each subsequent revision. A point is reached where changes produce only minor improvements. The system is not perfect, but it is just not worthwhile making any more revisions as most of the learners are succeeding most of the time. This point is often determined by a criterion level of achievement such as a ninety percent success rate by ninety percent of the learners. The implication is that those who do not succeed will need to take remedial instruction. It has never been claimed that all of this is entirely satisfactory. However, instruction that is developed in this way is generally effective and reposes on well developed and researched theories of human learning, on learner analysis, and on empirical evidence gathered through field-testing.

Where is instructional development going?

The need for empirical testing of any instruction developed to meet the needs of a curriculum shows up the major weakness in the instructional development process: even the strictest application of the scientific method and the soundest basis of instructional decisions made from learning theory and knowledge of the learners, cannot guarantee the success of what is developed. Revision will always be necessary. This has led some critics of the science of education, and of educational technology in particular, to declare that instructional development models do not work and that trying to use them is a waste of time. What is more, it seems that every development project

375

produces its own model of the development process. Consequently, attempts to come up with the model have produced monstrosities of great complexity which require so much effort and time to use that no-one tries. The critics appear to be justified. What is the point of following a complicated and time-consuming set of procedures if the end result is going to need extensive revision anyway? Yet development models exist and are used. The dilemma can be resolved if developers undertake to abide by three precepts.

An instructional development model should provide a developer with a framework for organizing ideas and should not be constraining. Even minimal experience in curriculum development should be enough to convince a developer that sets of procedures should be deviated from whenever it is necessary. Developers who feel that they cannot do what seems reasonable because the model says they should do something else are bound to fail. The model is a guideline, a general strategy, rather than a specific plan.

Instructional developers should, at times, play hunches as well as apply the scientific method. This is not true when a careful task analysis is required, or when exact performance objectives can be written. However, when it comes to deciding what materials, strategies and activities best suit a particular group of learners and a particular body of content, the developer should rely as much upon informal experiences as upon data gathered from formal experimentation. This lets some fresh air into the process and often leads to innovation in instruction. It also allows the developer to fill in the gaps that are inevitably found in a search for applicable instructional theory.

Instructional developers should get away from thinking in a linear fashion to a position where they can view the whole development process at once. Often, revision after field-testing is not the most efficient way to debug an instructional system. Some development models show revision

376

occurring at every step of the way. There is also
a tendency for subject-matter specialists to turn
tail and run if the first thing they are asked by
a curriculum developer is what their objectives
are. It helps, then, if the steps of the development process are seen as all interacting together
at once, rather than following each other in linear
fashion and only interacting with their immediate
neighbours. Nord[72], who identified for us the three
phases of input, process and output, suggests that
instructional development models might be based on
a different configuration:

Here, each phase retains something unique, has
something that it shares with each of the other two
phases, and something that it shares with both
others. If this occurs, then it is quite likely
that occasions will arise where little attempt is
made to analyze the learners before field-testing,
where objectives are changed because of difficulties in the production of materials, and even where
objectives are written after instruction has been
developed so as to describe what it can do rather
than prescribe what it should do.

     In our survey of the curriculum development
process, let us not lose sight of the fact that our
interest lies with the curriculum and instruction
specialist. We need for a moment to return to the
idea that the curriculum and instruction specialist
translates curriculum into instructional activity
by applying educational theory through the scientific method. To do this, as the discussion has
suggested, this person must possess a variety of
skills. These can be summarized as follows:

377

1. To determine what should be taught, and
to convert this into the broad objectives
and guidelines typically found in provincial
guides, a feeling for the needs of society
is required. The curriculum and instruction
(C & I) specialist should therefore keep up
to date with what is going on socially and
politically at the local and provincial
levels. Activities of the local school board
must be closely watched, as well as the
activities of the provincial curriculum committees. Often, the C & I specialist will
be asked to serve on such committees. This
is a necessary and valuable part of his
role.

2. The translation of these broad objectives
into curriculum begins with an awareness of
the philosophical orientations that a curriculum can take. The C & I specialist will
often be called upon to justify curriculum
to teachers, school board officials, and
members of provincial departments of education in terms of the basic premises upon
which a curriculum is built. This may take
the form, for example, of pointing out inconsistencies of orientation in early drafts
of goal statements in a new provincial
curriculum, or of getting pre- or in-service
teachers to think consistently and rationally
about their curricular and instructional
decisions. In this role the C & I specialist
consults with curriculum committees, gives
courses and workshops, or meets informally
with educators involved in curriculum development.

3. The development of instruction to implement the curriculum demands the ability
to carry out needs assessment, itself requiring knowledge of various testing techniques. The C & I specialist must be able
to conduct surveys and construct survey
questionnaires. For needs assessment in
particular subject areas and levels of

378

instruction, the C & I specialist must be capable of constructing, validating, administering, scoring and analyzing diagnostic achievement tests. This requires skill in psychometrics and statistics. The C & I specialist will also use and interpret tests of learner ability. The development of instruction is not possible without accurate information on what learners already know, and on their general aptitude for learning.

4. The C & I specialist will spend a good deal of time conducting task analysis. This requires a thorough understanding of what is to be learned, and the application of procedures which allow the identification of sequences of steps the learners have to go through in order to learn. Based on these steps, the C & I specialist will write the objectives of instruction by means of which curriculum will be implemented.

5. The C & I specialist designs instruction. This requires the application of instructional principles, derived from learning theory, by means of instructional strategies. The C & I specialist relies upon research-based knowledge of how people learn, results of other development projects and personal experience in order to determine the most effective way to teach the learners what they have to learn. Since there is no magic formula for arriving at the right decisions in this process, experience and intuition are often as important as instructional principles derived from research.

6. The C & I specialist must be an evaluator of some skill who knows what data are needed in order that instruction may be revised. This requires that the C & I specialist decide what to evaluate and how to do it. The specialist will determine the content areas to be tested, for example, and will

379

construct achievement tests in order to
see if the instruction was successful in
meeting the objectives of the curriculum.
After studying the results of curricular
evaluation, the C & I specialist makes
recommendations concerning revisions to the
curriculum and/or to the instruction by
means of which it was implemented.

If in addition to this we take into account
that curriculum and instruction specialists are
also often specialists in a particular academic
discipline, the scope of their activities appears
to be very wide indeed. But this is necessary if
theory is to become practice, and if the profession
of education is to benefit from the contributions
made to it by the discipline of education.

RESEARCH PERSPECTIVES

The contributions that curriculum and instruction specialists make to educational research
lie in both the pure and applied areas. The former
is usually characterized by a laboratory setting
where all variables are controlled except one or a
few independent variables manipulated by the researcher. Applied research takes place in as
realistic a classroom setting as possible with very
few variables controlled.[73]

Pure research in the area of curriculum and
instruction contributes to the body of knowledge
comprising educational theory. A typical research
study will have as its independent variable instructional method or stimulus characteristic and
will attempt to control all other effects by sampling techniques, control over the experimental
setting, or statistical procedures such as the
analysis of covariance. In this way, precise and
narrowly focused hypotheses can be tested concerning specific parts of instructional activities or
materials. Dependent variables are measures of
learning, but tend to measure one or two discreet
cognitive or psycho-motor skills rather than the

overall impact of an instructional treatment on the student's learning, attitude and intellectual development.

Data from empirical hypothesis-testing that the C & I specialist gathers in this way allow conclusions to be drawn about how people learn from different types of material and from different methods. This particular mode of inquiry permits generalization to different subject areas about very specific instructional phenomena. Within this research paradigm, curriculum and instruction researchers are turning more and more to the methodology of aptitude-treatment interaction research[74] whose main aim is to study the relationships between student achievement, instructional variables and student aptitudes. For example, a C & I specialist might investigate the relationships between student performance after verbal or audiovisual instruction in mitosis as a function of the students' verbal ability, or anxiety. In this way, testable hypotheses are being explored which will enable the curriculum specialist to prescribe different instructional activities and materials to learners according to their performance on aptitude tests. This is a first step towards the individualization of instruction based on empirical data.

A second mode of inquiry used by the curriculum and instruction specialist is research carried out in the field. Variously called "action research" "operations research" or "applied research" the purpose of these studies is not to generate data from which generalizations can be made, but rather to solve particular instructional problems in a given setting and often within a given period of time.[75] Little attempt is made to control peripheral variables, though instructional treatments may be varied as in pure research. The hypotheses tested are not focused narrowly on one or two characteristics of stimulus materials nor on small, sharply defined variations in method. Rather, whole systems of instruction are compared and the data gathered concern all aspects of the learners' performances, not specific discreet tasks. By and large, the conclusions that C & I specialists draw are valid only for the particular group and setting that were studied and action is taken on the basis of which method is better rather than only if results are significantly different statistically.

Often, of course, the C & I specialist does not compare two methods or sets of materials, but is simply concerned with whether instruction that has been developed works at all. This is the case, for example, when new curriculum is piloted in schools. We are now back with field-testing pure and simple, and this was discussed at some length above. Yet whether it is a question of a comparison of methods or of field-testing, the curriculum and instruction specialist doing applied research is always less concerned about the generalizability of the data and sacrifices statistical precision and experimental control in order to get the job done and to put something useful into the classroom.

It is wrong to say that pure research is more valid than applied research or vice versa. Both are important. The difference lies in whether what needs to be found out lies on the "theory" or the "practice" side of the division that runs through everything the curriculum and instruction specialist does. The researcher should be equally able to do both.

TEACHER TRAINING

This chapter began with the idea that curriculum and instruction bridges the gap between the discipline and the profession of education. Nowhere is this felt more keenly than in the preparation of teachers. Most curriculum and instruction specialists have the responsibility for preparing teachers to work in the schools. In university departments of curriculum, this responsibility boils down to four areas, and student teachers have

382

to be proficient in all four if they are to succeed as professionals.

The first area is quite simply the curriculum itself. When entering the classroom, a teacher must know what has to be taught. This is simple enough to achieve. A glance at a curriculum guide will give a general idea, and meetings with departments in the schools, together with advice from instructors, should supply sufficient details for the beginning teacher to get started. However, there is another side to this which is sometimes neglected: why what is taught in the schools is in fact taught there. The mark of all professionals is that they can justify what they are doing by referring it to a body of knowledge.[76] This is no less true of the teaching profession. Teachers therefore should understand the needs upon which the curriculum is built and should be sensitive to social trends which determine where the curriculum will go in the future. In this way the teacher will have a discipline as well as a trade to ply, and will be far more confident and effective in the classroom.

The second area concerns what we have been referring to as "educational theory". However good the curriculum, and however effective the instructional activities and materials that have been developed, no teacher can be one hundred percent effective unless there is an understanding of how people learn. Even in the classroom, there is a need for the teacher to straddle theory and practice. Each child is different, and the only person capable of noticing these differences is the teacher on the spot. No curriculum developer can provide a curriculum and instructional prescription that covers all eventualities and all types of learner. It is therefore up to the teacher to do some curriculum development as the need arises. To do this, there must be a grasp of educational theory for both the diagnosis of learner needs and the development of suitable instruction for them.

Next, there is the question of instructional

methods. The teacher has to learn the complete
range of instructional methods and materials that
are pertinent to a particular discipline. These
are the teacher's stock in trade. Emphasis must
be placed on variety, as it is impossible for a
teacher to tell which methods will be appropriate
in a particular instructional setting before
arriving in it. The curriculum and instruction
specialist knows the methods and where they are
effective. They should be demonstrated to the
student teacher and practiced at appropriate points
throughout the programme.

Finally, the professional teacher needs to
be trained in those procedures that permit the
application of theory to practice. We have already
seen that from time to time the teacher will be
called upon to do some curriculum development.
Curriculum determination and instructional development should be subjects studied by all student
teachers, for another mark of the professional is
the ability to apply theory to practice. In addition to supplying the teacher with skills that will
be needed from time to time, the study of curriculum
development will help the teacher understand why
the curriculum is as it is and also the strengths
and weaknesses of curriculum decisions. We have
seen that the curriculum development process does
not guarantee a good curriculum and effective instructional systems. If teachers know this and
understand why, then if they are asked they will be
able to make useful suggestions as to how it might
be improved. Even if they are not asked, understanding the difficulties of curriculum development
might well help teachers overcome some of the frus-
tration they often feel in the face of ineffective
curriculum decisions and materials.

Most university teacher-training programmes
endeavour to expose students to these four areas,
and C & I specialists may be called upon to teach
courses in any or all of them. There is a trend,
however, away from the academic towards the practical brought about largely by students' pleas for
"relevance" and an increasingly strong job orienta-

tion among students because of diminishing employment opportunities. It would be wrong, though, if
curriculum and instruction, the discipline, were to
cater exclusively to the practical demands of teaching. Without the research, theory and discipline
that curriculum and instruction specialists can
bring to teacher training, teachers will undergo
little more than an apprenticeship, and the profession will rapidly become little more than a
trade. This would be a serious set-back for educators and for schooling, since it would lead to
stagnation in the curriculum and to a lack of the
instructional innovation needed to improve education
as we find out more about cognitive processes and
individual differences in learners.

The key to success for curriculum and instruction within the enterprise of education lies
in curriculum development. To succeed here, there
has to be a balance between theory and practice
brought about by a sensitivity to the needs of society, a knowledge of how people learn, an understanding of learners and a commitment to the scientific approach to problem solving. But once the
constraints of particular sets of procedures are
felt, there must also be a flexibility that permits
innovation and intelligent guessing. Above all,
there must be the patience to keep trying until the
curriculum works as best it can, and a stoicism in
the face of the realization that nothing ever works
perfectly and that someone will always be dissatis-
fied with what you do.

FOOTNOTES

1. This distinction is not without precedent, though. Robert Heinich, in Technology and the Management of Instruction (Washington, Association for Educational Communication and Technology, 1970), p. 127, makes the distinction between "curriculum determination" and "curriculum planning". Hilda Taba, in Curriculum Development: Theory and Practice (New York: Harcourt, Brace and World, 1962), discusses curriculum development in terms of its foundations, which include such things as the needs of society, culture, learning theory and knowledge, and in terms of the planning process itself.

2. There are many extant definitions of curriculum. This particular one brings together the reasonable and recurring features of many others. It is essentially an expansion of the definition offered by James Popham and Eva Baker in the book Systematic Instruction (Englewood Cliffs: Prentice-Hall, 1970), p. 48: "Curriculum is all the planned learning outcomes for which the school is responsible". Strictly speaking, curricular experiences do not have to be planned, nor institutionalized. However, the narrower definition is more manageable and more relevant to the question of curriculum development, which is usually conducted for educational institutions.

3. Summaries of major learning theories are offered by Hilgard and Bower (E.R. Hilgard and G.H. Bower, Eds., Theories of Learning, Englewood Cliffs: Prentice Hall, 1975, 4th edition), and in most psychology textbooks.

4. The "scientific method" is the foundation of both the natural and the social sciences. It consists of the formulation of highly specific hypotheses and testing them under carefully prescribed conditions. A good description of this is given by Carl Hempel (Philosophy of Natural Science, Englewood Cliffs: Prentice-Hall, 1966), and ways of applying it to the behavioural sciences

are described by Fred Kerlinger (Foundations of Behavioural Research, New York: Holt, Rinehart and Winston, 1973, 2nd edition). The presence of the scientific method in education is not new in itself. As a general methodology for scholarship, it can be traced as far back as Aristotle. The advantage of the "problem-solving" approach is that it embodies the scientific method. This is because it requires that problems be carefully analyzed and described before hypotheses concerning solutions are written and tested. Proponents of this approach to curriculum development, such as Roger Kaufman (Educational System Planning, Englewood Cliffs: Prentice-Hall, 1972) and Derek Rowntree (Educational Technology in Curriculum Development, London: Harper and Row, 1974) have succeeded in developing systematized sets of procedures which, in theory at least, leave little of curriculum development to chance.

5. P.H. Taylor, How Teachers Plan their Courses, London: National Foundations for Educational Research, 1970.

6. G.R. Koopman, Curriculum Development, New York: Centre for Applied Research in Education, 1966, pp. 4-5.

7. John Dewey, The Child and the Curriculum, Chicago: University of Chicago Press, 1902, and also John Dewey, The Sources of a Science of Education, New York: Liveright, 1926.

8. E.L. Thorndike, The Psychology of Learning, New York: Teachers College, 1913.

9. These early attempts to make psychology an empirical science required that data be gathered only about observable behaviours. The resulting interest in stimulus-response relationships gave us "behavioural" psychology. Even today, the greatest efforts of curriculum developers go towards developing instruction from behavioural objectives that will teach observable, and therefore testable skills and knowledge. The dangers of the inherent

limitations of this are discussed below.

10. These notions led eventually to such reforms, now familiar aspects of education, as integrated curricula, where, for example, social studies activities rely upon and develop skills in language arts through report writing and discussions, and consumer education helps develop skills in mathematics through comparison shopping and the calculation of mortgage rates.

11. A good summary is given by R.W. Tyler, "Curriculum Development in the Twenties and Thirties", in R.M. McClure (Ed.), The Curriculum: Retrospect and Prospect, Chicago: National Society for the Study of Education, 1971, pp. 26-44.

12. The Curriculum, Boston: Houghton Mifflin Co., 1918, p. 42.

13. The Foundations and Technique of Curriculum-Making, Bloomington, Illinois: Public School Publishing Company, 1927, Part I, Curriculum-Making: Past and Present, p. 51.

14. Basic Principles of Curriculum and Instruction, Chicago: University of Chicago Press, 1949.

15. What happened after Sputnik I is just one example of ex post facto curriculum development. Two other notable examples are the more integrated curricula in natural and social sciences concerned with man and the environment spurred by the "ecology movement" of the middle and late sixties; and the "back-to-the-basics" movement, partly in reaction against the earlier reforms, and partly due to a swing to a more conservative stance in society and politics in the middle seventies.

16. See, for example, B.F. Skinner, "Teaching Machines", Science 128 (October 1958), 137-158.

17. Heinich, pp. 103-149, has discussed this development in detail, citing the adoption of tech-

nological principles by educators as an example of
"paradigm change" in the sense of the term as used
by Thomas Kuhn in his book The Structure of Scientific Revolutions (Chicago: University of Chicago
Press, 1970, 2nd. edition). The movement of education to a new orientation based upon technology
has been a radical one.

18. Characterizations of a technological, as
opposed to an industrial society, are given by
Jaques Ellul (The Technological Society), New York:
Random House, 1964) and by John Kenneth Galbraith
(The New Industrial State, Boston: Houghton Mifflin, 1967). Industrialization gave us uniformity,
regimentation and cybernetic models of processes
and behaviours. Technology has given us variety
and organic models of processes and behaviours.
The increased complexity and sophistication of a
technological society allows for more variation and
diversity, and subsequently creates a greater need
for organization, logistical planning and management.

19. Charles F. Hoban, "From Theory to Policy
Decisions", Audiovisual Communication Review 13
(1965), 121-139.

20. D.P. Ely (Ed.), "The Field of Educational
Technology: A Statement of Definition". Audiovisual Instruction 17 (1972), No. 8), 36-43.

21. Galbraith, p. 12.

22. Commission on Instructional Technology,
To Improve Learning. Washington: United States
Government, 1970, This is, in fact, just the second
part of the definition. The first part refers to
"media born of the communications revolution which
can be used for instructional purposes alongside
the teacher." So the Commission on Instructional
Technology was looking at both the old and the new
faces of technology in education. Other definitions
abound. Several are compared in a report of the
Ford Foundation on Instructional Technology (J.W.
Armsey and N.C. Dahl, An Inquiry Into the Uses of

389

Instructional Technology. New York: Ford Foundation, 1973). All of these definitions, the majority
of which were written after the report of the
Commission to the United States Congress, mention
something about technology and curriculum development, problem-solving, and so on.

23. The "systems" concept was borrowed by
educators from the natural sciences. In 1945, the
biologist von Bertalanffy first proposed General
System Theory (Ludwig von Bertalanffy, General System Theory, New York: Braziller, 1968), which
offered generalized mathematical models of the behaviour of closed and open systems derived from
models of the behaviour of living organizms, particularly of metabolic processes. Systems, then,
are organic in the sense that every part and function depends on every other part and function to
some degree. As a metaphor, the model serves education well, for it too is a complex "organism" of
many interrelated parts and functions.

24. They are described in detail by Roger
Kaufman, op.cit.

25. Taba's set of procedures was selected
because it typifies curriculum development, is
general enough to apply to most curriculum development projects, and is reasonably well known.

26. Examples of the influence of pressure
groups on curriculum are many. Some are: the
refusal, on religious grounds, of school boards to
allow the teaching of the theory of evolution; the
dismissal of teachers who discuss Marxism in Social
Studies; the removal of books by authors such as
Vonnegut and Salinger from school libraries; the
abandoning of family life (sex education) programmes.

27. The traditional academic disciplines are
not static. For example, until the late nineteenth
century, psychology was taught as a branch of
philosophy. Today, there is a move towards an
integration of life sciences and social sciences

390

into environmental studies, a merging of history, geography, economics and sociology into social studies, and the integration of the language arts of reading, writing and speaking.

28. A.R. King and J.A. Brownell, The Curriculum and the Disciplines of Knowledge. New York: Wiley, 1966, p. 26.

29. J. Dewey, The Child and the Curriculum. Chicago: University of Chicago Press, 1902.

30. Lawrence Cremin, The Genius of American Education. New York: Random House, 1966.

31. Jerome Bruner, Toward a Theory of Instruction. New York: Norton, 1966.

32. Jean Piaget and Barbel Inhelder, The Psychology of the Child. New York: Basic Books, 1969.

33. Several attempts to apply Piagetian theory to the classroom are presented by I.J. Athey and D.O. Rubadeau (Eds.), Educational Implications of Piaget's Theory. Waltham: Xerox College Publishing, 1970. There is, in these attempts, a tendency to treat content as a means to an end, the end being the acquisition of general intellectual abilities. It has been shown experimentally that the acquisition of these abilities can sometimes be accelerated in the classroom. J. Smedslund, "The Acquisition of the Conservation of Substance and Weight in Children: VI. Practice on Continuous versus Non-continuous Material in Conflict Situations Without Reinforcement". Scandinavian Journal of Psychology 2 (1961), 203-210. E.L. Palmer, "How Elementary Schoolchildren Resolve Experimentally Produced Conflicts in Thinking". United States Office of Education Cooperative Project No. 3216, August 1966. G.E. Gruen, "Experiences Affecting the Development of Number Conservation in Children". Child Development 36 (1965), 963-980.

34. Bruner, op.cit. p. 96, discusses learning

by discovery.

35. The Harvard Committee, <u>General Education in a Free Society.</u> Cambridge: Harvard University Press, 1945.

36. B.O. Smith, W.O. Stanley and J.H. Shores, <u>Fundamentals of Curriculum Development.</u> New York: Harcourt, Brace and World, 1957. In this regard, Urie Bronfenbrenner has provided an insightful and thought-provoking study of the new status of the North American child in the family ("The Changing American Child", in R. Havinghurst, B. Newgarten and J. Falk, <u>Society and Education.</u> Boston: Allyn and Bacon, 1967, pp. 67-73). J.S. Coleman ("The Adolescent Subculture and Academic Achievement", in Havinghurst, Newgarten and Falk, op.cit., pp. 109-115) even suggests that the child-rearing skills of many parents are obsolete. The social systems of high schools are far more meaningful to adolescents than the adult social systems encountered in the home. If this is in fact true, then the social responsibilities of the schools and the curriculum increase enormously.

37. Bruner has gone so far as to imply that political biases permeate even into instructional processes. In an article published in 1968 ("Culture, Politics and Pedagogy", <u>Saturday Review</u> 51 (May 18, 1968), 69-72), he asserts that pedagogical theory, inasmuch as it exists, is not normative in that it cannot be entirely prescriptive. It is rather "political" because it depends largely on prior decisions as to who shall be educated and for what purpose. In <u>Toward a Theory of Instruction,</u> Bruner again stresses the need for a prescriptive theory of instruction, which is rendered politically neutral by being based on notions of individual development rather than societal need.

38. H.S. Brandy, B.O. Smith and J.R. Burnett, <u>Democracy and Excellence in American Secondary Education.</u> Chicago: Rand McNally, 1964.

39. This idea is refined to a great degree by

Cecil Parker and Louis Rubin in their "Principle of Cross Application" (Process as Content: Curriculum Design and the Application of Knowledge. Chicago: Rand McNally, 1966). Beginning with the idea of transfer, they suggest that the curriculum should be concerned with teaching content that will improve the transfer process itself within each learner. With "application" as part of the curriculum, learners will become active in the acquisition and utilization of information instead of passive recipients. At this point, the pragmatic basis for curriculum determination becomes blurred with the personal development orientation.

40. J.B. Conant, Slums and Suburbs. New York: McGraw-Hill, 1961, p. 45.

41. It is intriguing to look at the other side of the coin and to wonder whether we should be educating for leisure. Though the predictions of the sixties that by 1980 all work necessary to keep a developed country running could be done by something like two percent of the population obviously will not be borne out, people are having more and more time to spend on leisure pursuits. It seems reasonable that education should prepare people to use this time wisely.

42. Future Shock. New York: Bantam, 1971.

43. The Most Probable World. New York: Harper and Row, 1968.

44. Of the many attempts to foresee the future of education, one of the most imaginative (some might say fanciful) is the vision of what school will be like in the year 2000 described by George Leonard in Education and Ecstasy (New York: Dell, 1968). While hardly a scientific basis for curriculum reform, this book paints a picture of a world where education is thoroughly enjoyable, stimulating and learner-centred. Emotion is cultivated as much as behaviours are developed. And children still learn.

45. Many jurisdictions report increases in enrolment in continuing education courses of one hundred percent and more.

46. The rightness of these arguments is open to discussion. History has both proved and disproved them. A hungry person without work is a social malcontent as the social upheavals of the nineteenth century have demonstrated. But on the other hand, a rational man is often employable in areas he has not been trained for, as was the case of most graduates of liberal arts programmes before the days of degree inflation.

47. Alberta Education, Curriculum Guide for Biology 10, 20, 30. Edmonton: Government of Alberta, 1977.

48. J.R. Nord, "A Search for Meaning". Audiovisual Instruction (December 1971), 11-17.

49. Rowntree, op.cit.

50. For alternative models, the reader can refer to Kaufman, op.cit.; J. Barson, Instructional Systems Development: A Demonstration and Evaluation Project. East Lansing: Michigan State University, 1967; R.M. Gagne and L. Briggs, Principles of Instructional Design. New York: Holt, Rinehart and Winston, 1974; and C.E. Cavert, An Approach to the Design of Mediated Instruction. Washington: The Association for Educational Communication and Technology, 1974. The contrasts will be obvious. Kaufman's approach is general and reasonably flexible. Cavert's model is complex, detailed and prescriptive. Each has its advantages and disadvantages. Kaufman leaves more up to the developer to decide. Cavert tends to over-restrict him.

51. Op.cit., p. 8.

52. Doing, knowing and feeling refer to three domains of human behaviour, the psychomotor, the cognitive and the affective. The idea of domains owes much to the preparation of a taxonomy

of types of behavioural objective by B.S. Bloom
(Taxonomy of Educational Objectives. Handbook I:
Cognitive Domain. New York: David McKay, 1956) and
D.R. Krathwohl (Taxonomy of Educational Objectives.
Handbook II: Affective Domain. New York: David
McKay, 1964). While Bloom and Krathwohl divide
human behaviour into two domains, it is interesting
that other researchers have added more. E.J.
Simpson deals with a taxonomy for the psychomotor
domain (The Classification of Educational Objectives in the Psychomotor Domain. Urbana, Illinois:
University of Illinois, 1966), and Gagne and Briggs
discuss five: intellectual skill, cognitive
strategy, verbal information, motor skill and attitude (op.cit., p. 26).

53. T.M. Schwen ("Learner Analysis: Some
Process and Content Concerns", Audiovisual Communication Review 21 (1973), 44-72) distinguishes
between three types of learner analysis commonly
used by developers. Selection analysis uses criterion and aptitude measures which, through regression
techniques, predict a person's success in something,
like college grades. Pre-knowledge analysis measures existing knowledge and enables learners to be
judged fit or unfit for a particular piece of instruction, or to be placed at a particular point in
it. Aptitude-treatment analysis uses measures of
one or more learner aptitudes in order to prescribe
the most effective instructional treatment from
among several alternatives. All of these can be
used in needs assessment.

54. I.K. Davies ("Task Analysis: Some Process and Content Concerns", Audiovisual Communication Review 21 (1973) 73-86) goes further and
identifies six bases for task analysis: objectives,
identifying terminal behaviour; behavioural analysis, which describes sequences of skills, concepts,
and so on; information processing, which identifies
cognitive processes enabling the task to be completed; decision-making, which analyzes the decisions a person has to make to complete the task;
subject-matter structure; and vocation schemata.
Obviously, the appropriateness of these approaches

varies from task to task. Davies summarizes these by saying that task analysis can either fit the person to the task, the task to the person, or both.

55. For example, J.G. Greeno, "Cognitive Objectives of Instruction: Theory of Knowledge for Solving Problems and Answering Questions", in D. Klahr (Ed.), Cognition and Instruction. New York: Wiley, 1976, 123-159; and L.B. Resnick, "Task Analysis in Instructional Design: Some Cases from Mathematics", in Klahr op.cit., 51-80.

56. The classic work in this area is by R.F. Mager (Preparing Instructional Objectives. Palo Alto: Fearon Publishers, 1962), who gives careful procedures to follow in order to define the the behaviour that will be accepted as evidence that the learner has achieved the objective, to describe the conditions under which the behavour will occur and to specify criteria for acceptable performance (p. 12). There is a danger inherent in this, and that is that teaching will be limited to only what is observable and measurable, reducing all human endeavour and human nature to overt behaviour. P.D. Mitchell ("The Sacramental Nature of Behavioural Objectives", paper presented to the International Conference on Educational Technology, Bath, England, March 1972) deplores the lack of attention paid to "latent capability ... the potential for acting, thinking, feeling and becoming." W.D. Winn ("Cognitive Objectives: an Alternative to the B.S. in Instruction", Audiovisual Instruction (December 1977) discusses problems inherent in taking behavioural science as the basis for education.

57. R.M. Gagne, The Conditions of Learning. New York: Holt, Rinehart and Winston, 1977, 3rd. Edition.

58. Gagne's eight types of learning are, in sequence: learning stimulus-response connections, learning motor chains, learning verbal chains, learning discriminations, learning concrete concepts, learning rules and defined concepts, and

problem solving.

59. Op.cit.

60. Op.cit.

61. As a reminder, these categories are, for
the cognitive domain: knowledge, comprehension,
application, analysis, synthesis and evaluation;
for the affective domain: receiving, responding,
valuing, organizing and characterizing by a value
or value system. For the psychomotor domain,
Simpson (op.cit.) lists handling, gripping, moving,
and other similar kinds of motor skill.

62. B.S. Bloom, J.T. Hastings and G.F. Madaus,
Handbook on Formative and Summative Evaluation of
Student Learning. New York: McGraw-Hill, 1971.

63. Toward a Theory of Instruction, p. 21.

64. J.S. Bruner, Studies in Cognitive Growth.
New York: Wiley, 1967.

65. In addition, Bruner points out that mode,
economy and power vary according to learners' ages,
their learning styles, and the structure of the
content. This is developed in Toward a Theory of
Instruction, p. 44.

66. Loc.cit., p. 64.

67. By way of example, Resnick discusses a
study where five models, varying in complexity, of
different ways of doing subtraction were examined
(S.S. Woods, L.B. Resnick and G.J. Groen, "An Experimental Test of Five Process Models for Subtraction". Journal of Educational Psychology 67
(1975), 17-21). Response latencies were predicted
from the number of steps required by each model.
Observed and predicted latencies were fit using
regression analysis to determine which model each
child in the experiment was using. In this way,
a variety of methods of processing information were
studied, and different children were found to pro-

cess information by means of different methods.

68. Greeno, loc.cit., p.123.

69. Other ways of mapping cognitive processes
and structures are offered by D.A. Norman, D.R.
Gentner and A.L. Stevens, "Comments on Learning
Schemata and Memory", in Klahr, o.cit., pp. 177-
196, who demonstrate semantic networks of concepts,
and more extensively by D.A. Norman and D.E. Rumel-
hart, Explorations in Cognition. San Francisco:
Freeman, 1975.

70. Typical of these summaries are those by
M.L. Fleming and W.H. Levie, Instructional Message
Design: Principles from the Behavioral Sciences.
Englewood Cliffs: Educational Technology Publications, 1978; W.H. Levie and K.E. Dickie, "The
Analysis and Application of Media" in R.M.W.
Travers (Ed.), Second Handbook of Research on Teaching. Chicago: Rand McNally, 1973, bringing together research in characteristics of stimulus
materials and learning, and W.H. Allen, "Intellectual Abilities and Instructional Media Design",
Audiovisual Communication Review 23 (1975), 133-
170, on aptitude-treatment interaction research.

71. Formative and summative evaluation techniques are familiar to most researchers. The purpose of formative evaluation is to gather data
throughout the instructional sequence so that weaknesses can be spotted and revisions made. Summative
evaluation gathers data on the whole instructional
sequence and is carried out at the end. Its purpose is more to validate the instruction by evaluating the students. The subject is dealt with in
detail by Bloom, Hasting and Madaus op.cit. It is
important to remember that the primary emphasis
during instructional development is evaluation of
instruction, not students.

72. Loc.cit.

73. E.R. Hilgard discusses in more detail a
continuum of research types from pure to applied

398

("A Perspective of the Relationship between Learning Theory and Educational Practices" in E.R.
Hilgard (Ed.), Theories of Learning and Instruction.
Chicago: University of Chicago Press, 1964, 402-
415.

74. L.J. Cronbach and R.E. Snow, Aptitudes
and Instructional Methods. New York: Irvington,
1977.

75. Several researchers have develped rationales and methodologies for this kind of research.
C.F. Hoban ("The Usable Residue of Educational Film
Research", New Teaching Aids for the American
Classroom. Palo Alto: Stanford University Press,
Institute for Communication Research, 1960), described operations research as the gathering of data
upon which policy and operating decisions can be
made with confidence (p. 171). R.A. Stowe
("Research and the Systems Approach as Methodologies
for Education", Audiovisual Communication Review
21 (1973), 165-175), advocates the systems approach
as a methodology for educational research permitting
the study of learners in complex real-world settings.
R.E. Snow ("Representative and Quasi-Representative
Designs for Research on Teaching", Review of Educational Research 44 (1974), 265-291), suggests
"representative" research designs for "ecologically
oriented and non-manipulative research" where, at
the expense of statistical precision and experimental control, experiments would be more "natural".
U. Bronfenbrenner ("The Experimental Ecology of
Education", Educational Researcher 5 (1976), 5-15)
makes a similar plea and emphasizes the value of
asking learners what they feel about the instruction
they receive.

76. Several definitions and characteristics
of professions are offered in J.A. Jackson, Professions and Professionalization. Cambridge: Cambridge University Press, 1970. Among them, in a
chapter on "Teaching as a Profession" (p. 155) is a
statement by T. Leggatt that "Practice is founded
upon a base of theoretical, esoteric knowledge".
In many instances, this knowledge base is weak, and

as a result of readier access to education by most
people, it is no longer esoteric. For these
reasons among others, Leggatt concludes that teaching is certainly not an elite profession even if
it can be called a profession at all.

ADDITIONAL REFERENCES

Anderson, V.E. *Principles and Procedures of Curriculum Development*. 2nd ed. New York: Ronald Press, 1965.

Babcock, C.D., ed. *New Insights in the Curriculum*. Washington: Association for Supervision and Curriculum Development, 1963.

Barrow, R. *Common Sense and the Curriculum*. London: Allen and Unwin, 1976.

Beaird, J.H. "Learner Variables and the Instructional Technologist". In National Special Media Institutes, *Contributions of Behavioral Science to Instructional Technology*. Volume II: Cognitive Domain. Washington: Gryphon House, 1972. 133-160.

Beauchamp. G.E. *Curriculum Theory*. Wilmette, Illinois: The Kagg Press, 1975.

Bellack, A. and Kliebard H. (Eds.). *Curriculum and Evaluation*. Berkeley: McCutcheon, 1977.

Broudy, H.S., Smith, B.O. and Burnett, J.R. *Democracy and Excellence in American Education*. Chicago: Rand McNally, 1964.

Eisner, E.W., ed. *Confronting Curriculum Reform*. Boston: Little Brown, 1971.

Eisner, E.W. and Vallance, E. eds. *Conflicting Conceptions of the Curriculum*. Berkeley: McCutcheon, 1974.

Elam, S., ed. *Education and the Structure of Knowledge*. Chicago: Rand McNally, 1964.

Eble, K.E. *A Perfect Education*. New York: Collier, 1966.

Ferkiss, V.C. *Technological Man: The Myth and the Reality*. New York: Braziller, 1969.

Ford, G.W. and Pugno, L. The Structure of Knowledge and the Curriculum. Chicago: Rand McNally, 1964.

Gagne, R.M. Psychological Principles in System Development. New York: Holt, Rinehart and Winston, 1962.

Galbraith, J.K. The Affluent Society. Boston: Houghton Mifflin, 1958.

Gilchrist, R.S. and Roberts, B.R. Curriculum Development: A Humanized Systems Approach. Belmont, California: Fearon, 1974.

Hass, G., Bondi, J. and Wiles, J. Curriculum Planning: A New Approach. Boston: Allyn and Bacon, 1974.

Hirsch, W. Inventing Education for the Future. San Francisco: Chandler, 1967.

Holland, J.G., Solomon, C., Doran, J. and Frezza, D.A. The Analysis of Behavior in Planning Instruction. Reading, Massachussetts: Addison-Wesley, 1976.

Hook, S. Education for Modern Man. New York: Knopf, 1963.

Hooper, R., Ed. The Curriculum: Context, Design and Development. Edinburgh: Oliver and Boyd in Association with The Open University Press, 1971.

Hudgins, B.B. The Instructional Process. Chicago: Rand McNally, 1971.

Joyce, B. and Weil, M. (Eds.). Models of Teaching. Englewood Cliffs: Prentice-Hall, 1972.

Keppel, F. The Necessary Revolution in American Education. New York: Harper and Row, 1966.

Kibler, R.J., Barker, L.L. and Miles, D.J.

Behavioral Objectives and Instruction. Boston: Allyn and Bacon, 1970.

McClure, R.M. "The Reforms of the Fifties and Sixties: A Historical Look at the Near Past". in R.M. McClure, Ed., The Curriculum: Retrospect and Prospect. Chicago: National Society for the Study of Education, 1971, 45-75.

McDonald, J.B. and Leeper, R.R. Theories of Instruction. Washington: Association for Supervision and Curriculum Development, 1965.

Mead, M. The School in American Culture. Cambridge: Harvard University Press, 1964.

Means, R.K. Methodology in Education. Columbus: Charles Merrill, 1968.

Monson, C.H., Ed. Education for What? Readings in the Ends and Means of Education. Boston: Houghton Mifflin, 1970.

National Education Association Center for the Study of Instruction. Rational Planning in Curriculum and Instruction. Eight Essays. Washington: National Education Association, 1967.

Nerboving, N.H. Unit Planning: A Model for Curriculum Development. Worthington, Ohio: Charles A. Jones, 1970.

Passow, A. Reactions to Silberman's 'Crisis in the Classroom'. Worthington, Ohio: Charles A. Jones, 1971.

Popham, W.J. (Ed.). Evaluation in Education: Current Applications. Berkeley: McCutcheon, 1974.

Poulliotte, C.A. and Peters, M.G. Behavioral Objectives: A Complete Bibliography. Boston: Northwestern University, 1971.

Pula, F.J. and Goff, R.G. Technology and Education:

Challenge and Change. Worthington, Ohio:
Charles A. Jones, 1972.

Reid, W.A. and Walker, D.F. Case Studies in
Curriculum Change. Boston: Routledge and
Kegan Paul, 1975.

Reynolds, J. and Skilbeck, M. Culture and the
Classroom. London: Open Books, 1967.

Rugg, H. The Foundations and Technique of Curriculum-Making. Part I, Curriculum Making: Past
and Present. Bloomington, Illinois: Public
School Publishing, 1927.

Schaefer, R.J. "Retrospect and Prospect" in R.M.
McClure, The Curriculum: Retrospect and
Prospect. Chicago: National Society for the
Study of Education, 1971.

Schaffarzick, J. and Hampson, D.H., Eds. Strategies for Curriculum Development. Berkeley:
McCutcheon, 1975.

Schalock, H.D. "Learner Outcomes, Learning Pro-
cesses and the Conditions of Learning" in
National Special Media Institutes, Contribu-
tions of Behavioral Science to Instructional
Technology. Volume II: The Cognitive Domain.
Washington: Gryphon House, 1972, pp. 37-131.

Silberman, C.A. Crisis in the Classroom. New
York: Random House, 1970.

Skinner, B.F. "The Science of Learning and the Art
of Teaching". Harvard Educational Review 24
(November 1954), 99-113.

Skinner, B.F. "The Steep and Thorny Way to a
Science of Behavior". American Psychologist
30 (January 1975), 42-49.

Socket, H. Designing the Curriculum. London:
Open Books, 1976.

Thompson, K. and White, J. Curriculum Development: A Dialogue. New York: Pitman, 1975.

Tosti, D.T. and Ball, J. A Behavioral Approach to Instructional Design and Media Selection. Albuquerque: Westinghouse, 1969.

Tyler, R.W., Gagne R.M. and Scriven, M. Perspectives of Curriculum Evaluation. Chicago: Rand McNally, 1967.

Zalatimo, S. and Sleeman, P., Eds. A Systems Approach to Learning Environments. Roselle, New Jersey: MEDED Inc., 1975.

CHAPTER 6

EDUCATIONAL ADMINISTRATION

Educational administration is a field of practice. It is also an area of study. The relationship between the two is complex and intriguing for, although the former constitutes the chief raison d'etre for the latter, and although enrolments in graduate programs in educational administration continue to be very healthy, it is by no means easy to see very precisely in what ways the practice of educational administration has been improved by its study. While the relationship concerns equally those who practice and those who profess, it is generally the latter who are most likely to explore its complexities and to find the exploration intriguing.

In the study of educational administration there has recently emerged a substantial and controversial debate about the nature of that study. Although the debate necessarily involves a consideration of the nature of the field of practice, it has as its prime focus the nature and use of theory in the study of educational administration: a hitherto accepted set of theories and assumptions which has underpinned research, scholarship and the preparation of administrators for some two decades, now may require complete re-examination or, in the opinion of some, rejection. It has been asserted that those whose approach has been attacked have "read the warning as a threat to their priesthood."[1] It is an extension of this metaphor which leads us (somewhat "playfully", to use March's notion)[2] to write of orthodoxy and heterodoxy. The suggestions of a temple-like arena, of ritual and of conformity which the metaphor invokes are exaggerated, but perhaps not entirely inappropriate. The first two sections of this chapter examine respectively the orthodoxy and the heterodoxy and the main aspects of the debate between their proponents. In the third section we shall attempt to look beyond the debate

407

and assess its implications for both the study and
practice of educational administration.

THE "THEORY MOVEMENT" IN
EDUCATIONAL ADMINISTRATION

The so-called "theory movement" in educational administration was begun in the 1950s.
Twenty years after its first beginnings, Griffiths,
one of its originators, described some of its
results:

> While, certainly, no group has
> felt recently that enough was
> known, there was the belief that
> educational administration was
> on the right track. Most, if not
> all, dissertations employed theo-
> retical concepts and structures,
> textbooks contained descriptions
> of several theories, and adminis-
> trators were taught to make theo-
> retical analyses. In Kuhn's
> language, there was an accepted
> paradigm, and the processes of
> "normal science" were ongoing.[3]

In order to understand what was the "accepted
paradigm" referred to by Griffiths it will be
useful to examine the origin of the "theory movement" and the lines of inquiry which were proposed. From this background it will be possible
to see the emergence of an orthodoxy and to examine its character.

The Origins of the "Theory Movement"

Before the early 1950s, study in educational administration was couched in essentially
practical terms, and programs of administrator
preparation were discernably influenced by management approaches current at different points in
time. Most notably influential were, first, the

408

ideas of Frederick Winslow Taylor and, later, the managerial concepts which arose from Elton Mayo's work. Frederick Taylor's The Principles of Scientific Management was published in 1911 and its promise of economy and increased productivity by the application of the basic principles of scientific management attracted a wide audience in the public school system. In 1913 the National Society for the Study of Education devoted a major part of its yearbook to the efficient management of education[4] and during the next several years widely read texts pursued the same theme.[5] One of the most interesting descriptions of the power of industrial and business leaders to impose their views of industrial management upon school administrators is contained in Callahan's Education and the Cult of Efficiency in which he notes that educators, "and especially the leaders in administration ... outdid themselves in bowing to the dominant pressures."[6]

However, by the late 1930s, Taylorism in public school administration yielded to yet another set of ideas gaining favour in American industry which were based upon the work of Elton Mayo.[7] "Human relations" or "democratic administration"--a set of managerial notions which emphasized interpersonal factors, especially employee morale and group dynamics, in administering organizations--became a common theme in the literature of educational administration, persisting into the 1950s.[8]

With the onset of the 1950s, the reliance of educational administration upon practical principles of organization and upon managerial techniques derived from industry came under strong criticism. In place of those practical and technical bases for administration, and in addition to a narrow concern for training, a more theoretical orientation was urged upon the field. Along with this urging came the specific suggestion that empirical research driving from theory in the social sciences must become more important and that administrative behavior should be a critical

409

focus of inquiry. The seminal statement of this view and its justification was presented in an influential monograph by Coldarci and Getzels in 1955:

> The most immediate bases for this monograph lie in (1) the observation that there are profound and identifiable in-adequacies in the practice of education; (2) the conviction that these inadequacies and the very real complexities and magnitude of the educational task call for better and more explicit theoretical orienta-tions; and (3) the assumption that administrative functions and structures, because of their influence in the determination of the total educative enterprise, are the most strategic targets for our theses.[9]

The development of this theory movement was assisted by other developments occurring at the time. The creation of the National Conference of Professors of Educational Administration (NCPEA) in 1947, the Kellogg Foundation support for the Cooperative Program in Educational Admin-istration (CPEA), begun in 1950, and the formation of the University Council for Educational Adminis-tration (UCEA) in 1956, served primarily to bring together educational administrators and social scientists. Their quest for theoretical bases was directed initially at sources outside educational administration and then increasingly became a quest for theories in the field itself. In 1958 Halpin summarized the trend thus:

> During the post-war period ... administrators have become in-creasingly aware of the role of theory and have come to recognize the contributions that social

410

scientists can make to our understanding of educational administration ... Those of us responsible for training administrators
have welcomed research findings
on leadership and group behavior,
and we have found ourselves drawing heavily upon insights about
administration derived from other
disciplines. But at the same time
we have been abashed by the poverty
of theory within our own field,
and have been dismayed by the extent to which our own research has
been anchored to "naked empiricism".
Out of this realization has grown
our present attempt to develop
theory in educational administration.[10]

Lines of Inquiry and the Quest for Theory

What main lines of inquiry and what key
ideas about the meaning and use of theory were
initially suggested as appropriate to guide the
needed developments in educational administration?
A review of the content of Halpin's Administrative
Theory in Education, a product of the first UCEA-
sponsored seminar on theory and research in educational administration in 1958, helps to answer
these questions. Of this volume, Griffiths has
contended that four chapters might be termed
"announcements" of lines of inquiry which were to
become the major focuses of research attention in
subsequent years.[11]

In one of these four chapters, Getzels
suggested that administrative behavior could be
understood as a reconciliation of the nomothetic
or institutional dimension of activity in a social
system (roles) and the idiographic or individual
dimensions of activity (personality) in that same
social system.[12] This line of inquiry, which came
to be labelled "social systems theory" or the
Getzels/Guba model[13] of research, was the first

411

and, until recently, one of the most frequently
used approaches to an examination of administrative behavior in education. Indeed, ten years
later it formed the substance of a major text book
in the field.[14]

Another of the lines of inquiry was that
proposed by Hemphill who considered the leadership
component of administration.[15] Hemphill's ideas,
together with the work of Halpin on leader be
behavior,[16] have inspired a great number of leadership studies in educational administration. Such
studies always used some form or adaptation of
the Leader Behavior Description Questionnaire
(LBDQ) originally developed by Hemphill and
Coons.[17] "Without question," Griffiths has observed, "the LBDQ has been the most widely used
research instrument in the past two decades."[18]

A third focus of inquiry--administration
as decision-making--was suggested in the chapter
by Griffiths.[19] Simon's book, Administrative Behavior,[20] and the ideas of Parsons[21] were the
chief sources of Griffiths' view that administration in education be considered not as deriving
from the educational nature of the service it
directs and supports but rather for the generalized
process which it is. Said Griffiths:

> ... the desired theory must deal
> with the substance of administration
> and not its form. The reverse has
> too long been the case in educational
> administration.... This means that
> educational administration's pre-
> occupation with the adjective rather
> than the noun must change. Not only
> have we been concerned almost ex-
> clusively with the adjective "educa-
> tional" but we have been spending
> our time looking at, for instance,
> the field of secondary school admin-
> istration and saying that it differs
> substantially from elementary school
> administration .... no case can be

made for the exclusive study of
"adjectival" administration.[22]

It appears that the line of inquiry suggested by Griffiths was not as popular as the two
previous ones in stimulating research. Griffiths'
own assessment, in 1969, was that research using
a decision theory base "has just gotten underway,
and, as yet, has not been the subject of critical
analysis."[23]

A fourth line of inquiry was proposed by
Parsons.[24] Parsons' chapter outlined an approach
to the analysis of the formal school organization
in terms of a general theory of social systems.[25]
Although the terminology is the same, the so-called
"social systems theory" of Getzels and Guba outlined earlier should not be confused with Parsons'
proposal. The Getzels and Guba model is psycho-
sociological in emphasis and is, in a sense, merely
a part of Parsons' scheme. In Parsons' analysis,
an organization was defined as a particular social
system oriented to the attainment of a relatively
specific type of goal, which contributed to a
major function or functions of a more comprehensive
system, usually the society. An organization was,
therefore, to be examined in terms of an institutionalized value system which defined and legitimized its goal, and in terms of the mechanisms or
sub-systems by which the organization is articulated with the rest of the society. In capsule
form, this is the "structural-functionalist" mode
of conceptualization, analysis and interpretation
which Selznick has neatly summarized:

> Structural-functional analysis
> relates contemporary and variable
> behavior to a presumptively stable
> system of needs and mechanisms.
> This means that a given empirical
> system is deemed to have basic
> needs, essentially related to self-
> maintenance; the system develops
> repetitive means of self-defense;
> and day-to-day activity is inter-

preted in terms of the function
served by that activity for
the maintenance and defense of
the system.[26]

Applied to the formal organization of the
school, Parsons' conceptualization meant, for
example, that the levels of authority in school
systems could be examined in terms of three
functional sub-systems: "technical" "managerial"
and "institutional". The technical functions
were the actual processes of teaching. The
"managerial system" consisted of administrators
who controlled the technical system. The "institutional system" (the community), legitimized the
managerial system through agencies (e.g. school
boards) or procedures (e.g. voting and policy-
making) designed for the control of schools.
Hills is one of the few scholars in educational
administration who has ever attempted a systematic
exploration of ways in which Parsons' work may be
considered as forming the essential basis for a
science of organization.[27]

At the same time as lines of inquiry were
being suggested, scholars were also pursuing questions of the meaning and use of theory itself.
Halpin maintained that it was of prime importance
to recognize that scholars in the field did not
share a common understanding of the term "theory".
He further suggested that two other major problems
were involved in developing useful theory: the
difficulties of communication between social
scientists and practising administrators, and the
delicate issue of personal motives in the search
for theory.[28]

On the first issue, that of the need for a
common understanding of the term "theory", Halpin
proposed that his colleagues examine the advantages
and disadvantages of using Feigl's definition:

... I propose to define a "theory"
as a set of assumptions from which
can be derived by purely logico-

mathematical procedures, a larger
set of empirical laws.[29]

Further, even if a common understanding on the
meaning of theory could be reached (Halpin did
not intend that Feigl's definition be adopted),
there were still major questions about the domain
of theory which had to be examined:

> The first is: what is the
> minimum number of value assump-
> tions we must invoke in order
> to construct a satisfactory
> theory of educational adminis-
> tration? And the corollary:
> Can we agree on these assump-
> tions? The second question
> concerns the molar-molecular
> issue. Should we seek to
> articulate molar theories such
> as Parsons' ... with theories
> of a more molecular type, such
> as Hemphill's and Getzels'?
> If we agree this is desirable,
> then how do we achieve artic-
> ulation? The third question
> relates to possible differences
> between administration qua ad-
> ministration and the special
> province of educational adminis-
> tration. Obviously, business
> administration, hospital adminis-
> tration, public administration and
> educational administration have
> many characteristics in common,
> and to the extent that we can iden-
> tify a g (or general) factor, a
> theory of administration is meaning-
> ful. But there are s (or specific)
> factors too, that distinguish edu-
> cational administration from other
> forms of administration. These g
> and s factors require examination.[30]

On the issue of communication between

scholars and practitioners, Halpin warned that
it was vitally important that bridges be built
between the two groups, each of which had its own
defense mechanism which would inhibit exchanges
between them. The issue of motivation in the
search for theory was expressed in the form of
the question, "Are we seeking a better <u>under-
standing</u> of theory, or are we trying to <u>promote</u>
the idea of theory?"[31] He cautioned that "administrative theory" would become another empty
slogan if it were used simply as a rallying cry.

Somewhat less concerned than Halpin with
anticipating the social dynamics of using theory,
Thompson seemed to represent some degree of emerging consensus in his attempt to describe what
the characteristics of an adequate theory would
be when it was achieved.[32] He identified five
such characteristics: (1) the variables and con-
stants would be selected for their logical and
operational properties rather than for their congruence with common sense, (2) an adequate theory
would be generalizable and hence abstract, (3)
the values which might be attached to education
and administration would be treated as variables
and not incorporated into the theoretical system
itself, (4) any adequate theory of administration
would be rooted in the basic social and behavioral
sciences, and (5) the focus would be on processes
rather than on correlations.

Each of these criteria was designed to com-
bat weaknesses in traditional approaches to theory
in administration. Thus, the use of common sense
terms such as "line" or "staff" was imprecise and
failed to order experience in the ways required
for systematic theory. An abstract theory was a
necessary antidote to the tendency to "regard educational administration as unique and to deny
prematurely the relevance of that which is known
about business administration, or military or
church administration."[33] If values such as democracy, for example, were treated as variables, then
it would be possible to account for administrative
behavior and processes not only in cases where

416

other ideals were highly valued. The use of the
social and behavioral sciences would require some
developmental work, but without the foundations
they provide, the task of developing a theory of
administration would be hopeless. Finally,
Thompson suggested that to show correlations between particular patterns of administrative behavior and performance was insufficient, and that
it was necessary to be able to explain how the
relationship occurred. This meant, he emphasized,
that structural concepts--those which tell us
"what"--are insufficient:

> We must also have "how" concepts.
> The structural concept "role",
> for example, gives us guide lines
> (sic) regarding the future behavior
> of a supervisor, but it does not
> explain how members of the work
> group gain understanding of the
> supervisor's role or how various
> roles articulate and operate within
> the work group or how roles change.
> Structural concepts seem to be in-
> dispensible but are not sufficient
> for a really useful theory.[34]

Halpin's Administrative Theory in Education,
from which so much of the foregoing material has
been taken, was a landmark in the development of
the field. One year later, in 1959, in a work
which was also to be influential, Griffiths wrote:

> If any one statement could be made
> concerning educational administration
> at this time, it would be that as a
> field of study it is undergoing
> radical change ... characterized
> by a search for the substance of
> administration and for the theory
> which binds the substance together.[35]

What might also be observed is that the
search itself appears to have bound scholars in
educational administration together. It is true

that the names of some of these early writers--
particularly those like Thompson whose academic
allegiances were to a broader field than educational administration[36]--appear less frequently
in subsequent publications in the field. But it
is equally true that many of the other contributors to the development of the theory movement
became (and still remain) identified as an influential group of scholars in educational administration.

The Emergent Orthodoxy

If Halpin's Administrative Theory in Education was the landmark which identified the intellectual excitement accompanying the birth of the
"new movement", then the sixty-third Yearbook of
the National Society for the Study of Education,
edited by Griffiths in 1964, was the work which
heralded its coming of age.[37] In the first chapter of the book, Griffiths et al convey a sense
of emancipation as they describe the difference
between educational administration as it had been
described in 1947 and educational administration
as it had now become.[38] Three aspects of this new
emancipated state merit attention: first, its
general characteristics; second, the kind of research it fostered; third, its diffusion beyond
the United States.

Hoyle has identified four main characteristics of the "new movement".[39] First, there was
a great emphasis on the need for careful theory
construction. It is interesting to note that
Feigl's definition of theory (which, it will be
recalled, Halpin has used in an attempt to start
a discussion of the meaning of theory) came to be
the most frequently used definition and, indeed,
was claimed by Griffiths to be one which could be
accepted.[40] Hoyle notes three associated aspects
of this first characteristic: a stress on the
need for operational definitions, a fondness for
the use of models in research, and a devaluation
of the role of classification in theory construc-

tion. The second characteristic was an emphasis
on the multi-disciplinary nature of the study of
educational administration, with particular use
being made of the social sciences. Third, the
movement became characterized by a rejection of
the "adjectival" approach, and hence a focus on
theories of general administration which might be
applicable to educational contexts rather than a
focus on the construction of specific theories of
educational administration. Finally, the movement
was characterized by an approach which sought to
make the study of educational administration
value-free by avoiding moral judgements in theory
construction and by treating values as variables.

These characteristics observed by Hoyle in
1969 capture the essence of that which was described in the 1964 Yearbook and which ran throughout textbooks produced during the 1960s.[41]
Essentially, the focus was on organizations and
their structures which not only provided the context for individuals' behavior, but also, to a
large extent, shaped and directed it.[42]

This stance towards theory and concepts of
organization dictated certain approaches to research. Particular methods of research were also
suggested by other developments in the social
sciences which provided a set of tools for the researcher. "These tools," wrote Griffiths et al,
"include concepts and theories of human behavior,
research designs, statistical insights, computers
and the logic of these modes of inquiry."[43]
Studies--and particularly dissertations--in educational administration fell heavily under the influence of these technologies. Correlational
analysis and more and more sophisticated techniques
of factor analysis characterized (and still
characterize) much of the work produced. Leadership, organizational climate and the bureaucratic
structure of schools became widely researched
themes for which data were collected by questionnaires often adapted from those devised in the
study of industrial and business organizations.
Investigations frequently built on those which had

preceded them so as to result in bodies of work which produced an intensive examination of particular variables and their correlates.[44]

The diverse locations from which many of these studies drew their samples is good evidence of the diffusion process which characterized the new movement. Canada provided an early centre and the University of Alberta was one of the first members of the prestigious University Council for Educational Administration. Contacts with Australia and Britain led to the emergence there of programmes in educational administration and to the subsequent formation in 1970 of the Commonwealth Council for Educational Administration which has joined with UCEA in supporting a quadrennial series of International Intervisitation Programmes begun in 1966.[45] In Canada, Britain and Australia the dominant emphasis originally was that provided by the movement which began in the United States. The texts of Downey and Enns in Canada, and of Baron and Taylor in Britain marked a consolidation of interest in those countries.[46], [47] The earlier issues of the Canadian Administrator and the Australian Journal of Educational Administration provide good evidence of the way in which the new movement spread.

It seems clear that the study of educational administration had found a strength which it had not before possessed, and that this strength came in large part from the so-called "theory movement" and the work associated with it. It is true that exciting new work was also being done which was not related to this movement, particularly in the economics of education.[48] It is also true that within the theory movement itself there was a good deal of variety. Nevertheless there was an identifiable stance as to what the study of educational administration was and how it should be prosecuted. That stance might never have deserved our title of "orthodoxy" had it not been for the attack mounted upon it in 1974 and the debate which the attack generated.

420

EMERGING DISSATISFACTIONS AND
THE "HETERODOXY"

In 1974 Greenfield presented a paper in which he attacked the orthodox approach to study in educational administration and advocated a phenomenological perspective.[49] This paper sparked the debate which has been known variously as "the paradigm debate" and "the Greenfield-Griffiths debate" and which has been carried on in the UCEA Review. At the time of writing, this debate is current and it is as well to step back from it and ask to what extent Greenfield's paper really constitutes a sudden and unexpected attack on a well established stance. The indications are that in proposing what he did, Greenfield did make a sudden and, for most observers, unexpected challenge. In addressing criticism to the theory movement, however, Greenfield was not alone. Cautions and criticisms had already been expressed. Before examining Greenfield's challenge and the current debate, it is useful to review some of these earlier cautions and criticisms.

Dissatisfaction: A Promise Only Part-Fulfilled

Among the more thoughtful of the instigators of the theory movement, Halpin had expressed some cautionary notes. He had suggested a need to guard against a search for the theory of educational administration and had, as we have already noted, cautioned against proselytizing in the name of theory. In an insightful essay entitled "Ways of Knowing" he had urged a recognition of different routes to knowledge.[50] Perhaps the movement grew too fast, was too exciting, for such cautions to be heeded to the full. In any case, by 1969, a loss of momentum or lack of fulfillment was observed by Halpin which led him to describe administrative theory as "the fumbled torch."[51]

The reasons for fumbling of the torch lay, according to Halpin, in the way the theory movement was originated and developed. The idea of

administrative theory, he claimed, was oversold.
Too much was expected too quickly. Interestingly,
Griffiths more recently has touched on the same
idea:

> Possibly, in an effort to over-
> come the nontheoretical, anti-
> intellectualism of the times,
> several of us attempted to con-
> struct highly abstract and
> formally elaborate theories.
> While it was good fun at the time
> it was not particularly helpful
> and, in fact, might even have
> been harmful because people were
> led to believe we were much
> farther along than we actually
> were.[52]

Recapitulating a theme from his earlier
work, Halpin noted that not only was the idea of
theory oversold, but those who bought it frequently did so because it seemed like a good bandwagon
and many of them became promoters of theory
rather than doers of theoretical work. Too few
of those who entered graduate programmes in the
1960s had fresh research talent or respect for
the craft of the researcher and many dissertations
exhibited methodological weaknesses. Moreover,
many of those who inspired the movement moved to
higher administrative posts where they could no
longer continue theoretical and research work.
Halpin summed up his view and created his cele-
brated metaphor thus:

> During the period from 1954 to
> 1964, several of us ... carried
> torches that burned with a
> bright and fervent flame. But
> as the race continued, few of us
> found another runner to whom we
> could pass the torch. In short,
> the torch has been fumbled, and
> there it lies on the ground in
> the middle of the arena.[53]

422

In a later (1975) review, Willower is less
pessimistic than Halpin about the future of theory
in educational administration, but notes some
additional reasons for the movement's loss of
momentum.[54] Too little attention, he suggests,
has been paid to a number of issues involved in
theory development, including the question of
what form an adequate theory might take--he notes
that Feigl's definition, advocated by Griffiths,
"sets a standard that would exclude virtually
everything done in educational administration to
date."[55] Willower notes also the emergence of
some dilletantism and grantsmanship among professors in the field, the latter closely connected
with another weakness, the pursuit of fads and
trivia. Although Willower notes the lack of any
serious epistemological debate in educational administration, his overall conclusions call less
for such a debate than for efforts in the direction
of integration to overcome the fragmentation which
he sees as having occurred in much of the research.

What is noteworthy about the explanations
offered for the less than complete fulfillment of
the movement's early promise is that they do not
question the basic stance which it enshrined.
Thus when Hoyle assessed the value of the movement
as it spread to Britain and discerned two weaknesses in it (an overemphasis on general as
opposed to specifically educational theories, and
a preoccupation with socio-psychological approaches), he saw them not as fundamental problems, but
simply as imbalances to be redressed.[56] Similarly
Campbell reviewing the field in 1972 wrote:

> We know that there are no miracles
> waiting for us. We realize that
> many of the concepts have little
> utility ... and those that do may
> have to be adapted and modified to
> our purpose. We are more problem
> oriented and we continue to ask
> what light the respective disci-
> plines can shed on the problems.[57]

Weaknesses there may be, slowing down there may have been, the promise of theory may not have been achieved, but, claimed Griffiths, "this is because we have not done our homework, not because the promise is unrealistic".[58] According to these explanations the torch may have been fumbled, but its flame still burned and it needed only to be picked up. It was Greenfield's denial of the absolute value of that flame that diverted the attention of some of the torch bearers to the sparks of a new debate.

Dissent: The New Critique

It is interesting to speculate whether or not Greenfield's views would have become so quickly talked of had he not chosen to present them in such a grand arena as that of the 1974 International Intervisitation Programme and had not Griffiths chosen to take them up in the UCEA Review. An earlier statement of much of his critique had appeared in print the previous year,[59] but it is the IIP '74 presentation[60] which has been the focus of most of the attention given to his work. Since that presentation, Greenfield has restated and amplified his theme in at least three papers,[61, 62, 63] and the description of it which follows is drawn from all of these sources.

What emerges as a dominant theme in Greenfield's work was initially stated in the 1973 paper:

> Most theories of organization
> grossly simplify the nature of
> the reality with which they deal.
> The drive to see the organization
> as a single kind of entity with a
> life of its own apart from the
> perceptions and beliefs of those
> involved in it blinds us to its
> complexity and the variety of
> organizations people create around
> themselves. It leads us to believe

that we must change some
abstract thing called "organization" rather than socially
maintained beliefs about how
people should relate to one
another and how they may attain
desired goals. The more
closely we look at organizations, the more likely we are
to find expressions of diverse
human meanings. The focus of
investigation should not be,
"What should be done to improve
this organization?" but, "Whose
meanings define what is right to
do among people here involved
with one another?"[64]

It was this theme which provided the
dominant thrust in the 1974 paper. In this 1974
paper, however, there was a more emphatic identification of the shortcomings of traditional ways
of viewing organizations and a more detailed
examination of the alternative. As a framework
for this examination, Greenfield wrote of "two
views of social reality", and suggested as labels
for them "the naturalistic view" and "the phenomenological view". The former was chosen to evoke
the imagery of systems theory including the structural-functionalist approach; the latter was
chosen to suggest "that view which sees organizations as the perceived social reality within which
individuals make decisions".[65] In the restatement
of his arguments in the UCEA Review, Greenfield
ordered them around four key questions: What are
organizations?   What is theory about them?   How
should research into them proceed?   What are the
implications for the training of administrators?

Greenfield's answer to the first of these
questions is that organizations are "definitions
of social reality",[66] or "a kind of invented social
reality".[67] The words he uses vary, but they are
less important than the idea they attempt to capture, namely that it is the composite of the

425

beliefs, perceptions, ideologies of those who are
members of an organization which define that organization. The contrast is between this view
and a natural systems view which sees organizations as entities which can, for example, serve
functions, have goals or act to implement policy.

In his various discussions of the second
question, "What is theory about organizations?"
Greenfield makes the point, following Kuhn, that
theory serves as a consensual agreement among
scientists about what explanations shall count as
scientific explanations. Theories are not simply
possible explanations of reality, they are sets
of instructions for looking at reality. Hence,
argues Greenfield, the choice of a particular
theory involves a value judgement and, in the
social sciences a moral judgement. In administrative studies, the choice of "naturalistic"
theory is an advocacy of a vision of reality which
ignores the humanness of the inventions we call
organizations. Such theories restrict our understanding:

> We have been caught in a trap
> which requires us in the name
> of theory to hold a single image
> up to reality and test whether
> it is true--or at least, whether
> it is a 'better' and more
> accurate representation of
> reality than any other image.
> But what is truth and falsity
> in social reality? If we are
> to understand organizations as
> containing multiple meanings, we
> must abandon the search for a
> single best image of it (sic) and
> recognize ... that the study of
> organizations can best advance by
> admitting multiple realities and
> multiple expressions of it ....
> A number of scholars now ... argue
> that such a shift requires us to
> abandon the attempt to construct

> a value-free theory of social
> reality. Instead we must
> recognize social and organiza-
> tional theories as expressions
> of ideology and as moral judge-
> ments about the world.[68]

As to the third question, "How should research proceed?" Greenfield argues for a mode of
research which aims at <u>understanding</u> the complex
reality of a given social situation at a given
time. The target for attack by Greenfield is
clearly the kind of sophisticated quantitative
research which has come to be common in the study
of organizations and which can seduce us into
thinking that correlations are explanations and
which can lead to socially disastrous actions if
we base decisions on the unthinking acceptance
of the findings of such research. In his earlier
paper, Greenfield is not able to be very specific
about what alternative kinds of research might
look like other than to note the value of case
studies and historical and philosophical needs.
In one of the later papers, however, he is able
to be more constructive.[69] He suggests four
"images of reality" which might lend themselves
to fruitful research. One of these suggestions
concerns the view of an organization in its environment. Whereas the traditional view holds
that the environment is something to which organizations adapt and that this adaptation process is
almost independent of the people of the organization, Greenfield suggests that to consider the
reverse situation would be both justifiable and
useful: it <u>does</u> sometimes happen that organizations control their environments which are adapted
to the ends of the people who make up the organization. Greenfield is not suggesting research
problems or designs, he is advocating new stances
for research methodologies which spring from new
views of organizations:

> I have suggested some alternative
> images or conceptions of what
> organizations are and what processes

427

> go on within them .... Accepting
> such ideas ... raises a consider-
> able difficulty for research in
> the field. The methodologies
> appropriate to the assumptions
> I am making about organizations
> are not well developed. It seems
> to me, however, better to set out
> on these uncharted seas with what-
> ever means reason and insight offer
> than to continue believing that
> our present methodologies offer
> reliable and accurate maps of what
> these domains contain.[70]

Whereas the two later (1977) papers show
developments in Greenfield's thinking about the
nature of theory and research in the "phenomenological" perspective, his answer to the last of
his four questions remains tentative:

> I confess I am not sure where my
> critique of organization theory
> leaves the field of educational
> administration and the consider-
> able service industry which is
> engaged in training people in a
> science which will make them better
> administrators.[71]

Of one thing he is sure, however, organization theorists cannot continue justifiably to
claim that they hold the keys which will unlock
the mysteries of administration for the neophyte.
He advocates a greater emphasis on clinical programs informed by critical and reflective perspectives on moral and social issues in organizations. Art, literature and history may well be
the means by which such perspectives can be
fostered.[72]

Debate: Politics and Inquiry

The first considered extensive reaction

to Greenfield's work was by Hills and was circu-
lated only to members of the Canadian Society for
the Study of Educational Administration.[73] While
Hills commended Greenfield for having written so
provocative an essay, he found serious flaws in
his arguments, and suggested that the opposition
discerned by Greenfield between the "naturalistic"
and "phenomenological" approaches was in large
measure due to his lack of understanding of the
structural-functionalist approach.

Kendell and Byrne make a similar suggestion,
but do so in the context of a distinction between
the political and the academic aspects of the debate.[74] While it might be preferable here to concentrate simply on the academic aspects of the
matter, it is interesting to note that the politics
of the exchange between Greenfield and Griffiths
may well have had an effect on its substance in
one rather important particular, namely the degree
to which each rejects the theoretical perspective
favoured by the other. In the 1973 paper Greenfield implies a partnership between the two perspectives. Discussing the kinds of questions we
must ask about organizations, he writes that these
questions "direct attention not only to goals and
technologies but also to the process by which
people come to believe in goals and work to achieve
them."[75] In the 1974 paper he is even more explicit, and asserts that, as one of five suggested
lines of development, "a continued study of organizations from the perspectives of the social sciences is certainly warranted."[76] In the later
papers however, the suggestion is never as explicit as in the 1974 paper. More importantly,
in terms of the political aspects of the debate,
his rhetoric becomes more aggressive. His counter
to Griffiths refers to "the tiny and threadbare
fabric of existing theory" and "its irrelevance
to most of what goes on in the world of practical
administrative affairs."[77] His A.E.R.A. paper
has: "Systems theory and structural-functionalist
thinking ... is demonstrably bad theory and leads
to sterile research."[78] Such a rhetoric can all
too easily lead to a polarization of ideas which

are not fully enough explored to justify that
polarization. The effects of polarization go
beyond the protagonists themselves and, in Kendell
and Byrne's view, the effect in the present case
is to some extent to force the field to make an
either/or choice on one side or the other.[79]

        Or, of course, in the middle. Another
major contribution to the debate, that of Gibson,
takes this approach,[80] and argues persuasively
that the "naturalistic" and "phenomenological"
views are complementary--"The question ... is not
which but how both."[81] Gibson's contribution is
interesting in the light of the distinction made
by Kendell and Byrne between the political and
academic dimensions of the debate. Although what
Gibson writes is clearly in the academic dimension, what he has chosen to write about is the
very polarity which characterizes the political
dimension. Gibson makes certain inferences
(highly plausible ones, but inferences for all
that) about the meaning to be attached to the two
poles and builds his argument convincingly on
those meanings. What Kendell and Byrne point out
is that while the pole represented by Griffiths
is reasonably clearly distinguishable as being in
the positivist tradition, Greenfield's description
of the point of view he has chosen to call "phenomenological" is much muddier.[82] Rather than too
readily accepting the phenomenological label, the
debate might make more substantive progress if it
were to probe more fully the stance underlying the
label.

        It is this kind of probing which has not
yet been widely carried out in the debate. To the
extent that it happens the debate will shift from
being political to being academic. Interestingly,
both of the contributions to date which have subjected Greenfield's work to probing analysis have
found in it inconsistencies, inadequacies and am-
biguities, but they have done so from different
points of view. Hill finds Greenfield's understanding of the natural systems position and of
the philosophy and methodology of science to be

430

deficient. Kendall and Byrne find his explanation of phenomenology to be inadequate. The very great merit of such contributions is that they call into question the too readily assumed definitions of the polarities and in doing so move the debate in academically more productive directions.

The demerit of those contributions, of course, is that jointly they appear to show that Greenfield has made no sort of contribution at all. But Greenfield has issued a challenge, and it is a challenge which has been taken seriously at both "political" and "academic" levels. To be sure, the UCEA Review is not the only journal in the field, and there are many activities going on in departments of educational administration which are apparently untouched by the debate, but it is difficult to see how a debate which purports to be about the very thing--theory--which gave the field its impetus can fail to have widespread implications. Some of these implications are discussed in the final section.

THEORY, METHODOLOGY AND PRACTICE

Although the debate which we have discussed purports to be about theory, it might be argued that its cutting edge really concerns methodology. In concluding this chapter we shall argue that such is the case, and that methodologies need to be examined not only in terms of doing research, but also in terms of the preparation of educational administrators.

Neither Griffiths nor Greenfield has "a theory" of organizations. Both of them, however, have a theoretical perspective on organizations. It is these perspectives that are important, not whether either of them can be elevated to the status of theory in Feigl's terms. Indeed, the quest for a definition of "theory" and the pursuit of theory for its own sake appear now to be as sterile as Halpin originally suggested they would be.[83] Hills has noted how, for him, the activity of "theorizing" has changed:

431

> Time was when my activities con-
> cerned with epistemology and the
> philosophy and methodology of
> science were conducted in one set
> of terms and concepts, and my
> activities concerned with organi-
> zations, societies and the people
> who populate them were conducted
> in another. More recently, that
> distinction has collapsed and the
> manner in which I now think about
> theories and theorizing is, in a
> sense, indistinguishable from the
> manner in which I think about
> societies, organizations and their
> members.[84]

Hill goes on to describe his own perspective
on man and organizations, but notes also that some
of the most insightful observations about organizations have been expressed in terms of concepts
other than those he has used in his description.
If the serious epistemological debate suggested
by Willower[85] emerges from the current controversy,
then it will need to be concerned with the variety
of perspectives which might be of value. It will
be concerned, in Halpin's phrase, with "ways of
knowing".

Greenfield has now raised for us the possibility that one of those ways of knowing may
lie in a phenomenological approach. He has also
asked us to question a too heavy reliance on the
traditional methods of the social sciences in the
design of our preparation programs. We shall return to this second point later. First it is
important to assess how the phenomenological approach may be useful.

Spiegelberg has addressed this question in
terms of the utility of phenomenology for the
individual:

> I suggested that phenomenology
> in its descriptive stage can

432

stimulate our perceptiveness
for the richness of our experience in width and in depth;
that in its search for essences
it can develop imaginativeness
and the sense for both what is
essential and what is accidental;
that, in its attention to ways
of appearance, it can heighten
the sense for the inexhaustibility
of the perspectives through which
our world is given; that, in its
study of their constitution in
consciousness it can develop the
sense for the dynamic adventure in
our relationship with the world;
that by the suspending of existential judgement it can make us more
aware of the precariousness of all
our trans-subjective claims to
knowledge, a ground for epistemological humility; and that in its
hermeneutic phase it can keep us
open for concealed meanings in the
phenomena.[86]

Beyond this, however, how can the phenomenological approach be used in the study of organizations? An excellent answer lies in the study of
a Mental Health Centre reported by Jehenson.[87]
Jehenson views the formal organization as a psycho-
social reality resulting from the subjective interpretations of its members. In his analysis he
deals with aspects which a more traditional organizational sociologist might refer to as hierarchy,
formal structures, standardization, roles, informal
structures and the like, but he is able to conclude
something which the use of those concepts does not
appear to have revealed, namely that the characteristics of a professional organization are
determined very closely by the technical knowledge
associated with the profession. He concludes:

The recourse to a phenomenological
approach, with its commitment to

433

the analysis of the meanings of
action based on the typifications
used by actors, would allow for
differentiations much more radical
than have formerly been made. By
viewing the formal organization as
a psycho-social reality built out
of the human actors' subjective
interpretations, and considering
the typifying mode of awareness
as constitutive of daily life, it
would be possible to describe each
type of professional organization
as a sui generis reality whose
specific characteristics are closely
determined by the epistemic community
to which its members are connected.[88]

Jehenson's study is worth reading in detail
not only for the insights it gives into professional organizations, but also for the exposure which
it provides to a set of potentially rich concepts
through which to think about the way people interpret others' actions and motives, and the effects
this may have on an organization.

It appears, then, that a new "way of
knowing" has been indicated which has potential
for the student of organizations. We have also
suggested earlier that there are implications in
the issues Greenfield has raised for the way we
prepare administrators. It may be useful to consider two kinds of implications: those deriving
from our having been forced to question our by now
traditional reliance on the social sciences and in
particular the "theory movement", and secondly,
those deriving from thinking about what phenomenology has to offer.

Although Greenfield has little to say about
the preparation of administrators, others, quite
independently of the debate, have raised serious
questions on the topic. Mann,[89] March,[90] and
Hills[91] have all addressed the preparation question
in new ways. Although their proposals are different

434

they have certain marked similarities. All three
are concerned with what it is that a university
can do best, and all three are concerned with the
"educational" aspect of educational administration.
What the university can do better than other
agencies is to provide rational modes of inquiry.
Hill's proposal for what the rationality should
be addressed to, and some of the means by which
it should be done, are wider-ranging than those
of the other two. March's work treats the topic
in greater depth. Mann summarizes nicely what
all three authors seem to include as important
when he writes that professors would be well ad-
vised to do "a better job at that part of the
professorial task which stresses the analysis of
important problems of practice which are accessible to reasoned intervention."[92] Seen in the
light of the development of educational administration as a field of study which prepares people
for practice, these contributions seem to have
two major points of interest quite apart from the
intrinsic merits of what they propose. First,
like Greenfield's contribution, they implicitly
question the exclusive utility of teaching organization theory as it has come to be taught in
departments of educational administration. Second,
much more than Greenfield, they reawaken the much
earlier questions about the respective merits of
the study of general as distinct from specifically
educational administration. The dominant trend of
the "theory movement" towards the former has been
shown throughout this chapter. The emphasis
placed by Hills, March and Mann on the specifically
educational character of the enterprise is, perhaps, an overdue recognition of the attention which
should have been paid to Halpin's raising of the
question almost twenty years ago.

The skills of analysis proposed by Hills,
March and Mann and a sensitivity to different ways
of knowing suggested by Greenfield, can make a
powerful combination. It is likely that sensitivity in particular can be enhanced by using some of
what may be suggested by the phenomenological
approach. At the very least, such an approach

might suggest attention to work which presents a subjective view of administrative processes. We might observe, however, that this is not unknown in present preparation programs--Farquhar has noted the existence of several which, in various ways, incorporate the humanities into their curricula.[93] It is nevertheless possible that the current debate may make some difference of emphasis in the use of such content.

What is rather more intriguing about the phenomenological perspective is that it appears to hold some promise for how we might use the humanities. An example might make the point. It is by no means uncommon for coffee shop conversation between professors and students of educational administration to refer to C.P. Snow as a novelist who can teach much about administration. It is rare, however, for such discussion to address systematically the question of what he teaches. We suggest that one reason for this is that the only tools available for many in educational administration have been those of the "theory movement" and its associated literature. It is difficult to go very far in an analysis of The Masters or Corridors of Power by using such concepts as "role" or "bureaucracy" or "organizational structure". To use concepts of the kind which Jehenson uses, however, opens up new possibilities. It seems likely that an analysis of the interpretation of motives and its dependence on typification could reveal some of the lessons which Snow may have for administrators.

"Phenomenology" may well in time come to be transmuted into other terms in educational administration. It is not the only truth, but it is one which holds some promise. To call it a heterodoxy is to claim too much, but the metaphor does at least recognize that there is a challenge to the orthodoxy and that we may enjoy some alternative answers to what is, after all, the crucial question: How shall we think about the administration of educational organizations so as to be able to study them in ways which will permit us to be of help to those who will have to administer them?

FOOTNOTES

1. Daniel E. Griffiths, "Some Thoughts about theory in Educational Administration--1975." UCEA Review, XVII, 1 (October 1975), p. 12.

2. James G. March, "Analytical Skills and the University Training of Educational Administrators." Journal of Educational Administration, 12: 1 (May 1974), p. 42.

3. Daniel E. Griffiths, "The Individual in Organization: A Theoretical Perspective." Educational Administration Quarterly, 13: 2 (Spring 1977), p. 1. The reference to Kuhn is to Thomas Kuhn, The Structure of Scientific Revolutions (Chicago: University of Chicago Press, 1970).

4. Franklin Bobbitt, "The Supervision of City Schools." Twelfth Yearbook of the National Society for the Study of Education (Chicago: The Society and the University of Chicago Press, 1913).

5. See, for example, J.B. Sears, Classroom Organization and Control (Boston: Houghton Mifflin, 1918); Elwood P. Cubberley, The Principal and His School: The Organization, Administration and Supervision of Instruction in an Elementary School (Boston: Houghton Mifflin, 1927). Taylor's ideas are evident in Cubberley's efforts to formulate "right principles of action" for administrators.

6. Raymond H. Callahan, Education and the Cult of Efficiency (Chicago: University of Chicago Press, 1962), p. 259.

7. Mayo's ideas were derived from a series of studies during 1927-1932 at the Hawthorne plant of the Western Electric Company in Chicago. Collectively called the "Hawthorne Studies" or the "Western Electric Studies", they are reported in F.J. Roethlisberger and W.J. Dickson, Management and the Worker (Cambridge: Harvard University

Press, 1939). For a fascinating critique of these studies see Alex Carey, "The Hawthorne Studies: A Radical Criticism." American Sociological Review, 32: 3 (June 1967), pp. 403-416.

8. See, for example, John A. Bartky, Supervision as Human Relations (Boston: Heath, 1953) and D.E. Griffiths, Human Relations in School Administration (New York: Appleton-Century Crofts, 1956).

9. Arthur P. Coldarci and Jacob W. Getzels, The Use of Theory in Educational Administration (Stanford: Board of Trustees of the Leland Stanford Junior University, 1955), p.1.

10. Andrew W. Halpin (Ed.), Administrative Theory in Education (The University Council for Educational Administration and the Midwest Administration Center, 1958), p. 1. A view similar to Halpin's was expressed in John Walton, "The Theoretical Study of Educational Administration." Harvard Educational Review, XXV (1955), pp. 169-178.

11. D.E. Griffiths, "Administrative Theory," in Robert E. Ebel (Ed.), Encyclopedia of Educational Research (Fourth Edition) (London: Collier-MacMillan, 1969), pp. 17-24. In this work Griffiths presents a detailed description and assessment of research which followed the four "lines of inquiry".

12. Jacob W. Getzels, "Administration as a Social Process," in Andrew W. Halpin (Ed.), Administrative Theory in Education, op.cit., pp. 150-165.

13. Originally this model was developed by Getzels in collaboration with Egon Guba in an investigation of types of conflict in a training centre for air force officers. See J.W. Getzels and E.G. Guba, "Role, Role Conflict, and Effectiveness: An Empirical Study." American Sociological Review, 19 (April 1954), pp. 164-175.

14. Jacob W. Getzels, James M. Lipham and Roald F. Campbell, _Educational Administration as a Social Process_ (New York: Harper and Row, 1968).

15. J.K. Hemphill, "Administration as Problem-Solving," in Andrew W. Halpin (Ed.), _Administrative Theory in Education_, op.cit., pp. 89-118. Hemphill's own work on leadership had begun earlier in 1950 when he was involved in several studies conducted by the Personnel Research Board at Ohio State University.

16. See, for example, A.W. Halpin and B.J. Winer, _The Leadership Behavior of the Airplane Commander_ (Ohio State University Press, 1952), and Andrew W. Halpin, _Theory and Research in Administration_ (New York: MacMillan, 1966), pp. 22-130.

17. John K. Hemphill and Alvin E. Coons, _Leader Behavior Descriptions_ (Ohio State University Press, 1950).

18. Griffiths, "Administrative Theory," op.cit., p. 18.

19. D.E. Griffiths, "Administration as Decision-Making," in Andrew W. Halpin (Ed.), _Administrative Theory in Education_, op.cit., pp. 119-149.

20. Herbert A. Simon, _Administrative Behavior_ (New York: MacMillan, 1950).

21. See, for example, Talcott Parsons, Some Ingredients of a General Theory of Formal Organization," in Andrew W. Halpin (Ed.), _Administrative Theory in Education_, op.cit., pp. 40-72. Griffiths seems to have relied most directly on Talcott Parsons, "Suggestions for a Sociological Approach to the Theory of Organizations I." _Administrative Science Quarterly_, 1 (June 1956), pp. 63-85.

22. Griffiths, "Administration as Decision-

making." op.cit., pp. 120-121.

23. Griffiths, "Administrative Theory." op.cit., p. 20.

24. Talcott Parsons, "Some Ingredients of a General Theory of Formal Organization." op.cit.

25. The proposal was based on ideas elaborated earlier in Talcott Parsons and Edward A. Shils (Eds.), Towards a General Theory of Action (Cambridge: Harvard University Press, 1951).

26. Philip Selznick, "Foundations of the Theory of Organization." American Sociological Review, 13: 1 (February 1948), p. 29. C.f. also Robert K. Merton, Social Theory and Social Structure: Toward the Codification of Theory and Research, Revised Edition (Glencoe: Free Press, 1958 (1949)).

27. R. Jean Hills, Toward a Science of Organization (Eugene: Center for the Advanced Study of Educational Administration, 1968).

28. A.W. Halpin, "The Development of Theory in Educational Administration," in Andrew W. Halpin (Ed.), Administrative Theory in Education op.cit., pp. 1-19.

29. Herbert Feigl, "Principles and Problems of Theory Construction in Psychology," in Wayne Dennis (Ed.), Current Trends in Psychological Theory (Pittsburgh: University of Pittsburgh Press, 1951), p. 182.

30. Halpin, "The Development of Theory in Educational Administration." op.cit., p. 10.

31. Ibid., p. 14.

32. James D. Thompson, "Modern Approaches to Theory in Administration," in Andrew W. Halpin (Ed.), Administrative Theory in Education, op.cit. pp. 20-39.

33. Ibid., pp. 30-31.

34. Ibid., pp. 32-33.

35. D.E. Griffiths, Administrative Theory (New York: Appleton-Century Crofts, 1959), pp. 1-2.

36. Although not written for educational administration, Thompson's later work became often cited in organizational studies in education. See especially his Organizations in Action (New York: McGraw-Hill, 1967).

37. Daniel E. Griffiths (Ed.), Behavioral Science and Educational Administration (The sixty-third Yearbook of the National Society for the Study of Education, Part II) (Chicago: N.S.S.E., 1964).

38. Daniel E. Griffiths, Richard O. Carlson, Jack Culbertson and Richard C. Lonsdale, "The Theme" in Daniel E. Griffiths (Ed.), Behavioral Science and Educational Administration, op.cit., pp. 1-7.

39. Eric Hoyle, "Organisation Theory and Educational Administration" in George Baron and William Taylor (Eds.), Educational Administration and the Social Sciences (London: Athlone Press, 1969), pp. 36-59.

40. Daniel E. Griffiths, "The Nature and Meaning of Theory," in Daniel E. Griffiths (Ed.), Behavioral Science and Educational Administration, op.cit., p. 118.

41. See, for example, Willard R. Lane, Ronald G. Corwin and William G. Monahan, Foundations of Educational Administration: A Behavioral Analysis (New York: MacMillan, 1967). See also Jacob W. Getzels et al., Educational Administration as a Social Process, op.cit.

42. Griffiths et al., "The Theme," op.cit., p.5.

43. Ibid., pp. 2-3.

44. See, for example, the summaries of such research provided throughout Jacob W. Getzels et al., Educational Administration as a Social Process, op.cit. As examples of reviews of work with a particular focus see T.B. Greenfield, "Research on the Behaviour of Leaders: Critique of a Tradition." Alberta Journal of Educational Research, 14: 1 (March 1968), pp. 55-76; and D.A. MacKay, "Research on Bureaucracy in Schools: The Unfolding of a Strategy." Journal of Educational Administration, 7 (1969), pp. 37-44.

45. For an account of this diffusion see William G. Walker, "UCEA's Bright Son at Morning: The Commonwealth Council for Educational Administration." Educational Administration Quarterly, 8: 2 (Spring 1972), pp. 16-25.

46. Lawrence W. Downey and Frederick Enns (Eds.), The Social Sciences and Educational Administration (Edmonton: University of Alberta, 1963).

47. George Baron and William Taylor (Eds.), Educational Administration and the Social Sciences (London: Athlone Press, 1969).

48. See, for example, Charles S. Benson, Perspectives on the Economics of Education (Boston: Houghton Mifflin, 1963); and, by the same author, The School and the Economic System (Chicago: Science Research Associates, 1966).

49. T.B. Greenfield, "Theory in the Study of Organizations and Administrative Structures: A New Perspective." Paper presented to the Third International Intervisitation Programme on Educational Administration, Bristol, England (July 1974). The paper was subsequently published in M.E. Hughes (Ed.), Educational Administration: International Challenge (London: Athlone Press, 1975), pp. 71-99.

50. Andrew W. Halpin, "The Development of Theory in Educational Administration." op.cit.; and "Ways of Knowing," in Roald F. Campbell and James M. Lipham (Eds.), Administrative Theory as a Guide to Action (Chicago: Midwest Administration Center, University of Chicago, 1960), pp. 3-20.

51. Andrew W. Halpin, "Administrative Theory: The Fumbled Torch," in Arthur M. Kroll (Ed.), Issues in American Education (New York: Oxford University Press, 1970), pp. 156-183. See also A.W. Halpin, "A Foggy View from Olympus." Journal of Educational Administration, 7 (May 1969); and L. Iannaccone, "Interdisciplinary Theory Guided Research in Educational Administration: A Smoggy View from the Valley." Teachers College Record, 75 (September 1973).

52. Griffiths, "The Individual in Organization: A Theoretical Perspective." op.cit., pp. 15-16.

53. Halpin, "Administrative Theory: The Fumbled Torch." op.cit., p. 173.

54. Donald J. Willower, "Theory in Educational Administration." UCEA Review, XVI, 5 (July 1975), pp. 1-5.

55. Ibid., p. 3.

56. Hoyle, "Organisation Theory and Educational Administration." op.cit., p. 38.

57. Roald F. Campbell, "Educational Administration--A Twenty-five Year Perspective." Educational Administration Quarterly, 8: 2 (Spring 1972), pp. 1-15.

58. Griffiths, "Some Thoughts about Theory in Educational Administration." op.cit. (ref. 1), p. 18.

59. T. Barr Greenfield, "Organizations as

Social Inventions: Rethinking Assumptions About Change." Journal of Applied Behavioral Science, 9: 5 (1973), pp. 551-574.

60. T.B. Greenfield, "Theory in the Study of Organizations and Administrative Structures: A New Perspective." op.cit.

61. T. Barr Greenfield, "Theory About What? Some More Thoughts about Theory in Educational Administration." UCEA Review, XVII, 2 (February 1976), pp. 4-9.

62. Thomas B. Greenfield, "Organization Theory as Ideology." Paper presented to the American Research Association, New York, April 1977.

63. Thomas B. Greenfield, "Ideas vs Data, or How Can the Data Speak for Themselves?" Paper presented to the Career Development Seminar, "Research in Educational Administration" sponsored by the University of Rochester and the UCEA (Rochester: May 1977). (To be published in the proceedings of the seminar.)

64. Greenfield, "Organizations as Social Inventions." op.cit., p.571.

65. Greenfield, "Theory in the Study of Organizations." op.cit., p. 3.

66. Ibid., p. 11.

67. Greenfield, "Organizations as Social Inventiona." op.cit., p. 556.

68. Greenfield, "Organization Theory as Ideology." op.cit., p. 14.

69. Greenfield, "Ideas vs. Data. . ." op. cit.

70. Ibid., p. 22.

71. Greenfield, "Theory About What?" op. cit., p. 9.

72. Ibid.

73. Jean Hills, "Some Comments on T.B. Greenfield's Theory in the Study of Organizations and Administration (sic) Structures." Canadian Association for the Study of Educational Administration, Occasional Papers, 1975.

74. Richard Kendell and David R. Byrne, "Thinking About the Greenfield-Griffiths Debate," UCEA Review, XIX, 1 (October 1977), pp. 6-16.

75. Greenfield, "Organizations as Social Inventions." op.cit., p. 571.

76. Greenfield, "Theory in the Study of Organizations." op.cit., p. 13.

77. Greenfield, "Theory About What?" op. cit., p. 4.

78. Greenfield, "Organization Theory as Ideology." op.cit., p. 1.

79. Kendell and Byrne, "Thinking About the Greenfield-Griffiths Debate." op.cit., p. 7.

80. R. Oliver Gibson, "Reflections on a Dialogue." UCEA Review, XVIII, 2 (January 1977), pp. 35-39.

81. Ibid., p. 38.

82. Kendell and Byrne, "Thinking About the Greenfield-Griffiths Debate." op.cit., pp. 10-11.

83. Halpin, "The Development of Theory in Educational Administration." op.cit.

84. Jean Hills, "A Perspective on Perspectives." UCEA Review, XIX, 1 (October 1977), pp. 1-5.

85. Willower, "Theory in Educational Administration." op.cit.

86. Herbert Spiegelberg, "On Some Human Uses of Phenomenology," in F.I. Smith (Ed.), Phenomenology in Perspective (The Hague: Martinus Nijhoff, 1970), p. 18.

87. Roger Jehenson, "A Phenomenological Approach to the Study of the Formal Organization," in George Psathas (Ed.), Phenomenological Sociology (New York: Wiley, 1973), pp. 219-247.

88. Ibid., p. 243.

89. Dale Mann, "What Peculiarities of Educational Administration Make it Difficult to Profess: An Essay." Journal of Educational Administration, 13: 1 (May 1975), pp. 139-147.

90. James G. March, "Analytical Skills and the University Training of Educational Administrators." Journal of Educational Administration, 12: 1 (May 1974), pp. 17-44.

91. Jean Hills, "Preparation for the Principalship: Some Recommendations from the Field." Administrators Notebook, XXIII, 9 (1975).

92. Mann, "What Peculiarities of Educational Administration Make it Difficult to Profess: An Essay." op.cit., p. 147.

93. Robin H. Farquhar, "New Directions in the Content of Canadian Preparation Programs for Educational Administrators." Paper presented to the Annual Conference of the Canadian Society for the Study of Education, Queen's University, May 1973.

CHAPTER 7

EDUCATIONAL KNOWLEDGE AND THE
SCHOOL PROFESSIONAL

This attempt to provide a sound description of the nature and purpose of each of the basic disciplines in the study of education is meant to present to the student the basic material of which educational decisions come to be made. What we have presented here is then the farthest thing from a mere exercise preceding live questions of educational practice. It is, in our view, an outline of the foundation of knowledge on which educational policy, and ultimately practice are based and from which reason and direction are derived. It is true that there has never been in education, nor in the social sciences generally, a totally clear conclusion from the fields of applied research or a perfect fit of the research findings and professional judgment with institutional practice. Thus, some would say that the state of knowledge in the fields presented here should be but are not the institutional foundations we suggest. Others might say that the gap between the scholar's perspective and that of the practitioner has proved to be too wide in education for such a connection to be claimed. While we would have some agreement with the first contention, we would maintain that the gaps respectively of time and application, as problematic as they are, are nevertheless bridged in a continuous, uneven, dynamic way. The history of education is in fact a history of institutional inclusion of intellectual efforts to accommodate social ideas and appropriate specific knowledge to education and schooling.

Through most of western history, however, educational knowledge, as in the case of the discrete social sciences, was studied synthetically with other studies of man and his works, and derived from whatever general conclusions were pertinent to the time. Only in the modern period, with some independence given to the institutional

449

and professional requirements of education, and with the discrimination of studies of social phenomena and institutions generally, was there a serious attempt to organize scientifically the sectors of study pertaining to particular requirements of educational activity. Even then, it was and remains difficult for those involved in higher studies, for the public at large, and sometimes for professional educators themselves to accept the finer distinctions among educational functions, considered over age groups, institutional requirement (e.g. administration, curriculum, didactics), and social-philosophical framework, which have been isolated in the research and which are revealed to some degree in the chapters.

The attempt, over most of this century, to fashion school education to meet better the demands of contemporary living was in fact an attempt to utilize the best judgment from available knowledge in order to energize the substance of education. It was an attempt to emphasize the content of educational skills, the thinking process, the structure of disciplines, to incorporate new learnings, long overdue, in the curriculum; to define literature more broadly so as to include social, scientific, and political literacy; to open up new media of learning which might accommodate a wider range of individual modes; to remove the artificial distinctions between vocational and intellectual education and between the groups of children predetermined for these respective types of schooling. These ideas were in no way impetuous. They were derived from social and philosophical analyses, by curriculum studies and psychological research. Essentially, they signified a change based on three premises: (1) that various sequences of learning could be devised for a much greater population than had been in school heretofore; (2) that, since neither the rudimentary learning of the elementary level nor the literary-philosophical learning of the academic upper level could be predicted to transfer functionally as they were once assumed to do, instruction in all subjects should be designed for specific relevance to life,

450

vocation, or intellectual objectives; (3) education for this age should have its reference in the conditions and requirements of its own present society. It might be said that, for the first time, changes determined from specific study projected education independently into the future of the society.

The independence of scientific studies of education varies according to the specificity of knowledge in the particular area and the link to cognate areas. For example, studies in psychology of education rely most heavily on the state of psychological knowledge pertaining to the particular educational problem or function; studies of administration refer primarily to the objective facts of institutional organization and to the application of organizational knowledge to that reality; studies of curriculum are based on the characteristics of knowledge in the respective fields incorporated in the school curriculum; studies of instructional method, while amenable to some degree of independent treatment, must also relate in specific ways to the characteristics of content and to the psychology of the learner. The integrative complications must finally be resolved in the separate studies of education. In certain areas, though, in sociology of education for instance, there is in the field as a whole virtually no independence. For the conclusions most important to the application of educational studies, the independence of research paradigms is irrelevant, and the independence of findings is forcibly adapted to overriding policy decisions.

When a broad policy objective is defined, a number of tasks are imposed on scholars, administrators, and teachers, which ideally are elaborated in a sequence from available knowledge to practice. Some of those tasks are more directly related to the convergence of judgment from the disciplines. To exemplify, with reference to a broad policy decision favoring promotion of equal educational opportunity, a first task might be the specification of intermediate organizational objectives.

451

Thus, change might require: (1) equalization of resources available to children in order to compensate for school-district differences; (2) preelementary preparation and instructional flexibility in the elementary school; (3) post-secondary opportunities, including variability in admission criteria and degree programs of universities.

A second task might be the discrimination among policy objectives in the target area from those in other areas, with the possibility of supportive changes being required in the latter. If, again for example, equal opportunity provisions are applied to the system of general education, while vocational education remains peripheral to this system and confined to a given social and ability group, the effect of target policies may be lost or at least diluted by the continuation of contradictory policy in the system as a whole. This conclusion has to do with solution of the problem, not with evaluation of the basic decision.

A third task involves identification of potential normative conflicts arising in implementation of policy. If specialized technical competence is the norm for performance in the work world, but non-vocational general education provides the norm for educational performance, which in turn stipulates access to respective occupations, the criteria for educational success may be irrelevant to those for social and economic opportunity. The discrepancy may then be mediated by advantages or disadvantages of social class or intellectual environment, thus subverting the goal without necessarily contradicting it in either educational or occupational practices.

A fourth task requires reconciliation of the policy objectives with principles of the institution. Without further elaboration, these task sequences show (1) that the proper study of education is in education, thus not defined in subject terms outside of education; (2) that educational studies cannot be ignored in the practical conduct of schooling; and (3) that, while the studies must be pursued independently and to some extent separately, they derive from and converge in the practice. In classic formulation, the principles of education are elaborated out of the practice, becoming then a base for the process of education; reflections on the _praxis_ become at once directives for action _and_ for study. Some of this may sound abstract. Abstraction is the shadow of reality, but the stuff of theory, without which a Peter Pan practice searches vainly for purpose. Within this abstraction, however, is a consistent emphasis on specifics of _knowledge_ and of action.

Probably the biggest problem in the organization of learning and of teaching learning is the serious split between institutional rigidity of process and perceived individual autonomy. Before addressing that, however, there is a prior question of knowledge substance.

There would seem to be little question that any university program is based on knowledge, that the schools transmit knowledge as a primary function, and that the numerous divisions of knowledge require selection, synthesis, and application in teacher-training and in teaching. It follows that teachers should not be denied that liberal education which allows them to know something of the best that has been thought about man and society, about heaven and earth, to know of the arts and sciences, to be able to discern and discriminate. It follows that they should be able to teach the most fundamental knowledge of the culture, which is all they are asked to do, and that their professional conduct and practice rest firmly on knowledge of the institution of education, its environment, and of the tasks they are expected to perform within it. The cultural and the professional basics go without saying. What is problematic is the tendency to diminish the importance of that critical learning mass, to equate all subjects and types of learning, and especially to fall into an academic version of the bureaucratic society, in which talk, procedure, and routine substitute for knowledge--and whereby a colonial clerical mentality may be perpetuated.

In the argument over teaching the "basics",
the negative position taken by professional educators (which may be well taken against sometimes
extreme threats), frequently ignored the realities
of mass education, and almost always, used a veil
of pseudo-social-science jargon to mask thinly a
position in favor of knowing less and doing less.
What passed too often as creative teaching was
actually a dignifying of opinion, interpersonal
relationship, and pleasurable activity--rococo
education: miniature, delicate, charming, and un-
substantive. Serious creative application, as
serious dissent and innovation, is a counterpart
of knowledge in the make-up of ability, but the
knowledge comes first.

The organization of knowledge for teaching,
while subject to endless debate, is properly bound
by some straightforward assumptions regarding
knowledge, priority, and sequence. First, the
knowledge assumption: that teacher education requires (1) the liberal education requisite to
membership in the cultural leadership; (2) professional training, which implies a basic integrated
core of functional knowledge, made up of (a) the
professional foundation: child development,
teacher's role between school and community, principles and procedures of educational policy-making,
identification of the school as a social institution in Canada, and ability to comprehend and
criticize the meaning of education as conducted in
schools; and (b) the teaching foundation: field
mastery, translation of field knowledge into teaching practice, including design, transmission, and
evaluation of content, recognition and promotion
of disabilities and talents in learning, use of
instructional media, and ability to respond to
individual differences with a sense of collective
values; (3) specialization, which is validated in
the discipline but also in institutional requirements, and yields at any one time a limited set of
professional options.

The priority assumption determines that choices must be made, of course, not only in the specializations that characterize the profession but also in the basic knowledge competencies identified. Present professional priorities are clearly in understanding and competence to deal with the disadvantaged--the physically, socially, economically handicapped; in developing a working knowledge of communities so as to utilize their total resources for the benefit of children and schools and so as to address educationally the potentially calamitous effects of transitional problems; in preparatory learning and socialization of young children; in using information technology; in teaching for scientific and political literacy; in using research findings and evaluation techniques; in promoting a sense of group identity synthesized from community and possibly nation; a sense of society which accounts for technological reality and moral dimensions of life, and a sense of other cultures here and elsewhere.

The sequence assumption is probably the most variable, given that there is little on which to validate any particular program sequence. Logically, the liberal studies should precede professional studies. Professional basics, preferably as complementary components, of variable length and with current content applicable to field situations, should follow. Ideally continuous study of the teaching subject or subjects and a vertical core theoretical study in education should run parallel through both stages, and a preliminary specialization package should follow. However organized, the body of cultural and professional knowledge required for the teacher should be built from the best common knowledge available, should be supplemented by specialized knowledge beyond subject-teaching competency, and should be internalized as a personal teaching style and attitude. The knowledge requirement includes then: (1) vertical integration (depth) of learning in and for the teaching specialty, (2) horizontal integration (synthesis) of learning of cultural and

455

professional basics, (3) learning of the relevant para-specializations likely to be needed over a long period of time, (4) career continuity in learning, (a) new content or methodologies in the subject, (b) skills and behaviors related to educational functions outside the classroom, and (c) advanced knowledge and research skills.

One version of the form-substance dichotomy is the separation of concern with structure of organization from concern with program of activity. Such separation is disfunctional. Furthermore, either is important only as it reflects a collective attitude favorable to understanding and promoting the general imperatives and specific tasks incumbent on education in a given institutional form, and a willingness continually to reconstruct the work according to a dynamic of objectives. Such an attitude depends on competence of knowing and competence of doing, it depends on acute social, scientific, and institutional awareness; it depends on a sense of mission, a sense of community, and a balanced tension between authority, of form and person, and individual freedom to create and renew.

Following some rather static statements on knowledge and on program, it should be noted that a number of present changes bear on the general imperatives and specific tasks of teacher education. First, the explosive production of knowledge and revolutionary means of processing knowledge in this latter half of the 20th century make it no less necessary to identify basic knowledge, but more necessary to identify it in terms of form and means, that is, what are the essential components, how are they related, and how are specifics found and generated. Further, the instability and uncertainty of the new knowledge (what is an atom?) calls for a running thought pattern, capable of accommodating adjustments and maintaining a critical distance on almost everything.

This attitude, projecting from knowledge into individual and organizational behavior, has had certain extreme manifestations which have, without reflection, like Topsy, "just growed". For example, the extreme change in time reference, wherein the past has no authority; the future no certainty. This started perhaps in the early 20th century, possibly occasioned by world catastrophes, by changes in mobility, by industrial built-in obsolescence, by emphasis on social science, on experts rather than on conventional sources of authority (families, sages), as well as by knowledge change in general, and led first to the primary of the present, then to the extreme of the isolated present, i.e., first as dominance of the present, then as only the present. This reference, together with a narcissistic sacrifice of community, led to a widespread behavioral reflection of a view that the culture has no past worth attending to, no values or principles impinging on present social conduct, thus no authority; that the future is simply an ongoing "now", forged out of continuous present experiences, each for its own sake, predominantly for individual gratification.

Social and intellectual tendencies so strong that they can be designated movements or outcomes cannot be ignored in the work of institutions. In fact, it is another extreme manifestation that institutions, as conservers of tradition, tend to isolate themselves against revolutionary change while their members are swept along by it, or they yield to the invisible winds of change entirely; thus losing their reason for being. In either case there is no confrontation with the present issue of change and conservation in order to determine where the confluence is and to determine what the basis of institutional reconstruction can be, in effect, to determine which aspects of "nature" to work with and which to work against. Consequently dichotomies and disfunctions become commonplace. All organization becomes disorganized as efforts to separate, to secure individuality, to promote self, to avoid constraint of any kind--under the guise of benevolence and democracy, run up against efforts to mechanize procedures, to maintain recognizable institutional identity and function, to pin down those functions and limit variability through techniques of evaluation and goals of accountability--all also under the guise of benevolence and democracy. The loss of any genuine democracy and of any genuine leadership that results is due to an irresolvable conflict (in situational terms) between institutional rigidity and extreme individualism; or, in other words, between the impersonal objective momentum of system mechanics and the subjective ego-driven desires of disconnected persons. The attempt to bridge this gap, in numerous variations accounts for much of the pressure on institutional leaders, for they can only mediate instances of the tension, not resolve it.

It is for this reason that collective attitudinal response <u>in education</u> is so important. Education is the key to response in other institutions. The policy foundation appropriate to such response will have to emphasize contemporary <u>form</u> as opposed to idiosyncracy and will allow for the construction within that form of tentative but operational syntheses.

What are some of the meanings of this for the way universities approach teacher-education, for the way teachers approach their profession and their children, for the way school authorities approach their teachers and their public? In the first place although it is true that institutions exist to serve the needs of society, it is not everything in the society to which Education can or should respond; it is to those selected characteristics of the culture and present social reality which together form the basis of a positive future. Secondly, the attitude which should prevail in institutional planning as well as in classroom practice, at any level, is one congenial to a tentatively designed balance between change and stability, and that balance should support all intermediate decisions regarding structure and program. Institutional mechanics simply facilitate the present stabilization; they should not be allowed to obstruct critical reformulation. Nor

458

should persons pretending to champion "people" be allowed to protect self-interest against reformulation in the larger or longer interest. Facilitative mechanics and creative individuality should not, then, be subordinated to conservative self or institutional protection, but should contribute in the interactive field of community.

At present, we are engaged, through the various methods available, in the attempt to define more precisely those effects of and on education which result from given sets of social and educational conditions.

Before the growth of mass education, when the schools were the privilege of those able to afford them, the cost of schooling to society in general was low. This is not the case today. Although schools are still required to perform many of their traditional academic functions, they no longer cater only to a wealthy elite in society but to children from all socio-economic strata, and they are now expected to produce en masse some tangible result of the education process. Education studies are important in this respect since it is the scholar in this field who may be asked legitimately: What have been the functions of schools historically? What have schools been expected to produce? What may we ask of schools today? Who is able to ask such questions? Who determines what is asked or expected? How important are schools for political, social, and economic development, and how important is this development for schools? What are the sources and reasons for educational reform?

The different sections of this book are united by their concern for the convergence of such questions in the improvement of educational thought and practice. Just as Education must be related to the mainstream of social development, so must the specific studies of education finally come together to support policy decisions calculated to strengthen the quality and effectiveness of the institution as a whole.